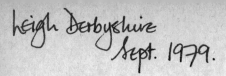

THE WORKS OF SHAKESPEARE

EDITED FOR THE SYNDICS OF THE
CAMBRIDGE UNIVERSITY PRESS

BY

JOHN DOVER WILSON

THE TRAGEDY OF HAMLET, PRINCE OF DENMARK

HAMLET

CAMBRIDGE
AT THE UNIVERSITY PRESS
1936

Published by the Syndics of the Cambridge University Press
Bentley House, 200 Euston Road, London, NW1 2DB
American Branch: 32 East 57th Street, New York, N.Y.10022

ISBNS:
0 521 07531 9 hard covers
0 521 09474 7 paperback

First published 1934
Second edition 1936
Reprinted 1941, 1948, *1954, 1957, 1961, 1964
First paperback edition 1968
Reprinted 1969, 1971, 1972

* Places where editorial changes or additions introduce
variants from the first edition are, when possible,
marked by a date [1954] in square brackets.

First printed in Great Britain at the University Press, Cambridge
Reprinted in Great Britain by Hazell Watson & Viney Ltd,
Aylesbury, Bucks

CONTENTS

PREFACE TO THE SECOND EDITION

Any new recension of a play like *Hamlet*, which is of universal interest and touches scholarship at numberless points, will provoke criticism and discussion from which the editor has much to learn. He will be fortunate too if friends and critics do not draw his attention to material already in print which he has overlooked. The call for a second edition within two years of publication comes too early for me to reap this aftermath to full advantage. Beyond correcting a few misprints I have, therefore, left the type of this volume as it stood in November, 1934, gathering together in supplementary pages additional notes and observations which it seemed profitable to Mr Child and myself to make at this juncture, in the hope of being able to incorporate them, with fresh additional matter, should a third edition ever be required. When these notes concern, by way of correction or expansion, the Introduction, Notes or Glossary of the 1934 edition, the reader's attention will be drawn to the fact by asterisks in the original text, though such notes, it may be observed, form only a part of the new matter. Meanwhile my grateful thanks are due to the many critics, private and public, who have tendered advice or admonition. Reasoned disagreement, indeed, is one of the greatest of services that an editor can receive. For even when the criticism cannot be accepted, it may, and often does, induce further elucidation, if not fresh discovery.

J. D. W.

September, 1936

To

Q.

HAMLET

I

The plays in this serial edition of Shakespeare have, in accordance with custom, hitherto followed the order originally laid down in the First Folio. With the completion of the fourteen Comedies, however, more than a third of the whole journey has been traversed, and to persevere in the wake of Messrs Heminge and Condell would mean a long trudge through the ten Histories. I therefore propose, not indeed to desert their guidance altogether, but to relieve the rather monotonous scenery of their second stage by an occasional excursion into the highlands of tragedy. The play that comes next to *The Winter's Tale* in the Folio is *King John*; this will be issued after the present volume, with *Richard II* to follow. Meanwhile, we turn aside from the frontiers of Angevin England to Denmark, a Denmark legendary in its setting but with an atmosphere and characters which clearly belong to the age of Elizabeth.

Hamlet has been chosen for several reasons, but chiefly for a personal one. With *The Winter's Tale* Sir Arthur Quiller-Couch ceased to captain the ship of this adventure. That I should wish to dedicate the next volume to him as a slight acknowledgment of encouragement and tolerance extended over twelve years of unclouded fellowship goes without saying. But I wished also to give him something different from the ordinary run of plays. And as I began working at *Hamlet* in 1917 and have been working at it, when time allowed, ever since, this seemed the most suitable offering. A sense of gratitude that spurs me on to undertake the most difficult of editorial tasks now, rather than in the sere and yellow leaf, leaves me more grateful than ever.

The longest of all Shakespeare's plays, and the turning-point of his spiritual and artistic development, *Hamlet* is also the cross-roads of Shakespearian criticism, at which all the highways and every conceivable lane and field-path seem to converge. Furness prudently included it among the earlier plays of his *Variorum Shakespeare*, and published it in 1877. But even at that date he found himself compelled to devote two volumes to it, a distinction not accorded to any text afterwards. The character of its hero, in the words of the best of modern Shakespearian critics, 'has probably exerted a greater fascination, and certainly has been the subject of more discussion, than any other in the whole literature of the world[1].' Yet the problems raised by the text are quite as baffling as those belonging to character, and even more complicated. They are, indeed, fit subject for a lifetime of study. And another life might well be spent upon its exegesis. Owing partly to Shakespeare's vocabulary, which seems richer here than ever before or after, partly to Hamlet's riddling habit of speech, which Shakespeare took over from his source with the 'antic disposition' and greatly elaborated, and partly to what Johnson called the 'excellent variety' of the scenes, which embrace almost every side of Elizabethan life, *Hamlet* stands in more need of commentary than any other play. Finally, there is the difficult and much debated question of topical allusion. While it seems to be agreed upon all hands that *Hamlet* is the most topical play in the whole corpus, unhappily when it comes to interpreting the supposed allusions, agreement almost entirely vanishes.

Even the shallow scratchings of a general editor must throw up more material in these various fields than can be conveniently gathered into a single volume, and, as I have said, my spade will strike somewhat deeper here than on previous occasions. The present volume is more

---

[1] A. C. Bradley, *Shakespearean Tragedy*, p. 90.

than twice as long as most of its fourteen predecessors, yet it must at the same time be more restricted in scope.

> Diseases desperate grown
> By desperate appliance are relieved
> Or not at all;

and the only 'appliance' adequate to the situation was the publication of auxiliary studies to ease the pressure upon this one. What follows is then the middle term of a series of three monographs on *Hamlet*, though it stands of course upon its own base and can be read independently of the others. The textual foundations, in previous plays dealt with in a 'note on the copy' running to a few pages, form the subject of the first monograph, already issued in the 'Shakespeare Problems' series under the title of *The Manuscript of Shakespeare's 'Hamlet,'* and that this monograph itself occupies two volumes will show something of the difficulties with which an editor must cope. On the other hand, it was found necessary to reserve full consideration of the dramatic problems for a third monograph called, *What happens in 'Hamlet,'* which is now being prepared and will appear shortly.[1] This does not mean that textual and dramatic topics will be excluded from the notes below. As I have just said, this book claims an independent existence of its own; and while utilising the results of the introductory monograph upon the text, it will also to some extent anticipate those of its sequel. Its own special contribution, however, apart from the presentation of a modernised text based upon the textual investigation just mentioned, is commentary, i.e. the interpretation of what is said and the glossing of words. And how much there was to do in this field alone may be gathered from the length of the glossary at the end of the volume.

The truth is that, despite the overwhelming tide of books and commentary upon *Hamlet*, its problems have never yet been tackled in any fashion that promises

[1] Third ed. published in 1951.

success. The proper foundations and an orderly method have alike been lacking. The literary and psychological critics for example, from Henry Mackenzie in the eighteenth century onwards, have one and all begun at the wrong end by attempting to solve the riddle of Hamlet's character before making sure that they understood the play in which he is the principal figure. As the subtlest of them excellently writes: 'The only way, if there is any way, in which a conception of Hamlet's character could be proved true, would be to show that it, and it alone, explains all the relevant facts presented by the text of the drama.' Unfortunately he continues: 'To attempt such a demonstration here would obviously be impossible, even if I felt certain of the interpretation of all the facts[1].' Yet without that certainty no reading of character possesses any secure foundation, as is evident enough in the ebb and flow of the various theories about Hamlet during the last century and a half. Furthermore, the 'facts' of a play are in their turn dependent on our understanding of the dialogue. Before we can be certain what is happening scene by scene we must first be certain that we fathom the meaning of what the characters say in each scene; or at least what they say at moments of dramatic significance. The existence of cruxes like 'the dram of eale' passage which lie off the main current does not seriously matter. But it does matter that we should follow the movement of Hamlet's mind when he is talking to the Ghost, Horatio and Marcellus in the Cellarage-scene, to Rosencrantz and Guildenstern in Act 2, Scene 2, or to Ophelia in the Nunnery-scene, because our whole conception of the play may turn upon the interpretation we put upon his words. Finally, before we can be certain what Hamlet or any other character says, we must be certain what Shakespeare wrote, or intended to write.

Thus the establishment of the text comes first, then

[1] Bradley, *op. cit.* p. 129.

the interpretation of the dialogue, then the elucidation of the plot, and only after all these matters have been settled are we in a position to estimate character. Yet so far no critic has seriously undertaken, or at least rightly undertaken, any of the three preliminary tasks, and the only critic who seems even to have been aware of their importance is Edward Dowden, whose edition of *Hamlet* in *The Arden Shakespeare*, though inconclusive and hesitating, is the most illuminating that has hitherto appeared. The three monographs above mentioned, of which the present volume is one, are then intended as distinct, related and progressive stages in preparation for an attack upon the greatest of all literary problems, the understanding of Shakespeare's *Hamlet*. They are preparatory only; they do not solve the enigma of Hamlet's character, still less do they provide that interpretation of the play as a whole which lies behind and beyond character in any great dramatic poem, as the world in our day is beginning to be aware. But studies of the kind must be undertaken before any aesthetic criticism of *Hamlet* is likely to achieve permanence. I am not so foolish as to expect finality for any of my three books, but I can at least claim that the method they exemplify is sound and has never before been tried.

It may appear strange to some that I do not include a history of the making of *Hamlet* among these prefatory studies. Textual history is a theme to which I have devoted a good deal of attention in the 'notes on the copy' of previous volumes, basing my conjectures for the most part upon a bibliographical analysis of the text in question. Such an analysis, however, forms no part of my present purpose. For one thing, I have my hands already overfull without it; for another, the history of a Shakespearian text should not, in my opinion, be attempted until we have made up our minds about Shakespeare's dramatic intentions, and this is just what, in regard to *Hamlet*, the world has hitherto found itself incapable of doing.

In other words, textual history, so far from being an instrument of dramatic criticism, as many modern Shakespearian students seem to imagine, is posterior not only to the three introductory stages just indicated, but also to that final appraisement of the play as a whole up to which they lead. When the dramatic situation is clear, as it is in most plays, to consider how the material (story or drama) from which Shakespeare started has influenced the final form is, of course, not merely interesting but highly instructive. But when this is not so, such an enquiry is attended with great risks. I touch here upon one of the capital fallacies of present-day Shakespearian scholarship to which I shall return later[1].

I do not then propose to pry into the processes of the creation of *Hamlet* or to launch out into speculations concerning the manner in which Shakespeare handled his sources. No introduction to *Hamlet* would, however, be complete without some account of the sources themselves, which are for the most part well known; and the account may be conveniently given before we proceed to our main task.

II

The origin of the story of Hamlet is lost in the mists of antiquity, through which, mingled as it were with sea-spray, we can dimly perceive the common ancestors of the English and Scandinavian races moving in their long ships about the southern shores of the Baltic and across the high seas that divide the Norwegian fiords from Iceland. The name Hamlet, in its Icelandic form of Amlóði, first crops up in an obscure fragment of verse from the Prose Edda composed about A.D. 1230[2], and a recent attempt has been made to identify the man to whom the Hamlet story belongs with a certain Swedish

[1] v. pp. xlvi–viii.
[2] I. Gollancz, *Sources of Hamlet*, p. 1.

King Onela, mentioned in *Beowulf*[1]. Whether or not, as the same writer claims, the name be separable into the components 'Anle,' a common Scandinavian name, and 'Óδι,' a by-name meaning originally 'furious in battle' and later 'mad,' there seems little doubt that feigned madness was an important element in the saga and a high probability that some folk-lore story of a hero who assumed madness for the purpose of revenge became attached to a historical or semi-historical figure, as apparently happened in the case of David among the Israelites and Lucius Junius Brutus among the Romans. It has even been suggested by some scholars that the Hamlet saga is nothing but a northern version of the tale of Brutus, and there are certainly striking points of similarity between the two, points which can however be explained as embellishments borrowed from Livy by the earliest writer to give the saga permanent literary form. This was Saxo Grammaticus, who at the end of the twelfth century compiled his Latin *Historia Danica*, the third book of which contains that part of the Hamlet story which Shakespeare later made famous. The following is a brief abstract of it.

The father of Amleth, for such is the form of the name in Saxo, a governor of Jutland, to whom the king of Denmark had given his daughter Gerutha in marriage, won fame by slaying the king of Norway in single combat, but encountered the jealousy of his brother Feng, who assassinated him, seized his office and married his wife, thus 'capping unnatural murder with incest[2].' Young Amleth determined to avenge his father, but in order to gain time and to allay the suspicions of his crafty

[1] Kemp Malone, *A Literary History of Hamlet*, and *Etymologies for Hamlet* (*Review of English Studies*, iii. pp. 259–71).

[2] The quotations are from the translation by Professor Oliver Elton, *The Tragical History of Amleth Prince of Jutland by Saxo Grammaticus*.

uncle, he feigned a 'foolish and grotesque madness' so that 'all he did savoured of utter lethargy.' Nevertheless, his mad speech concealed 'an unfathomable cunning' and 'he mingled craft and candour in such wise that, though his words did not lack truth, yet there was nothing to betoken the truth and betray how far his keenness went.' Two attempts were made to pierce this disguise: first by means of 'a fair woman' who had been his intimate since childhood and who was thrown in his path in order to seduce him; and secondly by 'a friend of Feng, gifted with more assurance than judgment,' who undertook to spy upon him when he was 'closeted alone with his mother in her chamber.' Of the former trap Amleth was warned by a faithful friend, 'a foster-brother who had not ceased to have regard to their common nurture.' From the second he was saved by his own caution; for, after searching the room, and detecting the man beneath the straw [of the bed], he 'drove his sword into the spot and impaled him who lay hid'; then 'cutting up the body into morsels, he seethed it in boiling water and flung it through the mouth of an open sewer for the swine to eat.' This done he upbraided his mother as 'the most infamous of women'; taxing her with 'wantoning like a harlot' and 'wheedling with filthy lures of blandishment him who has slain the father of thy son'; comparing her conduct with that of 'brute beasts' who 'are naturally incited to pair indiscriminately, and it would seem that thou, like them, hast clean forgot thy first husband'; and bidding her not to lament for his witlessness but rather 'weep for the blemish in thine own mind.' In this fashion, 'he rent the heart of his mother and redeemed her to walk in the ways of virtue; teaching her to set the fires of the past above the seductions of the present.'

Foiled of his purposes, Feng next dispatched Amleth to Britain with 'two retainers...bearing a letter graven on wood' which 'enjoined the king of the Britons to put

to death the youth who was sent over to him.' But while
the two slept, 'Amleth searched their coffers, found the
letter, and read the instructions therein. Whereupon he
erased all the writing on the surface, substituted fresh
characters and so changing the purport of the instructions, shifted his own doom upon his companions.. . .
Under this was falsely marked the signature of Feng.'
Upon reaching Britain, his companions were hanged
and Amleth was received with honour by the king, who
gave him his daughter in marriage and marvelled greatly
at the wisdom and subtlety of the young man. A year
later Amleth returned to Jutland where, having plied
Feng and his followers generously with drink, he set fire
to the palace, burnt alive all the drinkers within, and slew
Feng with his own hand, after first changing swords with
him, his own sword having been rendered useless by
treachery.

Such is the Hamlet story according to Saxo, and it will
be seen that, apart from the character of the hero, all the
elements of *Hamlet* are here in germ: fratricide, incest,
antic disposition, Ophelia, Horatio, Polonius, Rosencrantz and Guildenstern, the journey to England, the
changeling letter and the false seal, even the uncle's love
of drink and the exchange of swords in the final scene.
Most striking of all is Amleth's long speech to his mother
in her bedroom, which gives us the nucleus not only of
Hamlet's dagger-words which 'cleft' the heart of Gertrude but also of his first soliloquy. And though Amleth
is a very different person from Hamlet, we may find
a hint of the latter's melancholy and inaction in his
prototype's assumed 'lethargy.' Indeed, Saxo's words
'Quicquid opere exhibuit profundam redolebat inertiam'
might almost stand as a motto for Shakespeare's play.

I have emphasised the links between Saxo and
Shakespeare because it is generally assumed that the true
source of the play was an intermediary version of the
story to be found in Belleforest's *Histoires Tragiques*

(Paris, 1582). Belleforest borrowed from Saxo and
expanded the story somewhat; but apart from a definite
reference to Amleth's 'over-great melancholy' he made
only two new points of which Shakespeare later availed
himself, namely that Geruth and Fengon, as Amleth's
mother and uncle were now called, had committed
adultery before the murder[1] and that Amleth and the
'fair' temptress were lovers. On the other hand, some
of the germinal phrases in Saxo, such as the description
of Polonius's predecessor as 'praesumptione quam
solertia abundantior' and of Gerutha after her shending
as 'lacerata mater,' have no parallel in Belleforest. It
seems likely, therefore, that both versions influenced the
play, perhaps at different stages of its evolution. It should
be added that a contemporary English translation of
Belleforest, *The Hystorie of Hamblet* (1608), was in turn
influenced by the play, seeing that the author of it not
only added the words 'he cried, A rat, a rat!' to Belleforest's account of the Closet-scene, but also twice
translated 'loudier,' the counterpane beneath which the
spy hid himself (in place of the 'stramentum' of Saxo),
as 'arras' or 'hangings,' while he inserts 'behind the
hangings,' again without warrant, in an earlier passage.
Some have supposed that Shakespeare derived his plot
from a lost sixteenth-century edition of *The Hystorie*;
but there is no evidence of publication before 1608.

And even if an edition twenty or thirty years earlier
were discovered, it might still owe something to the play,
for it seems tolerably certain that a *Hamlet* was being
acted in London in 1589 and quite certain that one
existed by 1594. In a preface to the euphuistic romance
Menaphon, published by his friend Robert Greene in the
autumn of 1589, Thomas Nashe sets out in characteristic
vein to extol the university scholarship which they shared
and to decry other and more successful writers, especially
dramatists, who lacked such advantages. As, however,

[1] Cf. note 1. 5. 42–57.

while mentioning many poets and scholars of whom he approves, he carefully refrains from naming the 'mechanicall mates' and 'vaine glorious tragedians,' it is difficult for the modern reader to follow the drift of his invective; so that the following passage in the Preface has been the theme of much controversy:

It is a common practise now a dayes amongst a sort of shifting companions, that runne through euery Art and thriue by none, to leaue the trade of *Nouerint*, whereto they were borne, and busie themselues with the indeuours of Art, that could scarcely Latinize their neck verse if they should haue neede; yet English *Seneca* read by Candlelight yeelds many good sentences, as *Blood is a begger*, and so forth; and if you intreate him faire in a frostie morning, hee will affoord you whole Hamlets, I should say handfuls of Tragicall speeches. But O griefe! *Tempus edax rerum,* whats that will last alwayes? The Sea exhaled by droppes will in continuance bee drie, and *Seneca*, let blood line by line and page by page, at length must needes die to our Stage; which makes his famished followers to imitate the Kid in *Æsop*, who, enamoured with the Foxes newfangles, forsooke all hopes of life to leape into a newe occupation; and these men, renouncing all possibilities of credite or estimation, to intermeddle with Italian Translations: Wherein how poorely they haue plodded, (as those that are neither prouenzall men, nor are able to distinguish of Articles,) let all indifferent Gentlemen that haue travelled in that tongue discerne by their two-pennie Pamphlets[1].

If we assume that, though he uses the plural, Nashe is here attacking a single individual, an assumption which many think unwarranted, it would seem that the person in question had been a scrivener by profession, had written tragedies in the Senecan manner and had turned from these to making translations from the Italian. Not perhaps very distinctive marks of identity in an age when scriveners were many and Italian translations the fashion; yet since all three clues point to the author of *The*

[1] R. B. McKerrow, *Works of Nashe,* iii. 315–16.

Spanish Tragedy and the reference to 'the Kid in Æsop' looks like a pun upon his name, it has been widely supposed that Thomas Kyd was the target aimed at.

There will always be found people to challenge suppositions, however plausible; and this one has been questioned by critics as eminent as Sir Edmund Chambers[1] and Dr McKerrow[2]. But Herr V. Østerberg has recently brought it much more definitely into the area of probability and has, in my thinking, gone very near to proving it. Following up Koeppel's discovery[3] that the fable of the kid to which Nashe refers is to be found, not in Æsop as he avers[4], but under 'May' in Spenser's *Shepherd's Calendar*, he points out that nevertheless Nashe knew what he was doing and had Spenser clearly in mind, since the words 'enamoured with the Foxes newfangles' are a palpable echo of Spenser's lines

> He was so enamored with the newell,
> That nought he deemed deare for the jewell.

What then was the point of the allusion? The Spenserian fable, in which 'Kiddie' falls a prey to the Fox through curiosity, has little obvious reference to Nashe's version. Indeed, the sentence 'which makes his [Seneca's] famished followers to imitate the Kid in Æsop, who, enamoured with the Foxes newfangles, forsooke all hopes of life to leape into a newe occupation' shows that Nashe found some difficulty in dragging the fable in, seeing that the kid in Spenser was not famished and did not leap into a new occupation, nor did the followers of Seneca forsake all hopes of life. The conclusion is surely inescapable: his use of the story was not just a chance

[1] E. K. Chambers, *William Shakespeare*, i. 412.

[2] R. B. McKerrow, *op. cit*. iv. 449–52.

[3] *Englische Studien*, xviii. 130.

[4] Nashe was probably led astray by Spenser himself, who writes in the 'Glosse' to *May*: 'This tale is much like to that in Æsops fables, but the catastrophe and end is farre different.'

literary illustration; it was a deliberate fake to suit the
purpose of his satire. In other words Nashe could
not do without that 'Kid' because he wanted to hit at
Kyd in a punning allusion, just as in his *Anatomie of
Absurditie*[1] he hits at Philip Stubbes's earlier *Anatomie*
when he speaks of those who 'anatomize abuses and
stubbe vp sin by the rootes[2].'

Furthermore, if Kyd the dramatist be Nashe's mark,
then the sly allusion to 'whole Hamlets, I should say
handfuls of Tragicall speeches' would lose half its point
if Kyd were not known by the readers of *Menaphon* to
have written a play of that name. It must be remembered
too that Shakespeare's *Hamlet* belongs to the Senecan
tradition and is demonstrably full of links with *The
Spanish Tragedy*. I was for long extremely sceptical of
the theory connecting Kyd with an early *Hamlet*, but
the arguments of Herr Østerberg leave little doubt in
my mind that a Danish tragedy on the Hamlet theme by
Thomas Kyd was the talk of London in 1589.

The next historical clue we have is an entry in the
Diary, or account-book, of Philip Henslowe, the pawn-
broking financial manager of the Admiral's Company,
recording the performance of a *Hamlet* at the Newington
Butts playhouse on June 11, 1594; and as Henslowe
does not mark the play as 'ne,' it was presumably old
copy. The Newington Butts theatre was at the time in
joint-occupation by his company and the Chamberlain's
men, of which Shakespeare was a member at least as
early as Christmas in the same year. And that the
Hamlet belonged to the Chamberlain's and not the
Admiral's men is shown by a later reference to it,
this time in Thomas Lodge's *Wits Miserie* (1596),

[1] McKerrow, *op. cit.* i. 20.
[2] V. Østerberg, *Studier over Hamlet-teksterne*, Copenhagen, 1920. English scholars seem to have ignored this
important little book, perhaps because it is written in the
language of Hamlet's country. Cf. *R.E.S.* (1942), pp. 385 ff.

which speaks of a certain devil looking 'as pale as the Visard of the ghost which cried so miserably at the Theatre, like an oister wife, Hamlet, revenge'; inasmuch as the Theatre, a playhouse near Bishopsgate belonging to Burbadge, was then in use by his and Shakespeare's fellows. Yet a third reference occurs in Dekker's *Satiromastix*, a reply to Jonson's *Poetaster* and probably performed in the early autumn of 1601 shortly before the appearance of *Hamlet* as we now have it. The plays by Jonson and Dekker were salvos in the 'War of the Theatres' raging at that time, and their characters were mostly caricatures of persons on either side of the dispute. In Tucca, the braggart soldier-man, for example, Jonson had burlesqued a certain Captain Hannam, and Tucca reappears in Dekker's rejoinder, burning with resentment at the affront. He encounters Horace (Jonson) with his hanger-on Asinius Bubo, and taxes the latter with calling him names, whereupon the following dialogue takes place:

Asinius. Would I were hanged if I call you any names but 'Captain' and 'Tucca.'

Tucca. No fyest; my name's 'Hamlet revenge': thou hast been at Paris Garden, hast not?

Horace. Yes Captain, I ha' played Zulziman there.

The passage has long been a puzzle, because it seems to imply a performance of *Hamlet* at the Swan theatre in Paris Garden, a playhouse which the Chamberlain's men are not known to have used. It was left to the Danish critic aforementioned to point out that while the first half of Tucca's speech is spoken to Asinius, the question about the Paris Garden is addressed to Horace, and that there is no necessary connexion between the two[1]. I may add that the colon is a piece of dramatic pointing denoting the pause as Tucca turns from one to the other, and that the question to Horace was probably

[1] Østerberg, *op. cit.* pp. 24–5.

intended as an unpleasant reminder of the *Isle of Dogs*, a play performed at the Swan in 1597,* in which Jonson took part both as actor and author, and for which he fell into serious trouble with the authorities. This interpretation is borne out by Tucca's next speech, which gives a succinct biography of Jonson, including a mention of the *Isle of Dogs*, while it may even be that 'Zulziman[1]' was a character in that play whom Jonson impersonated. Dekker, therefore, had no intention of associating *Hamlet* with the Swan, and there is consequently no reason for supposing that the text of that play ever left the hands of Shakespeare's company from 1594 onwards.

How Kyd's play came into those hands in the first place is unknown but not difficult to guess. All the dramatic companies were in very low water during the plague years 1592–94, and there was much shifting of personnel and transference of playbooks. Moreover, the dramatic career of Kyd himself was brought to an untimely end by his arrest on May 11, 1593, upon the charge of being guilty of a 'libell that concernd the State[2].' There is thus nothing at all surprising in his *Hamlet*, for whatever company it may have been written, becoming part of the stock repertory of the Chamberlain's men, one of the two troupes which came best out of those troublous years; just as his *Spanish Tragedy* passed into the possession of their rivals, the Admiral's men. In any event, I regard it as certain as any deduction from the tangled and perplexing records of Elizabethan theatrical history can be, that it was purchased some time before June 1594 by Shakespeare's company, and that some time between then and the autumn of 1601 Shakespeare himself transformed it to the marvel of beauty and subtilty which his fortunate heirs call *Hamlet*.

Into the nature of that transformation I do not propose,

[1] Can this be a corruption of Zuleiman or Solyman, the Magnificent?
[2] F. S. Boas, *Works of Kyd*, p. lxvi.

as I have said, to enter at this time. It is enough to record first that the earliest mention of a Shakespearian *Hamlet* occurs in a note[1] by the Cambridge don, Gabriel Harvey, inscribed in the margin of his copy of Speght's *Chaucer* published in 1598, a note which speaks of the Earl of Essex as still living and must therefore have been penned before February 1601[2]; and secondly that certain passages in the final *Hamlet*, in particular the reference to the Children of the Chapel and the War of the Theatres at 2. 2. 340–65 and the glance at the defence of Ostend in the soliloquy of 4. 4., cannot have been written earlier than the summer or autumn of the same year[3]. It looks, therefore, as if Shakespeare may first have handled the play sometime after Lodge's reference of 1596 and then revised it in 1601[4].

Before leaving the question of origins a word must be said about a different source of the play from that considered above, an Italian and not a Danish source. We do not know what it was, but we can I think be certain that it existed. Of the circumstances and method of the murder of Hamlet's father, upon which so much hangs,

[1] The note, of considerable length, includes this statement: 'The younger sort takes much delight in Shakespeares *Venus, & Adonis*: but his *Lucrece* & his tragedie of *Hamlet, Prince of Denmarke*, haue it in them, to please the wiser sort.'

[2] E. K. Chambers (*William Shakespeare*, ii. 197) summing up the evidence writes 'On the whole any date from 1598 to the opening weeks of 1601 seem to me possible.' Cf. also G. C. Moore Smith, *Gabriel Harvey's Marginalia* (Preface); H. J. C. Grierson, *Modern Language Review*, xii. 218; F. S. Boas, *Shakespeare and the Universities*, pp. 27, 256–60.

[3] v. notes 2. 2. 335–36, 340–65, and 4. 4. 18 below.

[4] The reference to 'Hamlet revenge' in *Satiromastix* (1601) a cliché clearly belonging to the old *Hamlet*, does not preclude the existence of a Shakespearian *Hamlet* at that date, seeing that the expression continued in common use until 1620 (v. Chambers, *William Shakespeare*, i. 411).

and which are twice detailed, first in the account the Ghost renders of his own death, and again in the Gonzago play, or rather in the dumb-show that precedes it, there is no hint in either Saxo or Belleforest. The Danish story does not mention poison, sleep or orchard. On the contrary Belleforest expressly states that the deed was done by bloody violence in the banqueting-hall of the palace, while Amleth's father sat at meat. On the other hand, *The Murder of Gonzago* bears all the marks of being founded upon an Italian original; and I see no reason for doubting that Hamlet's words at 3. 2. 262, 'The story is extant, and written in very choice Italian,' were substantially correct. Indeed, there are even indications of a historical foundation for the tale, since according to Dowden, 'In 1538 the Duke of Urbino, married to a Gonzaga, was murdered by Luigi Gonzaga, who dropped poison into his ear[1].' What more likely than that Shakespeare, or Kyd, used a scene from a contemporary play upon this subject for his Play-scene, and in order to make the resemblance exact, altered the Hamlet-story to suit the story of Gonzago?

And if something like this happened, it follows that the character of Claudius was also in large measure derived from, or suggested by, the Gonzago-tale. The murderer in the Danish legend was crafty, it is true: 'The man,' Saxo tells us, ' veiled the monstrosity of his deed with such hardihood of cunning, that he made up a mock pretence of goodwill to excuse his crime, and glossed over fratricide with a show of righteousness.' But he was essentially a man of violence. The Claudius of *Hamlet* is effeminate and Italianate. Not without courage and possessed of considerable intellectual powers, he presents nevertheless a mean and contemptible figure. He is a prey to lust, works by spying, and listens behind

---

[1] Dowden unfortunately omits his authority. G. Sarrazin instances another Gonzaga murder on May 7, 1592 (*Sh. Jahrbuch*, 1895, p. 169).*

hangings; if murder is to be done, he eggs on others, when he can, to do it for him; and his trump card, when all else fails, is poison—poison in a 'vial,' a drinking-cup, or on the point of an unbated foil. It is in keeping with all this that he should put his brother out of the world by an act which could only have originated in decadent Italy, an act which revolts us less by its base treachery than by its hideous and unnatural character. Claudius was a 'politician' in the sixteenth-century meaning of that word, a man who lived by dropping poison into other people's ears, and his supreme crime is but the symbol of his personality. Such a being was bred not at Elsinore, but at some petty Italian court. Yet his insertion into the *Hamlet* frame was a masterly stroke. The man of violence, the Laertes type, is useful as a foil to Hamlet; but for his antagonist it was essential to have a man of great cunning, since one of the main interests of the play is the spectacle of two extraordinarily subtle men engaged in a deadly duel of wits.

Limitations of space forbid discussion of that fascinating and still largely unexplored topic, the intellectual sources of *Hamlet*, and in particular the books which Shakespeare was probably reading shortly before he wrote the play. Let it suffice to say that, as my notes show, I agree with Brandes in finding the influence of Montaigne throughout and with Dowden in believing that Shakespeare was well acquainted with a little book on psychology by Timothy Bright called *A Treatise of Melancholy* published in 1586. The most interesting point about this book is that while its phraseology and ideas seem to have influenced *Hamlet* at several places, the melancholy of the Prince was clearly not wholly derived from it. Apparently Shakespeare read it through with his notions of Hamlet already formed, and found Bright's conception of melancholy different from his own, although he used hints here and there and caught phrases from other parts of the treatise.

III

I turn to the main business of this Introduction, which is to give a brief summary of the book already published on the textual problems, so that the notes that follow may be intelligible, to discuss the exegetical problems which are the special concern of those notes and the glossary, and to glance at one or two outstanding dramatic problems.

Four *Hamlet* texts, belonging actually or by derivation to the period of Shakespeare's lifetime, have come down to us; but two are clearly of much greater authority than the others. Concerning the most debased of all, the German version, *Der bestrafte Brudermord,** little need here be said. The earliest copy known is a manuscript dated 1710; but the fact that its Polonius is called Corambus, of which the 'Corambis' in the First Quarto is a patent corruption, together with other clues, makes it certain that it is a degenerate scion of the main English stock and at least possible that its derivation belongs to a date before that at which Shakespeare's *Hamlet* took final shape. But though for this reason of some importance for the history of *Hamlet*, and though also at one or two points it throws light upon Shakespeare's meaning, it gives us no help in determining what Shakespeare actually wrote himself.

The First Quarto, which is a pirated text published in 1603 after Shakespeare's *Hamlet* was already in existence, is more to the purpose, though still only in a backhanded fashion. Ever since its discovery in 1821 critics have been debating its origin and composition, to which they have strangely devoted far more attention than to those of the two good texts. There are many theories; but on one point they all seem now to be agreed, namely that whatever may have been the nature of the piracy and however the pirate procured his copy, the book is in large measure based upon a memorised report of Shakespeare's *Hamlet* as performed in 1601 or 1602 on the Globe stage. Thus while its readings possess no independent authority whatever, though some may be relevant to the textual history of *Hamlet*, many of them are of use as corroborating readings in the other and better texts. Furthermore, its stage-directions, which are often fuller than those in the Second Quarto or the First Folio versions, are valuable for the information they give, on the whole probably reliable, about the stage-business at the Globe, and I have not hesitated to borrow one or two for the stage-directions in my text.

The Second Quarto followed the First at the beginning of 1605[1], and that it was intended to supersede it, as the authoritative edition, is clear from the title-page which proclaims it 'newly imprinted and enlarged to almost as much againe as it was, according to the true and perfect Coppie.' This and the First Folio text printed in 1623 are the only originals which can claim any material connexion with Shakespeare's manuscript. It is to them, therefore, and to them alone, that an editor must go for the construction of his own text. The *textus receptus* is based upon that of the First Folio and 'improved' by incorporation of a large number of readings from the Second Quarto, a few from the First Quarto, and a score or more arrived at by emendation. It is in short an eclectic text, which has varied a good deal from editor to editor, the main principle of choice between variant readings being the judgment and good taste of the editor in question. Judgment and good taste can never be dispensed with, but they may be assisted by critical bibliography, that is to say by a textual analysis which reveals, or at least enables us to surmise, the nature

[1] It was begun printing in 1604, three of the six extant copies being so dated, but not finished until 1605, this date appearing on the other three copies, the change being probably due to press-correction.

of the manuscripts used by the original printers. Readers of previous plays in this edition who have taken the trouble to study the 'note on the copy' preceding the notes in each volume will be familiar with the method. But whereas for none of the fourteen Comedies is there more than a single authoritative text to reckon with, in the case of *Hamlet* there are two, very different in character and each presenting most complicated problems of its own. Furthermore, when the two texts are analysed they disclose a situation exactly the reverse of that assumed by most editors since Rowe, and necessitate the working out of entirely fresh editorial principles.

In *The Manuscript of Shakespeare's 'Hamlet'* I have been able to prove—or so at least I hope—that the copy for *Hamlet* used by the printers of the First Folio, though ultimately derived from the author's autograph, reached them in a very corrupt condition. It was in short a transcript of a transcript: a transcript made in 1622 or 1623 for the publication of the Folio; made from the Globe prompt-book which, though itself in all probability taken direct from Shakespeare's manuscript, had been edited in a more or less high-handed fashion by the bookholder of the theatre; and made by a slovenly playhouse scribe, who to save himself the trouble of keeping his eye constantly on the prompt-book before him frequently trusted to a treacherous memory of the play as he had seen it performed. On the other hand, there is good reason for believing that the *Hamlet* of 1605 was printed, if badly printed, from Shakespeare's autograph, which the company sold to the publisher, the bookholder having no further use for it once he had prepared his prompt-copy for the actors. The text of the present volume is therefore based, not on that of the First Folio, but on the Second Quarto; and is, I believe, the first modernised edition of *Hamlet* to follow that printed 'according to the true and perfect Coppie.' Unfortunately, however perfect the copy, the printing of the

Second Quarto was far from being so, the compositor's worst fault being the omission of words, phrases, lines and occasionally of lengthy passages. He was also guilty of a large quantity of misprints, while his departures from Shakespeare were both complicated and obscured by an overlooker who took upon him to 'correct,' without reference to the manuscript copy, such of his sins of omission and commission as he detected or imagined that he detected. Thus, though the Second Quarto is the text to build upon, no editor can afford to neglect the First Folio, if only for the supply of omitted words and lines. Folio readings are often helpful too in the rectification of misprints, though in view of the corruption by double transcription they must be used with the utmost caution. Nevertheless, in one or two passages I have adopted Folio readings which have been rejected or ignored by all modern editors. For when one can see the ground upon which one treads, it is possible to take bold steps. Indeed, this sense of assurance, of knowing more or less exactly where one stands, is perhaps the greatest of all the rewards to be reaped from a definition of copy.

The foregoing paragraphs give the gist of the first volume of my monograph on the good *Hamlet* texts. The second is devoted to a detailed discussion of the editorial problems arising therefrom; a discussion which serves the purpose of the textual notes in other plays of the present edition and enables me very greatly to lighten the notes that follow in a manner set forth on p. 139. Here it only remains for me to indicate briefly the main trend of these editorial findings.

By editing the text which was printed directly from Shakespeare's manuscript instead of one printed from a careless copy of the prompt-book, and by thus using the latter merely as an auxiliary, it has been possible to decide with fair confidence a number of hitherto doubtful points and also to restore many readings which are not

accepted, for example, in standard modern texts like
The Cambridge Shakespeare and *The Arden Shakespeare.*
Here are some of the more important of these re-
storations, important inasmuch as the variants involve
difference in meaning or in poetic value:

'co-mart' (Q2) for 'covenant' (F1) at 1. 1. 93; 'new-
hatched unfledged courage' (Q2) for 'new-hatched unfledged comrade' (F1) at 1. 3. 65; 'a working mute and
dumb' (Q2) for 'a winking mute and dumb' (F1) at
2. 2. 137; 'repelléd' (Q2)[1] for 'repulsed' (F1) at 2. 2. 146; 'But
who, ah woe!' (Q2) for 'But who, O who' (F1) at 2. 2. 506;
'stallion' (Q2) for 'scullion' (F1) at 2. 2. 591; 'drift of
conference' (Q2) for 'drift of circumstance' (F1) at 3. 1. 1;
'co-medled' (Q2) for 'co-mingled' (F1) at 3. 2. 67; 'This
bad begins' (Q2) for 'Thus bad begins' (F1) at 3. 4. 179;
'like an apple' (Q2) for 'like an ape' (F1) at 4. 2. 17;
''pear' (Q2) for 'pierce' (F1) at 4. 5. 151; 'devise' (Q2)
for 'advise' (F1) at 4. 7. 52; 'preferred' (Q2) for 'prepared'
(F1) at 4. 7. 158; 'Therewith...make' (Q2) for 'There
with...come' (F1) at 4. 7. 167; 'lauds' (Q2) for 'tunes'
(F1) at 4. 7. 176; 'sage requiem' (F1) for 'a requiem' (Q2)
at 5. 1. 231; 'out of an habit' (Q2) for 'outward habit' (F1)
at 5. 2. 191; and 'O God, Horatio' (Q2) for 'Oh good
Horatio' (F1) at 5. 2. 342.

Passing from the choice of variants to the question of
emendation, bibliographical and literary arguments have
been advanced in support of the following solutions for
ten of the capital cruxes in the text:

'sullied flesh' (Q2 sallied flesh, F1 solid flesh) at 1. 2. 129;
'sanity' (Q2 safty, F1 sanctity) at 1. 3. 21; 'often most
select' (Q2, F1, Q1 of a most select) at 1. 3. 74; 'the dram
of evil' (Q2 the dram of eale) and 'often dout' (Q2 of a
doubt) at 1. 4. 36–7; 'peacock' (Q2, F1 paiock) at 3. 2. 284;
'brawls' (Q2 browes, F1 Lunacies) at 3. 3. 7; 'bait
and salary' (Q2 base and silly, F1 hyre and Sallery) at
3. 3. 79; 'of habits evil' (Q2 of habits deuill) at 3. 4. 162;
'parts' (Q2 part) at 5. 2. 115 and 'profound and winnowed'

---

[1] Q2 prints 'repell'd.'

(Q2 prophane and trennowed, F1 fond and winnowed) at
5. 2. 193.

Needless to say these emendations are proposed with
varying degrees of confidence, and some of them are not
included in the text.

In my opinion, however, the most important effect of
the new *apparatus criticus* is to make available for the
first time the stage-directions, speech-headings and
punctuation of the Second Quarto. By so doing it reveals,
for example, the second scene of the play as a meeting
of the King's Council, a Protestant minister conducting
the 'maimed rites' of Ophelia's funeral, and the true
character of the fencing-match in the final scene, while
it gives an entirely fresh turn both in sense and rhythm
to the most famous of Hamlet's prose speeches. For a
discussion of these and other new points, and of the
readings quoted above, the reader must be referred to
the notes. But a word in general must here be said on
the matter of punctuation.

Dr Johnson wrote 'In restoring the author's works to
their integrity, I have considered the punctuation as
wholly in my power,' and until Mr Percy Simpson
published his *Shakespearian Punctuation* in 1911 all
editors have cheerfully assumed a like tyrannical
authority. Mr Simpson's contention that Shakespeare's
punctuation was dramatic and rhetorical destroyed their
cheerfulness without entirely moving editorial sinners to
repentance. For though he made out a strong case in
many of his examples, he committed the mistake, natural
in the first flush of revolutionary discovery, of claiming
that dramatic punctuation was a general feature of all
plays printed in the First Folio. After editing fourteen
of them and examining as many more, I have come to
the reluctant conclusion that, while the original pointing
should always receive respectful consideration as being
ultimately derived from the playhouse, it is too often
overlaid and confused by the high-handed action of

compositors. The best we can hope for in most texts, as Dr Pollard has shown in his careful analysis of the punctuation of the quarto *Richard II*, is that in set speeches we may find the actual stops of Shakespeare himself[1]. Despite disappointment, however, I have always retained my faith in Shakespearian punctuation, for the simple reason that I studied it first in the Second Quarto of *Hamlet*, and that here its existence seems patent and indisputable.

The *Hamlet* of 1605, though set up from Shakespeare's manuscript, is, as I have said, a badly printed book. The compositor was probably a beginner, who had not learnt to carry words in his head, who had not mastered his printing-house spelling, and who, driven, as I suppose, to work at a speed beyond his powers, committed hundreds of misprints and left out words by the score. Yet his incompetence, once the simple little tricks of it are understood, opens up a rich mine to the enquirer. Behind his misprints and strange spellings may be detected Shakespeare's old-fashioned orthography and Shakespeare's wayward penmanship, while for punctuation, since he was too ignorant to possess more than the bare rudiments of a punctuation of his own, he must have relied almost entirely upon his copy. For the pointing of the Second Quarto is, in the main, a thing of beauty from beginning to end. There are passages in which the stops are obviously wrong or, as is more usual, have been omitted by accident. But these instances are surprisingly few, and there is no doubt whatever in my mind that the manuscript of *Hamlet*, the play to which Shakespeare gave more thought than any other, was carefully punctuated, and that the bulk of the stops in the Second Quarto are his. This punctuation I have endeavoured to reproduce in the reprint of the Second Quarto issued from the Cranach Press by Count Harry Kessler in

[1] *King Richard II: a new Quarto*, pp. 64 ff.

1930. In a modernised text like the present, it would not be appropriate to follow it with the same fidelity. It is a light pointing, corresponding with Hamlet's advice to the player to speak his lines 'trippingly on the tongue,' and I have therefore been obliged sometimes to add commas and more often to substitute dashes or periods for commas already there, in order to avoid ambiguity and bewilderment on the part of the reader. Except for such changes, which must go unregistered in the already overburdened notes, and a few more serious ones which will be recorded, together with the rectification of errors, a list of which may be found in *The Manuscript of Shakespeare's 'Hamlet,'* the punctuation of this edition is that of the Second Quarto, which is in the main, I believe, that of Shakespeare.

IV

When I first began editing Shakespeare in 1919 I was prepared for fresh tillage in the field of textual exploration and emendation, but in that of commentary I looked to find few stones unturned by editors of the eighteenth and nineteenth centuries. Nothing has surprised me more than the amount of work of this sort still to be done, not merely in comparatively neglected plays like *Love's Labour's Lost* and *All's Well*, but also in popular and constantly edited ones such as *The Tempest*, *The Merchant of Venice*, *As You Like It* and *Twelfth Night*. Indeed, the further I went upon my way the more the need for commentary forced itself upon my attention, and in *Hamlet*, the most popular and most frequently edited of them all, the task is heavier than ever.

Here, for example, is a list of some thirty of the more important passages upon which I think I have been able to throw fresh light, or upon which fresh light has been thrown by others during recent years:

to fast in fires (1. 5. 11); cursed hebona (1. 5. 62); now to

my word (1. 5. 110); yes, by St Patrick (1. 5. 136); I'll loose
my daughter to him (2. 2. 162); I know a hawk from a
handsaw (2. 2. 383); the law of writ and the liberty (2. 2.
406); like French falconers (2. 2. 434); the whips and scorns
of time (3. 1. 70); the undiscovered country (3. 1. 79);
inexplicable dumb-shows (3. 2. 12); I eat the air, promise-
crammed (3.2.91); I have nothing with this answer (3.2.93);
miching mallecho (3. 2. 135); Lucianus, nephew to the king
(3. 2. 243); these pickers and stealers (3. 2. 337); horrid hent
(3. 3. 88); enseaméd (3. 4. 92); lapsed in time and passion
(3. 4. 107); this piteous action (3. 4. 128); the body is with
the king, but the king is not with the body (4. 2. 26–7);
a thing of nothing (4. 2. 28–9); a little patch of ground
(4. 4. 18); nature is fine in love (4. 5. 161); O, how the wheel
becomes it! (4. 5. 171); a plurisy (4. 7. 116); a pair of indentures (5. 1. 107); drink up eisel, eat a crocodile (5. 1. 270);
a comma 'tween their amities (5. 2. 42); he hath laid on
twelve for nine (5. 2. 168); with the shell on his head
(5. 2. 186).

The principal reason why so much remains to do in
the exegesis of *Hamlet* and other plays is that *The New
English Dictionary*, or *The Oxford Dictionary* as we have
now been requested to call it, was not completed until
1928. So long as this incomparable editorial instrument
was in process of publication editors naturally did not
take it sufficiently seriously or consulted it half-heartedly.
They tended, for example, to seek help from it only in
the last resort, instead of cultivating the habit of consulting its pages on all sorts of passages which seem at
first sight to be perfectly plain.

If thou hast nature in thee bear it not,

says the Ghost to Hamlet; and what could be more
palpable or straightforward? Yet the discovery that the
simple-looking word 'nature' may mean 'natural
feeling,' and consequently 'filial affection,' illuminates
not only this line but four other passages in the play*
which have hitherto been misapprehended[1]. Editors too

[1] v. notes 4. 5. 161–63; 5. 2. 229 and cf. 1. 2. 102; 3. 2. 396.

grew weary in well-doing, and if they drew blank in the *Dictionary* under a substantive they might neglect to look for clues under the verb. Even Dowden, whose notes are richer than those of any previous editor, after rightly glossing 'mortal coil' at 3. 1. 67 as 'trouble or turmoil of mortal life,' continues

'In this sense "coil" occurs several times in Shakespeare, as in *Tempest*, 1. 2. 207. He nowhere uses it in the sense of concentric rings, nor does *The New English Dictionary* give an example earlier than 1627. The notion that "mortal coil" means the body, encircling the soul, may be set aside.'

Had he been inspired to turn from coil sb^2 to 'coil v^3' he would have found, quoted from Cotgrave's *French Dictionary* of 1611, 'to coil a cable, to wind or lay it up round or in a ring' under the very first heading, while above the heading stands a note: 'Goes with "coil sb^3" [to which the example from 1627 belongs], neither being as yet traced beyond 1611, though as nautical words they were no doubt in spoken use much earlier[1].' We need not hesitate, therefore, to credit Shakespeare with the quibble upon 'coil, a winding of rope,' or Hamlet with the notion of the body as a troublesome entanglement which the soul 'shuffles off' at death[2].

---

[1] That Dowden consulted the *N.E.D.* fitfully and carelessly is shown by his note upon 'comma' (5. 2. 42) in which he quotes from it under 'comma' 1 and yet misses the true explanation staring him in the face which it offers under 'comma' 2 *c*.

[2] 'shuffle off' means 'shirk' or 'evade' (cf. *Tw. Nt.* 3. 3. 16); its modern sense of disencumbering oneself hastily of some garment or wrap is derived from *Hamlet*. The original meaning of 'shuffle' is to 'shuffle with the feet' as one walks, and the image in Shakespeare's mind was, I think, that of the soul standing erect and freeing itself from the lifeless body which has fallen to the ground like a divested garment.

'A quibble,' wrote Dr Johnson, 'was to Shakespeare the fatal Cleopatra for which he lost the world and was content to lose it.' The relationship seems to me far more intimate and respectable. Shakespeare habitually thought in quibbles, if indeed 'quibble' be the right term for what was one of the main roots of his poetic expression. When he used a word, all possible meanings of it were commonly present to his mind, so that it was like a musical chord which might be resolved in whatever fashion or direction he pleased. To miss a quibble, then, is often to miss the interwoven thread which connects together a whole train of images; for imagery and double meaning are generally inseparable. It is therefore of first importance that an editor should know all the meanings of which Shakespeare might be aware, and this has only become feasible with the completion of *The Oxford Dictionary* in which the sixteenth and seventeenth century connotations of each word in the language are generally to be found in close proximity[1].

Shakespeare employs at least two distinct types of quibble. First there is what may be called the poetic quibble or conceit, of which an example has already been given in Hamlet's 'mortal coil.' This may be of almost every degree of complexity from the simple development of an image to an elaborate and lengthy interweaving of two or more strands of meaning derived from the same word or from an image either expressed or implied. How effective it may be dramatically is shown by Hamlet's 'table-book' speech at 1. 5. 95 ff.[2] and the opening episode of the play furnishes two good

---

[1] That there are still a few stray fish to be caught in the sea dredged by the *N.E.D.* may be seen by referring to the following items in the Glossary: cast beyond, cry on, days of nature, fishmonger (v. note), mallecho, ore, piece of work, rebel. It is also sometimes wrong, e.g. in regard to 'conscience' (3. 1. 83) as Bradley (p. 98 n.) points out.

[2] Cf. note 1. 5. 107–109.

instances of it in a more elementary form. In Horatio's lovely piece of scene-painting—

> But look, the morn in russet mantle clad
> Walks o'er the dew of yon high eastward hill—

the word 'russet,' used to describe the indeterminate reddish-brown or grey of the sky at daybreak, recalls the coarse homespun cloth, which is its original sense, and so gives birth to the image of Dawn as a labourer mounting the hill to his work of the day, his mantle thrown across his shoulder. Somewhat less obvious and more complicated is the train of imagery in the lines:

> Sharked up a list of lawless resolutes
> For food and diet to some enterprise
> That hath a stomach in't.

Here, as often, the clue to the picture in Shakespeare's mind is to be found in other plays. The ingredients of the witches' cauldron in *Macbeth* which include

> Maw and gulf
> Of the ravined salt-sea shark

give us a starting-point, which can be followed up in the lines of the 'Shakespearian' Addition to *Sir Thomas More*, describing More's warning to the rioters of the effects of social anarchy when 'other ruffians'

> Would shark on you, and men like ravenous fishes
> Would feed on one another.

These passages[1], both containing the word 'shark' together with the epithets 'ravined' or 'ravenous' which bear the same meaning, show us that voracious and promiscuous feeding was for Shakespeare the distinctive feature of the shark tribe. The phrase 'sharked up' therefore means 'swallowed up greedily and without discrimination,' while the notion of feeding has suggested

---

[1] For a discussion of that from *Sir Thomas More* v. articles by C. Spurgeon, *Review of English Studies*, vi. 257 and R. W. Chambers, *Modern Language Review*, xxvi. 265.

'food and diet' in the next line and 'stomach' in the line
following.

At the other extreme we have at 4. 7. 116–22 seven
lines of elaborate quibbling upon the word 'plurisy.'
A sixteenth-century spelling of 'pleurisy,' which is
rightly the inflammation of the pleura, i.e. the coverings
of the lungs, it came to mean figuratively 'superabun-
dance,' or 'excess,' through a mistaken etymological
connexion with 'plus.' Hence we get

> For goodness, growing to a plurisy,
> Dies in his own too-much;

and again

> And then this 'should' is like a spendthrift sigh,
> That hurts by easing,

which describes the pain in the chest and the difficult
breathing caused by pleurisy. Once the full connotation
of 'plurisy' in Elizabethan English is grasped it is not
difficult to follow the course of Shakespeare's thought.
But as often as not, especially in his later plays, the key-
image is suppressed altogether. When, for example,
Hamlet sums up Osric and his like in the words—

> Thus has he—and many more of the same bevy that
> I know the drossy age dotes on—only got the tune of the
> time and, out of an habit of encounter, a kind of yeasty
> collection, which carries them through and through the
> most profound and winnowed opinions, and do but blow
> them to their trial, the bubbles are out—

we understand them much better if we catch the hidden
picture of the fermentation of barley in a vat which un-
derlies them. Or again, the restored text of the opening
lines of the first soliloquy—

> O, that this too too sullied flesh would melt,
> Thaw and resolve itself into a dew—

ought not to trouble anyone who can see an image of
thawing snow behind the word 'sullied.'

But though the detection of poetic conceit or veiled metaphor is often of great help to an editor seeking to determine a reading or to elucidate a meaning, a conscious perception of them is not in most passages essential to appreciation. So much had the use of double meaning become a second nature with Shakespeare, that in all probability it was generally involuntary on his part; and that a reader should feel a connexion without being able to distinguish the separate links in the chain very often adds much to the pregnancy of the verse. Moreover, it must be remembered that Shakespeare wrote not for readers but for auditors, who would have no time to consider his linked metaphors too curiously. As a final example may be taken the following scrap of dialogue from the Bedroom-scene:

> *Queen.*   O Hamlet, speak no more.
> Thou turn'st my eyes into my very soul,
> And there I see such black and grainèd spots
> As will not leave their tinct.
> *Hamlet.*   Nay, but to live
> In the rank sweat of an enseamèd bed
> Stewed in corruption, honeying, and making love
> Over the nasty sty.

It is one of the most passionate passages in the most passionate scene of the play; and yet it is threaded on a string of images almost banal in character. For 'grainèd' and 'tinct,' being terms of wool-dyeing, have suggested 'enseamèd,' another technical word from the woollen industry meaning 'loaded with grease,' and that in turn, because the 'seam' employed in the greasing process was hog's-lard, has suggested the 'nasty sty.' It is very unlikely that Shakespeare himself was aware of this train of ideas; the son of the wool merchant of Stratford was unwittingly drawing from the well of early memories, that is all. It is even more unlikely that any reader or spectator would be aware of it, and in this instance the associations are probably too remote to

influence the imagination. Generally, however, such
associations are all the more potent for our being insensible of them. In his use of imagery, as in his creation
of character, Shakespeare's strength lies in the impression
of unfathomed and unfathomable depths which it is his
art to convey,*

> Because his touch is infinite and lends
>   A yonder to all ends.

But he was past-master also of a very different kind
of quibble, though it springs from the same root: the
quibble of wit and repartee. Here the situation is
reversed; for the quibble is the point of the jest, and if
it eludes the auditor the jest falls flat. That a large number
of his quibbles of necessity elude the modern reader and
have usually eluded his editors is the principal reason
why so much of his comic dialogue seems dead wood.
to-day. All the colour and sap of the fun has withered
like that of music-hall jokes fifty years old; we can no
more catch the trick of it than we can be born again into
the Elizabethan age. But editors have been over-modest
in this matter; and my experience with *Love's Labour's
Lost*, which probably seemed the most brilliant of all
Shakespeare's plays to his contemporaries, and in which
the quibbling is endless, has convinced me that enough
of it can be recovered for us to understand something
of the enthusiasm with which London hailed the advent
of this wittiest of Elizabethan poets. For his reputation,
at any rate at the time he was writing *Hamlet*, rested upon
'his facetious grace in writing,' as the apologetic Chettle
puts it, while a publisher exclaims, 'So much and such
savoured salt of wit is in his comedies that they seem, for
their height of pleasure, to be born in the sea that brought
forth Venus[1].'

Moreover, if more than half the point of Shakespeare's

---

[1] v. the *Epistle* to *Troilus and Cressida*, 1609.

clowning in plays like *Twelfth Night* and *As You Like It* has been missed because editors have not been sufficiently on the look-out for the double meaning, the loss is still more serious in *Hamlet*. Riddle and quibble are close of kin, and Shakespeare's Prince of Denmark inherited both from his legendary ancestor Amleth. To repeat the words of Saxo: 'astutiam veriloquio permiscebat, ut nec dictis veracitas deesset, nec acuminis modus verorum iudicio proderetur.' It would be difficult to find a more apt description of Hamlet's speech when he assumes his 'antic disposition,' and spectators or readers are robbed of the 'mirth' which, as Dr Johnson says, 'the pretended madness of Hamlet causes' if they do not attempt to detect the point of the 'acumen.' To write, as Aldis Wright does on one occasion, 'Hamlet is talking nonsense designedly' is to throw up the editorial sponge. Dowden saw deeper. 'If ingenuities are anywhere pardonable,' he concludes, 'it is in conjecturing the meaning of Hamlet's riddling speeches; it was not his use ever to talk sheer nonsense[1].' At his maddest, there is always an edge, a sharp edge, to what he says. We can be sure that Shakespeare's audience realised this to the full, and that the judicious among them took great pleasure in attempting to solve the enigmas which he set them. Stage-quibbling was indeed a kind of game, like the modern crossword puzzle or the problems with which writers of detective stories pose their readers; and in *Hamlet* it was 'performed at height.' The very first words Hamlet utters are a riddle. 'A little more than kin, and less than kind'—what might that mean? Obviously that he had suffered some unkindness at the hands of Claudius. But the full meaning, for those keen enough to see it, does not come before the end of the first soliloquy. Or take—

> *Hamlet.* The king is a thing—

---

[1] *Hamlet* (Arden Shakespeare), p. x.

Guildenstern. A thing, my lord!
Hamlet. Of nothing, bring me to him.

Editors rightly quote Ps. cxliv. 4 (Prayer Book version), 'Man is like a thing of nought,' but they forget to complete the verse—'his time passeth away like a shadow,' and so fail to catch Hamlet's point, which is that the King's days are numbered, as he has hinted in the scarcely less cryptic 'The body is with the king, but the king is not with the body' a moment before.

Elaborate and subtle conundrums of this kind raise a general question of some difficulty at first sight. If modern editors poring over their texts with the aid of dictionaries and glossaries have been foiled, how were even the swiftest Elizabethan intelligences expected to tackle them in the rapid give-and-take of spoken dialogue? A good deal, of course, depends upon whether the spectator or reader comes to the play in the proper frame of mind. Anyone who has watched a music-hall audience taking point after point in the gag of the funny man will know how quickly even the generality, when 'tickle o'th'sere,' will rise to the most far-fetched jest. Editors, on the other hand, have usually been of a temperament slow in such uptake, and have lacked the education a music-hall might provide. Again, Shakespeare no doubt relied to some extent upon the memory of his audience, and generally cast his quibbling riddles into a form which, in those days when verbal memory had not yet been swamped and corrupted by over-much reading, was easy to retain and ponder when the play was done. But he had something else besides memory to reckon with, a something the influence of which upon Elizabethan drama has been strangely neglected.

'My tables, meet it is I set it down,' exclaims Hamlet; and every Elizabethan gallant or inns-of-court man carried his table-book about him, for use on all sorts of occasions; to copy down 'saws of books' as he read, memorable passages from some sermon that took his fancy, witty remarks overheard in conversation, 'taffeta phrases, silken terms precise, three-piled hyperboles' that came his way and if captured might be used again by himself as opportunity offered. I call to mind an undergraduate of my acquaintance at Cambridge thirty years ago who filled note-books with epigrams from Oscar Wilde's plays and essays, with which he afterwards larded his own talk; and the young men of Shakespeare's day took the same path. The Osrics made a 'yeasty collection,' and the Benedicks 'guarded' 'the body of their discourse' 'with fragments' compiled in similar fashion. In *Have with you to Saffron Walden* Nashe gives us an imaginary picture of his enemy Gabriel Harvey pleading in the law-courts, and filling his speech with such strange ink-horn terms that 'we should haue the Proctors and Registers as busie with their Table-books as might bee, to gather phrases[1].' Above all, the tables came into play at the theatre; and where else in the whole history of the world has there been a richer harvest for such gleaning? 'I am one that hath seen this play often,' says a character in the Induction to Marston's *Malcontent*, which Shakespeare's company was playing within a year or so of *Hamlet*; 'I have most of the jests here in my table-book[2]'; and the unkindest cut in the attack upon an unnamed clown which appears in the First Quarto of *Hamlet*, but not in the Second Quarto or the Folio, is that he 'keeps one suit of jests, as a man is known by one suit of apparel' so that 'gentlemen quote his jests down in their tables *before* they come to the play.'* The subtilty of Shakespeare's jesting, the double and triple meanings of his quibbles, need not then disturb our sense of probability. The judicious, and no doubt often the injudicious also, the Master Slenders or Master Froths, brought their tables with them, took

---

[1] McKerrow, *op. cit.* iii. 46.
[2] Bullen, *Marston*, i. 200.

down what they could not fathom at first hearing, conned them over or discussed them with fellow playgoers at 'Yaughan's' and other taverns afterwards; and if they were still baffled, came again and yet again. The vogue must have afforded much entertainment, and of a kind perhaps not without its influence upon the takings at the theatre door.

But many of the sallies, intended to delight and at times to nonplus the wits of Bankside or Blackfriars, have become merely bewildering after three centuries of change in the language, and with the talk of the town—that amalgam of back-chat, topical allusion and passing cliché—faded beyond recall. The modern reader of Shakespeare needs all the help that can be given him; and though no editor, even with *The New English Dictionary* on his shelves, can hope to recover in full the luminous clarity and sparkling brilliance of the mirror in which Shakespeare reflected the very age and body of his time, its form and pressure, he can charwoman-like at least remove some of the worst of the weather-stains and brush away a little of the dust. In no play is such humble service needed more than in *Hamlet*.

Roughly, and upon no rigid principle of distinction, words and phrases needing comment have been dealt with in the following categories: those of special difficulty or dramatic importance, including most that occur in the speeches of Hamlet, will be explained by gloss or paraphrase in the Notes; others, of a kind in which the unlearned may expect help, will be found in the Glossary; lastly, an attempt has been made to draw attention to expressions which are especially misleading because they have altered their meaning since Shakespeare's day by mention in the notes and reference to the glossary.

Hamlet's quibbles, or difficult and obsolete phrasing elsewhere, are, however, by no means the most trouble-some hindrance to the full understanding of *Hamlet*.

There are the contemporary allusions already referred to, which I have attempted to deal with in the notes as they arise, and of which here no more need be said. There is a special group of hitherto misunderstood passages, connected with the fencing-match in the last scene, the details of which I hope have now been made clear by the aid of contemporary books upon sword-play and through conversation with modern practitioners of the art, among whom I am particularly indebted to Mr Evan John, actor, scholar and swordsman[1]. More formidable than all the rest is the failure of criticism to grapple with the question of what actually happens in the play scene by scene. The interpretation of some of the passages mentioned in the list at the beginning of this section depends upon the solution of such problems; and in order that my notes may be understood I must now briefly consider the matter in general terms.

V*

For the most part, the dramatic criticism of *Hamlet* during the past hundred and fifty years has been—rather wearisomely—revolving about the problem of Hamlet's character. That way lies psycho-analysis, and Dr Ernest Jones, president of the British Psycho-analytical Society, has duly obliged with the latest diagnosis of the Prince of Denmark's soul[2]. A fundamental misconception

---

[1] I have discussed the fencing-match at greater length than the notes below will allow in the introduction to a reprint of Silver's *Paradoxes of Defence* (1599), issued by the Shakespeare Association in 1933. Cf. also *Times Literary Supplement*, Jan. 11, 18, 25, 1934.

[2] *Essays in Applied Psycho-analysis*, 1923. In impugning psycho-analysis as an instrument of dramatic criticism, I cast of course no reflexion upon its therapeutic virtues, for which I entertain considerable respect. Moreover, Dr Jones's essay, which is a development of Bradley, or rather

vitiates this and most previous attempts of the kind: that
of treating Hamlet as if he were a living man or a
historical character, instead of being a single figure, if
the central figure, in a dramatic composition. Prospero
Shakespeare has put his spell upon the world; he has
filled his plays with creatures so life-like that we imagine
they must have an existence beyond the element they
move in. Yet they are confined spirits; and though the
illusion of their freedom is perhaps the highest of all
tributes to the potency of the magician's wand, the fact
that he has thus enchanted his greatest critics gives rise
to grave errors concerning the nature of his art. Even
the young Goethe was bewitched. The hero of *Wilhelm
Meister* reveals his critical method: 'I sought,' he says,
'for every indication of what the character of Hamlet
was before the death of his father; I took note of all that
this interesting youth had been, independently of that
sad event, independently of the subsequent terrible
occurrences, and I imagined what he might have been
without them[1].' Dr Jones, crediting Hamlet with an
Œdipus complex, is only carrying the procedure a step
further. Apart from the play, apart from his actions,
from what he tells us about himself and what other
characters tell us about him, there is no Hamlet. He is
like a figure in a picture; his position therein, the light
and shade around him, the lines and curves which
constitute his form, are part of the composition of the
whole, and derive their sole life and significance from
their relation to the rest of the picture. Critics who
speculate upon what Hamlet was like before the play
opens, who talk about his life with Horatio at Wittenberg, discuss how he came to fall in love with Ophelia,

---

of Löning who anticipates Bradley, shows wider reading
of previous criticism, especially of German criticism, than
most English writings on the subject.

[1] *Wilhelm Meister*, Bk IV, ch. iii (trans. in Furness,
Variorum *Hamlet*, ii. 272).

or attribute his conduct to a mother-complex acquired
in infancy, are merely cutting the figure out of the canvas
and sticking it in a doll's-house of their own invention.
As for Hamlet-psychology, the best thing ever said on
that head came to us the other day from Australia: 'We
can find out no more secrets about Hamlet's motives.
A play is not a mine of secret motives. We persist in
digging for them; what happens usually is that our spade
goes through the other side of the drama[1].'

Partly in reaction against such theorising, a school
of recent critics, with Professor Stoll of Minnesota,
Professor Schücking of Breslau, and the late Mr J. M.
Robertson of this country at their head, have restated the
problem in historical instead of psychological terms.
They ask, not 'What is wrong with Hamlet?' but 'What
is wrong with *Hamlet*?' and the answer they give is that
nearly everything is wrong. Shakespeare, they inform
us, threw the cloak of his inimitable poetry over the
primitive construction of Kyd's drama, but he was quite
unable to bring it dramatically to life, so that the un-
accountable behaviour of the hero is simply one, though
the most flagrant, indication of what Mr T. S. Eliot,
dancing to Mr Robertson's pipe, has called 'most
certainly an artistic failure[2].' Yet the historians are even
further astray than the psychologists. They appear to
have no aesthetic, or at least dramatic, principles whatever, but seek to explain and appraise everything in
Shakespeare by reference to historical causes. Thus,
when they come upon passages, scenes or characters
which perplex them, instead of asking themselves what
Shakespeare's purpose might have been or what artistic
.function such passages, scenes or characters might conceivably possess in a play written for the Elizabethan

[1] *Hamlet: a study of critical method*, by A. J. A. Waldock,
1931, p. 98. Cf. an admirable footnote on p. 158 of
Schücking's *Character Problems in Shakespeare's Plays*.
[2] *The Sacred Wood* (2nd ed.), p. 98.

stage and for an Elizabethan audience, they label them 'relics of an old play' and talk of the stubbornness of Shakespeare's material or the crudity of Elizabethan drama.

But before Shakespeare be dismissed from the rank of dramatist and degraded to that of a mere poetical decorator of other people's plays, a word or two may perhaps be found in his defence. There are dozens of problems, large and small, in *Hamlet* which have never been satisfactorily explained, and of which quite a fair proportion have never even been noticed. Some are probably due to 'historical' causes, that is to say they are discrepancies arising out of revision. I doubt, however, whether any of these are to be set down to the intractability of the inherited plot, and I am certain that they vanish one and all in the illusion of the theatre. The most famous of them, for example, the puzzle of Hamlet's age, which seems to be about eighteen at the opening of the play and is inferentially fixed at thirty by the words of the sexton in the last act, looks like a consequence of revision, but has obviously nothing to do with any difficulty in the original play and passes entirely unnoticed by spectators in the theatre, seeing that their Hamlet is an actor made up to represent a certain age, which they accept without question[1]. Shakespeare's critics have seldom recognised that he enjoyed, and of right exercised, a liberty denied to the novelist and eschewed by the modern dramatist whose production in an age dominated by the printing-press is consciously or unconsciously conditioned by the terms of publication. Verisimilitude and not consistency or historical accuracy is the business of drama, and its Elizabethan artists, working in a theatre without drop-curtain or act-pauses, knew that the audience could not ponder or check the

[1] Cf. Bradley, *op. cit.* p. 73, 'the moment Burbage entered it must have been clear whether the hero was twenty or thirty.'

coherence of events or character as a reader can. 'From the very outset of his career,' I have written elsewhere, 'Shakespeare took advantage of this freedom, but as time went on and as his sense of mastery of his instrument, the Elizabethan stage, grew upon him, he availed himself of it more and more boldly, not because he was becoming careless, but quite legitimately in the service of his art, in order to heighten his effects and to increase the volume and complexity of his theatrical orchestration[1].'

Once this point of Elizabethan dramatic technique is grasped, a number of other problems in *Hamlet* are seen to be mere devices similar to those by which a painter secures perspective or balance. The analysing scholar, for instance, is puzzled by certain 'difficulties' connected with the character of Horatio. He is now a foreigner to whom Hamlet is obliged to explain the customs and outstanding personalities of Denmark, and now a Dane, who knows the latest rumours at court, has seen King Hamlet, and can command the respectful hearing of Fortinbras and the rest after Prince Hamlet's death. The explanation is, of course, that he is not a person in actual life or a character in a novel but a piece of dramatic structure. His function is to be the chief spokesman of the first scene and the confidant of the hero for the rest of the play. As the former he gives the audience necessary information about the political situation in Denmark, as the latter he is the recipient of information even more necessary for the audience to hear. The double rôle involves some inconsistency, but rigid logical or historical consistency is hardly compatible with dramatic economy which requires all facts to be communicated through the mouths of the characters. Yet only a very indifferent playwright will allow an audience to perceive such joins in his flats. And Shake-

---

[1] *Aspects of Shakespeare* (British Academy Lectures), 1933, p. 208.

speare is able to give his puppets an appearance of life so overwhelming that his legerdemain remains unperceived not only by the spectator, who is allowed no time for consideration, but even by most readers. In the case of Horatio he secures this end by emphasising his humanity at three critical moments of the play: in the first scene, just before the Gonzago play, and in the finale. In short, we feel we know Hamlet's friend so well that it never occurs to us to ask questions about him.

Apart, however, from dramatic artifice or the possible effects of revision, there is a third group of problems in *Hamlet* which concern matters vital to our understanding of what is actually happening upon the stage. To cite a handful of examples: What is the meaning of Hamlet's extraordinary behaviour towards his father's spirit in the Cellarage-scene? Why do Rosencrantz and Guildenstern lure Hamlet on to discuss ambition with them? Does Hamlet know that Claudius, or Polonius, or both, are behind the hangings in the Nunnery-scene, and if so how does he learn it? Why does not Claudius break off the Gonzago play when he sees the Dumbshow, which represents all the circumstances of his crime, including the poisoning through the ear of the victim? Why does Hamlet make Lucianus the 'nephew' and not the brother of the murdered King of the play? What is the explanation of Hamlet's consistent use of obscene or insulting language to Ophelia or about her? The reply which the historical critics would furnish to these queries is a simple one, namely the ramshackle character of Elizabethan drama in general and of *Hamlet* in particular. Even Mr Granville-Barker declares that 'the plot, as a plot, is worked out with scandalous ineptitude[1].' Yet before we can decide whether a plot works effectively we ought at least to enquire whether all the parts of the plot are in working order. It is my

[1] v. *Aspects of Shakespeare*, p. 64.

contention that important elements of the plot of *Hamlet* have been lost or overlaid, and that the real 'problem' is to recover these elements.

The main trouble with the 'historical' critics is their ignorance of history and their lack of historical curiosity. On the one hand, they assume without evidence and in the teeth of all probability, that the aesthetic sensibility of the Elizabethans as regards drama was crude and infantile compared with our own; on the other hand, they make little or no attempt to study Shakespeare in the light of Elizabethan politics and cosmology.

The Ghost-scenes in *Hamlet*, for instance, cannot rightly be understood without some study of Elizabethan spiritualism, which was a very different thing from modern spiritualism. Practically everyone in that age, including probably Shakespeare himself, believed in ghosts. Reginald Scot, one of the few exceptions, wrote a notorious book entitled *The Discoverie of Witchcraft*, 1584, which contained an elaborate *Discourse upon Divels and Spirits* explaining ghosts as either the illusion of persons suffering from 'melancholy' or else flat knavery on the part of some rogue. Shakespeare knew the book and used it for *Macbeth*, while the attitude of Horatio towards the apparition in the first scene of *Hamlet* is probably a stage-reflexion of Scot's. But Scot was battling against the flowing tide and King James ordered his treatise to be publicly burnt by the hangman after his accession. Far more representative was another controversy about ghosts, which exercised some of the wisest minds of that time, and concerned their provenance, not their objectivity. The traditional view, coming down from the middle ages, and held by most unthinking persons, was that they were the spirits of the departed who were permitted to return from Purgatory to communicate with living men and women. But Protestants had ceased to believe in Purgatory; and they could hardly suppose that souls in bliss in Heaven would willingly re-

turn to earth or that souls might be released from Hell
to do so. Many of them, therefore, came to the conclusion that ghosts could not possibly be the dead, and
must be spirits of another sort. They might conceivably
be angels, but in most instances they were undoubtedly
devils who 'assumed'—such was the technical word—
the forms of the departed for their own evil purposes.
Catholic theologians, on the other hand, defended the
traditional explanation with much learning and industry.
The dispute was one of the major interests of the period.
'Of all the common and familiar subjects of conversation,' writes one of the controversialists, 'that are entered
upon in company concerning things remote from nature
and cut off from the senses, there is none so ready to
hand, none so usual, as that of visions of Spirits, and
whether what is said of them is true. It is the topic that
people most readily discuss and on which they linger the
longest, because of the abundance of examples; the
subject being fine and pleasing and the discussion the
least tedious that can be found[1].'

All this, the controversy and the various points of view
belonging to it, is mirrored, very faithfully and in-
terestingly mirrored, in *Hamlet*. The 'philosopher'
Horatio and the simple soldier-man Marcellus stand
respectively for the sceptical and the traditional interpretations. But Hamlet, the student of Wittenberg, is
chiefly swayed by Protestant prepossessions. When he
first hears of the Ghost he says

> If *it* assume my noble father's person,
> I'll speak to it though hell itself should gape
> And bid me hold my peace;

---

[1] v. p. 222 of Lewes Lavater, *Of Ghostes and Spirites
walking by Nyght* (1572), ed. by J. Dover Wilson and
May Yardley, 1929. In my Introduction and Miss Yardley's
essay on 'The Catholic position of the Ghost Controversy
of the Sixteenth Century' will be found a lengthy treatment
of the spiritualistic problems of *Hamlet*.

and when the apparition is before his eyes, the opening
words of his speech—

> Angels and ministers of grace defend us!
> Be thou a spirit of health, or goblin damned,
> Bring with thee airs from heaven, or blasts from hell,
> Be thy intents wicked, or charitable—

voice the orthodox Protestant standpoint. While he is
actually talking with the Ghost he is convinced: it is the
spirit of his beloved father. But directly the vision
disappears the doubts return:

> O all you host of heaven! O earth! what else?
> And shall I couple hell? O fie!

He shuts down the thought of hell; but the thought is
there, to prey upon him with added force in moods of
depression later.

> The spirit that I have seen
> May be a devil, and the devil hath power
> T'assume a pleasing shape, yea, and perhaps
> Out of my weakness and my melancholy,
> As he is very potent with such spirits,
> Abuses me to damn me—

he declares at the end of Act 2; and in the deep despondency of the 'To be or not to be' soliloquy in the
scene following he has clearly so far given up belief in
the 'honesty' of the Ghost that he speaks of the world
beyond the grave as

> The undiscovered country, from whose bourn
> No traveller returns.

Thus a passage, which has long been a stone of stumbling
to critics ignorant of Elizabethan spiritualism, which
Professor Stoll has stigmatised as a piece of careless
writing on Shakespeare's part, 'an unguarded word such
as we find not in Ibsen[1]', and Mr J. M. Robertson has

---

[1] E. E. Stoll, *Hamlet: an historical and comparative Study*,
1919, p. 35. Professor Stoll alone among the 'historical'
critics seems to realise that Elizabethan spiritualism is

disposed of by declaring that the whole soliloquy is misplaced and 'properly would come before the Ghost scene[1],' is seen to fall into its natural and unobtrusive position as a detail in the dramatic structure.

A little history, of the right kind, throws a flood of new light over the events of the first act and, moreover, greatly assists the working of the plot, since it makes it natural for Hamlet to hesitate and assume his 'antic disposition,' while it explains his need for the Gonzago play to test the truth of the Ghost's story. Nor is that all; both the Cellarage-scene and the apparition in the Queen's bedroom lose half their meaning unless illumined by contemporary notions about the spirit-world.

History too helps us to apprehend the political situation in *Hamlet*. How would this present itself to an Elizabethan audience? We need not go further back than Dr Johnson to enquire. Like other eighteenth-century critics, he always calls Claudius 'the Usurper.' In other words, Hamlet was thought of as the rightful heir to the throne who had been robbed of his inheritance by an uncle whom he himself describes as 'a cutpurse of the empire.' Of course he had suffered a more overwhelming wrong in the degrading incestuous marriage of his mother; and this second wrong quite overshadows the other in his thoughts. But he is not unmindful of the crown; and, far more important, Claudius is not unmindful either. In short, Hamlet's ambitious designs, or rather what his uncle takes to be such, form a very significant element in the relations between the two men right through the play. During the first half Claudius is constantly trying to probe them; they explain much in

relevant to *Hamlet*, and insists that Hamlet's doubts are honest and natural. Yet he entirely fails to see their bearing not only on 'To be or not to be' but also on the evolution of the main plot; his blindness being chiefly due to his anxiety to explain away the 'delay' motive.

[1] J. M. Robertson, *The Problem of Hamlet*, p. 55.

liv HAMLET

the conversations between Hamlet and the two spies, Rosencrantz and Guildenstern; they clarify the whole puzzling situation after the Play-scene; and they add surprising force and meaning to one of the most dramatic moments in the Play-scene itself.

I shall be told that had Shakespeare intended all this he would have made it plainer. The argument really cuts the other way. That Shakespeare did intend it is proved by Hamlet's two references to his loss of the crown: the one I have just referred to at 3. 4. 99, and the words

Popped in between th'election and my hopes,

spoken to Horatio in the last scene. And the fact that these references occur so late in the play proves that Shakespeare did not need to make it plainer, that he knew his audience would assume the situation from the start. The events and speeches of the first half of the second scene of the play could leave no doubt in the minds of spectators at the Globe, as they clearly left no doubt in those of most eighteenth-century readers. The dejected air of the crown prince, the contrast between his black doublet and the bright costumes of the rest, his strange and (as it would seem) sulky conduct towards his uncle, above all the hypocritical and ingratiating address of the uncle to him, bore only one possible interpretation—usurpation; and that Hamlet never mentions the subject in his first soliloquy but reveals a far more horrible wrong must have seemed to the original audience one of the most effective dramatic strokes of the play.

But I shall be told further that Denmark was an elective monarchy, as Hamlet's own words testify, and that, though disappointed perhaps, he had no legal case against Claudius. This objection offers a pretty illustration of the dangers of the 'historical' method, that is of explaining situations in Shakespeare by reference to his hypothetical sources. I say 'hypothetical' because there is no question of an elective monarchy in Saxo and Belle-forest, who tell us that Amleth's father and uncle were governors or earls of Jutland appointed by the King of Denmark. Possibly it was Kyd who enlarged the scene to include the whole kingdom and possibly he made a point of the elective character of the Danish monarchy in his lost *Hamlet*[1]. But had Shakespeare intended himself to make use of this constitutional idea, we can be certain not only that he would have said more about it, but that he must have said it much earlier in the play. He could assume the audience would realise the fact of usurpation without any underlining on his part, because such realisation merely meant interpreting the Danish constitution in English terms. But it is absurd to suppose that he wished his spectators to imagine quite a different constitution from that familiar to themselves, when he makes no reference to it until the very last scene. My own belief is that in putting the term 'election' into Hamlet's mouth, he was quite unconscious that it denoted any procedure different from that which determined the succession in England. After all, was not the monarchy of Elizabeth and James an 'elective' one? The latter like Claudius owed his throne to the deliberate choice of the Council, while the Council saw to it that he had the 'dying voice' of Elizabeth, as Fortinbras has that of Hamlet[2]. In any event, we can be certain that few if any spectators and readers of *Hamlet* at the beginning of the seventeenth century gave even a passing

[1] There are indications that at some period the *Hamlet* play was handled by a dramatist who knew more about Denmark than Shakespeare appears to have done; cf. Notes, *Names of the Characters* and G. 'Dansker.'

[2] v. note 5. 2. 354 below. Steevens first pointed out that the throne of Denmark was elective; Blackstone corroborated with all the weight of his legal authority, and since he oped his lips not a dog among the critics has dared to bark. v. Boswell's *Malone: Hamlet*, pp. 199–200.

thought to the constitutional practices of Denmark. And if after the accession of the Scottish King James and his Danish consort, Queen Anne, Shakespeare's audience came to include a few 'judicious' courtiers more knowing than the rest, what then? The election in Denmark was in practice limited to members of the royal house; in other words, the choice lay between Hamlet and his uncle. In the eyes of such spectators, therefore, Hamlet's disappointment would seem just as keen and his ambitious designs just as natural as if the succession had followed the principle of primogeniture. However it be looked at, an elective throne in Shakespeare's Denmark is a critical mare's nest.*

One more dramatic problem must here be glanced at, that of Hamlet's attitude towards Ophelia, an attitude which seems very perplexing to the ordinary reader and playgoer, which the psychologists explain as sex-nausea induced by his mother's behaviour and the historians as an ill-digested lump of the old play by Kyd, whose Ophelia, as they infer from Belleforest, was merely a female decoy employed by Hamlet's uncle to seduce him. There seems plausibility in both suggestions, but they fail to satisfy. Certainly Hamlet often treats Ophelia as if she were a decoy, or even a prostitute, when we see them together or when he speaks to Polonius about her; and yet she is as certainly nothing of the kind in Shakespeare's play. On the other hand, however great his disgust with life, Hamlet's outrageous language to her cannot be excused on that ground alone, can indeed only be excused if he had good grounds for supposing her to be that which he appears to assume. Something is lost, some clue to the relationship between them, some accidental misunderstanding which would explain Hamlet's conduct and render her fate even more pathetic. And what is lost is a very simple thing—a single stage-direction, giving Hamlet an entry (on the inner Elizabethan stage) nine lines before his entry on the other stage at 2. 2. 167, an entry which enables him accidentally and unseen to overhear the eavesdropping plot hatched between Polonius and Claudius, and so implicates Ophelia beyond possibility of doubt in his ears as one of his uncle's minions. The stage-direction is found in neither of the good texts; but the double-entry in Shakespeare's manuscript would naturally puzzle compositor and copyist; while omission, especially of stage-directions, is so common a feature of both texts that the absence of this one need not seriously disturb us, when weighed against the evidence of the surrounding dialogue, evidence which seems overwhelming. Here are the relevant lines according to the Second Quarto text:

King. How may we try it further?
Pol. You know sometimes he walkes foure houres
    together 160
Heere in the Lobby.
Quee. So he dooes indeede.
Pol. At such a time, Ile loose my daughter to him,
Be you and I behind an Arras then,
Marke the encounter, if he loue her not,
And be not from his reason falne thereon 165
Let me be no assistant for a state
But keepe a farme and carters.
King. We will try it.

           Enter Hamlet.

Quee. But looke where sadly the poore wretch comes
    reading.   (*Queene.*
Pol. Away, I doe beseech you both away, *Exit King and*
Ile bord him presently, oh giue me leaue, 170
How dooes my good Lord *Hamlet*?
Ham. Well, God a mercy.
Pol. Doe you knowe me my Lord?
Ham. Excellent well, you are a Fishmonger.

Polonius's words 'I'll loose my daughter to him' offer the leading clue. The expression 'loose,' notes Dowden, 'reminds the King and Queen that he has restrained Ophelia from communicating with Hamlet'; but it has also another meaning, still connected with the breeding of horses and cattle, which would not be missed by an Elizabethan audience and of which Shakespeare makes use again in *The Tempest*[1], when the cynic Sebastian sneers at Alonso because he would not marry his daughter to a European prince,

> But rather loose her to an African.

And that some shade of this meaning was in the mind of Polonius is strongly supported by the reference to 'a farm and carters' that follows, according to Shakespeare's usual practice of sustained metaphor noted in section IV above. Nor does the chain of significance cease there; for when Hamlet calls Polonius a 'fishmonger' in line 174, that is to say a bawd or pandar, and when he goes on immediately afterwards to compare his daughter to 'carrion' flesh and to speak of her 'conception,' the words are clearly related to those of Polonius just before and are indeed hardly intelligible without them. In short, 'loose,' 'fishmonger' and 'carrion' are so linked together as to make it impossible, for me at any rate, to escape the conclusion that Shakespeare intended Hamlet to overhear Polonius's unhappy jest.*

Though the rest is conjecture, we are even yet not entirely without Shakespeare's guidance, inasmuch as Polonius's words 'Here in the lobby' (coupled, we may suppose, with a jerk of the thumb towards the inner-stage, which lies behind them as they speak) are a direct invitation to the audience to look thither, and thus are almost as good as a stage-direction, marking with practical certainty, as I think, the point at which Hamlet comes in, and the place of his entry.* The entry must, of course, seem unpremeditated and no impression must be given of deliberate spying on Hamlet's part; it would never do, for example, to let him linger in his place of concealment. The nine lines between the King's question 'How

---

[1] 2. 1. 124.

may we try it further?' and his conclusion 'We will try
it' give Hamlet just time to enter with his eyes upon his
book, to catch the sound of voices on the outer-stage, to
pause for a moment beside the entrance thereto, to
compose his features and to come forward. But brief as
the interval is, it has been long enough for him to take
in the whole plot. And the stage-direction, once in place
at line 159, is seen to affect far more than Hamlet's
relations to Ophelia; it is the mainspring of the events
that follow in Acts 2 and 3; it renders the Nunnery-scene
playable as never before; it adds all kinds of fresh light
and shade to the Play-scene.

VI

Restoration along these lines, I believe, makes the plot
of *Hamlet* work properly for the first time since Shakespeare's day. And what of the mystery of Hamlet's
character? It frames it in more delicate dramatic tracery,
but it does not solve it. The mystery remains, deeper perhaps than that which enshrouds Iago and Cleopatra (or
the figures of Rembrandt) but not different in kind. I do
not attempt a solution, but I may note three points about
it by way of bringing these remarks to a conclusion. In the
first place, Hamlet's procrastination, which is considered
his most mysterious feature, was certainly intended by
Shakespeare. Indeed, the clearer the lines of the plot
become, the more obvious it is that Shakespeare went
out of his way to emphasise it. From time to time a critic
will arise to maintain that there is no delay in *Hamlet*, or
at least none that an audience need bother about. It is
true that, apart from the second and fourth soliloquies,
very little is said directly about the deferred revenge, and
that when the fourth is omitted, as it was from the First
Folio and as it commonly is upon our stage, the impression of delay is greatly weakened. Yet there the two
soliloquies are—ninety lines of them—and I do not

think that even the most hardened of 'historical' critics has ventured to write them off as relics of the old play. Whatever else Shakespeare may have inherited in *Hamlet*, these are his own, and that he took the trouble to write them is proof to my mind that he attached considerable importance to the delay-motive and wished his audience to do so likewise.*

Professor Stoll, in the latest instalment of his perennial endeavour to exhibit Shakespeare as a dramatist not for all time but of an age, argues with great elaboration and learning that Hamlet's self-accusation of delay must not be taken at its face value but as 'the sort of charge that Elizabethan and ancient tragedy, concerned with ethical rather than psychical defects, made no further account of'; that 'even if Shakespeare had desired it, he could scarcely, on the contemporary stage, have introduced so fundamental an innovation as, in the place of a popular heroic revenger, a procrastinator, lost in thought and weak of will'; that the reproaches 'motive the delay, not in the sense of grounding it in character, but of explaining it and bridging it over; they motive it by reminding the audience that the main business in hand, though retarded, is not lost to view[1].' In a word, the soliloquies were not intended to reveal any flaw in the character of the hero, but to 'save the story[2]' and spin it out for five acts. Professor Stoll is inspired by the worthiest of ambitions; he is in effect defending *Hamlet* against Mr Eliot's charge of 'artistic failure'; he is turning the weapons of the 'historical' critics against themselves, against his own self of earlier books; he is fighting in the last ditch to keep the tattered shreds of what was once the royal banner of Shakespeare's reputation still flying. Yet that his thesis is moonshine any unprejudiced reader of the soliloquy in 4. 4. may see for himself. Not that the evi-

---

[1] E. E. Stoll, *Art and Artifice in Shakespeare*, pp. 94–5.
[2] Stoll, *op. cit.* p. 101.

dence of the soliloquies by any means stands alone. Hamlet's sense of frustration, of infirmity of purpose, of character inhibited from meeting the demands of destiny, of the futility of life in general and action in particular, finds utterance in nearly every word he says. His melancholy and his procrastination are all of a piece, and cannot be disentangled. Moreover, his feelings are shared and expressed by other characters also. The note of 'heart-sickness' is struck by the sentry Francisco nine lines from the beginning of the play; the Player King holds up the Play-scene for several minutes with an elaborate disquisition upon human instability; Claudius himself embroiders the same topic in conversation with Laertes[1]. In short, that

> the native hue of resolution
> Is sicklied o'er with the pale cast of thought,

is not merely the constant burden of Hamlet's meditation but the key-note of the whole dramatic symphony. I refrain from dwelling upon the use which Shakespeare makes of Fortinbras and Laertes as foils to Hamlet; for that is critical commonplace, though ignored by Professor Stoll. But one last piece of evidence, at which he shies in a footnote, must be mentioned, because I think its relevance and force have escaped notice; for, though Dr Bradley with his usual perspicacity has seen it clearly enough[2], his successors have not.

> Do not forget! this visitation
> Is but to whet thy almost blunted purpose

says the Ghost to Hamlet in the Bedroom-scene. And what the Ghost says is true, whatever else be dramatic convention, since, as every Elizabethan who believed in the 'honesty' of ghosts would acknowledge, the Ghost sees Hamlet *sub specie eternitatis* and follows the secret motions of his heart.*

---

[1] v. note 4. 7. 117–22.
[2] Bradley, *op. cit.* p. 139.

The second point I wish to make about Hamlet concerns his behaviour rather than his 'character.' The fact that he is liable to sudden attacks of ungovernable excitement or anger has not passed unobserved by critics, but they seem scarcely to have made as much of it as the text warrants; and since it is a matter of vital concern not only for the performance of the part but also for the interpretation of the action, I make no apology for stressing it. Hamlet appears to be subject to such an attack on at least six occasions and possibly on a seventh also. The first is in the Cellarage-scene, when in reaction from the tension of his interview with the Ghost he gives way to a fit of extravagant levity and utters those 'wild and whirling words' for which Horatio gently rebukes him, words which later become still wilder. Of the second we learn from Ophelia's account of his strange conduct in her closet; the words—

> And with a look so piteous in purport
> As if he had been looséd out of hell
> To speak of horrors—

clearly denoting, to my mind, the after-effects of some delirium, for which he sought consolation in her presence. He works himself up to a third attack as he unpacks his heart with words of self-reproach in the soliloquy at the end of 2. 2. The Nunnery-scene, after the question 'Where's your father?' affords the fourth instance, the latter half of the Bedroom-scene gives the fifth, and the Graveyard-scene the sixth, while I think there is a display of uncontrolled excitement, again marked by a moderating comment from Horatio, after the exit of the King in the Play-scene.

These outbursts are different in tone; some are delirious, some savage, some sarcastic; but they possess one feature in common, hysteria or lack of balance. Moreover, they seem to be quite involuntary, and to be generally associated with a mood from the opposite end of the emotional scale, a mood of tenderness, solemnity or extreme dejection. Thus the ill-timed, not to say profane, merriment of 1. 5. follows immediately upon the most solemn moment of the play, the talk with the Ghost and the oath of consecration, while it is succeeded by that ominous and despondent couplet

> The time is out of joint, O curséd spite,
> That ever I was born to set it right!

Or take the interview with Gertrude. The first hundred lines compose a crescendo of excitement, which is interrupted by the apparition of the Ghost. This restores Hamlet's pulse to its 'healthful music,' and after the Ghost disappears we get forty lines of exquisite tenderness, a tenderness that even embraces Polonius. The episode ends with a couplet which suggests an exit, and had the scene finished there, it would have made a perfect close. But, as in the Nunnery-scene, Hamlet only goes to the door to turn back again, and the whole effect is destroyed by the hysterical violence and cynicism of what comes after.

This convulsive oscillation between extremes of frenzy and tranquillity is so marked a feature of the Prince's behaviour and provides so large an element of the rhythm of the whole play, that to miss it is to miss one of the principal clues to the understanding of *Hamlet*[1]. It is obviously of great importance theatrically, since Hamlet's excitement in its various forms adds much to the excitement of the audience. But it is no mere theatrical trick or device; it is meant to be part of the nature of the man. His mother is made to describe it for us after the 'towering passion' of the Funeral-scene:

> And thus awhile the fit will work on him.
> Anon as patient as the female dove
> When that her golden couplets are disclosed
> His silence will sit drooping.

---

[1] Dr Bradley (*op. cit.* p. 124) notices it but fails, I think, to appreciate its true importance.

Claudius refers to it in his words about 'turbulent and dangerous lunacy.' Hamlet himself admits it to his father's spirit:

> Do you not come your tardy son to chide,
> That *lapsed in time and passion* lets go by
> Th'important acting of your dread command?—

a passage which has been overlooked because the italicised words, which I interpret 'the prisoner of circumstance and of passion,' have not been understood. He tacitly admits it again in the pathetic address to Horatio at the beginning of 3. 2. in which the lines—

>   and blest are those
> Whose blood and judgement are so well co-medled,
> That they are not a pipe for Fortune's finger
> To sound what stop she please: give me that man
> That is not passion's slave, and I will wear him
> In my heart's core, ay in my heart of heart—

form a most revealing piece of self-criticism. Finally, he admits it in the apology to Laertes before the fencing-match, which has likewise been generally misapprehended[1]. What then? Was Hamlet mad? To suppose this might perhaps add pathos to his figure, but would rob it of all respect: he would, as Dr Bradley says, 'cease to be a tragic character[2].' Hamlet is one of the greatest and most fascinating of all Shakespeare's creations; he is a study of genius. To call him insane is absurd; but when he tells us that he is 'punished with a sore distraction' I think we are intended to believe his words, since he is throughout the play obviously subject to paroxysms of passion, which while they last are akin to insanity. He struggles against them, as Othello struggles with his jealousy and Macbeth with his moral instability; and that struggle is in large measure the groundwork of his tragedy. Robert Bridges, in his remarkable, if at

---

[1] v. note 5. 2. 230.
[2] *Shakespearean Tragedy*, p. 14.

times perverse, essay, *The influence of the audience on Shakespeare's drama*[1], faces the facts of Hamlet's behaviour as no other writer has done, and though he puts a construction upon them somewhat different from mine, both are covered by the shrewd criticism in *The Testament of Beauty*:

Hamlet himself would never hav been aught to us, or we to Hamlet, wer't not for the artful balance whereby Shakespeare so gingerly put his sanity in doubt without the while confounding his Reason[2].

So I come to my last point. If Shakespeare knew someone in real life possessed of such greatness and struggling with such weakness, someone whom he perhaps admired this side idolatry or in whom he was deeply interested, someone too whose fame and worth

> Stood challenger on mount of all the age
> For his perfection,

would he not have put him into a play? By this I do not of course mean that Hamlet *was* such a man, but merely that Shakespeare's knowledge of such a man may have provided the leaven of feeling which set working the creative ferment that produced *Hamlet*. Hamlet, I say again, is a character in a play, not a historical figure, however much his genesis may owe to the relations between two men once living at the end of the sixteenth century. He is as genuine a child of Shakespeare's imagination as Mark Antony or Macbeth; he has no existence outside the frame of his drama; and it would be as futile to try and explain him by discussing the 'psychology' of his supposed original, as it is to try and explain the play in the light of what we surmise about the lost *Hamlet* of Kyd. But if, as many have believed and as I have elsewhere maintained[3], the emotional stimulus for his

---

[1] *Collected Essays, etc. of Robert Bridges* (Oxford), i. 25–27.   [2] I. ll. 577–80.
[3] *The Essential Shakespeare*, pp. 95–107.

creation came to Shakespeare from the career and personality of the most conspicuous figure in England during the last decade of the sixteenth century, namely the brilliant, the moody, the excitable, the unstable, the procrastinating, the ill-fated Earl of Essex, one thing at least may be said. That being so, the contemporary audience must have pondered the character of Hamlet free from the bewilderment that afflicts modern critics and readers, though with a sense of mystery not a whit less profound.

Yet it is just this mystery, emanating maybe from a man long since dust, which sets Hamlet in the timeless and universal theatre of our imagination, which so liberates him from his Elizabethan shell that we forget it altogether and count him a king of infinity. One does not usually look to the Gallic muse for songs in honour of Shakespeare. But I know no better tribute to the eternal Hamlet than a prose apostrophe by Anatole France after an evening at the Comédie-Française. And as it puts the commentators in their right place, these comments shall end with it.

Vous êtes de tous les temps et de tous les pays. Vous n'avez pas vieilli d'une heure en trois siècles. Votre âme a l'âge de chacune de nos âmes. Nous vivons ensemble, prince Hamlet, et vous êtes ce que nous sommes, un homme au milieu du mal universel. On vous a chicané sur vos paroles et sur vos actions. On a montré que vous n'étiez pas d'accord avec vous-même. Comment saisir cet insaisissable personnage? a-t-on dit. Il pense tour à tour comme un moine du moyen âge et comme un savant de la Renaissance; il a la tête philosophique et pourtant pleine de diableries. Il a horreur du mensonge et sa vie n'est qu'un long mensonge. Il est irrésolu, c'est visible, et pourtant certains critiques l'ont jugé plein de décision, sans qu'on puisse leur donner tout à fait tort. Enfin, on a prétendu, mon prince, que vous étiez un magasin de pensées, un amas de contradictions et non pas un être humain. Mais c'est là, au contraire, le signe de votre profonde humanité. Vous êtes prompt et lent, audacieux et timide, bienveillant et cruel, vous croyez et vous doutez, vous êtes sage et par-dessus tout vous êtes fou. En un mot, vous vivez. Qui de nous ne vous ressemble en quelque chose? Qui de nous pense sans contradiction et agit sans incohérence? Qui de nous n'est fou? Qui de nous ne vous dit avec un mélange de pitié, de sympathie, d'admiration et d'horreur: "Good night, sweet prince!"[1]

1934   J. D. W.

[1] *La Vie Littéraire*, i. 7–8.

THE STAGE-HISTORY
OF *HAMLET*

Several books of this size could easily be filled with the stage-history of *Hamlet*. None of Shakespeare's plays has been so often acted in Great Britain, nor in so many foreign countries; and probably more actors have appeared in the part in which, according to Macready, 'a total failure is of rare occurrence' than in any other. Each of these actors must have expressed something of his own intelligence and personality through Hamlet; but not all the individual touches in all the renderings, could they be collected, would be of great interest, since by no means all of them arose out of any fresh conception of the character or threw new light on Shakespeare's meaning. Many pages could be filled with details about the presentation of the two pictures, the conduct of the duel, the 'business' of the Play-scene, the death of Hamlet and other such matters. But many of these, and many of the emphases on words, the pauses and so forth, must have been devices for doing something different from other people in a part that was always being acted and was known by heart, during a long period of the play's history, by most of the audience. Many of them may have been (to quote Macready again) 'innovations and traps for applause, which the following words of the text have shown to be at utter variance with the author's intention.'

Hamlet in foreign countries is another subject far too wide for such a study at the present. From Lewis Hallam in Philadelphia in 1759 to Walter Hampden in New York in 1918, and doubtless others later, Hamlets have been many in America. Since Ducis's version was staged in Paris, *Hamlet* has attracted (in Talma, Mounet-

Sully, Sarah Bernhardt and many another) the best of French acting; and Germany, which first came to know Shakespeare's *Hamlet* within at latest ten years after Shakespeare's death, has brought, with Schröder and the two Devrients, the romantic Hamlet to his height, and in Reinhardt has added to the great producers of the tragedy[1].

In a study of this length, therefore, it is best to attempt no more than a sketch of the play in the hands of the leading actors in the theatres of London, including foreigners only when they have contributed something interesting or valuable to the conception of the character or the play. In London the performances would be the best that the times could offer (although in old days, Bath, Dublin or Edinburgh, and some other provincial towns saw Hamlets that London never saw); and the London stage is the best field in which to observe the changes that have come in the conception of Hamlet and the staging of the tragedy. Those changes have never been more than slight. The text of *Hamlet* was left alone —except for cutting down—until the brief vogue of the version made by Garrick in his last years at Drury Lane; and even Frederic Reynolds respected it. *Hamlet*, therefore, has no such history of adaptation and a gradual return to purity as have (to take two notable instances) *King Lear* and *King Richard III*.

The play of *Hamlet* entered by the Stationers to James Roberts on July 26, 1602, was 'latelie Acted by the Lord Chamberleyne his servantes.' The title-page of the First Quarto (1603) states that *Hamlet* had been acted 'by his Highnesse seruants in the Cittie of London: as also in the two Vniuersities of Cambridge and Oxford, and else-where.' The mention

[1] For the stage-history of *Hamlet* in Germany and Austria see W. Widmann, *Hamlets Bühnenlaufbahn (1601–1877)*; Schriften der Deutschen Shakespeare-Gesellschaft; Leipzig, Tauchnitz, 1931.

of the universities gives a means of checking the date. It
has been shown that the performances at Cambridge and
at Oxford had no warrant from either university, and
that 'in the university towns' would be a more correct
statement. Some think that these performances may have
been as early as 1593; others would put them as late as
1599 or 1600. The next spark of evidence comes in
Ratseis Ghost, the second instalment (printed 1605) of
the life of Gamaliel Ratsey, the highwayman, who, in
counselling a strolling player to go to London, told him,
'if one man were dead, they will haue much neede of
such a one as thou art. There would be none in my
opinion, fitter then thy selfe to play his parts: my con-
ceipt is such of thee, that I durst venture all the mony in
my purse on thy head, to play Hamlet with him for a
wager.' That 'one man' is almost certainly Richard
Burbadge, whose funeral elegy mentions among his parts
'young Hamlett.' Rowe was told that the top of Shakespeare's performance was the Ghost in his own *Hamlet*.
On September 5, 1607, and again probably in March,
1608, *Hamlet* was acted on board Captain William
Keeling's ship, the *Dragon*, at Sierra Leone, as entertainment for Portuguese and English guests and as beneficial
occupation for the crew. Richard Burbadge, who may
be accepted as the first actor of the part of Hamlet, died
on March 13, 1619; and someone else must have played
the part when the tragedy was performed at Court in the
winter of 1619–20; almost certainly Joseph Taylor, who
joined the company in May, 1619, and acted Hamlet
'incomparably well.' It was probably he also who acted
the part at Hampton Court on January 24, 1637; and
his influence seems to have lasted on into the succeeding
era. Downes, in *Roscius Anglicanus*, says that Betterton
was taught 'in every Particle of it' by Sir William
D'Avenant, who had seen Taylor, who had been 'Instructed by the Author Mr. Shaksepeur.' Taylor can
hardly have been directly taught by Shakespeare, seeing

that he did not join the King's company till three years after Shakespeare's death. That, however, is no reason for doubting that Betterton inherited the tradition of the original performances.

Hamlet was one of the plays allotted to D'Avenant for the Duke's company by the warrant of December 12, 1660; but there is no record of his producing it before the summer of 1661. Pepys saw it at 'the Opera' (the playhouse in Lincoln's Inn Fields) for the first time on August 24 of that year, 'done with scenes very well, but above all, Betterton did the prince's part beyond imagination.' He saw it again on November 27 and December 5, 1661, on May 28, 1663 ('giving us fresh reason never to think enough of Betterton'), and again on August 31, 1668, when he was 'mightily pleased with it; but, above all, with Betterton, the best part, I believe, that ever man acted.' Pepys had a great admiration for *Hamlet*. On November 13, 1664, he 'spent all the afternoon with my wife within doors, and getting a speech out of Hamlett, "To bee or not to bee" without book.' A setting of that soliloquy to music for a single voice (possibly composed by Matthew Locke and arranged for the guitar by Cesare Morelli) is among the Pepys manuscripts at Magdalene College, Cambridge; and it has been (perhaps not altogether fancifully) suggested that the music may to some extent represent the intonations given to the speech by Betterton on the stage (the corruptions in the text may or may not be due to the same source). Evelyn did not share Pepys's enthusiasm. When he saw the play on November 26, 1661, he only remarked that 'the old plays begin to disgust this refined age.' But Pepys rather than Evelyn seems, in this case, to speak for the age, which was slow to show its disgust with *Hamlet*. 'No succeeding Tragedy for several Years,' wrote Downes, 'got more Reputation, or Money to the Company than this.' Betterton's acting of the part was praised by Downes, by Colley Cibber, by Rowe, by many others. He went on acting it for nearly fifty years, until, indeed, Tony Aston, and perhaps others, thought him too old and stiff and grave; but his last recorded performance, which was given at the Haymarket on September 20, 1709, when he must have been between 71 and 74 years old, drew from Steele this commendation in the *Tatler*: 'Had you been to-night at the play-house, you had seen the force of Action in perfection: your admired Mr Betterton behaved himself so well, that, though now about seventy, he acted youth, and by the prevalent power of proper manner, gesture, and voice, appeared through the whole drama a young man of great expectation, vivacity, and enterprize.' The last words give a hint of his reading of the part—not as a languid, ineffectual dreamer. 'When I acted the Ghost with Betterton,' said Barton Booth, 'instead of my awing him, he terrified me.' Cibber records his mixture, in that scene, of terror with filial reverence and impatience to know the truth; he was 'manly, but not braving; his voice never rising into that seeming outrage or wild defiance of what he naturally revered.' Davies quotes the statement that on the appearance of the Ghost Betterton's face turned suddenly 'as pale as his neck-cloth,' and that he trembled all over. That white neck-cloth, with bands, his full-bottomed wig, cocked hat and black clothes gave him the appearance often called 'clerical,' but meant to signify a scholar.

In that first production at Lincoln's Inn Fields Ophelia was acted by Mrs Sanderson (afterwards Mrs Betterton), Horatio by Harris, the Ghost by Richards, Polonius by Lovel, the First Gravedigger by Cave Underhill, the King by Lilliston, and the Queen by Mrs Davenport. If the quarto edition of 1676 is (as Mr Hazelton Spencer argues in his *Shakespeare Improved*) the text prepared by D'Avenant for his stage, it can be seen from it and from the quartos of 1683, 1695 and 1703 that during the Betterton period *Hamlet* was

not much 'reformed.' But it was considerably shortened.
Valtemand, Cornelius and Reynaldo are clean gone.
Fortinbras only comes in at the very end, and his Captain
is not seen. The longer speeches (except 'To be or not
to be') are severely cut—even most of Hamlet's first
address to the Ghost. Polonius's advice to Laertes is
gone, partly, perhaps, because Polonius was (or soon
came to be) played as a wholly comic character; and the
advice to the players is also all cut out. On the other
hand, the Dumb Show, and the scene of the King's
prayer and Hamlet's speech in sparing his life are retained very nearly complete. Much, therefore, of what
the study has considered the true poetic and philosophic
worth of the play was omitted; but the contentions of
Mr Alfred Hart about the cutting of plays for performance in the Elizabethan playhouse (*Review of English
Studies*, Vol. VIII, Nos. 30, 32; Vol. X, No. 37) suggest
the possibility that the Restoration versions of *Hamlet*
may preserve in this matter the tradition of the original
performances, and that in both instances the robust
action, rather than the profound thought of the poet, was
what the theatre aimed at representing. To D'Avenant
only, and not to his predecessors in deletion, it is safe to
ascribe the many tiresome little verbal alterations and
excisions made, after his usual manner, in the cause of
decency, clearness or 'politeness.'

Cibber has left a vivacious account of the 'rude and
riotous havock' at Drury Lane after the secession of
Betterton and other good players from the united companies in 1695. 'Shakespeare was defaced and tortured
in every signal character.—Hamlet and Othello lost in
one hour all their good sense, their dignity, and fame.'
It was probably about that time that Wilks took up the
acting of Hamlet, and almost certainly Wilks at whom
Cibber was hitting in his reference to a Hamlet, 'who,
on the first appearance of his Father's Spirit, has thrown
himself into all the straining vociferation requisite to

express rage and fury, and the house has thundered with applause, though the misguided actor was all the while (as Shakespeare terms it) tearing a passion into rags.' Aaron Hill in *The Prompter* for October 24, 1735, said very much the same. Wilks rushed at the Ghost much too soon, with precipitate clamour, 'hurrying on the whole [scene with] Smartness and Alacrity.' He threatened the Ghost, and turned his sword against it, not against those who were trying to hold him back (it was not by such means that Betterton's Hamlet had frightened Booth's Ghost). In the scene with Ophelia he was too light and airy all through, with no sign of sadness even when she was not observing him. On the other hand, in the Play-scene he showed an 'unforced, soft, becoming Negligence.' Thomas Davies differed from Hill on certain points. He thought that Wilks acted the scene with Ophelia like a lover and a gentleman, and the Closet-scene with warm indignation, tempered with the most affecting tenderness; and, while regretting Wilks's restlessness, he commended the pleasing melancholy of countenance and grave despondency of action with which he spoke the 'To be or not to be' soliloquy. To Wilks's credit it must be added that (as Professor Odell has discovered) he restored to the stage the advice to the players; and his acting cannot fail to have had some share in the steady popularity of the tragedy. In January, 1708, when the once more united companies appeared at Drury Lane, *Hamlet*, with Wilks as the Prince, was the opening play. On that occasion Booth played the Ghost; Mills, Horatio; Powell, Laertes; Johnson, Polonius; Cibber, Osric; Estcourt, the First Gravedigger; Mrs Knight, the Queen; and Mrs Mountfort, Ophelia. During the rule of Cibber and his partners at Drury Lane, 1710–33, *Hamlet* was given every year except two; and Wilks went on playing the Prince as late as February, 1732, the month in which he died. In the earlier part of that period the great cast would have been Wilks as Hamlet, Mills as Horatio, Barton Booth as the Ghost, Ryan or Powell as Laertes, Mrs Knight or Mrs Porter as the Queen, the 'majestic' Keene as the King, Dogget or Johnson as the First Gravedigger, and Mrs Mountfort or Miss Santlow (who became Mrs Barton Booth) as Ophelia. As time went on, other Hamlets were many. Thurmond first took up the part in 1708, Elrington in 1716, and Ryan (one of the best) in 1719; and in 1733 Mills, then between sixty and seventy years of age, suddenly and unwisely made a first appearance in the character. He had been (as had Barton Booth also) an excellent Horatio, others worthy of commendation in that part being Lee, Walker, and Milward. To the Ophelias must be added Mrs Bracegirdle, Mrs Cross, Mrs Bradshaw, Mrs Thurmond, and—to Ryan's Hamlet in March, 1728, two months after the first wild welcome of her Polly Peachum—no less a light than Lavinia Fenton. Quin made his first appearance as the King in 1719, and Milward in 1733. Hippisley was a favourite Polonius; Johnson the greatest of all First Gravediggers after Underhill, with Bullock for his only serious rival. 'Ostrick,' or the Fop, passed from Colley Cibber to his son Theophilus; and in 1731 Quin, copying Booth as closely as possible, must have made a very impressive Ghost. These lists of names could be greatly lengthened. Unfortunately, they do no more than show that the tragedy was steadily popular at all three playhouses and that everyone wanted to act most of the parts in it. They can tell nothing about how those parts were acted. From the want of advertisements of scenic displays it has been judged that *Hamlet* was one of the plays that were soberly (when they were not meanly) staged; one of what Cibber calls 'select plays that were able to be their own support, and in which we found our constant account without painting and patching them out like prostitutes with these follies in fashion.' We may imagine the players costumed in the conventional plumes, trains, and other signs of tragedy, Hamlet himself in a full-bottomed wig, and the play cut for performance very much as it had been in the time of Betterton.

A little oddity of 1736 may help to turn our eyes in the direction they must now take, away from the three legitimate playhouses to the unlicensed Goodman's Fields. On February 9 of that year, with Giffard playing Hamlet, Woodward as 'Ostrick' and Pinkethman clowning it as the First Gravedigger, there was introduced 'the Ceremony of Hamlet's Lying in State after the Manner of his Grace the Duke of Buckingham. With new music proper to the occasion, set by Mr Carey, words by Henry Saville, Esq.'—a topical variation from the sort of musical, scenic and choreographical entertainment then regularly tacked on to the tragedy. Nearly six years later, on December 9, 1741, Giffard was again acting Hamlet at Goodman's Fields, with Miss Hippisley as his Ophelia, and for the Ghost David Garrick. (He was to play that part again twenty-seven years later on his own stage of Drury Lane, for Palmer's benefit.) In August, 1742, Garrick was acting Hamlet in Dublin, with Mrs Woffington for his Ophelia; and in November he made his first appearance in the part at Drury Lane. Mrs Clive was his Ophelia; Mrs Pritchard the Queen, Havard Horatio, Delane the Ghost, Hallam Laertes, Taswell Polonius, and Macklin the First Gravedigger. In that, his first season, he acted the part some thirteen times. Hamlet was always one of his most popular successes; and though he resigned the part now and then to Spranger Barry, to Holland, to Smith, or to Sheridan, he played it himself every season throughout his career. His last appearance in it was on May 30, 1776, when he gave the performance in aid of the Theatrical Fund on the eve of his retirement.

From the writings of Thomas Davies and of Georg Christoph Lichtenberg, a German who was deeply impressed by Garrick's acting in 1775, from some papers signed 'Hic et Ubique' in the *St James's Chronicle* in February and March, 1772, from Fielding's *Tom Jones* and from other sources it is possible to put together some notion of Garrick's production and acting of *Hamlet*. He did away with the full-bottomed wigs and the plumes of tragedy. He himself wore black (the only character in the play seen in mourning) with a cloak and hat, knee breeches, and shoes which increased his height. The Ghost wore armour with steel-blue satin underneath it, and showed nothing of his face except the nose and a little of the cheek on either side of it. Horatio and Marcellus wore some sort of military dress. Ophelia had long, fair hair, and in her mad scene carried a neatly arranged handful of straw. In the version which he presented during most of his career Garrick kept the advice to the players, spoke more of the soliloquy, 'O, what a rogue and peasant slave am I!' than others had, and cut out the soliloquy during the King's prayer, either altogether or at least from 'Up, sword' to the last line and a half. It appears also that he took from the Ghost and gave to Hamlet the line 'O, horrible! O, horrible! most horrible!' and this soon established itself as a 'stage tradition.' The impression conveyed by Fielding that the Closet-scene came before the Play-scene must be due to inadvertence; but it may be accepted that the Ghost appeared in that scene in a flash of fire and disappeared down a trap. It was in that scene also that Garrick used a trick chair which would fall over (as tradition demanded) very easily when Hamlet sprang up on seeing the Ghost. When he spoke the lines, 'For some must watch,' he invariably walked about, vehemently twirling a white handkerchief. Macready borrowed this action from him, and it was that which Edwin Forrest hissed at the Theatre Royal, Edinburgh, in 1846, thus preparing the way for the fatal riot in New York in 1849.

The finest thing in Garrick's performance was evidently his meeting with the Ghost. He made Bransby, who was 'tolerably substantial,' seem 'incorporeal'—which means that he so acted terror as to make his audience share it. Lichtenberg describes the deathly stillness over the whole house while Hamlet, after standing up-stage with his hat pulled over his eyes and his arms folded under his cloak, is turning slightly away to the left, when Horatio suddenly points to the right with 'Look, my lord, it comes!' and the Ghost is there, motionless, before the audience is aware of it. Then 'Garrick turns abruptly round and at the same moment totters backward two or three steps, his knees knocking together beneath him, his hat falls on the ground, his arms, especially the left, are almost fully opened, the hand on a level with his head, the right arm bent with the hand hanging down, the fingers wide apart, the mouth open, so he stands, widely astride but not ungainly, as if turned to stone, held up by his friends, who have seen the Ghost before and are afraid he will fall. His face expressed such horror that shudder after shudder ran through one before he began to speak. The almost appalling silence of the audience, which began before this scene and made one feel scarcely safe, probably contributed not a little to the effect. At last he speaks, not with the beginning but with the end of a breath, and says in trembling tones, "Angels and ministers of grace defend us!" words which supply whatever might still be lacking to make this scene one of the greatest and most dreadful of which, perhaps, the stage is capable. The Ghost beckons him, then you should see him, never moving his eyes from the Ghost, even while he is talking to his friends and breaking away from them when they hold him back and warn him not to follow. But at last, his patience exhausted, he turns his eyes on them, tears himself violently away, and with a swiftness that makes one shudder draws his sword on

them, saying, "By heaven, I'll make a ghost of him that
lets me." So much for them! Then he turns his sword
toward the Ghost: "Go on, I'll follow thee"; and the
Ghost goes off. Hamlet remains standing still, with his
sword held out before him, so as to gain more distance,
and at last, when the Ghost is out of sight of the audience,
he begins to follow slowly, now stopping, now going on
again, but always with his sword held out before him, his
eyes fixed on the Ghost, his hair dishevelled, breathless
still, until he too passes out of sight behind the scenes.
You can easily imagine what loud applause this exit
wins. It begins as soon as the Ghost is gone, and lasts
until Hamlet likewise disappears'—lasts, as Davies would
add, until they both appeared again.

One of Johnson's many sneers at his beloved Davy
implied that he overacted this terror. 'Hic et Ubique'
complained of that long stretch of silent 'business' before
he began 'Angels and ministers of grace,' and found him
too violent with Horatio and Marcellus; and even the
devoted Lichtenberg blamed him for acting his feelings
too long in silence before he began to reveal them in
'O all you host of heaven.' But his triumph seems to
have lain in first arousing terror and then softening it
with the filial love which he made the keynote of the
character. Further details have been preserved. When
he came on to speak 'To be or not to be,' he was already
feigning distraction, his hair hanging about his shoulders,
one black stocking down, with the red garter showing.
With his chin on his right hand and his left hand sup-
porting his right elbow, he stood looking sideways down
on the ground and began very quietly, the audience
listening as reverently as if it was in church. In the scene
with Ophelia, some held him to be too boisterous and
harsh, where Barry was much gentler and graver; and
again in the scene with his mother he was occasionally too
rough and loud, where both Wilks and Barry always
preserved 'the delicacy of address to a lady.' He is

accused, again, of overacting in the soliloquy, 'O, what a rogue and peasant slave am I!' but Davies thought him unmatched in it. 'His self-expostulations, and upbraidings of cowardice and pusillanimity, were strongly pointed, and blended with marks of contemptuous indignation; the description of his uncle held up, at once, a portrait of horror and derision. When he closed his strong paintings with the epithet, *kindless* villain! a tear of anguish gave a most pathetic softness to the whole passionate ebullition.' The advice to the players he spoke well, but more like a stage-manager than a Prince.

Garrick's best Ophelia was Mrs Cibber. As she warmed to the part, she dropped her 'chanting' mode of speech, and she preserved favour and prettiness through all her grief and terror. Mrs Smith (whom Lichtenberg saw and admired) was also very pathetic in the part, and sang the songs beautifully (as, no doubt, did Susannah Cibber also). Mrs Clive was not so good, nor was Mrs Abington. Of the Queens none could touch Mrs Pritchard, who, indeed, was the only great actress of the time with the sense to see the worth of the part and the industry to study it. She had a way, at 'Do you see nothing there?' of turning her head slowly with a glare in her eye that made her audience tremble. The best Polonius was Baddeley, who played the part, like the others, as low comedy, but was not 'nauseously ridiculous.' Garrick's attempt to rescue Polonius from degradation failed. He persuaded Woodward to dress the part richly and to act it seriously; but Woodward made little of it and the audience nothing. Packer had decent merit as Horatio, but the part was always 'kept down' so as not to get in the way of Hamlet. Of Kings (another part despised by the players of the time) Jefferson took the palm, and after him Sparks (was it he whom Partridge in *Tom Jones* thought the best player in the cast because 'he speaks all his words distinctly, half as loud again as the other'?); and next to Johnson Yates was liked as the First Gravedigger.

In December, 1772, after he had been acting and staging *Hamlet* for more than thirty years, Garrick produced his own version of the tragedy. Since his visits to Paris on his tour of 1763–65 he had been more sensitive than before to French opinion; and in spite of his professed abhorrence of Voltaire, he seems to have been pondering some of his strictures on Shakespeare, and especially the very inaccurate account of *Hamlet* in the *Appel à toutes les nations de l'Europe des jugements d'un écrivain anglais* published in March, 1761. He had also read the version by Ducis, which had been staged in Paris in 1769, and which omitted the Ghost, the players and the fencing-match. But there was contemporary opinion in England also to encourage him to what he afterwards called 'the most impudent thing I ever did in all my life,' and 'rescue that noble play from all the rubbish of the fifth Act.' He never printed his version; and it survives only in the reports of others,* which have been collected by Professor Odell (*Shakespeare from Betterton to Irving*, i. 385–89). Garrick made some minor alterations in the first three Acts; but the greatest changes came later. The Gravediggers and the funeral of Ophelia were left out. Hamlet did not go to England, nor did Laertes plot with the King to murder him. Hamlet and Laertes quarrelled in the King's presence, and, on the King's intervening, Hamlet fought and killed him. Laertes then wounded Hamlet mortally, and, according to one account, himself died of his wounds; according to another account Hamlet, dying, prevented Horatio from avenging him and made Horatio and Laertes take hands. The Queen went mad and died off stage. Lichtenberg had known very well how the English audiences loved the Gravediggers (he had seen them at Covent Garden), and in his wordy, metaphysical way had discerned the fitness of the scene with its 'raw

strength.' But the public took to Garrick's version at least
kindly enough for Smith to continue it and for Henderson to take it up after Garrick's retirement, and for Tate
Wilkinson, denied a sight of the playbook, to make a
version of his own, something on the same lines and very
much worse. The last performance of Garrick's version
in London appears to have been at Drury Lane in
September 1779; but it is heard of at Bath in 1781.

During the era of Garrick at Drury Lane *Hamlet* was
played pretty regularly at Covent Garden, though not so
often as at the other house because none could compete
with Garrick. At the beginning of the period Ryan was
the Covent Garden Hamlet. Sheridan (wanting lightness, but original, and excellent in the graver scenes)
acted it next; and, when Barry followed, Ryan took up
the Ghost. In 1757 Smith appeared there for the first
time (he had, no doubt, by then dropped his youthful
practice of taking off his hat with a low bow as soon as he
had it from the Ghost's own mouth that it was his
father's spirit); and among others were Ross and, in
1768, Powell. After Quin, Macklin acted the Ghost and
also the Gravedigger (on one night both), or Polonius.
Dunstall was a popular Gravedigger. For Queen there
was Mrs Woffington, Mrs Elmy, and once Mrs Yates.
Sparks went over to Covent Garden to play the King,
and the 'useful but affected' Mrs Vincent did her best
to fill the gap left by Mrs Cibber's Ophelia, with Miss
Macklin and Mrs Mattocks coming later. The play
appears to have been shortened, but not otherwise altered. In (?) James Roberts's picture in the Garrick Club
Barry wears a black Court suit with a pale blue ribbon
(probably meant for the Order of the Elephant) over his
right shoulder and a white wig with hair hanging down
over his shoulders; and Mrs Barry (the scene is the
Closet-scene) is in full dress of the contemporary style
(*c.* 1775), with a white wig and many white plumes.

When Garrick had retired, Lacy at Drury Lane and

Lewis at Covent Garden each made a bid for his honours in *Hamlet*; but the largest measure of them (and none too great at that) went to Henderson, who had been acting the part at Bath and brought it to London, first to the Haymarket in June, 1777, and then, promptly engaged by R. B. Sheridan, to Drury Lane in September. Henderson, like Barry, was a graceful actor with a beautiful voice, and a very good speaker of verse. In the scene with the Ghost he differed from Garrick in endeavouring to subdue his terror and to address the Ghost calmly and firmly; and at Ophelia's funeral he showed singular tenderness and regret. But he had little greatness, and Bannister, junior, who sometimes took his place (he claimed to be the first to bring back the Gravediggers, and his *Hamlet* 'was always done twenty minutes sooner than anybody else'), had less. The play —like the theatre in general—had to wait for due consideration till the coming of John Philip Kemble.

The famous portrait by Lawrence would alone be enough to show that with Kemble comes a different sort of Hamlet from the vivacious, 'enterprising' Hamlet of Betterton or the bustling, histrionic Hamlet of Garrick. The romantic movement is upon the Theatre, and the keynote of the character is now an almost sepulchral melancholy. A fixed and sullen gloom was what Hazlitt, writing of John Kemble's later appearances, accused him of, and probably his earlier rendering differed little from his later. We may believe, too, that he was stiff, formal, deficient in the 'yielding flexibility' of Hamlet's character, and that, more even than his Coriolanus or his Macbeth, his Hamlet, with its little personal oddities, 'particular emphases, pauses and other novelties,' showed traces of Kemble's intense intellectual study and calculated art. But Scott thought his Hamlet equal to Garrick's. Lamb praised the 'playful court-bred spirit in which he condescended to the players' (at his first performance in London he left out the 'advice' through

modesty, but put it in on the second of his twelve nights);
and this 'sensible, lonely Hamlet,' intense, introspective,
abstracted, was the first of a good many such visions of
the character. On his first appearance at Drury Lane,
September 30, 1783, he wore 'a modern Court dress of
rich black velvet, with a star on the breast, the garter and
pendant ribbon of an order—mourning sword and
buckler, with deep ruffles; the hair in powder; which
in the scenes of feigned distraction, flowed dishevelled in
front over the shoulders' (which is very much what
Barry's does in the Garrick Club picture). On that occasion he had Bensley for the Ghost, Packer for the King,
Farren for Horatio, Suett for the Gravedigger, Baddeley
for Polonius, Mrs Hopkins for the Queen, and Miss
Field for Ophelia.

After his triumphant first season he produced the play
fairly often, but irregularly. His mature view of it is
best considered from the productions at Covent Garden
in 1803 and onwards, for which he printed his version of
the play. Introspective and melancholy though he was,
it must be noticed that all the important cuts were made
in order to keep the action of the play going, not to
emphasize the principal part. Fortinbras (some of
whose final lines are given to Horatio), the Ambassadors,
Reynaldo, the Dumb Show, the King's prayer and
Hamlet's soliloquy about it, are clean gone, and so are
Polonius's advice to Laertes and the talk about the boy
players. The King's part is a good deal shortened; most
of the soliloquy, 'O, what a rogue and peasant slave am
I!,' most of the Queen's description of Ophelia's drowning, and most of Hamlet's last two speeches to his mother
in the Closet-scene are cut out. Some of these cuts are
made, no doubt, to save time for the newly introduced
intervals between the setting of scenery, and some to
spare the delicacy which was now beginning to creep in
between the audience and the poet.

Only two can be held to throw light on his conception

of the character. He cut out a good many of Hamlet's most wild and whirling words to Horatio after the exit of the Ghost, which the earlier players had retained, and also (like Betterton and others after him) of those that follow the Play-scene. The suggestion is that of a Hamlet not only sane but also not wildly excited, and preserving the decorum of a 'classical' style throughout. Of the many small innovations much discussed by his contemporaries only two have much significance. Instead of keeping his sword pointed at the Ghost, as Garrick had, he kept it in his right hand but drooped the point behind him and held out his left hand to the Ghost; and on the Ghost's disappearance he kneeled to it in reverence. Henderson so admired this last that he adopted it himself. Perhaps another detail is worth preserving for its dramatic force. In the Closet-scene (where he was gentle and respectful to the Queen), when the Ghost appeared Hamlet's hand was on his mother's arm, his eyes fixed on the Ghost. He did not move his hand, and when the Ghost bade him speak to her, he did so mechanically without looking at her.

In spite of Munden as Polonius, Emery as the Grave-digger and Harley as Osric, the representative cast strikes rather chill: Cory, the King; Charles Kemble, Laertes; Brunton, Horatio; Murray, the Ghost; Mrs Chapman, the Queen; and Miss Mortimer, Ophelia. In the years between 1803 and his final performance at the time of his retirement in June, 1817, he had G. F. Cooke twice for the Ghost and Pope now and then. Liston, Blanchard, the elder Charles Mathews, Suett and Dowton played Polonius; Wewitzer the Grave-digger, Mrs Brereton and Mrs Weston the Queen, and among several Ophelias Mrs Charles Kemble, Miss Kelly and Miss Stephens. The researches of Mr Charles Beecher Hogan (kindly communicated to me) have discovered Mrs Siddons's 'second time of appearing' in the character of Hamlet at Manchester in March, 1777, and other appearances at Liverpool in the following December, at Bath in 1778, at Bristol in 1781 (in a version adapted by Lee from Garrick's), and at Dublin so late as 1802; but she played the Queen only three times, of which only one was in London, at Drury Lane in April, 1796, to the Hamlet of Wroughton, for King's benefit, and Ophelia only twice, at Drury Lane, for her own benefit, in April, 1786, and at Liverpool in June of the same year.

In 1785 at Covent Garden Holman first appeared in London as Hamlet (the elder Macready said that Kemble was the Prince, Holman was Hamlet, and Henderson was Hamlet Prince of Denmark); and ten years later it was he who was acting the part, to the Ophelia of Miss Poole, at that theatre when Hamlet was once more dressed in the 'Vandyke' style, and 'has ever since been fixed in costume of black satin and bugles.' In 1796 Mrs Powell was added to the large number of female Hamlets (yet another about this time was the Miss Edmead whom Parson Woodforde saw at Norwich in 1792). In 1802 Cooke failed in the part. In 1803 Charles Kemble gave his first performance of a Hamlet which differed from all others in being completely mad, 'an image,' wrote his daughter Fanny, 'of a distracted intellect and a broken heart.' In 1805 Master Betty entertained the town with his Hamlet; and in 1807 C. M. Young, not unworthy substitute and successor to J. P. Kemble, took up the part, which he played in his fine 'classical' manner until his farewell benefit in 1832, when Macready came to play the Ghost and old Charles Mathews, who had been his Polonius at his first appearance, came back to play it again at his last. None of these (not even Elliston, who acted Hamlet first in London in 1804 and, with a strong cast to support him, made the tragedy the opening performance of the rebuilt Drury Lane on October 10, 1812) need detain us long from the great event of March 12, 1814, when Edmund Kean first played Hamlet at Drury Lane.

The supposition of the romantic genius type of actor

—a Devrient or an Edmund Kean—that Shakespeare's characters were real people, who could be thoroughly understood by much brooding or 'moping about,' ought to have resulted in a unity of conception and presentation. With Kean it did not always. The gist of Hazlitt's famous criticism of his Hamlet is that he did not see the character as a whole. To John Kemble, to Macready, to Henry Irving, Hamlet was a consistent human being, or at the least a consistent part of a larger artistic design. To Kean the part was a sequence of impressive moments; and to make those moments effective he was not above self-assertion in the wrong places; he was 'too strong and pointed,' exaggerated in emphasis and manner, too much the performer, too little the impersonator of a gentleman and a scholar. Nevertheless, he brought to Hamlet certain things which others were glad to take over from him, notably an emphasis (apparently something other than part of a general exaggeration of points) on Hamlet's abiding passion for Ophelia, which led him to treat her without 'the conventional coarseness and almost brutal ferocity' (writing in 1812 Lamb had protested against that convention, thus proving its prevalence), and to come back to her at the end of the 'nunnery' scene, and kiss her hand. He did away, too, with the extreme physical terror of Hamlet on seeing the Ghost (he had a first-rate Ghost in Raymond); he called it 'Father' with intense pathos which thrilled the audience, and he followed it with eagerness and confidence, not at the sword's point. In this scene of the play he abated nothing of Hamlet's wildness, but in the Closet-scene Mrs Garrick found him 'too tame,' which meant tamer than Garrick had been. So masterly and graceful a fencer naturally made the most of the fight with Laertes, and after 'The rest is silence' he indulged in a very elaborate death by poison. Miss Smith (Mrs Bartley) was his Ophelia, Bannister the First Gravedigger and Dowton 'made nothing, or worse than nothing,' of Polonius.

Kean dressed Hamlet with short hair, black clothes with a handsome lace collar, and round his neck the then traditional blue ribbon meant for that of the Order of the Elephant. The portraits of Macready as Hamlet, as late as a dozen years after Kean's death, suggest that staginess must have come back and swept away all traces of the 'nature' which Kean, in his own way, brought into the part. His black hat has a forest of black feathers; his inky cloak trails on the ground. We do not need the addition of 'black silk gloves much too large for him,' and 'a dark beard close shaven to his square jaws, yet unsoftened by a trace of pigment' to complete a most depressing picture, which would more than justify a suspicion that Lewes was right when he called Macready's Hamlet 'lachrymose and fretful,' and 'too fond of a cambric handkerchief to be really affecting.' And yet, after calling him 'positively hideous,' Coleman goes on to say: 'But O ye gods, when he spoke...!'; and from Lady Pollock (and would that all critics of acting could make themselves as clear as she did!) and from others it is plain that Macready's Hamlet, ungraceful and laborious like nearly all his work, was still a thing of intellectual beauty and dramatic power. At Covent Garden in 1837 he mounted the play with the greatest care; and his diaries show how all through his career he laboured at the character, consistently exacting from himself more self-possession, finish, tenderness, earnestness and dignity. Lewes, with his head full of Wilhelm Meister and Fechter, may have found Macready's Hamlet a thing of shreds and patches, not a whole; but Bowes said that he was the only intelligible Hamlet that he had ever seen, and Spedding that it was easy to credit him with the thoughts that he uttered. He saw Hamlet as an agreeable, tender-natured prince, and a great lover of Ophelia before he learned of his father's murder. There was no physical fear in his meeting with the Ghost, only awe which was dominated by tenderness. Like John Kemble, he knelt to his father's spirit; but he convinced his audience that he had indeed seen and talked with a ghost and that he could never be the same again. He wept at the death of Polonius, pitied Ophelia without rancour, and was tenderly affectionate with Horatio. But his gentleness by no means implied dullness. He leapt into Ophelia's grave with the best. He brought back all the wild and whirling words after the Play which all others (even Betterton, who had not been afraid of 'old mole' and 'truepenny') had left out, and after them he broke down, with his head on Horatio's shoulder. And his dignity and gentleness were broken by moments of intense excitement. When Lady Pollock wrote to him in 1861 about Fechter's very quiet way of speaking the close of the soliloquy which ends with 'The play's the thing,' he replied that he 'conceived the excitement of that most excitable being to be carried to its highest pitch' at that point, and that therefore he 'must differ the whole heaven' from Fechter. Among the many who acted with him from time to time were Samuel Phelps as the Ghost, Mrs Warner as the Queen, Harley and Keeley as the First Gravedigger and Priscilla Horton as Ophelia. In his regular version he cut out Fortinbras, the Ambassadors, Reynaldo, the Dumb Show and all the scene of the King's prayer, and ended the play on 'The rest is silence.' When he took the play, with others, in 1845, to Paris, and acted it at the Tuileries before the King and Queen, he cut out also the Gravediggers.

The Hamlet of Charles Kean appears to have been, like most of his work, a respectable performance. He aimed at steering between the classical and the romantic; but, though he had never seen his father play the part, he was too much his father's son not to lean towards the romantic and to make more of certain moments than of the whole. Such moments were his cry of 'Is it the King?,' his speaking of 'O, what a rogue and peasant slave am I!' which he gave in full, his demeanour during

and after the Play, and (like his father) his elaborate
death-scene, following the words 'The rest is silence,'
with which he ended the play. In the scene with Ophelia
some found him too harsh, some too tender, which
proves mediocrity, while one friend congratulated him
on doing without the 'clapping and banging the doors,
and the maniac ravings of the old school.' In general he
was too lachrymose, too vehement, and too little of the
prince. His first performance in London was at Drury
Lane on January 8, 1838. After that the play was
among his most successful, and the staging of it at the
Princess's in 1850 and afterwards was in his usual careful
and elaborate style. But he brought back to the stage
scarcely anything that the others had left out; and he left
out all the scene of the King's prayer and Hamlet's
soliloquy thereon. The playbill of Samuel Phelps's
Hamlet, first produced at Sadler's Wells in July, 1844,
shows no Fortinbras, no Ambassadors, and no Reynaldo.

Barry Sullivan in 1852, with a flowing light brown
wig and his black relieved with purple, had given
London a taste of a completely sane Hamlet, with a robust temper, keen wits and a bitter tongue. And in 1861
Manchester (with Mr Henry Irving in its stock company
ready to play Laertes) was fortunate enough to see what
London had to wait for till 1880—the Hamlet of Edwin
Booth, sane, natural, graceful, melancholy, super-
sensitive, restless, and wildly impetuous, evidently a
many-sided and beautiful performance, of which the
abiding impression was that the prince was a haunted
man. (Booth, it should be added, played the most
nearly complete version of any on the English-speaking
stage.) It is tempting to believe that, if London could
have seen Booth's Hamlet before it saw, in March of that
very year 1861, Fechter's Hamlet, the innovations of the
'naturalistic' player might have been regarded more
steadily. But Fechter, knowing little of the English

theatrical tradition, was able to put much of the play in a new light when he produced it at the Princess's Theatre. He wore long flaxen curls and a small two-pointed beard, because Hamlet was a Dane; and he dressed his company in the style of the Viking era. He was delicate, handsome, graceful. He had a princely nonchalance and a pleasant way with his inferiors, and he could express emotion with sensibility. But he showed no awe nor depth of feeling. He thought that 'To be or not to be' was an impediment to the action, and spoke it fast and unimpressively, holding a drawn sword in his hand. He was never distraught, and seldom more than a little excited. His calm and self-possession were too much even for Lewes, who was prepared to see in him the pot-bound rose of Goethe, Hamlet with a burden laid on him too heavy for his soul to bear; but, lacking power, and too matter-of-fact and shallow, he robbed the play of true tragedy. Fechter doubtless cleared the way for others whom the tradition might have hampered. He appears to have retained the soliloquy during the King's prayer. According to one account his Hamlet did not see the King and Polonius spying on his meeting with Ophelia; according to another account he saw Polonius, but not the King. When he staged the play at the Lyceum in 1864, Kate Terry was his excellent Ophelia, and he knocked another nail into the coffin of the old manner of shouting at her in fury.

Ten years later, at that same theatre, came a hurried, shabby production of the play which ran for a hundred nights and revealed a Hamlet who owed something, no doubt, to the naturalism of Fechter (the new Hamlet himself had worn, in his provincial youth, a flaxen wig), something to the momentary fires of Edmund Kean, something to the consistent artistic unity of John Philip Kemble, and most of all to his own mind and his own personality. Henry Irving finally killed off the sepul-chral Hamlet and restored the intensity of thought

and feeling which had long been lacking. Between
his first appearance as Hamlet at the Lyceum in 1874
and his own production of the play in December,
1878, Salvini had shown tremendous dramatic power
and considerable beauty of idea in a performance
which in its signs of physical terror had gone back
to Garrick, and generally had escaped all influence from
the psychological analysis with which the critics for
something like a century had been making Hamlet more
and more difficult to act to the satisfaction of the educated
classes. Irving's dramatic power and beauty were altogether different from the robust Salvini's. He had the
many-sidedness, the 'yielding flexibility,' as Hazlitt
would have called it, of Edwin Booth's Hamlet, with a
poetry of aspect and an intensity of passion all his own.
One critic, Edward Russell, credited him with a stroke
of genius: he had discovered that Hamlet 'fosters and
aggravates his own excitements'; and hence came his
moments of 'vivid, flashing, half-foolish, half-inspired,
hysterical power.' He cut out Fortinbras, the Ambassadors, the Dumb Show, and the soliloquy during the
King's prayer—followed in the main, in fact, the
traditional cuts; he very much shortened the plotting
between the King and Laertes, and he ended the
play at 'The rest is silence.' But he was not afraid of the
wild and whirling words after the Ghost's departure and
was frantic with excitement after the Play. Yet he never
overacted; and at first some at least among his audience
wondered at his quiet in certain scenes—a quiet which
thrilled with the intensity behind it. In the production of
1874 his Ophelia was Isabel Bateman; in that of 1878
the matchless Ellen Terry. In both productions Miss
Pauncefort played the Queen, Chippendale Polonius
and Mead the Ghost. The staging in 1878 was beautiful
(the scene of the cemetery was especially admired); but
it was not so elaborate as to demand more cutting of the
play than was usual. In costume he made no attempt at

the Viking period, and himself wore no tragic trappings nor Orders.

Briefer notice must suffice for some subsequent productions, each of which, no doubt, has added something to the infinite variety of Hamlet in the theatre. At the Princess's Theatre in October, 1884, Wilson Barrett appeared as a sane and resolute youth of eighteen. His low-cut neck, his innovations in wording and his rearrangement of scenes were more discussed than his conception of the character. In January, 1892, Beerbohm Tree staged at the Haymarket a very elaborate production, which concluded on the words, 'Flights of angels sing thee to thy rest,' with an angelic chorus. He inclined strongly to the sentimental: A. B. Walkley called him a 'Werther Hamlet.' He cut out Osric and much shortened the Gravediggers. In September, 1897, at the Lyceum came one of the most beautiful of all Hamlets, Johnston Forbes-Robertson's, with Mrs Patrick Campbell for Ophelia. He followed, in the main, the usual cuts, leaving out the Ambassadors and the Dumb Show; but he restored, after several centuries, Fortinbras to give the play its proper ending (Hamlet himself lying dead on the throne which had been his for the last few breaths of his life); he kept a little of Reynaldo and he spoke Hamlet's soliloquy during the King's prayer. His conception was of a sane, indeed a reasonable Hamlet; and the beauty of its execution has influenced all that have followed. H. B. Irving's princely, intellectual Hamlet was first seen at the Adelphi in 1905, and for the last time, enriched and mellowed, at the Savoy in 1917. He went back to the old cuts for the most part; but he left in the first part of the Dumb Show, up to the entrance of the poisoner; he rearranged the scenes of the second and third Acts for a purpose which it is hard to detect; and he contrived to throw more emphasis than was usual on the mission to England. He too saw Hamlet as sane, except momentarily after the departure of the Ghost; but as lonely, resentful, and weak, a quick and youthful nature over-burdened by love for his father and instinctive loathing of his uncle. His Ophelia in his later performances was Miss Gertrude Elliott (Lady Forbes-Robertson). In May, 1905, at the Lyric Theatre Sir John Martin-Harvey gave the first of many performances of *Hamlet*. His Hamlet was a beautiful and passionate study in the romantic tradition; and in the course of a long series of productions—the last of which up to the present was that, played with curtains and tableaux, at Covent Garden in December, 1919—he so simplified his staging that he was able to include part of Reynaldo, Fortinbras in the final scene, the soliloquy during the King's prayer and the questioning of Hamlet about the disposal of the body of Polonius. The Dumb Show he left out; and a distinctive feature of his production was that neither Hamlet nor Ophelia knew that their meeting was being spied upon by Polonius and the King. The effect of terror conveyed in the first scene of all was to be noticed also, to a remarkable degree, in the production by the American actor Mr E. H. Sothern (with Miss Julia Marlowe for Ophelia) at the Waldorf (now the Strand) Theatre in May, 1907. He too kept in the soliloquy during the King's prayer. A hearty, straightforward performance at cheap prices by Mr Matheson Lang at the Lyceum in May, 1909, possibly conveyed an idea of what *Hamlet* meant to the groundlings at the Globe. A production by Mr L. E. Berman at the Prince of Wales's Theatre in May, 1925, kept in all the scenes following the Closet scene, and also the Dumb Show, which was mimed as a comic interlude to music and made the King laugh. The Hamlet was Mr Godfrey Tearle, who at the Haymarket in March, 1931, showed a winning, warm-hearted Hamlet, even gentler with Ophelia (Miss Fay Compton) than most modern Hamlets are. The Stratford-upon-Avon Festival Company, under Mr Bridges Adams, has given several versions of the play. Fortinbras is always retained; the Dumb Show is always omitted. For ordinary purposes, Reynaldo and the Ambassadors are cut down, but the soliloquy during the King's prayer is always retained. A Hamlet in itself beautiful and moving and rich in promise of future greatness was that of Mr John Gielgud at the Old Vic in 1929–30 and at the Queen's Theatre in 1930. In this version also the Dumb Show is retained, but passes unnoticed by the King.

Hamlet having suffered very little from the restorers and adapters, there has been no very urgent demand for its restoration to purity. Nevertheless the many cuts demanded by time and determined, in some cases, by taste, have roused in recent years the desire to see the play 'whole.' The first to gratify this desire was Sir F. R. Benson who, first in 1899, at the Shakespeare Memorial Theatre at Stratford, and again in July, 1911, and later in America, acted a composite text of the Second Quarto and the First Folio. In April, 1916, and subsequent years the Old Vic Company acted the full text of the Second Quarto under Sir Philip Ben Greet, who had produced it in America in 1905. In April, 1881, the Elizabethan Stage Society,* under Mr William Poel, gave at the St George's Hall 'the first public performance in England before curtains' of the text of the Quarto of 1603, and again at Carpenters' Hall in February, 1900. This text has also been produced often in America, and in 1928, 1929, and 1933 in London, by Sir Philip Ben Greet. On January 27, 1914, at the Little Theatre, Mr Poel produced a version intended 'to show scenes never acted in versions given on the modern stage.' Act I, scene i was left out, and so was all the Ghost until the Closet-scene; and the effect was to lay stress on the importance of the King and of the foreign politics of Denmark. In 1924, at Oxford and in London, Mr Poel also staged *Fratri-cide Punished*, an English version of *Der bestrafte Brudermord*, which may have been derived from a version of *Hamlet* acted in Germany early in the seventeenth century. *Hamlet* was the first Shakespeare play to be acted in modern times in modern dress. The Birmingham Repertory Company, under Sir Barry Jackson, gave it at the Kingsway Theatre in August, 1925, and again at the Birmingham Repertory Theatre in the following November. A performance at the Sloane School, London, in March, 1933, adopted, among other suggestions made by Professor Dover Wilson, these two: in Act II, scene ii, Hamlet overheard Polonius proposing to 'loose my daughter to him' and eavesdrop on their meeting; and the Dumb Show was performed, the King being too deep in talk with Polonius and the Queen about Hamlet's behaviour to look at it, and Hamlet distressed at this unauthorised addition to the Play, which threatened to explode his mine too soon.

1934   HAROLD CHILD.

TO THE READER

The following is a brief description of the punctuation and other typographical devices employed in the text, which have been more fully explained in the *Note on Punctuation* and the *Textual Introduction* to be found in *The Tempest* volume:

An obelisk (†) implies corruption or emendation, and suggests a reference to the Notes.

A single bracket at the beginning of a speech signifies an 'aside.'

Four dots represent a *full-stop* in the original, except when it occurs at the end of a speech, and they mark a long pause. Original *colons* or *semicolons*, which denote a somewhat shorter pause, are retained, or represented as three dots when they appear to possess special dramatic significance. Similarly, significant *commas* have been given as dashes.

Round brackets are taken from the original, and mark a significant change of voice; when the original brackets seem to imply little more than the drop in tone accompanying parenthesis, they are conveyed by commas or dashes.

Single inverted commas (' ') are editorial; double ones (" ") derive from the original, where they are used to draw attention to maxims, quotations, etc.

The reference number for the first line is given at the head of each page. Numerals in square brackets are placed at the beginning of the traditional acts and scenes.

THE
Tragicall Historie of
HAMLET,

Prince of Denmarke.

By William Shakespeare.

Newly imprinted and enlarged to almost as much
againe as it was, according to the true and perfect
Coppie.

AT LONDON,
Printed by I. R. for N. L. and are to be sold at his
shoppe vnder Saint Dunstons Church in
Fleetstreet. 1605.

2

The scene: Denmark

CHARACTERS IN THE PLAY

CLAUDIUS, *King of Denmark*

HAMLET, *Prince of Denmark, son to the late, and nephew to the present king*

POLONIUS, *Principal Secretary of State*

HORATIO, *friend to Hamlet*

LAERTES, *son to Polonius*

VALTEMAND
CORNELIUS } *ambassadors to Norway*

ROSENCRANTZ
GUILDENSTERN } *formerly fellow-students with Hamlet*

OSRIC, *a fantastic fop*

A gentleman

A Doctor of Divinity

MARCELLUS
BARNARDO } *Gentlemen of the Guard*
FRANCISCO

REYNALDO, *servant to Polonius*

Four or five Players

Two grave-diggers

FORTINBRAS, *Prince of Norway*

A Norwegian Captain

English Ambassadors

GERTRUDE, *Queen of Denmark, mother to Hamlet*

OPHELIA, *daughter to Polonius*

Lords, Ladies, Soldiers, Sailors, Messenger, and Attendants

The GHOST *of Hamlet's father*

THE
TRAGEDY OF HAMLET
PRINCE OF DENMARK

[I. I.] *The castle at Elsinore. A narrow platform upon the battlements; turret-doors to right and left. Starlight, very cold*

FRANCISCO, *a sentinel armed with a partisan, paces to and fro. A bell tolls twelve. Presently* BARNARDO, *another sentinel likewise armed, comes from the castle; he starts, hearing Francisco's tread in the darkness*

Barnardo. Who's there?
Francisco. Nay, answer me. Stand and unfold yourself.
Barnardo. Long live the king!
Francisco. Barnardo?
Barnardo. He.
Francisco. You come most carefully upon your hour.
Barnardo. 'Tis now struck twelve, get thee to
     bed, Francisco.
Francisco. For this relief much thanks, 'tis bitter cold,
And I am sick at heart.
Barnardo. Have you had quiet guard?
Francisco.   Not a mouse stirring. 10
Barnardo. Well, good night:
If you do meet Horatio and Marcellus,
The rivals of my watch, bid them make haste.

       HORATIO and MARCELLUS come forth

Francisco [*listens*]. I think I hear them. Stand ho, who
     is there?
Horatio. Friends to this ground.
Marcellus.   And liegemen to the Dane.

Francisco. Give you good night.

Marcellus.   O, farewell honest soldier,
Who hath relieved you?

Francisco.   Barnardo hath my place;
Give you good night.   [*Francisco goes*

Marcellus.   Holla, Barnardo!

Barnardo.   Say,
What, is Horatio there?

Horatio.   A piece of him.

20 *Barnardo.* Welcome Horatio, welcome good Marcellus.

Horatio. What, has this thing appeared again to-night?

Barnardo. I have seen nothing.

Marcellus. Horatio says 'tis but our fantasy,
And will not let belief take hold of him
Touching this dreaded sight twice seen of us,
Therefore I have entreated him along
With us to watch the minutes of this night,
That if again this apparition come,
He may approve our eyes and speak to it.

30 *Horatio.* 'Tush, tush, 'twill not appear.

Barnardo.   Sit down awhile,
And let us once again assail your ears,
That are so fortified against our story,
What we have two nights seen.

Horatio.   Well, sit we down,
And let us hear Barnardo speak of this.

Barnardo. Last night of all,
When yon same star that's westward from the pole
Had made his course t'illume that part of heaven
Where now it burns, Marcellus and myself,
The bell then beating one——

A GHOST *appears; it is clad in armour from head to*
foot, and bears a marshal's truncheon

Marcellus. Peace, break thee off, look where it   40
        comes again!
Barnardo. In the same figure like the king
        that's dead.
Marcellus. Thou art a scholar, speak to it, Horatio.
Barnardo. Looks a' not like the king? mark it, Horatio.
Horatio. Most like, it harrows me with fear
        and wonder.
Barnardo. It would be spoke to.
Marcellus.   Question it, Horatio.
Horatio. What art thou that usurp'st this time of night,
Together with that fair and warlike form
In which the majesty of buried Denmark
Did sometimes march? by heaven I charge thee speak.
Marcellus. It is offended.
Barnardo.   See, it stalks away.   50
Horatio. Stay, speak, speak, I charge thee speak.
                              [*the Ghost vanishes*
Marcellus. 'Tis gone and will not answer.
Barnardo. How now Horatio, you tremble and
        look pale,
Is not this something more than fantasy?
What think you on't?
Horatio. Before my God, I might not this believe
Without the sensible and true avouch
Of mine own eyes.
Marcellus.   Is it not like the king?
Horatio. As thou art to thyself.
Such was the very armour he had on,   60
When he the ambitious Norway combated,
So frowned he once, when in an angry parle

He smote the sledded Polacks on the ice.
'Tis strange.
　Marcellus. Thus twice before, and jump at this
　　　　dead hour,
With martial stalk hath he gone by our watch.
　Horatio. In what particular thought to work I
　　　　know not,
But in the gross and scope of mine opinion,
This bodes some strange eruption to our state.
70 *Marcellus.* Good now sit down, and tell me he
　　　　that knows,
Why this same strict and most observant watch
So nightly toils the subject of the land,
And why such daily cast of brazen cannon
And foreign mart for implements of war,
Why such impress of shipwrights, whose sore task
Does not divide the Sunday from the week,
What might be toward that this sweaty haste
Doth make the night joint-labourer with the day,
Who is't that can inform me?
　Horatio.　　　　　　　　　That can I,
80 At least the whisper goes so; our last king,
Whose image even but now appeared to us,
Was as you know by Fortinbras of Norway,
Thereto pricked on by a most emulate pride,
Dared to the combat; in which our valiant Hamlet
(For so this side of our known world esteemed him)
Did slay this Fortinbras, who by a sealed compact,
Well ratified by law and heraldy,
Did forfeit (with his life) all those his lands
Which he stood seized of, to the conqueror,
90 Against the which a moiety competent
Was gagéd by our king, which had returned
To the inheritance of Fortinbras,

Had he been vanquisher; as by the same co-mart,
And carriage of the article designed,
His fell to Hamlet; now sir, young Fortinbras,
Of unimprovéd mettle hot and full,
Hath in the skirts of Norway here and there
Sharked up a list of lawless resolutes
For food and diet to some enterprise
That hath a stomach in't, which is no other,   100
As it doth well appear unto our state,
But to recover of us by strong hand
And terms compulsatory, those foresaid lands
So by his father lost; and this, I take it,
Is the main motive of our preparations,
The source of this our watch, and the chief head
Of this post-haste and romage in the land.

   Barnardo. I think it be no other but e'en so;
Well may it sort that this portentous figure
Comes arméd through our watch so like the king   110
That was and is the question of these wars.

   Horatio. A mote it is to trouble the mind's eye:
In the most high and palmy state of Rome,
A little ere the mightiest Julius fell,
The graves stood tenantless, and the sheeted dead
Did squeak and gibber in the Roman streets,
†And even the like precurse of fierce events,
As harbingers preceding still the fates
And prologue to the omen coming on,
Have heaven and earth together demonstrated   120
Unto our climatures and countrymen,
As stars with trains of fire and dews of blood,
Disasters in the sun; and the moist star,
Upon whose influence Neptune's empire stands,
Was sick almost to doomsday with eclipse.

The GHOST *reappears*

But soft, behold, lo where it comes again!
I'll cross it though it blast me...[*he 'spreads his arms'*
          Stay, illusion!
If thou hast any sound or use of voice,
Speak to me.
130 If there be any good thing to be done
That may to thee do ease, and grace to me,
Speak to me.
If thou art privy to thy country's fate
Which happily foreknowing may avoid,
O, speak!
Or if thou hast uphoarded in thy life
Extorted treasure in the womb of earth,
For which they say you spirits oft walk in death,
                                        [*a cock crows*
Speak of it—stay and speak—stop it, Marcellus!
140 *Marcellus.* Shall I strike at it with my partisan?
    Horatio. Do if it will not stand.
    Barnardo.   'Tis here!
    Horatio.   'Tis here!
    Marcellus. 'Tis gone!   [*the Ghost vanishes*
We do it wrong being so majestical
To offer it the show of violence,
For it is as the air, invulnerable,
And our vain blows malicious mockery.
    Barnardo. It was about to speak when the cock crew.
    Horatio. And then it started like a guilty thing,
Upon a fearful summons; I have heard
150 The cock that is the trumpet to the morn
Doth with his lofty and shrill-sounding throat
Awake the god of day, and at his warning
Whether in sea or fire, in earth or air,

Th'extravagant and erring spirit hies
To his confine, and of the truth herein
This present object made probation.

Marcellus. It faded on the crowing of the cock.
Some say that ever 'gainst that season comes
Wherein our Saviour's birth is celebrated
This bird of dawning singeth all night long,   160
And then they say no spirit dare stir abroad,
The nights are wholesome, then no planets strike,
No fairy takes, nor witch hath power to charm,
So hallowed, and so gracious is that time.

Horatio. So have I heard and do in part believe it.
But look, the morn in russet mantle clad
Walks o'er the dew of yon high eastward hill.
Break we our watch up and by my advice
Let us impart what we have seen to-night
Unto young Hamlet, for upon my life   170
This spirit dumb to us, will speak to him:
Do you consent we shall acquaint him with it,
As needful in our loves, fitting our duty?

Marcellus. Let's do't, I pray, and I this morning know
Where we shall find him most convenient.   [*they go*

[1.2.]   *The Council Chamber in the castle*

A 'flourish' of trumpets. 'Enter CLAUDIUS *King of Denmark,* GERTRUDE *the Queen, Councillors,* POLONIUS *and
his son* LAERTES,' VALTEMAND *and* CORNELIUS, *all
clad in gay apparel, as from the coronation; and last of
all Prince* HAMLET *in black, with downcast eyes. The
King and Queen ascend steps to the thrones*

King. Though yet of Hamlet our dear brother's death
The memory be green, and that it us befitted
To bear our hearts in grief, and our whole kingdom

To be contracted in one brow of woe,
Yet so far hath discretion fought with nature,
That we with wisest sorrow think on him
Together with remembrance of ourselves:
Therefore our sometime sister, now our queen,
Th'imperial jointress to this warlike state,
10 Have we as 'twere with a defeated joy,
With an auspicious, and a dropping eye,
With mirth in funeral, and with dirge in marriage,
In equal scale weighing delight and dole,
Taken to wife: nor have we herein barred
Your better wisdoms, which have freely gone
With this affair along—for all, our thanks.
Now follows that you know, young Fortinbras,
Holding a weak supposal of our worth,
Or thinking by our late dear brother's death
20 Our state to be disjoint and out of frame,
Colleaguéd with this dream of his advantage,
He hath not failed to pester us with message
Importing the surrender of those lands
Lost by his father, with all bands of law,
To our most valiant brother—so much for him:
Now for ourself, and for this time of meeting,
Thus much the business is. We have here writ
To Norway, uncle of young Fortinbras—
Who impotent and bed-rid scarcely hears
30 Of this his nephew's purpose—to suppress
His further gait herein, in that the levies,
The lists, and full proportions, are all made
Out of his subject. And we here dispatch
You good Cornelius, and you Valtemand,
For bearers of this greeting to old Norway,
Giving to you no further personal power
To business with the king, more than the scope

Of these delated articles allow:
Farewell, and let your haste commend your duty.
   Cornelius, Valtemand. In that, and all things, will we
      show our duty.   40
    King. We doubt it nothing, heartily farewell.
             [*Valtemand and Cornelius bow, and depart*
And now, Laertes, what's the news with you?
You told us of some suit, what is't, Laertes?
You cannot speak of reason to the Dane,
And lose your voice; what wouldst thou beg, Laertes,
That shall not be my offer, not thy asking?
The head is not more native to the heart,
The hand more instrumental to the mouth,
Than is the throne of Denmark to thy father.
What wouldst thou have, Laertes?
   Laertes.   My dread lord,   50
Your leave and favour to return to France,
From whence though willingly I came to Denmark,
To show my duty in your coronation;
Yet now I must confess, that duty done,
My thoughts and wishes bend again toward France,
And bow them to your gracious leave and pardon.
   King. Have you your father's leave? what
      says Polonius?
   Polonius. He hath, my lord, wrung from me my
      slow leave
By laboursome petition, and at last
Upon his will I sealed my hard consent.   60
I do beseech you give him leave to go.
   King. Take thy fair hour, Laertes, time be thine,
And thy best graces spend it at thy will...
But now my cousin Hamlet, and my son—
   (*Hamlet.* A little more than kin, and less than kind.
   King. How is it that the clouds still hang on you?

Hamlet. Not so, my lord, I am too much in the 'son.'
Queen. Good Hamlet, cast thy nighted colour off,
And let thine eye look like a friend on Denmark,
70 Do not for ever with thy vailéd lids
Seek for thy noble father in the dust,
Thou know'st 'tis common, all that lives must die,
Passing through nature to eternity.
Hamlet. Ay, madam, it is common.
Queen.   If it be,
Why seems it so particular with thee?
Hamlet. Seems, madam! nay it is, I know not 'seems.'
'Tis not alone my inky cloak, good mother,
Nor customary suits of solemn black,
Nor windy suspiration of forced breath,
80 No, nor the fruitful river in the eye,
Nor the dejected haviour of the visage,
Together with all forms, modes, shapes of grief,
That can denote me truly. These indeed seem,
For they are actions that a man might play,
But I have that within which passes show,
These but the trappings and the suits of woe.
King. 'Tis sweet and commendable in your
             nature, Hamlet,
To give these mourning duties to your father,
But you must know your father lost a father,
90 That father lost, lost his, and the survivor bound
In filial obligation for some term
To do obsequious sorrow. But to persever
In obstinate condolement is a course
Of impious stubbornness, 'tis unmanly grief,
It shows a will most incorrect to heaven,
A heart unfortified, a mind impatient,
An understanding simple and unschooled.
For what we know must be and is as common

As any the most vulgar thing to sense,
Why should we in our peevish opposition 100
Take it to heart? fie, 'tis a fault to heaven,
A fault against the dead, a fault to nature,
To reason most absurd, whose common theme
Is death of fathers, and who still hath cried,
From the first corse till he that died to-day,
'This must be so'...We pray you throw to earth
This unprevailing woe, and think of us
As of a father, for let the world take note
You are the most immediate to our throne,
And with no less nobility of love 110
Than that which dearest father bears his son,
Do I impart toward you...For your intent
In going back to school in Wittenberg,
It is most retrograde to our desire,
And we beseech you, bend you to remain
Here in the cheer and comfort of our eye,
Our chiefest courtier, cousin, and our son.
   Queen. Let not thy mother lose her prayers, Hamlet,
I pray thee stay with us, go not to Wittenberg.
   Hamlet. I shall in all my best obey you, madam. 120
   King. Why, 'tis a loving and a fair reply,
Be as ourself in Denmark. Madam, come.
This gentle and unforced accord of Hamlet
Sits smiling to my heart, in grace whereof,
No jocund health that Denmark drinks to-day,
But the great cannon to the clouds shall tell,
And the king's rouse the heaven shall bruit again,
Re-speaking earthly thunder; come away.
        ['*Flourish. Exeunt all but Hamlet*'
   Hamlet. O, that this too too sullied flesh would melt,
Thaw and resolve itself into a dew, 130
Or that the Everlasting had not fixed

His canon 'gainst self-slaughter. O God, God,
How weary, stale, flat, and unprofitable
Seem to me all the uses of this world!
Fie on't, ah fie, 'tis an unweeded garden
That grows to seed, things rank and gross in nature
Possess it merely. That it should come to this,
But two months dead, nay not so much, not two,
So excellent a king, that was to this
140 Hyperion to a satyr, so loving to my mother,
That he might not beteem the winds of heaven
Visit her face too roughly—heaven and earth
Must I remember? why, she would hang on him
As if increase of appetite had grown
By what it fed on, and yet within a month,
Let me not think on't...frailty thy name is woman!
A little month or ere those shoes were old
With which she followed my poor father's body
Like Niobe all tears, why she, even she—
150 O God, a beast that wants discourse of reason
Would have mourned longer—married with my
          uncle,
My father's brother, but no more like my father
Than I to Hercules, within a month,
Ere yet the salt of most unrighteous tears
Had left the flushing in her gallèd eyes
She married. O most wicked speed...to post
With such dexterity to incestuous sheets!
It is not, nor it cannot come to good,
But break my heart, for I must hold my tongue.

HORATIO, MARCELLUS and BARNARDO enter

160   Horatio. Hail to your lordship!
       Hamlet.   I am glad to see you well;
       Horatio—or I do forget my self!

Horatio. The same, my lord, and your poor
  servant ever.

Hamlet. Sir, my good friend, I'll change that name
  with you.   *[they clasp hands*
And what make you from Wittenberg, Horatio?
Marcellus.   *[he gives his hand*

Marcellus. My good lord!

Hamlet. I am very glad to see you—good even, sir.
         [he bows to Barnardo
But what in faith make you from Wittenberg?
         [he draws Horatio apart

Horatio. A truant disposition, good my lord.

Hamlet. I would not hear your enemy say so, 170
Nor shall you do mine ear that violence
To make it truster of your own report
Against yourself. I know you are no truant,
But what is your affair in Elsinore?
We'll teach you to drink deep ere you depart.

Horatio. My lord, I came to see your father's funeral.

Hamlet. I prithee thee do not mock me fellow-student;
I think it was to see my mother's wedding.

Horatio. Indeed, my lord, it followed hard upon.

Hamlet. Thrift, thrift, Horatio, the funeral
  baked meats   180
Did coldly furnish forth the marriage tables.
Would I had met my dearest foe in heaven
Or ever I had seen that day, Horatio—
My father, methinks I see my father.

Horatio. Where, my lord?

Hamlet.   In my mind's eye, Horatio.

Horatio. I saw him once, a' was a goodly king—

Hamlet. A' was a man, take him for all in all,
I shall not look upon his like again.

Horatio. My lord, I think I saw him yesternight.

190 *Hamlet*. Saw, who?

   Horatio. My lord, the king your father.

   Hamlet.   The king my father!

   Horatio. Season your admiration for a while

With an attent ear till I may deliver

Upon the witness of these gentlemen

This marvel to you.

                         [*he turns to Marcellus and Barnardo*

   Hamlet.   For God's love let me hear!

   Horatio. Two nights together had these gentlemen,

Marcellus and Barnardo, on their watch

In the dead waste and middle of the night,

Been thus encountered. A figure like your father

200 Arméd at point exactly, cap-a-pe,

Appears before them, and with solemn march,

Goes slow and stately by them; thrice he walked

By their oppressed and fear-surpriséd eyes

Within his truncheon's length, whilst they distilled

Almost to jelly with the act of fear,

Stand dumb and speak not to him; this to me

In dreadful secrecy impart they did,

And I with them the third night kept the watch,

Where, as they had delivered, both in time,

210 Form of the thing, each word made true and good,

The apparition comes: I knew your father,

These hands are not more like.

   Hamlet.   But where was this?

   Marcellus. My lord, upon the platform where

       we watch.

   Hamlet. Did you not speak to it?

   Horatio.   My lord, I did,

But answer made it none, yet once methought

It lifted up it head, and did address

Itself to motion like as it would speak:

But even then the morning cock crew loud,
And at the sound it shrunk in haste away
And vanished from our sight.

Hamlet. 'Tis very strange. 220

Horatio. As I do live my honoured lord 'tis true,
And we did think it writ down in our duty
To let you know of it.

Hamlet. Indeed, indeed, sirs, but this troubles me.
Hold you the watch to-night?

All. We do, my lord.

Hamlet. Armed, say you?

All. Armed, my lord.

Hamlet. From top to toe?

All. My lord, from head to foot.

Hamlet. Then saw you not his face.

Horatio. O yes, my lord, he wore his beaver up. 230

Hamlet. What, looked he frowningly?

Horatio. A countenance more in sorrow than in anger.

Hamlet. Pale, or red?

Horatio. Nay, very pale.

Hamlet. And fixed his eyes upon you?

Horatio. Most constantly.

Hamlet. I would I had been there.

Horatio. It would have much amazed you.

Hamlet. Very like, very like, stayed it long?

Horatio. While one with moderate haste might tell
a hundred.

Marcellus, Barnardo. Longer, longer.

Horatio. Not when I saw't.

Hamlet. His beard was grizzled, no? 240

Horatio. It was as I have seen it in his life,
A sable silvered.

Hamlet. I will watch to-night,
Perchance 'twill walk again.

Horatio.   I war'nt it will.

Hamlet. If it assume my noble father's person,
I'll speak to it though hell itself should gape
And bid me hold my peace; I pray you all
If you have hitherto concealed this sight
Let it be tenable in your silence still,
And whatsomever else shall hap to-night,
250 Give it an understanding but no tongue.
I will requite your loves, so fare you well:
Upon the platform 'twixt eleven and twelve
I'll visit you.

All.   Our duty to your honour.

Hamlet. Your loves, as mine to you. Farewell.

                              [*they bow and depart*

My father's spirit (in arms!) all is not well,
I doubt some foul play, would the night were come,
Till then sit still my soul, foul deeds will rise,
Though all the earth o'erwhelm them, to men's eyes.

                                        [*he goes*

[I. 3.]   *A room in the house of Polonius*

          '*Enter LAERTES and OPHELIA his sister*'

Laertes. My necessaries are embarked, farewell,
And sister, as the winds give benefit
And convoy is assistant, do not sleep,
But let me hear from you.

Ophelia.   Do you doubt that?

Laertes. For Hamlet, and the trifling of his favour,
Hold it a fashion, and a toy in blood,
A violet in the youth of primy nature,
Forward, not permanent, sweet, not lasting,

The perfume and suppliance of a minute,
No more.
  Ophelia. No more but so?
  Laertes.   Think it no more.   10
For nature crescent does not grow alone
In thews and bulk, but as this temple waxes
The inward service of the mind and soul
Grows wide withal. Perhaps he loves you now,
And now no soil nor cautel doth besmirch
The virtue of his will. But you must fear,
His greatness weighed, his will is not his own,
For he himself is subject to his birth.
He may not, as unvalued persons do,
Carve for himself, for on his choice depends   20
†The sanity and health of this whole state,
And therefore must his choice be circumscribed
Unto the voice and yielding of that body
Whereof he is the head. Then if he says he loves you,
It fits your wisdom so far to believe it
As he in his particular act and place
May give his saying deed, which is no further
Than the main voice of Denmark goes withal.
Then weigh what loss your honour may sustain
If with too credent ear you list his songs,   30
Or lose your heart, or your chaste treasure open
To his unmast'red importunity.
Fear it Ophelia, fear it my dear sister,
And keep you in the rear of your affection,
Out of the shot and danger of desire.
"The chariest maid is prodigal enough
"If she unmask her beauty to the moon."
"Virtue itself 'scapes not calumnious strokes."
"The canker galls the infants of the spring
"Too oft before their buttons be disclosed,   40

"And in the morn and liquid dew of youth
"Contagious blastments are most imminent."
Be wary then—best safety lies in fear,
Youth to itself rebels, though none else near.

  Ophelia. I shall the effect of this good lesson keep
As watchman to my heart. But good my brother
Do not, as some ungracious pastors do,
Show me the steep and thorny way to heaven,
Whiles like a puffed and reckless libertine
50 Himself the primrose path of dalliance treads,
And recks not his own rede.

POLONIUS enters

  Laertes.   O fear me not,
I stay too long—but here my father comes.
A double blessing is a double grace,   *[he kneels*
Occasion smiles upon a second leave.

  Polonius. Yet here Laertes? aboard, aboard for shame!
The wind sits in the shoulder of your sail,
And you are stayed for. There—my blessing with thee,
                [he lays his hand on Laertes' head
And these few precepts in thy memory
Look thou character. Give thy thoughts no tongue,
60 Nor any unproportioned thought his act.
Be thou familiar, but by no means vulgar,
Those friends thou hast, and their adoption tried,
Grapple them unto thy soul with hoops of steel,
But do not dull thy palm with entertainment
Of each new-hatched unfledged courage. Beware
Of entrance to a quarrel, but being in,
Bear't that th'opposéd may beware of thee.
Give every man thy ear, but few thy voice,
Take each man's censure, but reserve thy judgement.
70 Costly thy habit as thy purse can buy,

But not expressed in fancy; rich not gaudy.
For the apparel oft proclaims the man,
And they in France of the best rank and station,
†Or of a most select and generous, chief in that:
Neither a borrower nor a lender be,
For loan oft loses both itself and friend,
And borrowing dulls the edge of husbandry;
This above all, to thine own self be true
And it must follow as the night the day
Thou canst not then be false to any man...   80
Farewell—my blessing season this in thee.
 Laertes. Most humbly do I take my leave, my lord.
 Polonius. The time invites you, go, your servants tend.
 Laertes [*rises*]. Farewell, Ophelia, and remember well
What I have said to you.
 Ophelia.   'Tis in my memory locked,
And you yourself shall keep the key of it.
          [*they embrace*
 Laertes. Farewell.   [*he goes*
 Polonius. What is't, Ophelia, he hath said to you?
 Ophelia. So please you, something touching the
   Lord Hamlet.
 Polonius. Marry, well bethought.   90
'Tis told me he hath very oft of late
Given private time to you, and you yourself
Have of your audience been most free and bounteous.
If it be so—as so 'tis put on me,
And that in way of caution—I must tell you,
You do not understand yourself so clearly
As it behoves my daughter and your honour.
What is between you? give me up the truth.
 Ophelia. He hath, my lord, of late made many tenders
Of his affection to me.   100
 Polonius. Affection, pooh! you speak like a green girl

Unsifted in such perilous circumstance.
Do you believe his tenders as you call them?
  Ophelia. I do not know, my lord, what I should think.
  Polonius. Marry, I will teach you—think yourself
     a baby
That you have ta'en these tenders for true pay
Which are not sterling. Tender yourself more dearly,
Or (not to crack the wind of the poor phrase,
Running it thus) you'll tender me a fool.
110 *Ophelia.* My lord, he hath importuned me with love
In honourable fashion.
  Polonius. Ay, fashion you may call it, go to, go to.
  Ophelia. And hath given countenance to his speech,
     my lord,
With almost all the holy vows of heaven.
  Polonius. Ay, springes to catch woodcocks. I do know
When the blood burns, how prodigal the soul
Lends the tongue vows. These blazes daughter,
Giving more light than heat, extinct in both,
Even in their promise, as it is a-making,
120 You must not take for fire. From this time
Be something scanter of your maiden presence,
Set your entreatments at a higher rate
Than a command to parle; for Lord Hamlet,
Believe so much in him that he is young,
And with a larger tether may he walk
Than may be given you: in few Ophelia,
Do not believe his vows, for they are brokers
Not of that dye which their investments show,
But mere implorators of unholy suits,
130 Breathing like sanctified and pious bonds
The better to beguile...This is for all,
I would not in plain terms from this time forth
Have you so slander any moment leisure

As to give words or talk with the Lord Hamlet.
Look to't I charge you, come your ways.

  Ophelia. I shall obey, my lord.   *[they go*

[1. 4.]   *The platform on the battlements*

   HAMLET, HORATIO *and* MARCELLUS *come from
one of the turrets*

Hamlet. The air bites shrewdly, it is very cold.
Horatio. It is a nipping and an eager air.
Hamlet. What hour now?
Horatio.   I think it lacks of twelve.
Marcellus. No, it is struck.
Horatio. Indeed? I heard it not—it then draws near
    the season,
Wherein the spirit held his wont to walk.
      ['*a flourish of trumpets*,' *and ordnance shot off*
What does this mean, my lord?
  Hamlet. The king doth wake to-night and takes
    his rouse,
Keeps wassail and the swagg'ring upspring reels:
And as he drains his draughts of Rhenish down,   10
The kettle-drum and trumpet thus bray out
The triumph of his pledge.
  Horatio.   Is it a custom?
  Hamlet. Ay marry is't,
But to my mind, though I am native here
And to the manner born, it is a custom
More honoured in the breach than the observance.
This heavy-headed revel east and west
Makes us traduced and taxed of other nations.
They clepe us drunkards, and with swinish phrase
Soil our addition, and indeed it takes   20

From our achievements, though performed at height,
The pith and marrow of our attribute.
So, oft it chances in particular men,
That for some vicious mole of nature in them,
As in their birth, wherein they are not guilty
(Since nature cannot choose his origin),
By the o'ergrowth of some complexion,
Oft breaking down the pales and forts of reason,
Or by some habit, that too much o'er-leavens
30 The form of plausive manners—that these men,
Carrying I say the stamp of one defect,
Being nature's livery, or fortune's star,
His virtues else be they as pure as grace,
As infinite as man may undergo,
Shall in the general censure take corruption
From that particular fault: the dram of evil
†Doth all the noble substance of a doubt,
To his own scandal.

The GHOST appears

Horatio.   Look, my lord, it comes!
Hamlet. Angels and ministers of grace defend us!
40 Be thou a spirit of health, or goblin damned,
Bring with thee airs from heaven, or blasts from hell,
Be thy intents wicked, or charitable,
Thou com'st in such a questionable shape,
That I will speak to thee. I'll call thee Hamlet,
King, father, royal Dane. O, answer me!
Let me not burst in ignorance, but tell
Why thy canonized bones hearsèd in death
Have burst their cerements? why the sepulchre,
Wherein we saw thee quietly inurned,
50 Hath oped his ponderous and marble jaws
To cast thee up again? what may this mean

That thou, dead corse, again in complete steel
Revisits thus the glimpses of the moon,
Making night hideous, and we fools of nature
So horridly to shake our disposition
With thoughts beyond the reaches of our souls?
Say why is this? wherefore? what should we do?

[the Ghost " beckons"

  Horatio. It beckons you to go away with it,
As if it some impartment did desire
To you alone.
  Marcellus.   Look with what courteous action   60
It waves you to a more removéd ground,
But do not go with it.
  Horatio.   No, by no means.
  Hamlet. It will not speak, then I will follow it.
  Horatio. Do not my lord.
  Hamlet.   Why, what should be the fear?
I do not set my life at a pin's fee,
And for my soul, what can it do to that
Being a thing immortal as itself;
It waves me forth again, I'll follow it.
  Horatio. What if it tempt you toward the flood,
      my lord,
Or to the dreadful summit of the cliff   70
That beetles o'er his base into the sea,
And there assume some other horrible form,
Which might deprive your sovereignty of reason,
And draw you into madness? think of it—
The very place puts toys of desperation,
Without more motive, into every brain
That looks so many fathoms to the sea
And hears it roar beneath.
  Hamlet.   It waves me still.
Go on, I'll follow thee.

80 *Marcellus.* You shall not go, my lord.
    Hamlet.   Hold off your hands.
    Horatio. Be ruled, you shall not go.
    Hamlet.   My fate cries out,
And makes each petty artere in this body
As hardy as the Nemean lion's nerve;
Still am I called, unhand me gentlemen,
                    [*he breaks from them, drawing h s sword*
By heaven I'll make a ghost of him that lets me!
I say, away! go on, I'll follow thee.
                    [*the Ghost passes into one of the turrets,*
                        Hamlet following
    Horatio. He waxes desperate with imagination.
    Marcellus. Let's follow, 'tis not fit thus to obey him.
    Horatio. Have after—to what issue will this come?
90 *Marcellus.* Something is rotten in the state of Denmark.
    Horatio. Heaven will direct it.
    Marcellus.   Nay, let's follow him.
                                          [*they follow*

[1. 5.]   *An open space at the foot of the*
                            castle wall

A door in the wall opens; the GHOST *comes forth and*
HAMLET *after, the hilt of his drawn sword held crosswise*
before him

    Hamlet. Whither wilt thou lead me? speak, I'll go
        no further.
    Ghost [*turns*]. Mark me.
    Hamlet.   I will.
    Ghost.   My hour is almost come,
When I to sulph'rous and tormenting flames
Must render up myself.

Hamlet.   Alas poor ghost!

Ghost. Pity me not, but lend thy serious hearing
To what I shall unfold.

Hamlet.   Speak, I am bound to hear.

Ghost. So art thou to revenge, when thou shalt hear.

Hamlet. What?

Ghost. I am thy father's spirit,
Doomed for a certain term to walk the night,   10
And for the day confined to fast in fires,
Till the foul crimes done in my days of nature
Are burnt and purged away: but that I am forbid
To tell the secrets of my prison-house,
I could a tale unfold whose lightest word
Would harrow up thy soul, freeze thy young blood,
Make thy two eyes like stars start from their spheres,
Thy knotted and combinéd locks to part,
And each particular hair to stand an end,
Like quills upon the fretful porpentine.   20
But this eternal blazon must not be
To ears of flesh and blood. List, list, O list!
If thou didst ever thy dear father love——

Hamlet. O God!

Ghost. Revenge his foul and most unnatural murder.

Hamlet. Murder!

Ghost. Murder most foul, as in the best it is,
But this most foul, strange and unnatural.

Hamlet. Haste me to know't, that I with wings
        as swift
As meditation or the thoughts of love,   30
May sweep to my revenge.

Ghost.   I find thee apt,
And duller shouldst thou be than the fat weed
That rots itself in ease on Lethe wharf,
Wouldst thou not stir in this; now Hamlet hear,

'Tis given out, that sleeping in my orchard,
A serpent stung me, so the whole ear of Denmark
Is by a forgéd process of my death
Rankly abused: but know, thou noble youth,
The serpent that did sting thy father's life
40 Now wears his crown.

   Hamlet.   O, my prophetic soul!
My uncle?

  Ghost. Ay, that incestuous, that adulterate beast,
With witchcraft of his wit, with traitorous gifts,
O wicked wit and gifts, that have the power
So to seduce; won to his shameful lust
The will of my most seeming-virtuous queen;
O Hamlet, what a falling-off was there!
From me whose love was of that dignity,
That it went hand in hand even with the vow
50 I made to her in marriage, and to decline
Upon a wretch whose natural gifts were poor
To those of mine;
But virtue, as it never will be moved,
Though lewdness court it in a shape of heaven,
So lust, though to a radiant angel linked,
Will sate itself in a celestial bed
And prey on garbage.
But soft, methinks I scent the morning air,
Brief let me be; sleeping within my orchard,
60 My custom always of the afternoon,
Upon my secure hour thy uncle stole
With juice of cursed hebona in a vial,
And in the porches of my ears did pour
The leperous distilment, whose effect
Holds such an enmity with blood of man,
That swift as quicksilver it courses through
The natural gates and alleys of the body,

And with a sudden vigour it doth posset
And curd, like eager droppings into milk,
The thin and wholesome blood; so did it mine,   70
And a most instant tetter barked about
Most lazar-like with vile and loathsome crust
All my smooth body....
Thus was I sleeping by a brother's hand,
Of life, of crown, of queen at once dispatched,
Cut off even in the blossoms of my sin,
Unhouseled, disappointed, unaneled,
No reck'ning made, but sent to my account
With all my imperfections on my head.
O, horrible! O, horrible! most horrible!   80
If thou hast nature in thee bear it not,
Let not the royal bed of Denmark be
A couch for luxury and damnéd incest....
But howsomever thou pursues this act,
Taint not thy mind, nor let thy soul contrive
Against thy mother aught—leave her to heaven,
And to those thorns that in her bosom lodge
To prick and sting her. Fare thee well at once,
The glow-worm shows the matin to be near,
And 'gins to pale his uneffectual fire.   90
Adieu, adieu, adieu, remember me.
> [*the Ghost vanishes into the ground; Hamlet*
> *falls distraught upon his knees*

Hamlet. O all you host of heaven! O earth! what else?
And shall I couple hell? O fie! Hold, hold, my heart,
And you, my sinews, grow not instant old,
But bear me stiffly up...[*he rises*] Remember thee?
Ay thou poor ghost whiles memory holds a seat
In this distracted globe. Remember thee?
Yea, from the table of my memory
I'll wipe away all trivial fond records,

100 All saws of books, all forms, all pressures past
    That youth and observation copied there,
    And thy commandment all alone shall live
    Within the book and volume of my brain,
    Unmixed with baser matter—yes by heaven!
    O most pernicious woman!
    O villain, villain, smiling, damnéd villain!
    My tables, meet it is I set it down   [*he writes*
    That one may smile, and smile, and be a villain,
    At least I am sure it may be so in Denmark...
110 So, uncle, there you are. Now, to my Word,
    It is 'Adieu, adieu, remember me.'...
        [*he kneels and lays his hand upon the hilt of his sword*
    I have sworn't.   [*he prays*

      HORATIO and MARCELLUS come from the castle,
                  calling in the darkness

Horatio. My lord, my lord!
Marcellus.   Lord Hamlet!
Horatio.   Heaven secure him!
(Hamlet. So be it!   [*he rises*
Marcellus. Illo, ho, ho, my lord!
Hamlet. Hillo, ho, ho, boy! come, bird, come.
                          [*they see Hamlet*
Marcellus. How is't, my noble lord?
Horatio.   What news, my lord?
Hamlet. O, wonderful!
Horatio.   Good my lord, tell it.
Hamlet. No, you will reveal it.
120 *Horatio.* Not I, my lord, by heaven.
Marcellus.   Nor I, my lord.
Hamlet. How say you then, would heart of man once
       think it?
    But you'll be secret?

Horatio, Marcellus.   Ay, by heaven, my lord.

Hamlet. There's ne'er a villain dwelling in all
     Denmark
But he's an arrant knave.

Horatio. There needs no ghost, my lord, come from
     the grave,
To tell us this.

Hamlet.   Why right, you are in the right,
And so without more circumstance at all
I hold it fit that we shake hands and part,
You, as your business and desire shall point you,
For every man hath business and desire   130
Such as it is, and for my own poor part,
Look you, I will go pray.

Horatio. These are but wild and whirling words,
     my lord.

Hamlet. I am sorry they offend you, heartily,
Yes, faith, heartily.

Horatio.   There's no offence, my lord.

(*Hamlet* [*to Horatio*]. Yes, by Saint Patrick, but there
     is, Horatio,
And much offence too—touching this vision here,
It is an honest ghost that let me tell you—
For your desire to know what is between us,
O'ermaster't as you may. [*to both*] And now,
     good friends,   140
As you are friends, scholars, and soldiers,
Give me one poor request.

Horatio. What is't, my lord? we will.

Hamlet. Never make known what you have
     seen to-night.

Both. My lord, we will not.

Hamlet.   Nay, but swear't.

Horatio.   In faith,

My lord, not I.

Marcellus.   Nor I, my lord, in faith.

Hamlet [*draws*]. Upon my sword.

Marcellus.   We have sworn, my lord, already.

Hamlet. Indeed, upon my sword, indeed.

Ghost [*beneath*]. Swear.

150 *Hamlet.* Ha, ha, boy! say'st thou so? art thou
        there, truepenny?

Come on, you hear this fellow in the cellarage,

Consent to swear.

Horatio.   Propose the oath, my lord.

Hamlet. Never to speak of this that you have seen,

Swear by my sword.

                    [*they lay their hands upon the hilt*

Ghost [*beneath*]. Swear.

Hamlet. Hic et ubique? then we'll shift our ground:

Come hither gentlemen,

And lay your hands again upon my sword.

Swear by my sword,

160 Never to speak of this that you have heard.

Ghost [*beneath*]. Swear by his sword.

Hamlet. Well said, old mole! canst work i'th'earth
        so fast?   [*they swear again in silence*

A worthy pioner! Once more remove, good friends.

Horatio. O day and night, but this is wondrous
        strange!

Hamlet. And therefore as a stranger give it welcome.

There are more things in heaven and earth, Horatio,

Than are dreamt of in your philosophy.

But come—

Here as before, never, so help you mercy

170 (How strange or odd some'er I bear myself,

As I perchance hereafter shall think meet

To put an antic disposition on)

That you at such times seeing me, never shall
With arms encumbered thus, or this head-shake,
Or by pronouncing of some doubtful phrase,
As 'Well, well, we know,' or 'We could an if
      we would,'
Or 'If we list to speak,' or 'There be an if they might,'
Or such ambiguous giving out, to note
That you know aught of me—this do swear,
So grace and mercy at your most need help you!   180
  Ghost [*beneath*]. Swear.
  Hamlet. Rest, rest, perturbéd spirit! [*they swear a*
      third time] So, gentlemen,
With all my love I do commend me to you,
And what so poor a man as Hamlet is
May do t'express his love and friending to you
God willing shall not lack. Let us go in together,
And still your fingers on your lips I pray.
The time is out of joint, O curséd spite,
That ever I was born to set it right!
Nay come, let's go together.   [*they enter the castle* 190

        [*Some weeks pass*]

[2. 1.]   *A room in the house of Polonius*

       POLONIUS *and* REYNALDO

  Polonius. Give him this money, and these notes,
     Reynaldo,
  Reynaldo. I will, my lord.
  Polonius. You shall do marvellous wisely, good
     Reynaldo,
Before you visit him, to make inquire
Of his behaviour.
  Reynaldo.   My lord, I did intend it.

Polonius. Marry, well said, very well said; look
    you sir,
Inquire me first what Danskers are in Paris,
And how, and who, what means, and where they keep,
What company, at what expense, and finding
10 By this encompassment and drift of question
That they do know my son, come you more nearer
Than your particular demands will touch it,
Take you as 'twere some distant knowledge of him,
As thus, 'I know his father, and his friends.
And in part him'—do you mark this, Reynaldo?
  Reynaldo. Ay, very well, my lord.
  Polonius. 'And in part him, but,' you may say,
    'not well,
But if't be he I mean, he's very wild,
Addicted so and so.' And there put on him
20 What forgeries you please, marry none so rank
As may dishonour him, take heed of that,
But sir such wanton, wild, and usual slips,
As are companions noted and most known
To youth and liberty.
  Reynaldo.   As gaming, my lord.
  Polonius. Ay, or drinking, fencing, swearing,
    quarrelling,
Drabbing—you may go so far.
  Reynaldo. My lord, that would dishonour him.
  Polonius. Faith no, as you may season it in the
    charge.
You must not put another scandal on him,
30 That he is open to incontinency,
That's not my meaning, but breathe his faults
    so quaintly
That they may seem the taints of liberty,
The flash and outbreak of a fiery mind,

A savageness in unreclaiméd blood,
Of general assault.
  Reynaldo.   But, my good lord——
  Polonius. Wherefore should you do this?
  Reynaldo.   Ay my lord,
I would know that.
  Polonius.   Marry sir, here's my drift,
And I believe it is a fetch of warrant,
You laying these slight sullies on my son,
As 'twere a thing a little soiled i'th' working,   40
Mark you, your party in converse, him you
       would sound,
Having ever seen in the prenominate crimes
The youth you breathe of guilty, be assured
He closes with you in this consequence,
'Good sir,' or so, or 'friend,' or 'gentleman,'
According to the phrase, or the addition
Of man and country.
  Reynaldo.   Very good, my lord.
  Polonius. And then sir, does a' this, a' does, what was
       I about to say?
By the mass I was about to say something.
Where did I leave?
  Reynaldo.   At 'closes in the consequence,'   50
At 'friend, or so, and gentleman.'
  Polonius. At 'closes in the consequence.'
       ay marry—
He closes thus, 'I know the gentleman,
I saw him yesterday, or th'other day,
Or then, or then, with such or such, and as you say,
There was a' gaming, there o'ertook in's rouse,
There falling out at tennis,' or perchance,
'I saw him enter such a house of sale,'
Videlicet, a brothel, or so forth. See you now,

60 Your bait of falsehood takes this carp of truth,
    And thus do we of wisdom, and of reach,
    With windlasses, and with assays of bias,
    By indirections find directions out,
    So by my former lecture and advice
    Shall you my son; you have me, have you not?
    Reynaldo. My lord, I have.
    Polonius.   God bye ye, fare ye well.
    Reynaldo. Good, my lord.
    Polonius. Observe his inclination in yourself.
    Reynaldo. I shall, my lord.
70 *Polonius.* And let him ply his music.
    Reynaldo.   Well, my lord. [*he goes*
    Polonius. Farewell.

        OPHELIA *enters in perturbation*

              How now Ophelia, what's the matter?
    Ophelia. O my lord, my lord, I have been
          so affrighted!
    Polonius. With what, i'th'name of God?
    Ophelia. My lord, as I was sewing in my closet,
    Lord Hamlet with his doublet all unbraced,
    No hat upon his head, his stockings fouled,
    Ungart'red, and down-gyvéd to his ankle,
    Pale as his shirt, his knees knocking each other,
    And with a look so piteous in purport
80 As if he had been looséd out of hell
    To speak of horrors—he comes before me.
    Polonius. Mad for thy love?
    Ophelia.   My lord, I do not know,
    But truly I do fear it.
    Polonius.   What said he?
    Ophelia. He took me by the wrist, and held me hard,
    Then goes he to the length of all his arm,

And with his other hand thus o'er his brow,
He falls to such perusal of my face
As a' would draw it. Long stayed he so,
At last, a little shaking of mine arm,
And thrice his head thus waving up and down, 90
He raised a sigh so piteous and profound
As it did seem to shatter all his bulk,
And end his being; that done, he lets me go,
And with his head over his shoulder turned
He seemed to find his way without his eyes,
For out adoors he went without their helps,
And to the last bended their light on me.
   Polonius. Come, go with me. I will go seek the king.
This is the very ecstasy of love,
Whose violent property fordoes itself, 100
And leads the will to desperate undertakings,
As oft as any passion under heaven
That does afflict our natures: I am sorry—
What, have you given him any hard words of late?
   Ophelia. No, my good lord, but as you did command
I did repel his letters, and denied
His access to me.
   Polonius.   That hath made him mad.
I am sorry that with better heed and judgement
I had not quoted him. I feared he did but trifle
And meant to wreck thee, but beshrew my jealousy: 110
By heaven it is as proper to our age
To cast beyond ourselves in our opinions,
As it is common for the younger sort
To lack discretion; come, go we to the king.
This must be known, which, being kept close,
     might move
More grief to hide, than hate to utter love.
Come.   *[they go*

[2. 2.] *An audience chamber in the castle; at the back a lobby, with curtains to left and right of the entry and a door to the rear within*

A flourish of trumpets. The KING *and* QUEEN *enter followed by* ROSENCRANTZ, GUILDENSTERN *and attendants*

King. Welcome, dear Rosencrantz and Guildenstern!
Moreover that we much did long to see you,
The need we have to use you did provoke
Our hasty sending. Something have you heard
Of Hamlet's transformation—so call it,
Sith nor th'exterior nor the inward man
Resembles that it was. What it should be,
More than his father's death, that thus hath put him
So much from th'understanding of himself,
10 I cannot dream of: I entreat you both,
That being of so young days brought up with him,
And sith so neighboured to his youth and haviour,
That you vouchsafe your rest here in our court
Some little time, so by your companies
To draw him on to pleasures, and to gather
So much as from occasion you may glean
Whether aught to us unknown afflicts him thus,
That opened lies within our remedy.
Queen. Good gentlemen, he hath much talked of you,
20 And sure I am two men there are not living
To whom he more adheres. If it will please you
To show us so much gentry and good will
As to expend your time with us awhile,
For the supply and profit of our hope,
Your visitation shall receive such thanks
As fits a king's remembrance.
Rosencrantz.   Both your majesties
Might by the sovereign power you have of us,

Put your dread pleasures more into command
Than to entreaty.

Guildenstern. But we both obey,
And here give up ourselves in the full bent,   30
To lay our service freely at your feet
To be commanded.

   King. Thanks Rosencrantz, and gentle Guildenstern.

   Queen. Thanks Guildenstern, and gentle Rosencrantz,
And I beseech you instantly to visit
My too much changéd son. Go some of you
And bring these gentlemen where Hamlet is.

   Guildenstern. Heavens make our presence and
      our practices
Pleasant and helpful to him!

   Queen.   Ay, amen!

               *[Rosencrantz and Guildenstern bow
                  and depart*

   POLONIUS *enters, and speaks with the King apart*

Polonius. The ambassadors from Norway, my
     good lord,   40
Are joyfully returned.

   King. Thou still hast been the father of
     good news.

   Polonius. Have I, my lord? Assure you, my
     good liege,
I hold my duty as I hold my soul,
Both to my God and to my gracious king;
And I do think, or else this brain of mine
Hunts not the trail of policy so sure
As it hath used to do, that I have found
The very cause of Hamlet's lunacy.

   King. O speak of that, that do I long to hear.   50

   Polonius. Give first admittance to th'ambassadors.

Q.H. – 8

My news shall be the fruit to that great feast.
   King. Thyself do grace to them, and bring them in.

[Polonius goes out

He tells me, my dear Gertrude, he hath found
The head and source of all your son's distemper.
   Queen. I doubt it is no other but the main,
His father's death and our o'erhasty marriage.
   King. Wèll, we shall sift him.

POLONIUS returns with VALTEMAND and CORNELIUS

Welcome, my good friends!

Say Valtemand, what from our brother Norway?
60 *Valtemand.* Most fair return of greetings and desires;

[they bow

Upon our first, he sent out to suppress
His nephew's levies, which to him appeared
To be a preparation 'gainst the Polack,
But better looked into, he truly found
It was against your highness, whereat grieved
That so his sickness, age and impotence
Was falsely borne in hand, sends out arrests
On Fortinbras, which he in brief obeys,
Receives rebuke from Norway, and in fine,
70 Makes vow before his uncle never more
To give th'assay of arms against your majesty:
Whereon old Norway, overcome with joy,
Gives him threescore thousand crowns in annual fee,
And his commission to employ those soldiers,
So levied, as before, against the Polack,
With an entreaty, herein further shown,
That it might please you to give quiet pass
Through your dominions for this enterprise,
On such regards of safety and allowance
80 As therein are set down.   [<i>he proffers a paper</i>

King [*takes it*]. It likes us well,
And at our more considered time, we'll read,
Answer, and think upon this business:
Meantime, we thank you for your well-took labour.
Go to your rest, at night we'll feast together.
Most welcome home!

     [*Valtemand and Cornelius bow and depart*

Polonius.   This business is well ended....
My liege and madam, to expostulate
What majesty should be, what duty is,
Why day is day, night night, and time is time,
Were nothing but to waste night, day and time.
Therefore since brevity is the soul of wit,   90
And tediousness the limbs and outward flourishes,
I will be brief—your noble son is mad:
Mad call I it, for to define true madness,
What is't but to be nothing else but mad?
But let that go.

 Queen.   More matter, with less art.
 Polonius. Madam, I swear I use no art at all.
That he is mad 'tis true, 'tis true, 'tis pity,
And pity 'tis 'tis true—a foolish figure,
But farewell it, for I will use no art.
Mad let us grant him then, and now remains   100
That we find out the cause of this effect,
Or rather say, the cause of this defect,
For this effect defective comes by cause:
Thus it remains, and the remainder thus.
Perpend.   [*he takes papers from his doublet*
I have a daughter, have while she is mine,
Who in her duty and obedience, mark,
Hath given me this, now gather and surmise.
[*he reads*] 'To the celestial, and my soul's idol, the
most beautified Ophelia,'—   110

That's an ill phrase, a vile phrase, 'beautified' is a vile
phrase, but you shall hear. Thus: [*he reads*
     'In her excellent white bosom, these, &c.'—
Queen. Came this from Hamlet to her?
Polonius. Good madam stay awhile, I will
    be faithful—   [*he reads*

        'Doubt thou the stars are fire,
          Doubt that the sun doth move,
          Doubt truth to be a liar,
          But never doubt I love.

120   O dear Ophelia, I am ill at these numbers, I have not
art to reckon my groans, but that I love thee best, O
most best, believe it. Adieu.
                  Thine evermore, most dear lady, whilst
                      this machine is to him, HAMLET.'
This in obedience hath my daughter shown me,
And more above hath his solicitings,
As they fell out by time, by means, and place,
All given to mine ear.
    King.   But how hath she
Received his love?
    Polonius.   What do you think of me?
130   *King.* As of a man faithful and honourable.
    Polonius. I would fain prove so. But what might
        you think
When I had seen this hot love on the wing,
As I perceived it (I must tell you that)
Before my daughter told me, what might you,
Or my dear majesty your queen here think,
If I had played the desk or table-book,
Or given my heart a working mute and dumb,
Or looked upon this love with idle sight,
What might you think? no, I went round to work,
140 And my young mistress thus I did bespeak—

'Lord Hamlet is a prince out of thy star,
This must not be': and then I prescripts gave her
That she should lock herself from his resort,
Admit no messengers, receive no tokens.
Which done, she took the fruits of my advice:
And he repelléd, a short tale to make,
Fell into a sadness, then into a fast,
Thence to a watch, thence into a weakness,
Thence to a lightness, and by this declension,
Into the madness wherein now he raves,   150
And all we mourn for.
   King.   Do you think 'tis this?
   Queen. It may be, very like.
   Polonius. Hath there been such a time, I would fain
      know that,
That I have positively said "'Tis so,'
When it proved otherwise?
   King.   Not that I know.
   Polonius. Take this from this, if this be otherwise;
                [*he points to his head and shoulder*
If circumstances lead me, I will find
Where truth is hid, though it were hid indeed
Within the Centre.

[† *Hamlet, disorderly attired and reading a book, enters
the lobby by the door at the back; he hears voices from the
chamber and pauses a moment beside one of the curtains,
unobserved*]

   King.   How may we try it further?
   Polonius. You know sometimes he walks four
      hours together   160
Here in the lobby.
   Queen.   So he does, indeed.

Polonius. At such a time I'll loose my daughter to him.
Be you and I behind an arras then,
Mark the encounter, if he love her not,
And be not from his reason fall'n thereon,
Let me be no assistant for a state,
But keep a farm and carters.
　　King.　　　　　　　　　　We will try it.

　　　HAMLET comes forward, his eyes on the book

Queen. But look where sadly the poor wretch
　　　comes reading.
Polonius. Away, I do beseech you both away,
170 I'll board him presently, O give me leave.
　　　　　　　　　　[*the King and Queen hurry forth*
How does my good Lord Hamlet?
Hamlet. Well, God-a-mercy.
Polonius. Do you know me, my lord?
Hamlet. Excellent well, you are a fishmonger.
Polonius. Not I, my lord.
Hamlet. Then I would you were so honest a man.
Polonius. Honest, my lord?
Hamlet. Ay sir, to be honest as this world goes, is to
be one man picked out of ten thousand.
180 *Polonius.* That's very true, my lord.
Hamlet. For if the sun breed maggots in a dead dog,
being a good kissing carrion....have you a daughter?
Polonius. I have, my lord.
Hamlet. Let her not walk i'th'sun. Conception is a
blessing, but as your daughter may conceive, friend
look to't.　　　　　　　　　　　　　　[*he reads again*
(*Polonius.* How say you by that? still harping on my
daughter, yet he knew me not at first, a' said I was a
fishmonger. A' is far gone, far gone, and truly in my
190 youth I suffered much extremity for love, very near

this....I'll speak to him again....What do you read, my lord?

Hamlet. Words, words, words.

Polonius. What is the matter, my lord?

Hamlet. Between who?

Polonius. I mean the matter that you read, my lord.

Hamlet [*bears down upon him, Polonius retreating backwards*]. Slanders, sir; for the satirical rogue says here that old men have grey beards, that their faces are wrinkled, their eyes purging thick amber and plum-tree gum, and that they have a plentiful lack of wit, together with most weak hams—all which, sir, though I most powerfully and potently believe, yet I hold it not honesty to have it thus set down, for yourself, sir, shall grow old as I am...if like a crab you could go backward.   [*he reads again*

(*Polonius.* Though this be madness, yet there is method in't.

Will you walk out of the air, my lord?

Hamlet. Into my grave.

(*Polonius.* Indeed, that's out of the air; how pregnant sometimes his replies are! a happiness that often madness hits on, which reason and sanity could not so prosperously be delivered of. I will leave him, and suddenly contrive the means of meeting between him and my daughter.

My honourable lord, I will most humbly take my leave of you.

Hamlet. You cannot, sir, take from me any thing that I will more willingly part withal: except my life, except my life, except my life.

Polonius. Fare you well, my lord.   [*he bows low*

Hamlet. These tedious old fools!

                                    [*he returns to his book*

Rosencrantz and Guildenstern enter

Polonius. You go to seek the Lord Hamlet, there he is.

Rosencrantz [*to Polonius*]. God save you, sir!

[*Polonius goes out*

Guildenstern. My honoured lord!

Rosencrantz. My most dear lord!

Hamlet [*looks up*]. My excellent good friends! How
dost thou, Guildenstern? [*putting up the book*
Ah, Rosencrantz! Good lads, how do you both?

Rosencrantz. As the indifferent children of the earth.

230 *Guildenstern.* Happy, in that we are not over-happy,
On Fortune's cap we are not the very button.

Hamlet. Nor the soles of her shoe?

Rosencrantz. Neither, my lord.

Hamlet. Then you live about her waist, or in the
middle of her favours?

Guildenstern. Faith, her privates we.

Hamlet. In the secret parts of fortune? O most true,
she is a strumpet. What's the news?

Rosencrantz. None, my lord, but that the world's
240 grown honest.

Hamlet. Then is doomsday near. But your news is
not true. Let me question more in particular: what have
you, my good friends, deserved at the hands of Fortune,
that she sends you to prison hither?

Guildenstern. Prison, my lord!

Hamlet. Denmark's a prison.

Rosencrantz. Then is the world one.

Hamlet. A goodly one, in which there are many
confines, wards and dungeons; Denmark being one
250 o'th'worst.

Rosencrantz. We think not so, my lord.

Hamlet. Why, then 'tis none to you; for there is

nothing either good or bad, but thinking makes it so:
to me it is a prison.

Rosencrantz. Why, then your ambition makes it one:
'tis too narrow for your mind.

Hamlet. O God! I could be bounded in a nut-shell,
and count myself a king of infinite space; were it not
that I have bad dreams.

Guildenstern. Which dreams, indeed, are ambition: 260
for the very substance of the ambitious is merely the
shadow of a dream.

Hamlet. A dream itself is but a shadow.

Rosencrantz. Truly, and I hold ambition of so airy and
light a quality, that it is but a shadow's shadow.

Hamlet. Then are our beggars bodies, and our mon-
archs and outstretched heroes the beggars' shadows...
Shall we to th' court? for, by my fay, I cannot reason.

Rosencrantz, Guildenstern. We'll wait upon you.

Hamlet. No such matter: I will not sort you with the 270
rest of my servants; for to speak to you like an honest
man, I am most dreadfully attended....But, in the beaten
way of friendship, what make you at Elsinore?

Rosencrantz. To visit you, my lord, no other occasion.

Hamlet. Beggar that I am, I am even poor in thanks,
but I thank you—and sure, dear friends, my thanks are
too dear a halfpenny: were you not sent for? is it your
own inclining? is it a free visitation? come, come, deal
justly with me, come, come, nay speak.

Guildenstern. What should we say, my lord?   280

Hamlet. Why, any thing but to th'purpose...You
were sent for, and there is a kind of confession in your
looks, which your modesties have not craft enough to
colour—I know the good king and queen have sent for
you.

Rosencrantz. To what end, my lord?

Hamlet. That you must teach me: but let me conjure you, by the rights of our fellowship, by the consonancy of our youth, by the obligation of our ever-preserved
290 love, and by what more dear a better proposer can charge you withal, be even and direct with me whether you were sent for or no?

⟨*Rosencrantz.* What say you? ⟨*to Guildenstern*

⟨*Hamlet.* Nay then, I have an eye of you!

[*aloud*] If you love me, hold not off.

Guildenstern. My lord, we were sent for.

Hamlet. I will tell you why, so shall my anticipation prevent your discovery, and your secrecy to the king and queen moult no feather. I have of late, but where-
300 fore I know not, lost all my mirth, forgone all custom of exercises: and indeed it goes so heavily with my disposition, that this goodly frame the earth, seems to me a sterile promontory, this most excellent canopy the air, look you, this brave o'erhanging firmament, this majestical roof fretted with golden fire, why it appeareth nothing to me but a foul and pestilent congregation of vapours....What a piece of work is a man, how noble in reason, how infinite in faculties, in form and moving, how express and admirable in action, how like an angel
310 in apprehension, how like a god: the beauty of the world; the paragon of animals; and yet to me, what is this quintessence of dust? man delights not me, no, nor woman neither, though by your smiling you seem to say so.

Rosencrantz. My lord, there was no such stuff in my thoughts.

Hamlet. Why did ye laugh then, when I said 'man delights not me'?

Rosencrantz. To think, my lord, if you delight not in
320 man, what lenten entertainment the players shall receive

from you. We coted them on the way, and hither are
they coming to offer you service.

Hamlet. He that plays the King shall be welcome,
his majesty shall have tribute on me, the adventurous
Knight shall use his foil and target, the Lover shall not
sigh gratis, the Humorous Man shall end his part in
peace, the Clown shall make those laugh whose lungs
are tickle o'th'sere, and the Lady shall say her mind
freely...or the blank verse shall halt for't. What players
are they?   330

Rosencrantz. Even those you were wont to take such
delight in, the tragedians of the city.

Hamlet. How chances it they travel? their residence
both in reputation and profit was better both ways.

Rosencrantz. I think their inhibition comes by the
means of the late innovation.

Hamlet. Do they hold the same estimation they did
when I was in the city; are they so followed?

Rosencrantz. No, indeed, are they not.

Hamlet. How comes it? do they grow rusty?   340

Rosencrantz. Nay, their endeavour keeps in the wonted
pace; but there is, sir, an aery of children, little eyases,
that cry out on the top of question, and are most tyrannically clapped for't: these are now the fashion, and so
berattle the common stages (so they call them) that many
wearing rapiers are afraid of goose-quills, and dare
scarce come thither.

Hamlet. What, are they children? who maintains 'em?
how are they escoted? Will they pursue the quality no
longer than they can sing? will they not say afterwards 350
if they should grow themselves to common players (as
it is like most will if their means are not better) their
writers do them wrong, to make them exclaim against
their own succession?

Rosencrantz. Faith, there has been much to-do on both sides: and the nation holds it no sin to tarre them to controversy. There was, for a while, no money bid for argument, unless the Poet and the Player went to cuffs in the question.

360 *Hamlet.* Is't possible?

Guildenstern. O, there has been much throwing about of brains.

Hamlet. Do the boys carry it away?

Rosencrantz. Ay, that they do my lord, Hercules and his load too.

Hamlet. It is not very strange, for my uncle is king of Denmark, and those that would make mows at him while my father lived, give twenty, forty, fifty, a hundred ducats apiece for his picture in little. 370 'Sblood, there is something in this more than natural, if philosophy could find it out.

[*'A flourish' of trumpets heard*

Guildenstern There are the players.

Hamlet. Gentlemen, you are welcome to Elsinore [*he bows*]. Your hands? come then, th'appurtenance of welcome is fashion and ceremony; let me comply with you in this garb…[*he takes their hands*] lest my extent to the players, which I tell you must show fairly outwards, should more appear like entertainment than yours…You are welcome: but my uncle-father, and 380 aunt-mother, are deceived.

Guildenstern. In what, my dear lord?

Hamlet. I am but mad north-north-west; when the wind is southerly, I know a hawk from a handsaw.

POLONIUS enters

Polonius. Well be with you, gentlemen!

(*Hamlet.* Hark you Guildenstern, and you too, at each

ear a hearer—that great baby you see there is not yet out of his swaddling-clouts.

(*Rosencrantz.* Happily he is the second time come to them, for they say an old man is twice a child.

(*Hamlet.* I will prophesy, he comes to tell me of the 390 players, mark it.

[*raises his voice*] You say right sir, a Monday morning, 'twas then indeed.

Polonius. My lord, I have news to tell you.

Hamlet. My lord, I have news to tell you...When Roscius was an actor in Rome—

Polonius. The actors are come hither, my lord.

Hamlet. Buz, buz!

Polonius. Upon my honour—

Hamlet. 'Then came each actor on his ass'— 400

Polonius. The best actors in the world, either for tragedy, comedy, history, pastoral, pastoral-comical, historical-pastoral, tragical-historical, tragical-comical-historical-pastoral, scene individable, or poem unlimited. Seneca cannot be too heavy nor Plautus too light for the law of writ and the liberty, these are the only men.

Hamlet. O Jephthah, judge of Israel, what a treasure hadst thou!

Polonius. What a treasure had he, my lord? 410

Hamlet. Why

    'One fair daughter, and no more,
      The which he lovéd passing well.'

(*Polonius.* Still on my daughter.

Hamlet. Am I not i'th' right, old Jephthah?

Polonius. If you call me Jephthah, my lord, I have a daughter that I love passing well.

Hamlet. Nay, that follows not.

Polonius. What follows then, my lord?

420 *Hamlet*. Why,

> 'As by lot, God wot,'

and then you know

> 'It came to pass, as most like it was...'

the first row of the pious chanson will show you more,
for look where my abridgement comes.

'*Enter four or five Players*'

You are welcome masters, welcome all—I am glad
to see thee well—Welcome, good friends—O, my old
friend! why, thy face is valanced since I saw thee last,
com'st thou to beard me in Denmark?—What, my young
430 lady and mistress! by'r lady, your ladyship is nearer to
heaven than when I saw you last by the altitude of a
chopine. Pray God your voice, like a piece of uncurrent gold, be not cracked within the ring...Masters,
you are all welcome. We'll e'en to't like French falconers, fly at any thing we see, we'll have a speech
straight. [*to the First Player*] Come give us a taste of your
quality, come a passionate speech.

1 *Player*. What speech, my good lord?

Hamlet. I heard thee speak me a speech once, but it
440 was never acted, or if it was, not above once, for the
play I remember pleased not the million, 'twas caviary
to the general, but it was—as I received it, and others,
whose judgements in such matters cried in the top of
mine—an excellent play, well digested in the scenes, set
down with as much modesty as cunning....I remember
one said there were no sallets in the lines, to make the
matter savoury, nor no matter in the phrase that might
indict the author of affection, but called it an honest
method, as wholesome as sweet, and by very much more
450 handsome than fine: one speech in't I chiefly loved,
'twas Æneas' tale to Dido, and thereabout of it especi-

ally where he speaks of Priam's slaughter. If it live in
your memory begin at this line, let me see, let me see—
    'The rugged Pyrrhus, like th'Hyrcanian beast'—
'tis not so, it begins with Pyrrhus—
    'The rugged Pyrrhus, he whose sable arms,
    Black as his purpose, did the night resemble
    When he lay couchéd in th'ominous horse,
    Hath now this dread and black complexion smeared
    With heraldy more dismal: head to foot   460
    Now is he total gules, horridly tricked
    With blood of fathers, mothers, daughters, sons,
    Baked and impasted with the parching streets,
    That lend a tyrannous and a damnéd light
    To their lord's murder. Roasted in wrath and fire,
    And thus o'er-sizéd with coagulate gore,
    With eyes like carbuncles, the hellish Pyrrhus
    Old grandsire Priam seeks'...
So proceed you.
  Polonius. 'Fore God, my lord, well spoken, with 470
good accent and good discretion.
  1 *Player.*   'Anon he finds him
    Striking too short at Greeks, his antique sword,
    Rebellious to his arm, lies where it falls,
    Repugnant to command; unequal matched,
    Pyrrhus at Priam drives, in rage strikes wide,
    But with the whiff and wind of his fell sword
    Th'unnerved father falls: then senseless Ilium,
    Seeming to feel this blow, with flaming top
    Stoops to his base; and with a hideous crash   480
    Takes prisoner Pyrrhus' ear. For lo! his sword,
    Which was declining on the milky head
    Of reverend Priam, seemed i'th'air to stick,
    So as a painted tyrant Pyrrhus stood,
    And like a neutral to his will and matter,

Did nothing:
But as we often see, against some storm,
A silence in the heavens, the rack stand still,
The bold winds speechless, and the orb below
490   As hush as death, anon the dreadful thunder
Doth rend the region, so after Pyrrhus' pause,
A rouséd vengeance sets him new awork,
And never did the Cyclops' hammers fall
On Mars's armour, forged for proof eterne,
With less remorse than Pyrrhus' bleeding sword
Now falls on Priam.
Out, out, thou strumpet Fortune! All you gods,
In general synod take away her power,
Break all the spokes and fellies from her wheel,
500   And bowl the round nave down the hill of heaven
As low as to the fiends.'

Polonius. This is too long.

Hamlet. It shall to the barber's with your beard;
prithee say on—he's for a jig, or a tale of bawdry, or he
sleeps—say on, come to Hecuba.

1 *Player.* 'But who, ah woe! had seen the mobled
    queen—'

Hamlet. 'The mobled queen'?

Polonius. That's good, 'mobled queen' is good.

1 *Player.* 'Run barefoot up and down, threat'ning
    the flames
510   With bisson rheum, a clout upon that head
Where late the diadem stood, and for a robe,
About her lank and all o'er-teeméd loins,
A blanket in the alarm of fear caught up—
Who this had seen, with tongue in venom steeped,
'Gainst Fortune's state would treason have pro-
    nounced;
But if the gods themselves did see her then,
When she saw Pyrrhus make malicious sport

In mincing with his sword her husband's limbs,
The instant burst of clamour that she made,
Unless things mortal move them not at all, 520
Would have made milch the burning eyes of
  heaven,
And passion in the gods.'

Polonius. Look whe'r he has not turned his colour, and has tears in's eyes—prithee no more.

Hamlet. 'Tis well, I'll have thee speak out the rest of this soon. Good my lord, will you see the players well bestowed; do you hear, let them be well used, for they are the abstracts and brief chronicles of the time; after your death you were better have a bad epitaph than their ill report while you live. 530

Polonius. My lord, I will use them according to their desert.

Hamlet. God's bodkin, man, much better! use every man after his desert, and who shall 'scape whipping? Use them after your own honour and dignity—the less they deserve the more merit is in your bounty. Take them in.

Polonius. Come, sirs. [*he goes to the door*

Hamlet. Follow him, friends, we'll hear a play to-morrow; [*he stops the First Player*] dost thou hear me, 540 old friend, can you play The Murder of Gonzago?

1 *Player.* Ay, my lord.

Hamlet. We'll ha't to-morrow night. You could for a need study a speech of some dozen or sixteen lines, which I would set down and insert in't, could you not?

1 *Player.* Ay, my lord.

[*Polonius and the Players go out*

Hamlet. Very well. Follow that lord, and look you mock him not. [*First Player goes*
[*to Rosencrantz and Guildenstern*] My good friends,
I'll leave you till night. You are welcome to Elsinore. 550

Rosencrantz. Good my lord.   [*they take their leave*

Hamlet. Ay, so, God bye to you! now I am alone.

O, what a rogue and peasant slave am I!

Is it not monstrous that this player here,

But in a fiction, in a dream of passion,

Could force his soul so to his own conceit

That from her working all his visage wanned,

Tears in his eyes, distraction in his aspect,

A broken voice, and his whole function suiting

560 With forms to his conceit; and all for nothing!

For Hecuba!

What's Hecuba to him, or he to Hecuba,

That he should weep for her? what would he do,

Had he the motive and the cue for passion

That I have? he would drown the stage with tears.

And cleave the general ear with horrid speech,

Make mad the guilty and appal the free,

Confound the ignorant, and amaze indeed

The very faculties of eyes and ears; yet I,

570 A dull and muddy-mettled rascal, peak

Like John-a-dreams, unpregnant of my cause,

And can say nothing; no, not for a king,

Upon whose property and most dear life

A damned defeat was made: am I a coward?

Who calls me villain, breaks my pate across,

Plucks off my beard and blows it in my face,

Tweaks me by the nose, gives me the lie i'th'throat

As deep as to the lungs? who does me this?

Ha, 'swounds, I should take it: for it cannot be

580 But I am pigeon-livered, and lack gall

To make oppression bitter, or ere this

I should ha' fatted all the region kites

With this slave's offal. Bloody, bawdy villain!

Remorseless, treacherous, lecherous, kindless villain!

O, vengeance!
Why, what an ass am I. This is most brave,
That I, the son of a dear father murdered,
Prompted to my revenge by heaven and hell,
Must like a whore unpack my heart with words,
And fall a-cursing like a very drab;   590
A stallion! fie upon't! foh!
About, my brains; hum, I have heard
That guilty creatures sitting at a play
Have by the very cunning of the scene
Been struck so to the soul, that presently
They have proclaimed their malefactions:
For murder, though it have no tongue, will speak
With most miraculous organ: I'll have these players
Play something like the murder of my father
Before mine uncle, I'll observe his looks,   600
I'll tent him to the quick, if a' do blench
I know my course....The spirit that I have seen
May be a devil, and the devil hath power
T'assume a pleasing shape, yea, and perhaps
Out of my weakness and my melancholy,
As he is very potent with such spirits,
Abuses me to damn me; I'll have grounds
More relative than this—the play's the thing
Wherein I'll catch the conscience of the king. [*he goes*

[*A day passes*]

[3. 1.] *The lobby of the audience chamber, the walls hung with arras; a table in the midst; to one side a faldstool with a crucifix*

The KING *and the* QUEEN *enter with* POLONIUS, ROSENCRANTZ, *and* GUILDENSTERN; OPHELIA *follows a little behind*

  King. And can you by no drift of conference
Get from him why he puts on this confusion,
Grating so harshly all his days of quiet
With turbulent and dangerous lunacy?
  Rosencrantz. He does confess he feels himself
      distracted,
But from what cause a' will by no means speak.
  Guildenstern. Nor do we find him forward to
      be sounded,
But with a crafty madness keeps aloof
When we would bring him on to some confession
10 Of his true state.
    Queen.   Did he receive you well?
  Rosencrantz. Most like a gentleman.
  Guildenstern. But with much forcing of his disposition.
  Rosencrantz. Niggard of question, but of our demands
Most free in his reply.
    Queen.   Did you assay him
To any pastime?
  Rosencrantz. Madam, it so fell out that certain players
We o'er-raught on the way. Of these we told him,
And there did seem in him a kind of joy
To hear of it: they are here about the court,
20 And as I think, they have already order
This night to play before him.
    Polonius.   'Tis most true,

And he beseeched me to entreat your majesties
To hear and see the matter.

King. With all my heart, and it doth much content me
To hear him so inclined.
Good gentlemen, give him a further edge,
And drive his purpose into these delights.

Rosencrantz. We shall, my lord.

[*Rosencrantz and Guildenstern go out*

King. Sweet Gertrude, leave us too,
For we have closely sent for Hamlet hither,
That he, as 'twere by accident, may here   30
Affront Ophelia;
Her father and myself, lawful espials,
Will so bestow ourselves, that seeing unseen,
We may of their encounter frankly judge,
And gather by him as he is behaved,
If't be th'affliction of his love or no
That thus he suffers for.

Queen. I shall obey you—
And for your part, Ophelia, I do wish
That your good beauties be the happy cause
Of Hamlet's wildness, so shall I hope your virtues   40
Will bring him to his wonted way again,
To both your honours.

Ophelia. Madam, I wish it may.

[*the Queen goes*

Polonius. Ophelia, walk you here. Gracious, so
    please you,
We will bestow ourselves...Read on this book,

[*he takes a book from the faldstool*

That show of such an exercise may colour
Your loneliness; we are oft to blame in this,
'Tis too much proved, that with devotion's visage
And pious action we do sugar o'er

The devil himself.

 (*King.*   O, 'tis too true,

50 How smart a lash that speech doth give my conscience.
The harlot's cheek, beautied with plast'ring art,
Is not more ugly to the thing that helps it,
Than is my deed to my most painted word:
O heavy burden!

  Polonius. I hear him coming, let's withdraw, my lord.
      [*they bestow themselves behind the arras;*
       Ophelia kneels at the faldstool

   HAMLET enters, in deep dejection

 Hamlet. To be, or not to be, that is the question,
Whether 'tis nobler in the mind to suffer
The slings and arrows of outrageous fortune,
Or to take arms against a sea of troubles,
60 And by opposing, end them. To die, to sleep—
No more, and by a sleep to say we end
The heart-ache, and the thousand natural shocks
That flesh is heir to; 'tis a consummation
Devoutly to be wished to die to sleep!
To sleep, perchance to dream, ay there's the rub,
For in that sleep of death what dreams may come
When we have shuffled off this mortal coil
Must give us pause—there's the respect
That makes calamity of so long life:
70 For who would bear the whips and scorns of time,
Th'oppressor's wrong, the proud man's contumely,
The pangs of disprized love, the law's delay,
The insolence of office, and the spurns
That patient merit of th'unworthy takes,
When he himself might his quietus make
With a bare bodkin; who would fardels bear,
To grunt and sweat under a weary life,

But that the dread of something after death,
The undiscovered country, from whose bourn
No traveller returns, puzzles the will, 80
And makes us rather bear those ills we have,
Than fly to others that we know not of?
Thus conscience does make cowards of us all,
And thus the native hue of resolution
Is sicklied o'er with the pale cast of thought,
And enterprises of great pitch and moment
With this regard their currents turn awry,
And lose the name of action....Soft you now,
The fair Ophelia—Nymph, in thy orisons
Be all my sins remembered.

   Ophelia [*rises*].   Good my lord, 90
How does your honour for this many a day?
  Hamlet.   I humbly thank you, well, well, well.
  Ophelia.   My lord, I have remembrances of yours,
That I have longed long to re-deliver.
I pray you now receive them.
  Hamlet.   No, not I,
I never gave you aught.
  Ophelia.   My honoured lord, you know right well
       you did,
And with them words of so sweet breath composed
As made the things more rich. Their perfume lost,
Take these again, for to the noble mind 100
Rich gifts wax poor when givers prove unkind.
There, my lord. [*she takes jewels from her bosom and
             places them on the table before him*
  Hamlet [*remembers the plot*]. Ha, ha! are
     you honest?
  Ophelia. My lord?
  Hamlet. Are you fair?
  Ophelia. What means your lordship?

Hamlet. That if you be honest and fair, your honesty should admit no discourse to your beauty.

Ophelia. Could beauty, my lord, have better com-
110 merce than with honesty?

Hamlet. Ay truly, for the power of beauty will sooner transform honesty from what it is to a bawd, than the force of honesty can translate beauty into his likeness. This was sometime a paradox, but now the time gives it proof. I did love you once.

Ophelia. Indeed, my lord, you made me believe so.

Hamlet. You should not have believed me, for virtue cannot so inoculate our old stock, but we shall relish of it—I loved you not.

120 *Ophelia.* I was the more deceived.

Hamlet [*points to the faldstool*]. Get thee to a nunnery, why wouldst thou be a breeder of sinners? I am myself indifferent honest, but yet I could accuse me of such things, that it were better my mother had not borne me: I am very proud, revengeful, ambitious, with more offences at my beck, than I have thoughts to put them in, imagination to give them shape, or time to act them in: what should such fellows as I do crawling between earth and heaven? we are arrant knaves all, believe none
130 of us—go thy ways to a nunnery....[*suddenly*] Where's your father?

Ophelia. At home, my lord.

Hamlet. Let the doors be shut upon him, that he may play the fool no where but in's own house. Farewell.

[*he goes out*

Ophelia [*kneels before the crucifix*]. O help him, you sweet heavens!

Hamlet [*returns, distraught*]. If thou dost marry, I'll give thee this plague for thy dowry—be thou as chaste as ice, as pure as snow, thou shalt not escape calumny; get thee

to a nunnery, go, farewell....[*he paces to and fro*] Or if thou 140
wilt needs marry, marry a fool, for wise men know well
enough what monsters you make of them: to a nunnery,
go, and quickly too, farewell.   [*he rushes out*

Ophelia. O heavenly powers, restore him!

Hamlet [*once more returning*]. I have heard of your
paintings too, well enough. God hath given you one face
and you make yourselves another, you jig, you amble,
and you lisp, you nickname God's creatures, and make
your wantonness your ignorance; go to, I'll no more
on't, it hath made me mad. I say we will have no mo 150
marriage—those that are married already, all but one,
shall live, the rest shall keep as they are: to a nunnery, go.
                              [*he departs again*

Ophelia. O, what a noble mind is here o'erthrown!
The courtier's, soldier's, scholar's, eye, tongue, sword,
Th'expectancy and rose of the fair state,
The glass of fashion, and the mould of form,
Th'observed of all observers, quite quite down,
And I of ladies most deject and wretched,
That sucked the honey of his music vows,
Now see that noble and most sovereign reason   160
Like sweet bells jangled, out of tune and harsh,
That unmatched form and feature of blown youth,
Blasted with ecstasy! O, woe is me!
T'have seen what I have seen, see what I see! [*she prays*

The KING *and* POLONIUS *steal forth*
from behind the arras

King. Love! his affections do not that way tend,
Nor what he spake, though it lacked form a little,
Was not like madness—there's something in his soul,
O'er which his melancholy sits on brood,
And I do doubt the hatch and the disclose

170 Will be some danger; which for to prevent,
    I have in quick determination
    Thus set it down: he shall with speed to England,
    For the demand of our neglected tribute.
    Haply the seas, and countries different,
    With variable objects, shall expel
    This something-settled matter in his heart,
    Whereon his brains still beating puts him thus
    From fashion of himself. What think you on't?
                           [*Ophelia comes forward*

    Polonius. It shall do well. But yet do I believe
180 The origin and commencement of his grief
    Sprung from neglected love...How now, Ophelia?
    You need not tell us what Lord Hamlet said,
    We heard it all...My lord, do as you please,
    But if you hold it fit, after the play,
    Let his queen-mother all alone entreat him
    To show his grief, let her be round with him,
    And I'll be placed (so please you) in the ear
    Of all their conference. If she find him not,
    To England send him; or confine him where
190 Your wisdom best shall think.
    King.   It shall be so,
    Madness in great ones must not unwatched go.
                                 [*they depart*

[3. 2.] *The hall of the castle, with seats set to both sides as for a spectacle; at the back a dais with curtains concealing an inner-stage*

    'HAMLET, *and three of the Players' come from behind the curtains*

    Hamlet [*to the First Player*]. Speak the speech I pray you as I pronounced it to you, trippingly on the tongue,

but if you mouth it as many of your players do, I had as
lief the town-crier spoke my lines. Nor do not saw the air
too much with your hand thus, but use all gently, for in
the very torrent, tempest, and as I may say whirlwind
of your passion, you must acquire and beget a temper-
ance that may give it smoothness. O, it offends me
to the soul, to hear a robustious periwig-pated fellow
tear a passion to tatters, to very rags, to split the ears 10
of the groundlings, who for the most part are capable
of nothing but inexplicable dumb-shows and noise:
I would have such a fellow whipped for o'erdoing
Termagant, it out-herods Herod, pray you avoid it.

1 *Player.* I warrant your honour.

Hamlet. Be not too tame neither, but let your own discretion be your tutor, suit the action to the word, the
word to the action, with this special observance, that you
o'erstep not the modesty of nature: for any thing so
o'erdone is from the purpose of playing, whose end both 20
at the first, and now, was and is, to hold as 'twere the
mirror up to nature, to show virtue her own feature,
scorn her own image, and the very age and body of the
time his form and pressure...Now this overdone, or
come tardy off, though it make the unskilful laugh,
cannot but make the judicious grieve, the censure of the
which one must in your allowance o'erweigh a whole
theatre of others. O there be players that I have seen
play—and heard others praise, and that highly—not
to speak it profanely, that neither having th'accent of 30
Christians, nor the gait of Christian, pagan, nor man,
have so strutted and bellowed, that I have thought some
of nature's journeymen had made men, and not made
them well, they imitated humanity so abominably.

1 *Player.* I hope we have reformed that indifferently
with us, sir.

Hamlet. O reform it altogether, and let those that play
your clowns speak no more than is set down for them,
for there be of them that will themselves laugh, to set on
40 some quantity of barren spectators to laugh too, though
in the mean time some necessary question of the play be
then to be considered. That's villanous, and shows a most
pitiful ambition in the fool that uses it...Go, make you
ready.   [*the Players retire behind the curtains*

POLONIUS *enters with* ROSENCRANTZ *and* GUILDENSTERN

How now, my lord? will the king hear this piece of work?
  Polonius. And the queen too, and that presently.
  Hamlet. Bid the players make haste.
                       [*Polonius bows and departs*
Will you two help to hasten them?
  Rosencrantz. Ay, my lord.
            [*Rosencrantz and Guildenstern follow Polonius*
50   *Hamlet.* What, ho! Horatio!

HORATIO *comes in*

  Horatio. Here, sweet lord, at your service.
  Hamlet. Horatio, thou art e'en as just a man
As e'er my conversation coped withal.
  Horatio. O, my dear lord,—
  Hamlet.   Nay, do not think I flatter,
For what advancement may I hope from thee,
That no revenue hast but thy good spirits
To feed and clothe thee? why should the poor
         be flattered?
No, let the candied tongue lick absurd pomp,
And crook the pregnant hinges of the knee
60 Where thrift may follow fawning...Dost thou hear?
Since my dear soul was mistress of her choice,

And could of men distinguish her election,
Sh'hath sealed thee for herself, for thou hast been
As one in suff'ring all that suffers nothing,
A man that Fortune's buffets and rewards
Hast ta'en with equal thanks; and blest are those
Whose blood and judgement are so well co-medled,
That they are not a pipe for Fortune's finger
To sound what stop she please: give me that man
That is not passion's slave, and I will wear him   70
In my heart's core, ay in my heart of heart,
As I do thee. Something too much of this—
There is a play to-night before the king,
One scene of it comes near the circumstance
Which I have told thee of my father's death.
I prithee when thou seest that act afoot,
Even with the very comment of thy soul
Observe my uncle—if his occulted guilt
Do not itself unkennel in one speech,
It is a damnéd ghost that we have seen,   80
And my imaginations are as foul
As Vulcan's stithy; give him heedful note,
For I mine eyes will rivet to his face,
And after we will both our judgements join
In censure of his seeming.

   Horatio.   Well, my lord,
If a' steal aught the whilst this play is playing,
And 'scape detecting, I will pay the theft.

               [*trumpets and kettle-drums heard*
   Hamlet. They are coming to the play. I must be idle.
Get you a place.

The KING *and* QUEEN *enter, followed by* POLONIUS,
OPHELIA, ROSENCRANTZ, GUILDENSTERN, *and other
courtiers; they sit, the King, the Queen and Polonius
on this side, Ophelia with Horatio and others on that*

90 *King.* How fares our cousin Hamlet?

Hamlet. Excellent i'faith, of the chameleon's dish, I eat
the air, promise-crammed—you cannot feed capons so.

King. I have nothing with this answer, Hamlet. These
words are not mine.

Hamlet. No, nor mine now. [*to Polonius*] My lord,
you played once i'th'university, you say?

Polonius. That did I, my lord, and was accounted a
good actor.

Hamlet. What did you enact?

100 *Polonius.* I did enact Julius Cæsar. I was killed i'th'
Capitol, Brutus killed me.

Hamlet. It was a brute part of him to kill so capital a
calf there. Be the players ready?

Rosencrantz. Ay, my lord, they stay upon your
patience.

Queen. Come hither, my dear Hamlet, sit by me.

Hamlet. No, good mother, here's metal more at-
tractive. [*he turns towards Ophelia*

(*Polonius* [*to the King*]. O ho! do you mark that?

[*they whisper together, watching Hamlet*

110 *Hamlet.* Lady, shall I lie in your lap?

Ophelia. No, my lord.

Hamlet. I mean, my head upon your lap?

Ophelia. Ay, my lord. [*he lies at her feet*

Hamlet. Do you think I meant country matters?

Ophelia. I think nothing, my lord.

Hamlet. That's a fair thought to lie between maids'
legs.

Ophelia. What is, my lord?

Hamlet. Nothing.

Ophelia. You are merry, my lord. 120

Hamlet. Who, I?

Ophelia. Ay, my lord.

Hamlet. O God, your only jig-maker. What should a man do but be merry, for look you how cheerfully my mother looks, and my father died within's two hours.

> [*the Queen turns away and whispers with the King and Polonius*

Ophelia. Nay, 'tis twice two months, my lord.

Hamlet. So long? nay then let the devil wear black, for I'll have a suit of sables; O heavens, die two months ago, and not forgotten yet? then there's hope a great man's memory may outlive his life half a year, but 130 by'r lady a' must build churches then, or else shall a' suffer not thinking on, with the hobby-horse, whose epitaph is 'For O! for O! the hobby-horse is forgot.'

'*The trumpets sound*,' *the curtains are drawn aside, discovering the inner-stage, and a Dumb-Show is performed thereon*

The Dumb-Show

'*Enter a King and a Queen, very lovingly, the Queen embracing him and he her, she kneels and makes show of protestation unto him, he takes her up and declines his head upon her neck, he lies him down upon a bank of flowers, she seeing him asleep leaves him: anon comes in another man, takes off his crown, kisses it, and pours poison in the sleeper's ears and leaves him: the Queen returns, finds the King dead, and makes passionate action: the poisoner with some three or four mutes comes in again, seeming to condole with her: the dead body is carried away: the poisoner wooes*

the Queen with gifts, she seems harsh awhile, but in the
end accepts his love '　　　　　[*the curtains are closed*
　Hamlet seems troubled and casts glances at the King and
Queen as the show goes forward; they continue in talk
with Polonius throughout

Ophelia. What means this, my lord?
Hamlet. Marry, this is miching mallecho, it means
mischief.
Ophelia. Belike this show imports the argument of
the play.

　　　Enter a player before the curtains; the King and
　　　　　　　Queen turn to listen

Hamlet. We shall know by this fellow. The players
140 cannot keep counsel, they'll tell all.
Ophelia. Will a' tell us what this show meant?
Hamlet [*savagely*]. Ay, or any show that you will show
him—be not you ashamed to show, he'll not shame to tell
you what it means.
Ophelia. You are naught, you are naught, I'll mark
the play.
Player. For us and for our tragedy,
　　　　Here stooping to your clemency,
　　　　We beg your hearing patiently.　　　　[*exit*
150 *Hamlet.* Is this a prologue, or the posy of a ring?
Ophelia. 'Tis brief, my lord.
Hamlet. As woman's love.

　　　Enter on the dais two Players, a King and
　　　　　　　a Queen

Player King. Full thirty times hath Phœbus' cart
　　　gone round
Neptune's salt wash, and Tellus' orbéd ground,

And thirty dozen moons with borrowed sheen
About the world have times twelve thirties been,
Since love our hearts and Hymen did our hands
Unite commutual in most sacred bands.
  Player Queen. So many journeys may the sun
     and moon
Make us again count o'er ere love be done!   160
But woe is me, you are so sick of late,
So far from cheer, and from your former state,
That I distrust you. Yet though I distrust,
Discomfort you, my lord, it nothing must.
For women fear too much, even as they love,
And women's fear and love hold quantity,
†In neither aught, or in extremity.
Now what my love is proof hath made you know,
And as my love is sized, my fear is so.
Where love is great, the littlest doubts are fear,   170
Where little fears grow great, great love grows there.
  Player King. Faith, I must leave thee, love, and
     shortly too.
My operant powers their functions leave to do,
And thou shalt live in this fair world behind,
Honoured, beloved, and haply one as kind
For husband shalt thou—
  Player Queen.   O, confound the rest!
Such love must needs be treason in my breast,
In second husband let me be accurst,
None wed the second, but who killed the first.
  (*Hamlet.* That's wormwood, wormwood.   180
  Player Queen. The instances that second
     marriage move
Are base respects of thrift, but none of love.
A second time I kill my husband dead,
When second husband kisses me in bed.

Player King. I do believe you think what now
    you speak,
But what we do determine, oft we break.
Purpose is but the slave to memory,
Of violent birth but poor validity,
Which now like fruit unripe sticks on the tree,
190 But fall unshaken when they mellow be.
Most necessary 'tis that we forget
To pay ourselves what to ourselves is debt.
What to ourselves in passion we propose,
The passion ending, doth the purpose lose.
The violence of either grief or joy
Their own enactures with themselves destroy,
Where joy most revels, grief doth most lament,
Grief joys, joy grieves, on slender accident.
This world is not for aye, nor 'tis not strange
200 That even our loves should with our fortunes change:
For 'tis a question left us yet to prove,
Whether love lead fortune, or else fortune love.
The great man down, you mark his favourite flies,
The poor advanced makes friends of enemies,
And hitherto doth love on fortune tend,
For who not needs shall never lack a friend,
And who in want a hollow friend doth try,
Directly seasons him his enemy.
But orderly to end where I begun,
210 Our wills and fates do so contrary run,
That our devices still are overthrown,
Our thoughts are ours, their ends none of
    our own—
So think thou wilt no second husband wed,
But die thy thoughts when thy first lord is dead.
    Player Queen. Nor earth to me give food nor
        heaven light,

Sport and repose lock from me day and night,
To desperation turn my trust and hope,
An anchor's cheere in prison be my scope,
Each opposite that blanks the face of joy
Meet what I would have well and it destroy,   220
Both here and hence pursue me lasting strife,
If once a widow, ever I be wife!

Hamlet. If she should break it now!

Player King. 'Tis deeply sworn. Sweet leave me
   here awhile,
My spirits grow dull, and fain I would beguile
The tedious day with sleep.   [*he 'sleeps'*

Player Queen.   Sleep rock thy brain,
And never come mischance between us twain! [*exit*

Hamlet. Madam, how like you this play?

Queen. The lady doth protest too much methinks.

Hamlet. O, but she'll keep her word.   230

King. Have you heard the argument? is there no
offence in't?

Hamlet. No, no, they do but jest, poison in jest, no
offence i'th'world.

King. What do you call the play?

Hamlet. The Mouse-trap. Marry, how?—tropically.
This play is the image of a murder done in Vienna.
Gonzago is the duke's name, his wife Baptista, you shall
see anon, 'tis a knavish piece of work, but what of that?
your majesty, and we that have free souls, it touches 240
us not—let the galled jade wince, our withers are unwrung....

Enter First Player for LUCIANUS, *clad in a black doublet
and with a vial in his hand; he struts towards the sleeping
King making mouths and threatening gestures*

This is one Lucianus, nephew to the king.

Ophelia. You are as good as a chorus, my lord.

Hamlet. I could interpret between you and your love, if I could see the puppets dallying.

Ophelia. You are keen, my lord, you are keen.

Hamlet. It would cost you a groaning to take off mine edge.

250 *Ophelia.* Still better and worse.

Hamlet. So you mis-take your husbands....[*he looks up*] Begin, murderer. Pox! leave thy damnable faces and begin! Come——'the croaking raven doth bellow for revenge.'

Lucianus. Thoughts black, hands apt, drugs fit, and
    time agreeing,
Confederate season, else no creature seeing,
Thou mixture rank, of midnight weeds collected,
With Hecate's ban thrice blasted, thrice infected,
Thy natural magic and dire property
260 On wholesome life usurps immediately.

[*'pours the poison in his ears'*
Hamlet. A' poisons him i'th'garden for's estate, his name's Gonzago, the story is extant, and written in very choice Italian, you shall see anon how the murderer gets the love of Gonzago's wife.

[*the King, very pale, totters to his feet*
Ophelia. The king rises.

Hamlet. What, frighted with false fire!

Queen. How fares my lord?

Polonius. Give o'er the play.

King. Give me some light—away!

[*he rushes from the hall*
270 *Polonius.* Lights, lights, lights!

[*all but Hamlet and Horatio depart*
Hamlet. Why, let the stricken deer go weep,
        The hart ungallèd play,

> For some must watch while some must sleep,
>> Thus runs the world away.

Would not this, sir, and a forest of feathers, if the rest of my fortunes turn Turk with me, with two Provincial roses on my razed shoes, get me a fellowship in a cry of players, sir?

Horatio. Half a share.

Hamlet. A whole one, I.   280

> For thou dost know, O Damon dear,
>> This realm dismantled was
> Of Jove himself, and now reigns here
>> A very, very—peacock.

Horatio. You might have rhymed.

Hamlet. O good Horatio, I'll take the ghost's word for a thousand pound....Didst perceive?

Horatio. Very well, my lord.

Hamlet. Upon the talk of the poisoning?

Horatio. I did very well note him.   290

ROSENCRANTZ and GUILDENSTERN return

Hamlet. Ah, ha! [*turns his back upon them*] Come, some music! come, the recorders!

> For if the king like not the comedy,
>> Why then, belike,—he likes it not, perdy.

Come, some music!

Guildenstern. Good my lord, vouchsafe me a word with you.

Hamlet. Sir, a whole history.

Guildenstern. The king, sir,—

Hamlet. Ay, sir, what of him?   300

Guildenstern. Is in his retirement marvellous distempered.

Hamlet. With drink, sir?

Guildenstern. No, my lord, rather with choler.

Hamlet. Your wisdom should show itself more richer to signify this to the doctor. For, for me to put him to his purgation, would perhaps plunge him into more choler.

Guildenstern. Good my lord, put your discourse into 310 some frame, and start not so wildly from my affair.

Hamlet. I am tame, sir—pronounce.

Guildenstern. The queen your mother, in most great affliction of spirit, hath sent me to you.

Hamlet. You are welcome.

Guildenstern. Nay, good my lord, this courtesy is not of the right breed. If it shall please you to make me a wholesome answer, I will do your mother's commandment. If not, your pardon and my return shall be the end of my business.   [*he bows and turns away*

320 *Hamlet.* Sir, I cannot.

Rosencrantz. What, my lord?

Hamlet. Make you a wholesome answer—my wit's diseased. But, sir, such answer as I can make, you shall command, or rather as you say, my mother. Therefore no more, but to the matter—my mother, you say—

Rosencrantz. Then thus she says, your behaviour hath struck her into amazement and admiration.

Hamlet. O wonderful son that can so stonish a 330 mother! but is there no sequel at the heels of this mother's admiration? impart.

Rosencrantz. She desires to speak with you in her closet ere you go to bed.

Hamlet. We shall obey, were she ten times our mother. Have you any further trade with us?

Rosencrantz. My lord, you once did love me.

Hamlet. And do still, by these pickers and stealers.

Rosencrantz. Good my lord, what is your cause of

distemper? you do surely bar the door upon your own
liberty, if you deny your griefs to your friend.   340

Hamlet. Sir, I lack advancement.

Rosencrantz. How can that be, when you have the
voice of the king himself for your succession in Denmark?

Hamlet. Ay, sir, but 'While the grass grows'—the
proverb is something musty.

Players bring in recorders

O, the recorders, let me see one. [*he takes a recorder and
leads Guildenstern aside*] To withdraw with you, why
do you go about to recover the wind of me, as if you
would drive me into a toil?   350

Guildenstern. O, my lord, if my duty be too bold, my
love is too unmannerly.

Hamlet. I do not well understand that—will you play
upon this pipe?

Guildenstern. My lord, I cannot.

Hamlet. I pray you.

Guildenstern. Believe me, I cannot.

Hamlet. I do beseech you.

Guildenstern. I know no touch of it, my lord.

Hamlet. It is as easy as lying; govern these ventages 360
with your fingers and thumb, give it breath with your
mouth, and it will discourse most eloquent music—look
you, these are the stops.

Guildenstern. But these cannot I command to any
utt'rance of harmony, I have not the skill.

Hamlet. Why, look you now, how unworthy a thing
you make of me! you would play upon me, you would
seem to know my stops, you would pluck out the heart
of my mystery, you would sound me from my lowest
note to the top of my compass—and there is much music, 370

excellent voice, in this little organ, yet cannot you make
it speak. 'Sblood, do you think I am easier to be played
on than a pipe? call me what instrument you will,
though you can fret me, you cannot play upon me.

POLONIUS enters

God bless you, sir!

　Polonius. My lord, the queen would speak with you,
and presently.

　Hamlet. Do you see yonder cloud that's almost in
shape of a camel?

380　*Polonius.* By th'mass and 'tis, like a camel indeed.

　Hamlet. Methinks it is like a weasel.

　Polonius. It is backed like a weasel.

　Hamlet. Or, like a whale?

　Polonius. Very like a whale.

　Hamlet. Then I will come to my mother by and by.
[*aside*] They fool me to the top of my bent—
I will come by and by.

　Polonius. I will say so.

　　　　[*Polonius, Rosencrantz and Guildenstern depart*

　Hamlet. 'By and by' is easily said.

390 Leave me, friends.　　　　　　　　　　　　[*the rest go*
'Tis now the very witching time of night,
When churchyards yawn, and hell itself breathes out
Contagion to this world: now could I drink hot blood,
And do such bitter business as the day
Would quake to look on: soft, now to my mother—
O heart, lose not thy nature, let not ever
The soul of Nero enter this firm bosom,
Let me be cruel not unnatural.
I will speak daggers to her, but use none.
400 My tongue and soul in this be hypocrites,
How in my words somever she be shent,
To give them seals never, my soul, consent!　　[*he goes*

[3. 3.] *The lobby, with the faldstool as before; the audience chamber without*

The KING, ROSENCRANTZ *and* GUILDENSTERN

King. I like him not, nor stands it safe with us
To let his madness range. Therefore prepare you,
I your commission will forthwith dispatch,
And he to England shall along with you.
The terms of our estate may not endure
Hazard so near's as doth hourly grow
Out of his brows.

   Guildenstern.   We will ourselves provide.
Most holy and religious fear it is
To keep those many many bodies safe
That live and feed upon your majesty.   10

   Rosencrantz. The single and peculiar life is bound
With all the strength and armour of the mind
To keep itself from noyance, but much more
That spirit upon whose weal depends and rests
The lives of many. The cess of majesty
Dies not alone; but like a gulf doth draw
†What's near it with it. O, 'tis a massy wheel
Fixed on the summit of the highest mount,
To whose huge spokes ten thousand lesser things
Are mortised and adjoined, which when it falls,   20
Each small annexment, petty consequence,
Attends the boist'rous ruin. Never alone
Did the king sigh, but with a general groan.

   King. Arm you, I pray you, to this speedy voyage,
For we will fetters put about this fear,
Which now goes too free-footed.

   Rosencrantz.   We will haste us.
                                  [*they go*

POLONIUS enters

Polonius. My lord, he's going to his mother's closet—
Behind the arras I'll convey myself
To hear the process—I'll warrant she'll tax him home,
30 And as you said, and wisely was it said,
'Tis meet that some more audience than a mother,
Since nature makes them partial, should o'erhear
The speech of vantage; fare you well, my liege,
I'll call upon you ere you go to bed,
And tell you what I know.
     King.   Thanks, dear my lord....
                    [*Polonius goes; the King paces to and fro*
O, my offence is rank, it smells to heaven,
It hath the primal eldest curse upon't,
A brother's murder! Pray can I not,
Though inclination be as sharp as will.
40 My stronger guilt defeats my strong intent,
And like a man to double business bound,
I stand in pause where I shall first begin,
And both neglect. What if this curséd hand
Were thicker than itself with brother's blood,
Is there not rain enough in the sweet heavens
To wash it white as snow? whereto serves mercy
But to confront the visage of offence?
And what's in prayer but this two-fold force,
To be forestalléd ere we come to fall,
50 Or pardoned being down? then I'll look up....
My fault is past, but O, what form of prayer
Can serve my turn? 'Forgive me my foul murder'?
That cannot be since I am still possessed
Of those effects for which I did the murder;
My crown, mine own ambition, and my queen;
May one be pardoned and retain th'offence?

In the corrupted currents of this world
Offence's gilded hand may shove by justice,
And oft 'tis seen the wicked prize itself
Buys out the law. But 'tis not so above,   60
There is no shuffling, there the action lies
In his true nature, and we ourselves compelled
Even to the teeth and forehead of our faults
To give in evidence. What then? what rests?
Try what repentance can—what can it not?
Yet what can it, when one can not repent?
O wretched state! O bosom black as death!
O liméd soul, that struggling to be free,
Art more engaged; help, angels! Make assay,
Bow stubborn knees, and heart; with strings of steel,   70
Be soft as sinews of the new-born babe—
All may be well.   [*he kneels*

Hamlet enters the audience chamber and pauses,
seeing the King

Hamlet. [*approaches the entry to the lobby*] Now might
        I do it pat, now a' is a-praying—
And now I'll do't, [*he draws his sword*] and so a' goes to
        heaven,
And so am I revenged. That would be scanned:
A villain kills my father, and for that
I his sole son do this same villain send
To heaven....
†Why, this is bait and salary, not revenge.
A' took my father grossly, full of bread,   80
With all his crimes broad blown, as flush as May,
And how his audit stands who knows save heaven?
But in our circumstance and course of thought,
'Tis heavy with him: and am I then revenged
To take him in the purging of his soul,

When he is fit and seasoned for his passage?

No.   [*he sheathes his sword*

Up, sword, and know thou a more horrid hent,

When he is drunk asleep, or in his rage,

90 Or in th'incestuous pleasure of his bed,

At game, a-swearing, or about some act

That has no relish of salvation in't,

Then trip him that his heels may kick at heaven,

And that his soul may be as damned and black

As hell whereto it goes; my mother stays,

This physic but prolongs thy sickly days. [*he passes on*

   King [*rises*]. My words fly up, my thoughts

       remain below.

Words without thoughts never to heaven go.   [*he goes*

[3. 4.]   *The Queen's closet hung with arras, and with*
portraits of King Hamlet and Claudius upon one wall;
seats and a couch

The QUEEN *and* POLONIUS

Polonius. A' will come straight. Look you lay home
   to him,

Tell him his pranks have been too broad to bear with,

And that your grace hath screened and stood between

Much heat and him. I'll silence me even here—

Pray you be round with him.

   Hamlet [*without*]. Mother, mother, mother!

   Queen.   I'll war'nt you,

Fear me not. Withdraw, I hear him coming.

               [*Polonius hides behind the arras*

HAMLET *enters*

   Hamlet. Now, mother, what's the matter?

   Queen.   Hamlet, thou hast thy father much offended.

Hamlet. Mother, you have my father much offended. 10
Queen. Come, come, you answer with an
    idle tongue.
Hamlet. Go, go, you question with a wicked tongue.
Queen. Why, how now, Hamlet?
Hamlet.   What's the matter now?
Queen. Have you forgot me?
Hamlet.   No, by the rood not so,
You are the queen, your husband's brother's wife,
And would it were not so, you are my mother.
Queen. Nay then, I'll set those to you that can speak.
                                      [*going*
Hamlet [*seizes her arm*]. Come, come, and sit you
    down, you shall not budge,
You go not till I set you up a glass
Where you may see the inmost part of you.   20
Queen. What wilt thou do? thou wilt not murder me?
Help, help, ho!
Polonius [*behind the arras*]. What, ho! help,
    help, help!
Hamlet [*draws*]. How now! a rat? dead, for a
    ducat, dead.   [*he makes a pass through the arras*
Polonius [*falls*]. O, I am slain!
Queen. O me, what hast thou done?
Hamlet.   Nay, I know not,
Is it the king?
     [*he lifts up the arras and discovers Polonius, dead*
Queen. O what a rash and bloody deed is this!
Hamlet. A bloody deed—almost as bad, good mother,
As kill a king, and marry with his brother.
Queen. As kill a king!
Hamlet.   Ay, lady, it was my word....   30
[*to Polonius*] Thou wretched, rash, intruding
    fool, farewell!

I took thee for thy better, take thy fortune,
Thou find'st to be too busy is some danger.

                       [*he turns back, dropping the arras*

Leave wringing of your hands, peace, sit you down,
And let me wring your heart, for so I shall
If it be made of penetrable stuff,
If damnéd custom have not brassed it so,
That it be proof and bulwark against sense.

    Queen. What have I done, that thou dar'st wag
       thy tongue
40 In noise so rude against me?

    Hamlet.   Such an act
That blurs the grace and blush of modesty,
Calls virtue hypocrite, takes off the rose
From the fair forehead of an innocent love
And sets a blister there, makes marriage vows
As false as dicers' oaths, O such a deed
As from the body of contraction plucks
The very soul, and sweet religion makes
A rhapsody of words; heaven's face does glow,
†And this solidity and compound mass
50 With heated visage, as against the doom,
Is thought-sick at the act.

    Queen.   Ay me, what act,
That roars so loud, and thunders in the index?

    Hamlet [*leads her to the portraits on the wall*]. Look
       here, upon this picture, and on this,
The counterfeit presentment of two brothers.
See what a grace was seated on this brow—
Hyperion's curls, the front of Jove himself,
An eye like Mars to threaten and command,
A station like the herald Mercury,
New-lighted on a heaven-kissing hill,
60 A combination and a form indeed,

Where every god did seem to set his seal
To give the world assurance of a man.
This was your husband—Look you now what follows.
Here is your husband, like a mildewed ear,
Blasting his wholesome brother. Have you eyes?
Could you on this fair mountain leave to feed,
And batten on this moor? ha! have you eyes?
You cannot call it love, for at your age
The hey-day in the blood is tame, it's humble,
And waits upon the judgement, and what judgement   70
Would step from this to this? Sense sure you have
Else could you not have motion, but sure that sense
Is apoplexed, for madness would not err,
Nor sense to ecstasy was ne'er so thralled,
But it reserved some quantity of choice
To serve in such a difference. What devil was't
That thus hath cozened you at hoodman-blind?
Eyes without feeling, feeling without sight,
Ears without hands or eyes, smelling sans all,
Or but a sickly part of one true sense   80
Could not so mope: O shame, where is thy blush?
Rebellious hell,
If thou canst mutine in a matron's bones,
To flaming youth let virtue be as wax
And melt in her own fire. Proclaim no shame
When the compulsive ardour gives the charge,
Since frost itself as actively doth burn,
And reason pandars will.

  Queen.   O Hamlet, speak no more.
Thou turn'st my eyes into my very soul,
And there I see such black and grainéd spots   90
As will not leave their tinct.

  Hamlet.   Nay, but to live
In the rank sweat of an enseaméd bed

Stewed in corruption, honeying, and making love
Over the nasty sty—
   Queen.   O speak to me no more,
These words like daggers enter in mine ears,
No more, sweet Hamlet.
   Hamlet.   A murderer and a villain,
A slave that is not twentieth part the tithe
Of your precedent lord, a vice of kings,
A cutpurse of the empire and the rule,
100 That from a shelf the precious diadem stole
And put it in his pocket—
   Queen.   No more.
   Hamlet. A king of shreds and patches—

       '*Enter the* GHOST *in his night-gown*'

Save me and hover o'er me with your wings,
You heavenly guards!—What would your gracious
      figure?
   Queen. Alas, he's mad.
   Hamlet. Do you not come your tardy son to chide,
That lapsed in time and passion lets go by
Th'important acting of your dread command?
O, say!
110   *Ghost.* Do not forget! this visitation
Is but to whet thy almost blunted purpose—
But look, amazement on thy mother sits,
O step between her and her fighting soul,
Conceit in weakest bodies strongest works,
Speak to her, Hamlet.
   Hamlet.   How is it with you, lady?
   Queen. Alas, how is't with you,
That you do bend your eye on vacancy,
And with th'incorporal air do hold discourse?
Forth at your eyes your spirits wildly peep,
120 And as the sleeping soldiers in th'alarm,

Your bedded hairs like life in excrements
Start up and stand an end. O gentle son,
Upon the heat and flame of thy distemper
Sprinkle cool patience. Whereon do you look?
  Hamlet. On him! on him! Look you, how pale
        he glares!
His form and cause conjoined, preaching to stones,
Would make them capable. Do not look upon me,
Lest with this piteous action you convert
My stern effects, then what I have to do
Will want true colour, tears perchance for blood.   130
  Queen. To whom do you speak this?
  Hamlet.   Do you see nothing there?
  Queen. Nothing at all, yet all that is I see.
  Hamlet. Nor did you nothing hear?
  Queen.   No, nothing but ourselves.
  Hamlet. Why, look you there! look how it
        steals away!
My father in his habit as he lived,
Look where he goes, even now, out at the portal.
                              [*the Ghost vanishes*
  Queen. This is the very coinage of your brain!
This bodiless creation ecstasy
Is very cunning in.
  Hamlet.   Ecstasy!
My pulse as yours doth temperately keep time,   140
And makes as healthful music—it is not madness
That I have uttered, bring me to the test
And I the matter will re-word, which madness
Would gambol from. Mother, for love of grace,
Lay not that flattering unction to your soul,
That not your trespass but my madness speaks,
It will but skin and film the ulcerous place,
Whiles rank corruption mining all within
Infects unseen. Confess yourself to heaven,

150 Repent what's past, avoid what is to come,
And do not spread the compost on the weeds
To make them ranker. Forgive me this my virtue,
For in the fatness of these pursy times
Virtue itself of vice must pardon beg,
Yea curb and woo for leave to do him good.
   Queen. O Hamlet, thou hast cleft my heart in
      twain.
   Hamlet. O throw away the worser part of it,
And live the purer with the other half.
Good night, but go not to my uncle's bed,
160 Assume a virtue if you have it not.
That monster custom, who all sense doth eat
†Of habits evil, is angel yet in this,
That to the use of actions fair and good
He likewise gives a frock or livery
That aptly is put on. Refrain to-night,
And that shall lend a kind of easiness
To the next abstinence, the next more easy:
For use almost can change the stamp of nature,
†And either...the devil, or throw him out,
170 With wondrous potency: once more, good night,
And when you are desirous to be blessed,
I'll blessing beg of you. For this same lord,
                     [*pointing to Polonius*
I do repent; but heaven hath pleased it so,
To punish me with this, and this with me,
That I must be their scourge and minister.
I will bestow him and will answer well
The death I gave him; so, again, good night.
I must be cruel only to be kind.
This bad begins, and worse remains behind....
                   [*he makes to go, but returns*
180 One word more, good lady.

Queen.   What shall I do?
  Hamlet. Not this by no means that I bid you do—
Let the bloat king tempt you again to bed,
Pinch wanton on your cheek, call you his mouse,
And let him for a pair of reechy kisses,
Or paddling in your neck with his damned fingers,
Make you to ravel all this matter out
That I essentially am not in madness,
But mad in craft. 'Twere good you let him know,
For who that's but a queen, fair, sober, wise,
Would from a paddock, from a bat, a gib,   190
Such dear concernings hide? who would do so?
No, in despite of sense and secrecy,
Unpeg the basket on the house's top,
Let the birds fly, and like the famous ape,
To try conclusions in the basket creep,
And break your own neck down.
  Queen. Be thou assured, if words be made of breath,
And breath of life, I have no life to breathe
What thou hast said to me.
  Hamlet. I must to England, you know that?
  Queen.   Alack,   200
I had forgot, 'tis so concluded on.
  Hamlet. There's letters sealed, and my two
       school-fellows,
Whom I will trust as I will adders fanged,
They bear the mandate—they must sweep my way
And marshal me to knavery: let it work,
For 'tis the sport to have the enginer
Hoist with his own petar, and't shall go hard
But I will delve one yard below their mines,
And blow them at the moon: O, 'tis most sweet
When in one line two crafts directly meet.   210
This man shall set me packing,

I'll lug the guts into the neighbour room;
Mother, good night indeed. This counsellor
Is now most still, most secret, and most grave,
Who was in life a foolish prating knave....
Come, sir, to draw toward an end with you....
Good night, mother.
> [*he drags the body from the room; the Queen*
> *casts herself sobbing upon the couch*

[4. 1.] *After a short while the* KING *enters with*
ROSENCRANTZ *and* GUILDENSTERN

King [*raises her*]. There's matter in these sighs, these
     profound heaves,
You must translate, 'tis fit we understand them.
Where is your son?
Queen. Bestow this place on us a little while....
> [*Rosencrantz and Guildenstern depart*

Ah, mine own lord, what have I seen to-night!
King. What, Gertrude? how does Hamlet?
Queen. Mad as the sea and wind when both contend
Which is the mightier—in his lawless fit,
Behind the arras hearing something stir,
10 Whips out his rapier, cries 'A rat, a rat!'
And in this brainish apprehension kills
The unseen good old man.
King.   O heavy deed!
It had been so with us had we been there.
His liberty is full of threats to all,
To you yourself, to us, to every one.
Alas, how shall this bloody deed be answered?
It will be laid to us, whose providence
Should have kept short, restrained, and out of haunt
This mad young man; but so much was our love,

We would not understand what was most fit,   20
But like the owner of a foul disease,
To keep it from divulging, let it feed
Even on the pith of life: where is he gone?
  Queen. To draw apart the body he hath killed,
O'er whom his very madness, like some ore
Among a mineral of metals base,
Shows itself pure—a' weeps for what is done.
  King. O, Gertrude, come away!
The sun no sooner shall the mountains touch,
But we will ship him hence, and this vile deed   30
We must with all our majesty and skill
Both countenance and excuse. Ho! Guildenstern!

ROSENCRANTZ and GUILDENSTERN return

Friends both, go join you with some further aid—
Hamlet in madness hath Polonius slain,
And from his mother's closet hath he dragged him—
Go, seek him out, speak fair, and bring the body
Into the chapel; I pray you, haste in this.   [*they go*
Come, Gertrude, we'll call up our wisest friends,
And let them know both what we mean to do
And what's untimely done: [so haply slander,]   40
Whose whisper o'er the world's diameter,
As level as the cannon to his blank
Transports his poisoned shot, may miss our name,
And hit the woundless air. O, come away!
My soul is full of discord and dismay.   [*they go*

[4. 2.]   *Another room of the castle*

HAMLET enters

  Hamlet. Safely stowed.
  Calling without. Hamlet! Lord Hamlet!

Hamlet. But soft, what noise, who calls on Hamlet?
O, here they come!

*ROSENCRANTZ and GUILDENSTERN enter in
haste, with a guard*

Rosencrantz. What have you done, my lord, with the
dead body?

Hamlet. Compounded it with dust whereto 'tis kin.

Rosencrantz. Tell us where 'tis that we may take
it thence,

And bear it to the chapel.

Hamlet. Do not believe it.

10 *Rosencrantz.* Believe what?

Hamlet. That I can keep your counsel and not mine
own. Besides, to be demanded of a sponge, what replication should be made by the son of a king?

Rosencrantz. Take you me for a sponge, my lord?

Hamlet. Ay, sir, that soaks up the king's countenance,
his rewards, his authorities. But such officers do the
king best service in the end, he keeps them like an apple
in the corner of his jaw, first mouthed to be last swallowed—when he needs what you have gleaned, it is but
20 squeezing you, and, sponge, you shall be dry again.

Rosencrantz. I understand you not, my lord.

Hamlet. I am glad of it—a knavish speech sleeps in a
foolish ear.

Rosencrantz. My lord, you must tell us where the
body is, and go with us to the king.

Hamlet. The body is with the king, but the king is
not with the body. The king is a thing——

Guildenstern. A thing, my lord!

Hamlet. Of nothing, bring me to him. Hide fox, and
30 all after. [*he runs out; they pursue with the guard*

[4. 3.] *The hall of the castle, as before*

The KING seated at a table on the dais with 'two or three' councillors of state

King. I have sent to seek him, and to find the body.
How dangerous is it that this man goes loose!
Yet must not we put the strong law on him,
He's loved of the distracted multitude,
Who like not in their judgement but their eyes,
And where 'tis so, th'offender's scourge is weighed
But never the offence: to bear all smooth and even,
This sudden sending him away must seem
Deliberate pause. Diseases desperate grown
By desperate appliance are relieved, 10
Or not at all.

ROSENCRANTZ, GUILDENSTERN and others enter

How now! what hath befallen?
Rosencrantz. Where the dead body is bestowed, my lord,
We cannot get from him.
King. But where is he?
Rosencrantz. Without, my lord, guarded, to know your pleasure.
King. Bring him before us.
Rosencrantz. Ho! bring in the lord.

HAMLET enters guarded by soldiers

King. Now, Hamlet, where's Polonius?
Hamlet. At supper.
King. At supper? where?
Hamlet. Not where he eats, but where a' is eaten—
a certain convocation of politic worms are e'en at him: 20
your worm is your only emperor for diet, we fat all

creatures else to fat us, and we fat ourselves for maggots. Your fat king and your lean beggar is but variable service, two dishes, but to one table—that's the end.

King. Alas, alas!

Hamlet. A man may fish with the worm that hath eat of a king, and eat of the fish that hath fed of that worm.

King. What dost thou mean by this?

Hamlet. Nothing, but to show you how a king may go
30 a progress through the guts of a beggar.

King. Where is Polonius?

Hamlet. In heaven—send thither to see, if your messenger find him not there, seek him i'th'other place yourself. But if indeed you find him not within this month, you shall nose him as you go up the stairs into the lobby.

King [*to attendants*]. Go seek him there.

Hamlet. A' will stay till you come.   [*they depart*

King. Hamlet, this deed, for thine especial safety,
40 Which we do tender, as we dearly grieve
For that which thou hast done, must send thee hence
With fiery quickness. Therefore prepare thyself,
The bark is ready, and the wind at help,
Th'associates tend, and every thing is bent
For England.

Hamlet.   For England.

King.   Ay, Hamlet.

Hamlet.   Good.

King. So is it if thou knew'st our purposes.

Hamlet. I see a cherub that sees them. But, come, for England! [*he bows*] Farewell, dear mother.

King. Thy loving father, Hamlet.

50 *Hamlet.* My mother—father and mother is man and wife, man and wife is one flesh, and so my mother: [*he turns to his guards*] come, for England!   [*they go*

King [*to Rosencrantz and Guildenstern*]. Follow him
　　at foot, tempt him with speed aboard,
Delay it not, I'll have him hence to-night.
Away! for every thing is sealed and done
That else leans on th'affair—pray you, make haste....
　　　　　　　　　　　　　[*all depart save the King*
And, England, if my love thou hold'st at aught—
As my great power thereof may give thee sense,
Since yet thy cicatrice looks raw and red
After the Danish sword, and thy free awe　　　　　　　60
Pays homage to us—thou mayst not coldly set
Our sovereign process, which imports at full
By letters congruing to that effect,
The present death of Hamlet. Do it, England,
For like the hectic in my blood he rages,
And thou must cure me; till I know 'tis done,
Howe'er my haps, my joys were ne'er begun. [*he goes*

[4. 4.]　　*A plain near to a port in Denmark*

　　Prince FORTINBRAS, *with his army on the march*

Fortinbras. Go, captain, from me greet the
　　Danish king,
Tell him that by his license Fortinbras
Craves the conveyance of a promised march
Over his kingdom. You know the rendezvous.
If that his majesty would aught with us,
We shall express our duty in his eye,
And let him know so.
　　Captain.　　　　　　　I will do't, my lord.
　　　　　　　　　　　　　　　[*he turns one way*
　　Fortinbras [*to the troops*]. Go softly on.
　　　　　　　　[*Fortinbras and the army go forward
　　　　　　　　another way*

The Captain meets HAMLET, ROSENCRANTZ, GUIL-
DENSTERN *and the guard on their road to port*

Hamlet. Good sir, whose powers are these?
10 *Captain.* They are of Norway, sir.
Hamlet. How purposed, sir, I pray you?
Captain. Against some part of Poland.
Hamlet. Who commands them, sir?
Captain. The nephew to old Norway, Fortinbras.
Hamlet. Goes it against the main of Poland, sir,
Or for some frontier?
Captain. Truly to speak, and with no addition,
We go to gain a little patch of ground
That hath in it no profit but the name.
20 To pay five ducats, five, I would not farm it;
Nor will it yield to Norway or the Pole
A ranker rate should it be sold in fee.
Hamlet. Why, then the Polack never will defend it.
Captain. Yes, 'tis already garrisoned.
Hamlet. Two thousand souls and twenty
         thousand ducats
Will not debate the question of this straw!
This is th'imposthume of much wealth and peace,
That inward breaks, and shows no cause without
Why the man dies....I humbly thank you, sir.
30 *Captain.* God bye you, sir.   [*he goes*
Rosencrantz.   Will't please you go, my lord?
Hamlet. I'll be with you straight, go a little before....
       [*Rosencrantz, Guildenstern and the rest pass on*
How all occasions do inform against me,
And spur my dull revenge! What is a man,
If his chief good and market of his time
Be but to sleep and feed? a beast, no more:
Sure he that made us with such large discourse,

Looking before and after, gave us not
That capability and god-like reason
To fust in us unused. Now, whether it be
Bestial oblivion, or some craven scruple   40
Of thinking too precisely on th'event—
A thought which quartered hath but one
   part wisdom,
And ever three parts coward—I do not know
Why yet I live to say 'This thing's to do,'
Sith I have cause, and will, and strength, and means,
To do't...Examples gross as earth exhort me.
Witness this army of such mass and charge,
Led by a delicate and tender prince,
Whose spirit with divine ambition puffed
Makes mouths at the invisible event,   50
Exposing what is mortal and unsure
To all that fortune, death and danger dare,
Even for an egg-shell....Rightly to be great
Is not to stir without great argument,
But greatly to find quarrel in a straw
When honour's at the stake. How stand I then,
That have a father killed, a mother stained,
Excitements of my reason and my blood,
And let all sleep? while to my shame I see
The imminent death of twenty thousand men,   60
That for a fantasy and trick of fame
Go to their graves like beds, fight for a plot
Whereon the numbers cannot try the cause,
Which is not tomb enough and continent
To hide the slain? O, from this time forth,
My thoughts be bloody, or be nothing worth!
        [he follows on

   [Some weeks pass]

[4. 5.]   *A room in the castle of Elsinore*

The QUEEN *with her ladies,* HORATIO *and
a gentleman*

Queen. I will not speak with her.
Gentleman. She is importunate, indeed distract,
Her mood will needs be pitied.
Queen.   What would she have?
Gentleman. She speaks much of her father, says
she hears
There's tricks i'th'world, and hems, and beats her heart,
Spurns enviously at straws, speaks things in doubt
That carry but half sense. Her speech is nothing,
Yet the unshapéd use of it doth move
The hearers to collection—they aim at it,
10 And botch the words up fit to their own thoughts,
Which as her winks and nods and gestures yield them,
Indeed would make one think there might be thought,
Though nothing sure, yet much unhappily.
Horatio. 'Twere good she were spoken with, for she
may strew
Dangerous conjectures in ill-breeding minds.
Queen. Let her come in.   [*the gentleman goes out*
[*aside*] "To my sick soul, as sin's true nature is,
"Each toy seems prologue to some great amiss,
"So full of artless jealousy is guilt,
20 "It spills itself, in fearing to be spilt."

The gentleman returns with OPHELIA, *distracted, a lute
in her hands and her hair about her shoulders*

Ophelia. Where is the beauteous majesty of Denmark?
Queen. How now, Ophelia?
Ophelia [*sings*]. How should I your true love know
From another one?

> By his cockle hat and staff,
> And his sandal shoon.

Queen. Alas, sweet lady, what imports this song?

Ophelia. Say you? nay, pray you mark.

> [*sings*] He is dead and gone, lady,
> He is dead and gone, 30
> At his head a grass-green turf,
> At his heels a stone.

O, ho!

Queen.   Nay, but Ophelia—

Ophelia.   Pray you mark.

> [*sings*] White his shroud as the mountain snow—

The KING enters

Queen. Alas, look here, my lord.

Ophelia [*sings*]. Larded all with sweet flowers,

> Which bewept to the grave did not go,
> With true-love showers.

King. How do you, pretty lady?

Ophelia. Well, God dild you! they say the owl was a 40
baker's daughter. Lord, we know what we are, but
know not what we may be....God be at your table!

King. Conceit upon her father.

Ophelia. Pray you let's have no words of this, but
when they ask you what it means, say you this....

[*sings*]   To-morrow is Saint Valentine's day,
> All in the morning betime,
> And I a maid at your window
> To be your Valentine.

> Then up he rose, and donned his clo'es, 50
> And dupped the chamber door,
> Let in the maid, that out a maid
> Never departed more.

King. Pretty Ophelia!

Ophelia. Indeed, la, without an oath, I'll make an
end on't—

[*sings*]   By Gis and by Saint Charity,
        Alack and fie for shame!
     Young men will do't, if they come to't,
60   By Cock, they are to blame.
     Quoth she, Before you tumbled me,
        You promised me to wed.

(He answers.)
        So would I ha' done, by yonder sun,
        An thou hadst not come to my bed.

King. How long hath she been thus?

Ophelia. I hope all will be well. We must be patient,
but I cannot choose but weep to think they would lay
him i'th'cold ground. My brother shall know of it, and
70 so I thank you for your good counsel. Come, my coach!
Good night, ladies, good night. Sweet ladies, good night,
good night.   [*she goes*

   King. Follow her close, give her good watch, I
     pray you.

             [*Horatio and the gentleman follow her*
O, this is the poison of deep grief, it springs
All from her father's death—and now behold!
O Gertrude, Gertrude,
When sorrows come, they come not single spies,
But in battalions: first her father slain,
Next your son gone, and he most violent author
80 Of his own just remove, the people muddied,
Thick and unwholesome in their thoughts
     and whispers
For good Polonius' death—and we have done
     but greenly,
In hugger-mugger to inter him—poor Ophelia
Divided from herself and her fair judgement,

Without the which we are pictures or mere beasts,
Last, and as much containing as all these,
Her brother is in secret come from France,
Feeds on his wonder, keeps himself in clouds,
And wants not buzzers to infect his ear
With pestilent speeches of his father's death,   90
Wherein necessity, of matter beggared,
Will nothing stick our person to arraign
In ear and ear: O my dear Gertrude, this
Like to a murdering-piece in many places
Gives me superfluous death!   [*a tumult without*
  Queen.   Alack! what noise is this?
  King [*calls*]. Attend!   [*an attendant enters*
Where are my Switzers? let them guard the door.
What is the matter?
  Attendant.   Save yourself, my lord!
The ocean, overpeering of his list,
Eats not the flats with more impiteous haste   100
Than young Laertes in a riotous head
O'erbears your officers: the rabble call him lord,
And as the world were now but to begin,
Antiquity forgot, custom not known,
The ratifiers and props of every word,
They cry 'Choose we, Laertes shall be king!'
Caps, hands, and tongues applaud it to the clouds,
'Laertes shall be king, Laertes king!'
                              [*the shouts grow louder*
  Queen. How cheerfully on the false trail they cry!
O, this is counter, you false Danish dogs!   110
  King. The doors are broke.

        LAERTES, *armed, bursts into the room*
               with Danes following

Laertes. Where is this king? Sirs, stand you all without.

Danes. No, let's come in.

Laertes.   I pray you, give me leave.

Danes. We will, we will.

                              [*they retire without the door*

Laertes. I thank you, keep the door. O thou vile king,
Give me my father.

Queen.   Calmly, good Laertes.

Laertes. That drop of blood that's calm proclaims
     me bastard,
Cries cuckold to my father, brands the harlot,
Even here, between the chaste unsmirchéd brows
120 Of my true mother.

                         [*he advances upon them; the Queen
                              throws herself in his path*

  King.   What is the cause, Laertes,
That thy rebellion looks so giant-like?
Let him go Gertrude, do not fear our person,
There's such divinity doth hedge a king,
That treason can but peep to what it would,
Acts little of his will. Tell me, Laertes,
Why thou art thus incensed—let him go, Gertrude—
Speak, man.

  Laertes. Where is my father?

  King.   Dead.

  Queen.   But not by him.

  King. Let him demand his fill.

130 *Laertes.* How came he dead? I'll not be juggled with
To hell allegiance, vows to the blackest devil,
Conscience and grace to the profoundest pit!
I dare damnation. To this point I stand,
That both the worlds I give to negligence,
Let come what comes, only I'll be revenged
Most throughly for my father.

  King.   Who shall stay you

Laertes. My will, not all the world's:
And for my means, I'll husband them so well,
They shall go far with little.
  King.   Good Laertes,
If you desire to know the certainty   140
Of your dear father, is't writ in your revenge,
That, sweepstake, you will draw both friend
          and foe,
Winner and loser?
  Laertes. None but his enemies.
  King.   Will you know them then?
  Laertes. To his good friends thus wide I'll ope
          my arms,
And like the kind life-rend'ring pelican,
Repast them with my blood.
  King.   Why, now you speak
Like a good child and a true gentleman.
That I am guiltless of your father's death,
And am most sensibly in grief for it,   150
It shall as level to your judgement 'pear,
As day does to your eye.
  Shouting without.   Let her come in.
  Laertes. How now! what noise is that?

        OPHELIA re-enters with flowers in her hand

O heat, dry up my brains, tears seven times salt,
Burn out the sense and virtue of mine eye!
By heaven, thy madness shall be paid with weight,
Till our scale turn the beam. O rose of May,
Dear maid, kind sister, sweet Ophelia!
O heavens, is't possible a young maid's wits
Should be as mortal as an old man's life?   160
Nature is fine in love, and where 'tis fine,

It sends some precious instance of itself
After the thing it loves.

  Ophelia [*sings*].

        They bore him barefaced on the bier,
        Hey non nonny, nonny, hey nonny,
        And in his grave rained many a tear—

Fare you well, my dove!

  Laertes. Hadst thou thy wits, and didst persuade
      revenge,

It could not move thus.

170 *Ophelia.* You must sing, 'Adown adown,' an you call him adown-a. O, how the wheel becomes it! It is the false steward that stole his master's daughter.

  Laertes. This nothing's more than matter.

  Ophelia [*to Laertes*]. There's rosemary, that's for remembrance—pray you, love, remember—and there is pansies, that's for thoughts.

  Laertes. A document in madness, thoughts and remembrance fitted.

  Ophelia. [*to the King*] There's fennel for you, and 180 columbines. [*to the Queen*] There's rue for you, and here's some for me, we may call it herb of grace o'Sundays—O, you must wear your rue with a difference. There's a daisy. I would give you some violets, but they withered all, when my father died—they say a' made a good end——

[*sings*]   For bonny sweet Robin is all my joy—

  Laertes. Thought and affliction, passion, hell itself,
She turns to favour and to prettiness.

  Ophelia [*sings*]. And will a' not come again?
190   And will a' not come again?
                 No, no, he is dead,
                 Go to thy death-bed,
              He never will come again.

His beard was as white as snow,
All flaxen was his poll,
    He is gone, he is gone,
    And we cast away moan,
    God ha' mercy on his soul!—
And of all Christian souls I pray God. God bye you.

                                       [she goes

Laertes. Do you see this, O God?   200
  King. Laertes, I must commune with your grief,
Or you deny me right. Go but apart,
Make choice of whom your wisest friends you will,
And they shall hear and judge 'twixt you and me.
If by direct or by collateral hand
They find us touched, we will our kingdom give,
Our crown, our life, and all that we call ours,
To you in satisfaction; but if not,
Be you content to lend your patience to us,
And we shall jointly labour with your soul   210
To give it due content.
  Laertes.   Let this be so.
His means of death, his obscure funeral,
No trophy, sword, nor hatchment o'er his bones,
No noble rite, nor formal ostentation,
Cry to be heard as 'twere from heaven to earth,
That I must call't in question.
  King.   So you shall,
And where th'offence is let the great axe fall.
I pray you, go with me.   *[they go*

[4. 6.]   '*Horatio and others*' enter

  Horatio. What are they that would speak with me?
  Gentleman. Seafaring men, sir. They say they have
letters for you.

Horatio. Let them come in.   [*an attendant goes out*
[*aside*] I do not know from what part of the world
I should be greeted, if not from Lord Hamlet.

The attendant brings in sailors

1 *Sailor.* God bless you, sir.
Horatio. Let him bless thee too.
1 *Sailor.* A' shall, sir, an't please him. There's a letter
10 for you, sir, it came from th'ambassador that was bound
for England, if your name be Horatio, as I am let to
know it is.

(*Horatio* [*turns aside and reads*]. 'Horatio, when thou
shalt have overlooked this, give these fellows some
means to the king, they have letters for him...Ere we
were two days old at sea, a pirate of very warlike appointment gave us chase. Finding ourselves too slow of
sail, we put on a compelled valour, and in the grapple I
boarded them. On the instant they got clear of our ship,
20 so I alone became their prisoner. They have dealt with
me like thieves of mercy, but they knew what they did.
I am to do a good turn for them. Let the king have the
letters I have sent, and repair thou to me with as much
speed as thou wouldest fly death. I have words to speak
in thine ear will make thee dumb, yet are they much too
light for the bore of the matter. These good fellows will
bring thee where I am. Rosencrantz and Guildenstern
hold their course for England—of them I have much to
tell thee. Farewell.

30   He that thou knowest thine, HAMLET.'
Come, I will give you way for these your letters,
And do't the speedier that you may direct me
To him from whom you brought them.   [*they go*

[4. 7.]   *The KING and LAERTES return*

King. Now must your conscience my acquittance seal,
And you must put me in your heart for friend,
Sith you have heard and with a knowing ear
That he which hath your noble father slain
Pursued my life.
   Laertes.   It well appears: but tell me,
Why you proceeded not against these feats,
So crimeful and so capital in nature,
As by your safety, greatness, wisdom, all things else,
You mainly were stirred up.
   King.   O, for two special reasons,
Which may to you perhaps seem much unsinewed,   10
But yet to me they're strong. The queen his mother
Lives almost by his looks, and for myself,
My virtue or my plague, be it either which,
She is so conjunctive to my life and soul,
That as the star moves not but in his sphere
I could not but by her. The other motive,
Why to a public count I might not go,
Is the great love the general gender bear him,
Who dipping all his faults in their affection,
Would like the spring that turneth wood to stone,   20
Convert his gyves to graces, so that my arrows,
Too slightly timbered for so loud a wind,
Would have reverted to my bow again,
And not where I had aimed them.
   Laertes. And so have I a noble father lost,
A sister driven into desperate terms,
Whose worth, if praises may go back again,
Stood challenger on mount of all the age
For her perfections. But my revenge will come.

30 *King.* Break not your sleeps for that, you must
    not think
That we are made of stuff so flat and dull,
That we can let our beard be shook with danger
And think it pastime. You shortly shall hear more.
I loved your father, and we love ourself,
And that I hope will teach you to imagine—

      '*Enter a* MESSENGER *with letters*'

How now! what news?
  Messenger.   Letters, my lord, from Hamlet.
These to your majesty, these to the queen.
  King. From Hamlet! who brought them?
  Messenger. Sailors, my lord, they say, I saw them not.
40 They were given me by Claudio, he received them
Of him that brought them.
  King.   Laertes, you shall hear them...
Leave us.   [*the Messenger goes*
  [*reads*] 'High and mighty, you shall know I am set
naked on your kingdom. To-morrow shall I beg leave
to see your kingly eyes, when I shall, first asking your
pardon thereunto, recount the occasion of my sudden
and more strange return.   HAMLET.'
What should this mean? are all the rest come back?
Or is it some abuse, and no such thing?

50 *Laertes.* Know you the hand?
  King.   'Tis Hamlet's character....'Naked'—
And in a postscript here he says 'alone.'
Can you devise me?
  Laertes. I am lost in it, my lord, but let him come!
It warms the very sickness in my heart
That I shall live and tell him to his teeth
'Thus diest thou.'
  King.   If it be so, Laertes,—

As how should it be so? how otherwise?—
Will you be ruled by me?
  Laertes.   Ay, my lord,
So you will not o'errule me to a peace.
  King. To thine own peace. If he be now returned,   60
As checking at his voyage, and that he means
No more to undertake it, I will work him
To an exploit, now ripe in my device,
Under the which he shall not choose but fall:
And for his death no wind of blame shall breathe,
But even his mother shall uncharge the practice,
And call it accident.
  Laertes.   My lord, I will be ruled,
The rather if you could devise it so
That I might be the organ.
  King.   It falls right.
You have been talked of since your travel much,   70
And that in Hamlet's hearing, for a quality
Wherein they say you shine. Your sum of parts
Did not together pluck such envy from him,
As did that one, and that in my regard
Of the unworthiest siege.
  Laertes.   What part is that, my lord?
  King. A very riband in the cap of youth,
Yet needful too, for youth no less becomes
The light and careless livery that it wears,
Than settled age his sables and his weeds
Importing health and graveness; two months since,   80
Here was a gentleman of Normandy—
I have seen myself, and served against, the French,
And they can well on horseback—but this gallant
Had witchcraft in't, he grew unto his seat,
And to such wondrous doing brought his horse,
As had he been incorpsed and demi-natured

With the brave beast. So far he topped my thought,
That I in forgery of shapes and tricks
Come short of what he did.

   Laertes.   A Norman, was't?

90   *King.* A Norman.

   Laertes. Upon my life, Lamord.

   King.   The very same.

   Laertes. I know him well, he is the brooch indeed
And gem of all the nation.

   King. He made confession of you,
And gave you such a masterly report
For art and exercise in your defence,
And for your rapier most especial,
That he cried out 'twould be a sight indeed
If one could match you; the scrimers of their nation
100 He swore had neither motion, guard, nor eye,
If you opposed them; sir, this report of his
Did Hamlet so envenom with his envy,
That he could nothing do but wish and beg
Your sudden coming o'er to play with him.
Now, out of this—

   Laertes.   What out of this, my lord?

   King. Laertes, was your father dear to you?
Or are you like the painting of a sorrow,
A face without a heart?

   Laertes.   Why ask you this?

   King. Not that I think you did not love your father,
110 But that I know love is begun by time,
And that I see in passages of proof
Time qualifies the spark and fire of it.
There lives within the very flame of love
A kind of wick or snuff that will abate it,
And nothing is at a like goodness still,
For goodness, growing to a plurisy,

Dies in his own too-much. That we would do
We should do when we would: for this 'would' changes,
And hath abatements and delays as many
As there are tongues, are hands, are accidents,   120
And then this 'should' is like a spendthrift sigh,
That hurts by easing; but to the quick o'th'ulcer—
Hamlet comes back, what would you undertake
To show yourself your father's son in deed
More than in words?
 Laertes.   To cut his throat i'th'church.
 King. No place indeed should murder sanctuarize,
Revenge should have no bounds: but, good Laertes,
Will you do this, keep close within your chamber.
Hamlet returned shall know you are come home.
We'll put on those shall praise your excellence,   130
And set a double varnish on the fame
The Frenchman gave you, bring you in fine together,
And wager on your heads; he being remiss,
Most generous, and free from all contriving,
Will not peruse the foils, so that with ease,
Or with a little shuffling, you may choose
A sword unbated, and in a pass of practice
Requite him for your father.
 Laertes.   I will do't,
And, for the purpose, I'll anoint my sword.
I bought an unction of a mountebank,   140
So mortal, that but dip a knife in it,
Where it draws blood, no cataplasm so rare,
Collected from all simples that have virtue
Under the moon, can save the thing from death
That is but scratched withal. I'll touch my point
With this contagion, that if I gall him slightly,
It may be death.
 King.   Let's further think of this,

Weigh what convenience both of time and means
May fit us to our shape. If this should fail,
150 And that our drift look through our bad performance,
'Twere better not assayed. Therefore this project
Should have a back or second that might hold,
If this did blast in proof; soft, let me see,
We'll make a solemn wager on your cunnings—
I ha't!
When in your motion you are hot and dry,
As make your bouts more violent to that end,
And that he calls for drink, I'll have preferred him
A chalice for the nonce, whereon but sipping,
160 If he by chance escape your venomed stuck,
Our purpose may hold there...But stay, what noise?

The QUEEN *enters weeping*

Queen. One woe doth tread upon another's heel,
So fast they follow; your sister's drowned, Laertes.
Laertes. Drowned! O, where?
Queen. There is a willow grows askant the brook,
That shows his hoar leaves in the glassy stream,
Therewith fantastic garlands did she make
Of crow-flowers, nettles, daisies, and long purples
That liberal shepherds give a grosser name,
170 But our cold maids do dead men's fingers call them.
There on the pendent boughs her crownet weeds
Clamb'ring to hang, an envious sliver broke,
When down her weedy trophies and herself
Fell in the weeping brook. Her clothes spread wide,
And mermaid-like awhile they bore her up,
Which time she chanted snatches of old lauds,
As one incapable of her own distress,
Or like a creature native and indued

Unto that element. But long it could not be
Till that her garments, heavy with their drink,   180
Pulled the poor wretch from her melodious lay
To muddy death.
 Laertes.   Alas then, she is drowned?
 Queen. Drowned, drowned.
 Laertes. Too much of water hast thou, poor Ophelia,
And therefore I forbid my tears; but yet
It is our trick, nature her custom holds,
Let shame say what it will—when these are gone,
The woman will be out....Adieu, my lord!
I have a speech o' fire that fain would blaze,
But that this folly douts it.   [*he goes*
 King.   Let's follow, Gertrude.   190
How much I had to do to calm his rage!
Now fear I this will give it start again,
Therefore let's follow.   [*they follow*

[5. 1.] *A graveyard, with a newly opened grave;
cypress-trees, and a gate*

*Two clowns (a sexton and his mate) enter with spades
and mattocks; they make them ready to dig*

 1 *Clown.* Is she to be buried in Christian burial when
she wilfully seeks her own salvation?

 2 *Clown.* I tell thee she is, therefore make her grave
straight. The crowner hath sat on her, and finds it
Christian burial.

 1 *Clown.* How can that be, unless she drowned herself
in her own defence?

 2 *Clown.* Why, 'tis found so.

 1 *Clown.* It must be 'se offendendo,' it cannot be else.

10 For here lies the point, if I drown myself wittingly, it argues an act, and an act hath three branches, it is to act, to do, and to perform—argal, she drowned herself wittingly.

2 *Clown.* Nay, but hear you, goodman delver.

1 *Clown.* Give me leave. Here lies the water—good. Here stands the man—good. If the man go to this water and drown himself, it is, will he nill he, he goes, mark you that. But if the water come to him, and drown him, he drowns not himself—argal, he that is not guilty of his 20 own death, shortens not his own life.

2 *Clown.* But is this law?

1 *Clown.* Ay, marry is't, crowner's quest law.

2 *Clown.* Will you ha' the truth an't? if this had not been a gentlewoman, she should have been buried out a Christian burial.

1 *Clown.* Why, there thou say'st, and the more pity that great folk should have countenance in this world to drown or hang themselves more than their even-Christen...Come, my spade! there is no ancient gentle-30 men but gardeners, ditchers and grave-makers—they hold up Adam's profession.

> [*he goes down into the open grave*

2 *Clown.* Was he a gentleman?

1 *Clown.* A' was the first that ever bore arms.

2 *Clown.* Why, he had none.

1 *Clown.* What, art a heathen? how dost thou understand the Scripture? the Scripture says Adam digged; could he dig without arms? I'll put another question to thee. If thou answerest me not to the purpose, confess thyself—

40 2 *Clown.* Go to.

1 *Clown.* What is he that builds stronger than either the mason, the shipwright, or the carpenter?

2 *Clown.* The gallows-maker, for that frame outlives a thousand tenants.

1 *Clown.* I like thy wit well in good faith, the gallows does well—but how does it well? it does well to those that do ill. Now thou dost ill to say the gallows is built stronger than the church—argal, the gallows may do well to thee. To't again, come.

2 *Clown.* 'Who builds stronger than a mason, a ship- 50 wright, or a carpenter?'

1 *Clown.* Ay, tell me that, and unyoke.

2 *Clown.* Marry, now I can tell.

1 *Clown.* To't.

2 *Clown.* Mass, I cannot tell.

1 *Clown.* Cudgel thy brains no more about it, for your dull ass will not mend his pace with beating. And when you are asked this question next, say 'a grave-maker.' The houses he makes lasts till doomsday. Go, get thee to †Yaughan, and fetch me a stoup of liquor.   60

[*Second Clown goes*

HAMLET (*clad in sailor's garb*) *and* HORATIO *are seen entering the graveyard*

First Clown digs and sings

In youth when I did love, did love,
    Methought it was very sweet,
To contract o' the time for a my behove,
    O, methought there a was nothing a meet.

Hamlet. Has this fellow no feeling of his business that a' sings in grave-making?

Horatio. Custom hath made it in him a property of easiness.

Hamlet. 'Tis e'en so, the hand of little employment hath the daintier sense.   70

1 *Clown* [*sings*].

> But age with his stealing steps
> Hath clawed me in his clutch,
> And hath shipped me intil the land,
> As if I had never been such.

[*he throws up a skull*

Hamlet. That skull had a tongue in it, and could sing once! how the knave jowls it to the ground, as if 'twere Cain's jaw-bone, that did the first murder! This might be the pate of a politician, which this ass now o'er-reaches; one that would circumvent God, might it not?

80 *Horatio.* It might, my lord.

Hamlet. Or of a courtier, which could say 'Good morrow, sweet lord! how dost thou, good lord?' This might be my lord such-a-one, that praised my lord such-a-one's horse, when a' meant to beg it, might it not?

Horatio. It might, my lord.

Hamlet. Why, e'en so, and now my Lady Worm's, chopless and knocked about the mazzard with a sexton's spade; here's fine revolution an we had the trick to see't! did these bones cost no more the breeding, but to

90 play at loggats with them? mine ache to think on't.

1 *Clown* [*sings*].

> A pick-axe, and a spade, a spade,
> For and a shrouding sheet,
> O, a pit of clay for to be made
> For such a guest is meet.

[*he throws up a second skull*

Hamlet. There's another. Why may not that be the skull of a lawyer? Where be his quiddities now, his quillities, his cases, his tenures, and his tricks? why does he suffer this rude knave now to knock him about the sconce with a dirty shovel, and will not tell him of his

100 action of battery? [*he takes up the skull*] Hum! this fellow might be in's time a great buyer of land, with his

statutes, his recognizances, his fines, his double vouchers, his recoveries: is this the fine of his fines, and the recovery of his recoveries, to have his fine pate full of fine dirt? will his vouchers vouch him no more of his purchases, and double ones too, than the length and breadth of a pair of indentures? the very conveyances of his lands will scarcely lie in this box, [*he taps the skull*] and must th'inheritor himself have no more, ha?

Horatio. Not a jot more, my lord. 110

Hamlet. Is not parchment made of sheep-skins?

Horatio. Ay, my lord, and of calves'-skins too.

Hamlet. They are sheep and calves which seek out assurance in that. I will speak to this fellow.... [*they go forward*] Whose grave's this, sirrah?

1 *Clown.* Mine, sir—
   [*sings*] O, a pit of clay for to be made
            For such a guest is meet.

Hamlet. I think it be thine, indeed, for thou liest in't.

1 *Clown.* You lie out on't sir, and therefore 'tis not 120 yours; for my part I do not lie in't, and yet it is mine.

Hamlet. Thou dost lie in't, to be in't and say it is thine. 'Tis for the dead, not for the quick—therefore thou liest.

1 *Clown.* 'Tis a quick lie, sir, 'twill away again from me to you.

Hamlet. What man dost thou dig it for?

1 *Clown.* For no man, sir.

Hamlet. What woman then?

1 *Clown.* For none neither.

Hamlet. Who is to be buried in't? 130

1 *Clown.* One that was a woman, sir, but rest her soul she's dead.

Hamlet. How absolute the knave is! we must speak by the card or equivocation will undo us. By the Lord, Horatio, this three years I have took note of it, the age is grown so picked, that the toe of the peasant comes so

near the heel of the courtier he galls his kibe....How
long hast thou been grave-maker?

1 *Clown.* Of all the days i'th'year I came to't that
140 day that our last king Hamlet overcame Fortinbras.

Hamlet. How long is that since?

1 *Clown.* Cannot you tell that? every fool can tell that.
It was that very day that young Hamlet was born: he
that is mad and sent into England.

Hamlet. Ay, marry, why was he sent into England?

1 *Clown.* Why, because a' was mad: a' shall recover
his wits there, or if a' do not, 'tis no great matter there.

Hamlet. Why?

1 *Clown.* 'Twill not be seen in him there, there the
150 men are as mad as he.

Hamlet. How came he mad?

1 *Clown.* Very strangely, they say.

Hamlet. How strangely?

1 *Clown.* Faith, e'en with losing his wits.

Hamlet. Upon what ground?

1 *Clown.* Why, here in Denmark: I have been
sexton here man and boy thirty years.

Hamlet. How long will a man lie i'th'earth ere he rot?

1 *Clown.* Faith, if a' be not rotten before a' die, as we
160 have many pocky corses now-a-days that will scarce hold
the laying in, a' will last you some eight year, or nine
year. A tanner will last you nine year.

Hamlet. Why he more than another?

1 *Clown.* Why sir, his hide is so tanned with his trade,
that a' will keep out water a great while; and your water
is a sore decayer of your whoreson dead body. Here's a
skull now: this skull hath lien you i'th'earth three-and-
twenty years.

Hamlet. Whose was it?

170 1 *Clown.* A whoreson mad fellow's it was, whose do
you think it was?

Hamlet. Nay, I know not.

1 *Clown.* A pestilence on him for a mad rogue! a'
poured a flagon of Rhenish on my head once; this same
skull, sir, was, sir, Yorick's skull, the king's jester.

Hamlet. This?

1 *Clown.* E'en that.

Hamlet. Let me see. [*he takes the skull*] Alas, poor
Yorick! I knew him, Horatio—a fellow of infinite jest,
of most excellent fancy. He hath borne me on his back 180
a thousand times, and now how abhorred in my imagination it is! my gorge rises at it....Here hung those
lips that I have kissed I know not how oft. Where be
your gibes now? your gambols, your songs, your flashes
of merriment, that were wont to set the table on a roar?
not one now to mock your own grinning? quite chop-
fallen? Now get you to my lady's chamber, and tell her,
let her paint an inch thick, to this favour she must come.
Make her laugh at that....Prithee, Horatio, tell me one
thing.   190

Horatio. What's that, my lord.

Hamlet. Dost thou think Alexander looked o' this
fashion i'th'earth?

Horatio. E'en so.

Hamlet. And smelt so? pah! [*he sets down the skull*

Horatio. E'en so, my lord.

Hamlet. To what base uses we may return, Horatio!
Why may not imagination trace the noble dust of
Alexander, till a' find it stopping a bung-hole?

Horatio. 'Twere to consider too curiously, to consider so. 200

Hamlet. No, faith, not a jot, but to follow him thither
with modesty enough, and likelihood to lead it; as
thus—Alexander died, Alexander was buried, Alexander returneth to dust, the dust is earth, of earth we
make loam, and why of that loam whereto he was con-
verted might they not stop a beer-barrel?

Imperious Cæsar, dead and turned to clay,
Might stop a hole to keep the wind away.
O, that that earth, which kept the world in awe,
210   Should patch a wall t'expel the winter's flaw!
But soft, but soft, awhile—here comes the king,
The queen, the courtiers.

A procession enters the graveyard: the corpse of OPHELIA
in an open coffin, with LAERTES, *the* KING, *the* QUEEN,
courtiers and a Doctor of Divinity in cassock and
gown following

                      Who is this they follow?
And with such maiméd rites? This doth betoken
The corse they follow did with desp'rate hand
Fordo it own life. 'Twas of some estate.
Couch we awhile, and mark.

                           [*they sit under a yew*

    Laertes. What ceremony else?
    Hamlet.   That is Laertes,
A very noble youth—mark.
    Laertes. What ceremony else?
220   *Doctor.* Her obsequies have been as far enlarged
As we have warranty. Her death was doubtful,
And but that great command o'ersways the order,
She should in ground unsanctified have lodged
Till the last trumpet: for charitable prayers,
Shards, flints and pebbles should be thrown on her:
Yet here she is allowed her virgin crants,
Her maiden strewments, and the bringing home
Of bell and burial.
    Laertes. Must there no more be done?
    Doctor.   No more be done!
230 We should profane the service of the dead

To sing sage requiem and such rest to her
As to peace-parted souls.

   Laertes.   Lay her i'th'earth,
And from her fair and unpolluted flesh
May violets spring! [*the coffin is laid within the grave*]
       I tell thee, churlish priest,
A minist'ring angel shall my sister be,
When thou liest howling.

   Hamlet.   What, the fair Ophelia!
   Queen [*scattering flowers*]. Sweets to the sweet.
       Farewell!
I hoped thou shouldst have been my Hamlet's wife:
I thought thy bride-bed to have decked, sweet maid,
And not have strewed thy grave.

   Laertes.   O, treble woe   240
Fall ten times treble on that cursèd head
Whose wicked deed thy most ingenious sense
Deprived thee of! Hold off the earth awhile,
Till I have caught her once more in mine arms;
                   ['*leaps in the grave*'
Now pile your dust upon the quick and dead,
Till of this flat a mountain you have made
T'o'ertop old Pelion, or the skyish head
Of blue Olympus.

   Hamlet [*comes forward*]. What is he whose grief
Bears such an emphasis? whose phrase of sorrow
Conjures the wand'ring stars, and makes them stand   250
Like wonder-wounded hearers? This is I,
Hamlet the Dane.   ['*leaps in after Laertes*'
   Laertes [*grappling with him*]. The devil take thy soul
   Hamlet. Thou pray'st not well.
I prithee take thy fingers from my throat,
For though I am not splenitive and rash,
Yet have I in me something dangerous,

Which let thy wiseness fear; hold off thy hand.
  King. Pluck them asunder.
  Queen.   Hamlet, Hamlet!
  All. Gentlemen!
  Horatio.   Good my lord, be quiet.
                [Attendants part them, and they come
                      up out of the grave
260 *Hamlet.* Why, I will fight with him upon this theme
Until my eyelids will no longer wag.
  Queen. O my son, what theme?
  Hamlet. I loved Ophelia, forty thousand brothers
Could not with all their quantity of love
Make up my sum....What wilt thou do for her?
  King. O, he is mad, Laertes.
  Queen. For love of God, forbear him.
  Hamlet. 'Swounds, show me what thou't do:
Woo't weep? woo't fight? woo't fast? woo't tear thyself?
270 Woo't drink up eisel? eat a crocodile?
I'll do't. Dost thou come here to whine?
To outface me with leaping in her grave?
Be buried quick with her, and so will I.
And if thou prate of mountains, let them throw
Millions of acres on us, till our ground,
Singeing his pate against the burning zone,
Make Ossa like a wart! nay, an thou'lt mouth,
I'll rant as well as thou.
  Queen.   This is mere madness,
And thus awhile the fit will work on him.
280 Anon as patient as the female dove
When that her golden couplets are disclosed
His silence will sit drooping.
  Hamlet.   Hear you, sir,
What is the reason that you use me thus?
I loved you ever, but it is no matter,

Let Hercules himself do what he may,
The cat will mew, and dog will have his day. [*he goes*

   King. I pray thee, good Horatio, wait upon him....

                                  [*Horatio follows*

[*aside to Laertes*] Strengthen your patience in our last
     night's speech,
We'll put the matter to the present push....
Good Gertrude, set some watch over your son.   290
This grave shall have a living monument.
An hour of quiet shortly shall we see,
Till then, in patience our proceeding be.   [*they go*

[5. 2.]   *The hall of the castle; chairs of state,*
                benches, tables, etc.

     HAMLET *and* HORATIO *enter talking*

 Hamlet. So much for this, sir, now shall you see
     the other—
You do remember all the circumstance?
 Horatio. Remember it, my lord!
 Hamlet. Sir, in my heart there was a kind of fighting
That would not let me sleep—methought I lay
Worse than the mutines in the bilboes. Rashly,
And praised be rashness for it....let us know
Our indiscretion sometime serves us well,
When our deep plots do pall, and that should learn us
There's a divinity that shapes our ends,   10
Rough-hew them how we will—
  Horatio.   That is most certain.
 Hamlet. Up from my cabin,
My sea-gown scarfed about me, in the dark
Groped I to find out them, had my desire,

Fingered their packet, and in fine withdrew
To mine own room again, making so bold,
My fears forgetting manners, to unseal
Their grand commission; where I found, Horatio—
Ah, royal knavery!—an exact command,
20 Larded with many several sorts of reasons,
Importing Denmark's health and England's too,
With, ho! such bugs and goblins in my life,
That on the supervise, no leisure bated,
No, not to stay the grinding of the axe,
My head should be struck off.

    Horatio.   Is't possible?
    Hamlet. Here's the commission, read it at more leisure.
But wilt thou hear now how I did proceed?
    Horatio. I beseech you.
    Hamlet. Being thus be-netted round with villanies—
30 Or I could make a prologue to my brains
They had begun the play. I sat me down,
Devised a new commission, wrote it fair—
I once did hold it, as our statists do,
A baseness to write fair, and laboured much
How to forget that learning, but, sir, now
It did me yeoman's service. Wilt thou know
Th'effect of what I wrote?

    Horatio.   Ay, good my lord.
    Hamlet. An earnest conjuration from the king,
As England was his faithful tributary,
40 As love between them like the palm might flourish,
As peace should still her wheaten garland wear
And stand a comma 'tween their amities,
And many such like 'as'es' of great charge,
That on the view and knowing of these contents,
Without debatement further, more or less,
He should those bearers put to sudden death,

Not shriving-time allowed.
  Horatio.   How was this sealed?
  Hamlet. Why, even in that was heaven ordinant,
I had my father's signet in my purse,
Which was the model of that Danish seal,   50
Folded the writ up in the form of th'other,
Subscribed it, gave't th'impression, placed it safely,
The changeling never known: now, the next day
Was our sea-fight, and what to this was sequent
Thou knowest already.
  Horatio. So Guildenstern and Rosencrantz go to't.
  Hamlet. Why, man, they did make love to
        this employment,
They are not near my conscience, their defeat
Does by their own insinuation grow.
'Tis dangerous when the baser nature comes   60
Between the pass and fell incenséd points
Of mighty opposites.
  Horatio.   Why, what a king is this!
  Hamlet. Does it not, think thee, stand me now upon—
He that hath killed my king, and whored my mother,
Popped in between th'election and my hopes,
Thrown out his angle for my proper life,
And with such cozenage—is't not perfect conscience
To quit him with this arm? and is't not to be damned,
To let this canker of our nature come
In further evil?   70
  Horatio. It must be shortly known to him
        from England
What is the issue of the business there.
  Hamlet. It will be short, the interim is mine,
And a man's life's no more than to say 'One'...
But I am very sorry, good Horatio,
That to Laertes I forgot myself;

For by the image of my cause I see
The portraiture of his; I'll court his favours:
But sure the bravery of his grief did put me
80 Into a towering passion.

    Horatio.   Peace, who comes here?

*OSRIC, a diminutive and fantastical courtier, enters the
hall, wearing a winged doublet and a hat of latest
fashion*

  Osric [*doffs his hat and bows low*]. Your lordship is
right welcome back to Denmark.

  Hamlet. I humbly thank you, sir....[*aside*] Dost know
this water-fly?

  (*Horatio.* No, my good lord.

  (*Hamlet.* Thy state is the more gracious, for 'tis a vice
to know him. He hath much land, and fertile: let a
beast be lord of beasts, and his crib shall stand at the
king's mess. 'Tis a chough, but, as I say, spacious in the
90 possession of dirt.

  Osric [*bows again*]. Sweet lord, if your lordship were
at leisure, I should impart a thing to you from his
majesty.

  Hamlet. I will receive it, sir, with all diligence of
spirit. [*Osric continues bowing and waving his hat to
and fro*] Put your bonnet to his right use, 'tis for the
head.

  Osric. I thank your lordship, it is very hot.

  Hamlet. No, believe me, 'tis very cold, the wind is
100 northerly.

  Osric. It is indifferent cold, my lord, indeed.

  Hamlet. But yet, methinks, it is very sultry and hot for
my complexion.

  Osric. Exceedingly, my lord, it is very sultry—as
'twere—I cannot tell how...But, my lord, his majesty

bade me signify to you that a' has laid a great wager on
your head. Sir, this is the matter,—

Hamlet [*again moves him to put on his hat*]. I beseech
you remember—

Osric. Nay, good my lord, for mine ease, in good faith. 110
Sir, here is newly come to court Laertes—believe me,
an absolute gentleman, full of most excellent differences,
of very soft society, and great showing: indeed, to speak
sellingly of him, he is the card or calendar of gentry; for
you shall find in him the continent of what parts a
gentleman would see.

Hamlet. Sir, his definement suffers no perdition in
you, though I know to divide him inventorially would
dizzy th'arithmetic of memory, and yet but yaw neither
in respect of his quick sail, but in the verity of extolment 120
I take him to be a soul of great article, and his infusion
of such dearth and rareness, as to make true diction of
him, his semblable is his mirror, and who else would
trace him?—his umbrage, nothing more.

Osric. Your lordship speaks most infallibly of him.

Hamlet. The concernancy, sir? why do we wrap the
gentleman in our more rawer breath?

Osric. Sir?

Horatio. Is't not possible to understand in another
tongue? You will to't, sir, really.   130

Hamlet. What imports the nomination of this
gentleman?

Osric. Of Laertes?

(*Horatio.* His purse is empty already, all's golden
words are spent.

Hamlet. Of him, sir.

Osric. I know you are not ignorant—

Hamlet. I would you did, sir, yet in faith if you did,
it would not much approve me. Well, sir?

140   *Osric.* You are not ignorant of what excellence
Laertes is—

   Hamlet. I dare not confess that, lest I should compare
with him in excellence, but to know a man well were
to know himself.

   Osric. I mean, sir, for his weapon, but in the imputation laid on him by them in his meed, he's unfellowed.

   Hamlet. What's his weapon?

   Osric. Rapier and dagger.

   Hamlet. That's two of his weapons—but, well.

150   *Osric.* The king, sir, hath wagered with him six
Barbary horses, against the which he has impawned, as
I take it, six French rapiers and poniards, with their
assigns, as girdle, hangers, and so. Three of the carriages
in faith are very dear to fancy, very responsive to the
hilts, most delicate carriages, and of very liberal conceit.

   Hamlet. What call you the carriages?

   (*Horatio.* I knew you must be edified by the margent
ere you had done.

   Osric. The carriages, sir, are the hangers.

160   *Hamlet.* The phrase would be more germane to the
matter, if we could carry a cannon by our sides—I would
it might be hangers till then. But on! six Barbary
horses against six French swords, their assigns, and three
liberal-conceited carriages—that's the French bet against
the Danish. Why is this all 'impawned' as you call it?

   Osric. The king, sir, hath laid, sir, that in a dozen
passes between yourself and him he shall not exceed
you three hits. He hath laid on twelve for nine. And it
would come to immediate trial, if your lordship would
170 vouchsafe the answer.

   Hamlet. How if I answer 'no'?

   Osric. I mean, my lord, the opposition of your person
in trial.

Hamlet. Sir, I will walk here in the hall, if it please his majesty. It is the breathing time of day with me. Let the foils be brought, the gentleman willing, and the king hold his purpose, I will win for him an I can, if not I will gain nothing but my shame and the odd hits.

Osric. Shall I re-deliver you e'en so?

Hamlet. To this effect, sir,—after what flourish your 180 nature will.

Osric [*bows*]. I commend my duty to your lordship.

Hamlet. Yours, yours.

[*after another deep bow, Osric*
dons his hat and trips forth

He does well to commend it himself, there are no tongues else for's turn.

Horatio. This lapwing runs away with the shell on his head.

Hamlet. A' did comply, sir, with his dug before a' sucked it. Thus has he—and many more of the same bevy that I know the drossy age dotes on—only got the 190 tune of the time and, out of an habit of encounter, a kind of yeasty collection, which carries them through and through the most †profound and winnowed opinions, and do but blow them to their trial, the bubbles are out.

A lord enters

Lord. My lord, his majesty commended him to you by young Osric, who brings back to him that you attend him in the hall. He sends to know if your pleasure hold to play with Laertes, or that you will take longer time.

Hamlet. I am constant to my purposes, they follow the king's pleasure. If his fitness speaks, mine is ready; 200 now or whensoever, provided I be so able as now.

Lord. The king, and queen, and all are coming down.

Hamlet. In happy time.

Lord. The queen desires you to use some gentle entertainment to Laertes before you fall to play.

Hamlet. She well instructs me.　　　[*the lord departs*

Horatio. You will lose this wager, my lord.

Hamlet. I do not think so. Since he went into France, I have been in continual practice. I shall win at the odds; 210 but thou wouldst not think how ill all's here about my heart—but it is no matter.

Horatio. Nay, good my lord—

Hamlet. It is but foolery, but it is such a kind of gain-giving as would perhaps trouble a woman.

Horatio. If your mind dislike any thing, obey it. I will forestall their repair hither, and say you are not fit.

Hamlet. Not a whit, we defy augury. There is special providence in the fall of a sparrow. If it be now, 'tis not to come—if it be not to come, it will be now—if it be 220 not now, yet it will come—the readiness is all. Since no man, of aught he leaves, knows what is't to leave betimes, let be.

Attendants enter to set benches and carry in cushions for the spectators; next follow trumpeters and drummers with kettle-drums, the KING, the QUEEN and all the court, OSRIC and another lord, as judges, bearing foils and daggers which are placed upon a table near the wall, and last of all LAERTES dressed for the fence

King. Come, Hamlet, come and take this hand
　　　from me.
　　[*he puts the hand of Laertes into the hand of Hamlet;
　　　and after leads the Queen to the chairs of state*

Hamlet. Give me your pardon, sir. I have done
　　　you wrong,
But pardon't, as you are a gentleman.
This presence knows, and you must needs have heard,

How I am punished with a sore distraction.
What I have done
That might your nature, honour and exception
Roughly awake, I here proclaim was madness.   230
Was't Hamlet wronged Laertes? never Hamlet.
If Hamlet from himself be ta'en away,
And when he's not himself does wrong Laertes,
Then Hamlet does it not, Hamlet denies it.
Who does it then? his madness. If't be so,
Hamlet is of the faction that is wronged,
His madness is poor Hamlet's enemy.
Sir, in this audience,
Let my disclaiming from a purposed evil
Free me so far in your most generous thoughts,   240
That I have shot my arrow o'er the house,
And hurt my brother.

  Laertes.   I am satisfied in nature,
Whose motive in this case should stir me most
To my revenge, but in my terms of honour
I stand aloof, and will no reconcilement,
Till by some elder masters of known honour
I have a voice and precedent of peace,
To keep my name ungored: but till that time,
I do receive your offered love like love,
And will not wrong it.

  Hamlet.   I embrace it freely,   250
And will this brother's wager frankly play...:
Give us the foils, come on.

  Laertes.   Come, one for me.

  Hamlet. I'll be your foil, Laertes. In mine ignorance
Your skill shall like a star i'th'darkest night
Stick fiery off indeed.

  Laertes.   You mock me, sir.

  Hamlet. No, by this hand.

King. Give them the foils, young Osric.

> [*Osric brings forward some four or five foils;*
>   *Laertes takes one and makes a pass or two*

     Cousin Hamlet,
You know the wager?

Hamlet.   Very well, my lord.
Your grace has laid the odds o'th'weaker side.

260   *King.* I do not fear it, I have seen you both—
But since he is bettered, we have therefore odds.

Laertes. This is too heavy: let me see another.

> [*he goes to the table and brings from it the*
>   *poisoned and unbated rapier*

Hamlet [*takes a foil from Osric*]. This likes me well.
     These foils have all a length?

Osric. Ay, my good lord.

*The judges and attendants prepare the floor for the fence;
     Hamlet makes ready; other servants bear in flagons of
     wine with cups*

King. Set me the stoups of wine upon that table.
If Hamlet give the first or second hit,
Or quit in answer of the third exchange,
Let all the battlements their ordnance fire.
The king shall drink to Hamlet's better breath,
270 And in the cup an union shall he throw,
Richer than that which four successive kings
In Denmark's crown have worn: give me the cups,
And let the kettle to the trumpet speak,
The trumpet to the cannoneer without,
The cannons to the heavens, the heaven to earth,
'Now the king drinks to Hamlet.' Come, begin,
And you, the judges, bear a wary eye.

> *The cups are set at his side; trumpets sound;
>   Hamlet and Laertes take their stations*

Hamlet. Come on, sir.

Laertes.   Come, my lord.

They play

Hamlet.   One!

Laertes.   No.

Hamlet.   Judgement?

Osric. A hit, a very palpable hit.

   [*they break off; the kettle-drum sounds, the trumpets
     blow, and a cannon-shot is heard without*

Laertes.   Well, again.

King. Stay, give me drink. [*a servant fills a cup*]

     Hamlet, [*he holds up a jewel*], this pearl is thine. 280
Here's to thy health!   [*he drinks and then seems to cast
               the pearl into the cup*

     Give him the cup.

Hamlet. I'll play this bout first, set it by a while.

      [*the servant sets it on a table behind him*
Come.

They play again

     Another hit! What say you?

Laertes. A touch, a touch, I do confess't.

               [*they break off*

King. Our son shall win.

Queen.   He's fat, and scant of breath.
Here, Hamlet, take my napkin, rub thy brows.

      [*she gives it him, and going to the table
           takes up his cup of wine*
The queen carouses to thy fortune, Hamlet.

Hamlet. Good madam!

King.   Gertrude, do not drink.

Queen. I will, my lord, I pray you pardon me.

      [*she drinks and offers the cup to Hamlet*
(*King.* It is the poisoned cup, it is too late!   290

Hamlet. I dare not drink yet, madam—by and by.

Queen.   Come, let me wipe thy face.   [*she does so*

Laertes [*to the King*]. My lord, I'll hit him now.

King.   I do not think't.

(*Laertes*. And yet 'tis almost 'gainst my conscience.

Hamlet. Come, for the third, Laertes. You do
    but dally,

I pray you pass with your best violence.

I am afeard you make a wanton of me.

Laertes. Say you so? come on.

They play the third bout

Osric. Nothing neither way.   [*they break off*

300 *Laertes* [*suddenly*]. Have at you now!

> [*he takes Hamlet off his guard and wounds
> him slightly; Hamlet enraged closes with
> him, and "in scuffling they change rapiers"*

King.   Part them, they are incensed.

Hamlet·[*attacks*]. Nay, come again. [*the Queen falls*

Osric.   Look to the queen there, ho!

> [*Hamlet wounds Laertes deeply*

Horatio. They bleed on both sides!—how is it,
    my lord?   [*Laertes falls*

Osric [*tending him*]. How is't, Laertes?

(*Laertes*. Why, as a woodcock to my own
    springe, Osric!

I am justly killed with mine own treachery.

Hamlet. How does the queen?

King.   She swoons to see them bleed.

Queen. No, no, the drink, the drink—O my
    dear Hamlet—

The drink, the drink! I am poisoned!   [*she dies*

Hamlet. O villainy! ho! let the door be locked—

310 Treachery! seek it out.

Laertes. It is here, Hamlet. Hamlet, thou art slain,
No medicine in the world can do thee good,
In thee there is not half an hour of life,
The treacherous instrument is in thy hand,
Unbated and envenomed. The foul practice
Hath turned itself on me, lo, here I lie,
Never to rise again—thy mother's poisoned—
I can no more—the king, the king's to blame.

    Hamlet. The point envenomed too!—
Then, venom, to thy work.   *[he stabs the King* 320

    All. Treason! treason!

    King. O, yet defend me, friends, I am but hurt.

    Hamlet. Here, thou incestuous, murderous,
          damnéd Dane,   *[he forces him to drink*
Drink off this potion. Is thy union here?
Follow my mother.   *[the King dies*

    Laertes.   He is justly served,
It is a poison tempered by himself.
Exchange forgiveness with me, noble Hamlet,
Mine and my father's death come not upon thee,
Nor thine on me!   *[he dies*

    Hamlet. Heaven make thee free of it! I follow thee... 330
                [he falls
I am dead, Horatio. Wretched queen, adieu!
You that look pale and tremble at this chance,
That are but mutes or audience to this act,
Had I but time, as this fell sergeant, Death,
Is strict in his arrest, O, I could tell you—
But let it be; Horatio, I am dead,
Thou livest, report me and my cause aright
To the unsatisfied.

    Horatio.   Never believe it;
I am more an antique Roman than a Dane—
Here's yet some liquor left.   *[he seizes the cup* 340

Hamlet [*rises*].　　　　　As thou'rt a man,
Give me the cup, let go, by heaven I'll ha't!
　　　　　[*he dashes the cup to the ground and falls back*
O God, Horatio, what a wounded name,
Things standing thus unknown, shall live behind me!
If thou didst ever hold me in thy heart,
Absent thee from felicity awhile,
And in this harsh world draw thy breath in pain,
To tell my story...
　　　　　　　[*the tread of soldiers marching heard afar off,*
　　　　　　　　　and later a shot; Osric goes out
　　　　　　　　　What warlike noise is this?
　Osric [*returning*]. Young Fortinbras, with conquest
　　　come from Poland,
To th'ambassadors of England gives
350 This warlike volley.
　Hamlet.　　　　　O, I die, Horatio,
The potent poison quite o'er-crows my spirit,
I cannot live to hear the news from England,
But I do prophesy th'election lights
On Fortinbras, he has my dying voice.
So tell him, with th'occurrents more and less
Which have solicited—the rest is silence.　　　[*he dies*
　Horatio. Now cracks a noble heart. Good night,
　　　sweet prince;
And flights of angels sing thee to thy rest!
Why does the drum come hither?

　　　Prince FORTINBRAS, *the English ambassadors,*
　　　　　　and others enter

360　*Fortinbras*. Where is this sight?
　Horatio.　　　　　　　What is it you would see?
If aught of woe or wonder cease your search.

Fortinbras. This quarry cries on havoc. O
     proud death,
What feast is toward in thine eternal cell,
That thou so many princes at a shot
So bloodily hast struck?

  1 *Ambassador.*   The sight is dismal,
And our affairs from England come too late.
The ears are senseless that should give us hearing,
To tell him his commandment is fulfilled,
That Rosencrantz and Guildenstern are dead.
Where should we have our thanks?

  Horatio.   Not from his mouth, 370
Had it th'ability of life to thank you;
He never gave commandment for their death;
But since, so jump upon this bloody question,
You from the Polack wars, and you from England,
Are here arrived, give order that these bodies
High on a stage be placéd to the view,
And let me speak to th'yet unknowing world
How these things came about; so shall you hear
Of carnal, bloody and unnatural acts,
Of accidental judgements, casual slaughters,   380
Of deaths put on by cunning and forced cause,
And, in this upshot, purposes mistook
Fall'n on th'inventors' heads: all this can I
Truly deliver.

  Fortinbras.   Let us haste to hear it,
And call the noblest to the audience.
For me, with sorrow I embrace my fortune.
I have some rights of memory in this kingdom,
Which now to claim my vantage doth invite me.

  Horatio. Of that I shall have also cause to speak,
And from his mouth whose voice will draw on more. 390
But let this same be presently performed,

Even while men's minds are wild, lest more mischance
On plots and errors happen.

 Fortinbras.   Let four captains
Bear Hamlet like a soldier to the stage,
For he was likely, had he been put on,
To have proved most royal; and for his passage,
The soldiers' music and the rite of war
Speak loudly for him:
Take up the bodies—such a sight as this
400 Becomes the field, but here shows much amiss.
Go, bid the soldiers shoot.

*The soldiers bear away the bodies, the while a dead
march is heard; 'after the which a peal of ordnance is
shot off'*

NOTES

As the textual aspects of *Hamlet* have been dealt with comprehensively and in full detail in a publication shortly preceding this, entitled *The Manuscript of Shakespeare's 'Hamlet,'* it is unnecessary to record here, as in other volumes of this edition, the departures from the original texts or to reprint all the original stage-directions. Outstanding cruxes will, however, be briefly discussed, and readings taken from Q2 and F1 which are not accepted by the editors of *Hamlet* in the *Globe, Cambridge* or *Arden Shakespeare* will be registered, so as to make the position clear, while in the case of departures from Q2 and F1 the name of the critic or text responsible for the reading will be given in brackets. The line-numeration for reference to plays not yet issued in this edition is that used in the *Globe Shakespeare* and Bartlett's *Concordance*.

The following abbreviations are employed:

Q2 for the text of the *Second Quarto*; F1 for that of the *First Folio*; Q1 for that of the *First Quarto*; S.D. for stage-direction; G. for Glossary; N.E.D. for *The Oxford Dictionary*; Sh.Eng. for *Shakespeare's England* (Oxford, 1917); MSH. for *The Manuscript of Shakespeare's 'Hamlet'* (v. *Introd.* p. ix); Sh. for Shakespeare. The names of characters have also been abbreviated to save space.

Abbott for Abbott's *Shakespearian Grammar*; Aspects for *Aspects of Shakespeare: British Academy Lectures* (Oxford, 1933); Bond for *The Works of John Lyly* ed. by Warwick Bond; Bradley for *Shakespearean Tragedy* by A. C. Bradley; Brandes for *William Shakespeare* by Georg Brandes (1 vol. ed.); Bright for *A Treatise of Melancholie* by Timothy Bright, 1586; Camb. for *The Cambridge Shakespeare* ed. by Aldis

Wright; Chambers, *Will. Shak.* for *William Shake-speare* by E. K. Chambers; Chambers, *Eliz. Stage* for *The Elizabethan Stage* by E. K. Chambers; Clar. for *Hamlet* ed. by W. G. Clark and Aldis Wright (Clarendon Press Series); Dowden for *Hamlet* (4th ed.) by Edward Dowden (Arden Shakespeare); E.M.I. for *Every Man in his Humour*; E.M.O. for *Every Man out of his Humour*; Furness for *Hamlet* ed. by H. H. Furness, 1877 (Variorum Shakespeare); Globe for *The Globe Shakespeare*; Greg for *The Principles of Emendation in Shakespeare* (a lecture in 'Aspects' q.v.); Herford for *Hamlet* ed. by C. H. Herford (Eversley Shakespeare); Jonson for *Ben Jonson* ed. by C. H. Herford and Percy Simpson; Lavater for Lewes Lavater, *Of Ghostes and Spirites walking by Nyght*, 1572, ed. by J. Dover Wilson and May Yardley (Oxford, for the Shakespeare Association, 1929); Madden for *The Diary of Master William Silence* by D. H. Madden; M.L.R. for *The Modern Language Review*; Montaigne for *The Essayes of Montaigne* trans. by John Florio (The Museum Edition, 1906); R.E.S. for *The Review of English Studies*; Silver for G. Silver's *Paradoxes of Defence*, 1599, ed. with an Introduction (on the fencing-match in *Hamlet*) by J. Dover Wilson for the Shakespeare Association, 1933; Tilley for *Elizabethan Proverb Lore* by M. P. Tilley; T.L.S. for *The Literary Supplement of The Times*; Verity for *Hamlet* ed. by A. W. Verity (The Student's Shakespeare). Eighteenth-century edd. are generally quoted from Boswell's ed. of *Malone's Shakespeare* (1821).

Names of the Characters. A list first furnished by Rowe. The names in *Hamlet* deserve special study. Some appear to be perversions of Danish names,* perhaps derived from the visit to Denmark in 1586 of Leicester's players (v. Chambers, *Eliz. Stage*, ii. 272, *Will. Shak.* i. 39–40); others are borrowed from novels or plays of the early nineties; and one at least has been

deliberately altered (for reasons unknown) at some stage
in the history of the text. Cf. F. G. Stokes, *Dictionary
of Characters etc. in Shakespeare*. (i) *Claudius*. Not
named in the dialogue; appears in S.D. at head of 1. 2.
and in prefix to his first speech, but everywhere else in
Q2 described as 'King.' Possibly the name was spoken
in the sixteenth-century version of the play. (ii) *Hamlet*.
The traditional name, found in many variant forms, of
the hero of the old saga (v. *Introd*. pp. xii–xiii). It is
perhaps an accident that the name was current in
Warwickshire and that Shakespeare's own son (b. 1585)
was christened Hamnet, a variant of it. (iii) *Polonius*.
Called 'Corambis' in Q1 and 'Corambus' in the
Brudermord (cf. *Introd*. p. xxv). Until recently it
was assumed that 'Corambus' was the original name,
altered to 'Polonius' in Shakespeare's latest revision;
Chambers (*Will. Shak*. i. 417–18) challenges this,
I think unnecessarily. For the name Polonius and a
possible reference to Burleigh, v. Gollancz, *Book of
Homage*, pp. 173–77. Rowe described Polonius as
'Lord Chamberlain,' and Chambers (Sh.Eng. i. 85)
endorses this. But he is the most important person in the
state of Denmark after the royal family, and it appears
from 2. 2. 166 ('assistant for a state') and 1. 2. that he
is the chief of the King's Councillors, i.e. a statesman
and not a ceremonial official like the Lord Chamberlain.
I have little doubt that Shakespeare regarded him as
corresponding with the Principal Secretary of State
under Elizabeth and James I, a post held first by
Burleigh and later by his son Robert Cecil. (iv) *Horatio*.
Also the name of the murdered son of Hieronimo
in Kyd's *Spanish Tragedy* (c. 1589) and perhaps
borrowed from there. (v) *Laertes*. The name of the
father of Ulysses, referred to in Ovid, *Metam*. xiii. 48,
and in *Tit. And*. 1. 1. 380. (vi) *Valtemand*. The sp.
'Voltimand' (F2) has been universally adopted by edd.
I follow Q2, though this is, as Greg (*Aspects*, p. 198)

points out, 'presumably a corruption of "Waldemar,"' and the interesting Q 1 'Voltemar' may conceivably have been the actual form in the old *Hamlet*. (vii) *Cornelius*. The name occurs in *Dr Faustus*, a play also referring to Wittenberg. (viii) *Rosencrantz* and *Guildenstern*. The Q 2 sp. is 'Rosencraus and Guyldensterne.' Both names appear in the official records of the University of Wittenberg, and as Rosencrans and Guldensteren on a contemporary engraving of the portrait of Tycho Brahe (cf. Chambers, *Will. Shak.* i. 425).* (ix) *Osric*. Another Danish name; given to Hamlet's foster-brother in the Saxo Grammaticus story. (x) *Doctor of Divinity* (cf. note 5. 1. 212 S.D.). (xi) *Barnardo*. The Q 2 sp. Most edd. follow F 1 and print 'Bernardo.' (xii) *Reynaldo*. Called 'Montano' in Q 1, whether through forgetfulness of the reporter or because the name belonged to the old *Hamlet* it is impossible to say (cf. Corambus under *Polonius* above). 'Montano' appears in Sannazaro's *Arcadia*, 1504 (cf. *Ophelia*) and is used by Shakespeare in *Oth.* (xiii) *Gertrude*. Q 2 misprints 'Gertrard.' She is 'Geruth' in the Belleforest story, v. *Introd.* p. xvi. (xiv) *Ophelia*. In Sannazaro's *Arcadia* 'Ofelia' and 'Montano' are love-sick swains. For *Yorick* v. note 5. 1. 175, *Lamord* v. note 4. 7. 91.

Acts and Scenes. Q 2 contains no such divisions. F 1 prints 'Actus Primus. Scœna Prima,' 'Scena Secunda,' 'Scene Tertia,' 'Actus Secundus,' 'Scena Secunda'—and nothing more, v. MSH. p. 87. Rowe first introduced the traditional divisions.

Punctuation. The Q 2 punctuation, for which v. *Introd.* pp. xxx–xxxii and MSH. pp. 192–215, has been as closely followed as a modernised text allows.

Stage-directions. Directions from the original texts are indicated by inverted commas. Occasional use has been made of directions from F 1, while hints are even at times taken from Q 1, which is valuable as evidence of what the reporter saw taking place on the Globe stage. For a comparative table of S.D.s in Q2 and F1 v. MSH. pp. 353–69.

1.1.

S.D. *A narrow platform* etc. For 'platform' (first read by Theobald) cf. 1.2.213 'the platform where we watch,' and 1.2.252 'Upon the platform.' Its technical meaning in Sh.'s day was a raised level place or an open walk on the top of a building, for the emplacement of guns (v. N.E.D. 'platform' 6). Sh. probably imagined it as situated on the battlements of the castle, at once a look-out for guards and a commanding position for cannon. Theatrically, I take it, the word denotes the upper-stage, which would explain the unmotived disappearance of Bar. in 1.4., when his place is taken by Ham.; seeing that four characters besides the Ghost would have overcrowded the gallery, which for the rest, with its curtained recess in the middle, would be very convenient for the apparition. (For a different view, by Chambers, v. head-note 1.5.)

Francisco, a sentinel armed etc. Prob. the 'sentinels' all carried partisans (v. G.) like the Wardens of the Tower, whom Sh. seems to have in mind. As royal guards, too, they would rank as officers and gentlemen (a title Hor. expressly gives to Mar. and Bar. at 1.2.194), though Mar. seems to have been of higher military rank than Bar. (v. note 1.2.167). Perhaps Sh. intended him as captain of the guard and the others as lieutenants. Cf. Sh.Eng. i.138.

1. *Who's there?* The question and the dialogue that follows emphasise the darkness of the night and the jumpiness of the guards. It was for Fran., on guard, to give the challenge.

3. *Long live the king!* The watchword is dramatically ironical in view of all that follows.

8. *bitter cold* Sh. builds up the atmosphere of the frosty, star-lit, northern night as he proceeds; cf. I. I. 36–8 'yon same star...*burns.*'

9. *sick at heart* The solitary figure of Fran. with his heart-sickness foreshadows Ham.

13. *bid them make haste* Bar. is anxious not to be left alone.

19. *A piece of him.* Hor.'s jocularity is contrasted with the nervousness of the others; he does not believe in ghosts. The jest means, I take it, that he is pinched with the cold.

21. *What, has...to-night?* (Q2) F1, Q1, and most mod. edd. assign to Mar. Cf. MSH. p. 37. The contemptuous word 'thing' clearly comes from the sceptic, and Mar.'s speech beginning 'Horatio says' seems more natural, if Hor. has just spoken.

23. *Horatio...fantasy* Hor., philosopher and student, may be classed as one of the school of Reginald Scot. When he sees the Ghost, of course, his attitude changes. Cf. Lavater, p. xvii, and *Introd.* pp. l–liii.

29. *He may...speak to it.* Cf. note I. I. 42.

33. *two nights* Cf. I. 2. 196. The play opens on the eve of the coronation and marriage of Claudius; and the Ghost begins to walk three days before the ceremony. Cf. I. 2. head-note.

Well, sit we down Hor. is bored.

39. S.D. *clad in armour...truncheon* Cf. I. 2. 200–204, and notes. That the Ghost appears 'in arms' is clearly of great significance to all who speak of it; cf. also ll. 47–9, 60–3 below, I. 2. 200–204, 226–30, 255, and I. 4. 52. It gives Ham. the clue to the apparition before he sees it; and makes him suspect 'foul play' and the need for vengeance (I. 2. 255). That the armour was also dramatically extraordinarily effective, we cannot doubt; Sh. replaced the stock stage-spook from Tartarus clad in a leather pilch by a Christian spirit 'in his habit as he lived.' Cf. F. W. Moorman, *The Pre-Shake-*

spearian Ghost and *Shakespeare's Ghosts*, M.L.R. vol. i. and Sh.Eng. ii. 268.

42. *a scholar, speak to it* Hor. had been brought as a precaution; spirits could only be exorcised in Latin formulae, and therefore it was safe for scholars alone to hold converse with ghosts. Cf. l. 29 above and Beaumont and Fletcher, *Night Walker*, 2. 1.

> Let's call the butler up, for he speaks Latin,
> And that will daunt the devil.

43. *Looks a'* For Q 2's frequent use of this colloquial form v. MSH. pp. 230–1.

45. *It would be spoke to.* Ghosts could not speak until spoken to. Dowden cites Boswell's *Johnson* (ed. Birkbeck Hill, iii. 307).

46. *usurp'st* Hor. implies that it is some impostor or an evil spirit, which has assumed the form of the dead King. No wonder 'it is offended.' v. note l. 23 above and *Introd.* pp. l–lii.

63. *sledded Polacks* (Malone) Q 2, Q 1 'sleaded pollax,' F 1 'sledded Pollax.' Some have imagined a reference to a 'leaded (or 'sledged') poleaxe'; but Malone is clearly right, cf. 'the Polack' (2. 2. 75; 4. 4. 23). A battle upon the ice is not at all impossible on or near the Baltic. The sp. 'pollax' is phonetic. For 'sledded' v. G.

65. *dead hour* Cf. 1. 2. 198 'dead waste and middle of the night.'

85. *this side...world* = the whole western world (as we should say).

87. *heraldy* (Q 2) The older form; cf. G. Tournaments and state combats were regulated by the Earl Marshal, head of the College of Heralds, and his staff. Cf. *Ric. II*, 1. 3.

89. *conqueror*, Q 2 'conqueror.'

90. *moiety competent* = equal share.

93. *co-mart* (Q 2) F 1 'Cou'nant'—which most

mod. edd. read. Malone followed Q2 and explained: 'a joint bargain, a word perhaps of our poet's coinage'; and Warburton notes that since 'the article designed' means 'the covenant entered into to confirm that bargain' the F1 reading 'makes a tautology.'

94. *carriage*...*designed*=process or tenour of the clause in the 'sealed compact' drawn up covering the point.

98. *Sharked up*=Swept up speedily and indiscriminately. v. *Introd*. pp. xxxvi–xxxvii.

lawless (Q2, Q1) F1 'Landlesse.' MSH. pp. 150, 268.

100. *stomach* v. G.

108–25. *I think...eclipse.* F1 omits these lines. MSH. pp. 25, 168.

112. *mote* (Q5) Q2 'moth'—a common sp., cf. *L.L.L.* 4. 3. 158. Hor., recovering his balance, belittles the Ghost; the apparition, he says, is nothing to what happened before Caesar's death or to more recent portents.

113–16. *In the most...Roman streets* Cf. *Jul. Caes.* 2. 2. 18–24. One of the indications of the close connexion between the two plays. Both owe something to North's *Plutarch* ('Julius Caesar').

117–21. *And even...countrymen.* 122–25. *As stars ...eclipse.* Q2 prints these passages in the reverse order, and edd. at a loss to interpret have supposed something lost. My rearrangement, following a suggestion by Gerald Massey (*Secret Drama of Shakespeare's Sonnets*, 1872, Sup. p. 46), who notes that lunar eclipses are not mentioned in Plutarch, restores the sense. The Q2 inversion would be explained if Sh. crowded additional matter into the foot of a MS. page. Cf. note ll. 122–25, and MSH. pp. 222–25.

122–25. *As stars...eclipse.* Sh. is referring to contemporary events. Solar eclipses were visible in England on Feb. 25, 1598, July 10, 1600, and Dec. 24,

1601, and lunar ones on Feb. 11 and Aug. 6, 1598 (and again in Nov. 1603). The year 1598 was thus rich in eclipses, those of Feb. 11 and Aug. 6 being total, and therefore particularly terrifying to the superstitious populace of those days. On the other hand, astrologers foretold that the evil effects of the 'disaster in the sun' of July 1600 would be felt between Jan. 20, 1601 and July 12, 1603, and the Essex rising of Feb. 1601 was hailed as a direct fulfilment of this. Cf. Introd. by D. C. Collins to Norden's *Vicissitudo Rerum*, 1600 (Shak. Assoc. Facs. 1931), and a thesis by the same writer which I have had the privilege of consulting. At any time between 1598 and 1602 Hor.'s words here, and Ham.'s at 3. 4. 48–51 (q.v.), would have made a special appeal to a London audience. The 'moist star' is, of course, the moon.

125. *almost to dooomsday* i.e. 'almost to the point of complete darkness, alluding to the biblical prophecy that at the second coming of Christ "the moon shall not give her light" (Matt. xxiv. 29),' Herford. Cf. also Luke xxi. 25–7.

127. *cross it,* i.e. cross its path, stop it. To cross or be crossed by a spirit or demon, which often took the form of a man or animal, was considered exceedingly dangerous; and Ferdinando Stanley, Earl of Derby, one-time patron of Sh.'s company, died in 1594, as many thought, because he had been thus crossed (cf. Furness).

S.D. *he spreads his arms* (Q. 1676) Q2 'It spreads his armes' Carelessly written, 'he' might be taken for 'yt,' and the S.D. seems clearly connected with 'I'll cross it though it blast me,' signifying that Hor. steps in the path of the Ghost and spreads his arms across the narrow platform (the upper-stage) so as to stop its passage.

Stay, illusion! Hor. still retains shreds of scepticism.

138. S.D. *a cock crows* The crowing distracts the audience for a moment, and the Ghost slips into the

recess at the back of the upper-stage, while the three men cover the action by scuffling together in a knot.

150. *trumpet* = trumpeter.

153–55. *Whether in sea...confine* 'According to the pneumatology of that time, every element was inhabited by its peculiar order of spirits. The meaning therefore is, that all *spirits extravagant*, wandering out of their element, whether aerial spirits visiting earth, or earthly spirits ranging the air, return to their station, to their proper limits, in which they are *confined*' (Dr Johnson). Cf. *Temp.* 4. 1. 120 'Spirits, which by mine art/I have from their confines called,' and v. G. 'confine' and I. 5. 11.

158–60. *Some say...all night long* I have not been able to trace any source for this legend. But a correspondent in T.L.S. (Ap. 7, 1932) quotes R. Jefferies, *Wild Life in a Southern Country* (ch. xvii): 'Towards the end of December the cocks, reversing their usual practice, crow in the evening, hours before midnight. The cockcrow is usually associated with the dawn, and the change of habit, just when the nights are longest, is interesting.' It is not difficult to imagine the legend springing from these facts.

165. *in part* Hor. continues to affect scepticism.

166. *russet* v. *Introd.* p. xxxvi.

170. *young Hamlet* Perhaps so called to distinguish him from the Hamlet they had just seen.

175. *convenient* (Q2) F1, Q1 and all edd. read 'conveniently.' Sh. prefers the more unusual form; cf. MSH. p. 278 for other examples.

I. 2.

S.D. Q2 'Florish. Enter Claudius, King of Denmarke, Gertrad the Queene, Counsaile: as Polonius, and his Sonne Laertes, Hamlet, Cum Alijs.' For

'Counsaile: as' which I take for a misp. of 'Counsailors,' v. MSH. p. 110. The occasion of the scene, as is clear from the business transacted, is a meeting of the King's Council, the first since the double event just celebrated of the royal marriage and coronation. The entry of Ham. is significant; it is his first, and he comes in, with dejected mien, last of the court figures, a black figure against a blaze of colour. The F1 S.D., universally followed, ruins this effect by leaving out the Councillors, introducing Oph., and giving Ham. his entry in order of rank immediately after the Queen. Cf. Sh.Eng. ii. 271 and MSH. pp. 34, 183.

14–16. *nor have we…thanks* These words, addressed directly to the Lords of the Council, show that Claudius has secured the succession by winning them over, no doubt with the aid of Pol.

17. *know, young* Q2 and F1 omit comma. Edd. print 'know: young' The 'that' = that which.

21. *Colleaguéd* The antecedent is 'supposal'; 'advantage' = superiority.

24. *bands* (Q2) F1 'Bonds' The two forms are used indifferently by Sh., v. G.

26–7. *Now…time of meeting…business is* This, if nothing else, would stamp the scene as a formal meeting of the Council.

28. *Fortinbras—* Q2 'Fortenbrasse' 30. *purpose—* Q2 'purpose;' The Q2 semicolon gives the same effect as the dashes, which will be more easily understood by the modern reader.

34. *Valtemand* v. *Names of the Characters* above.

44–9. *You cannot…thy father* The K. thus gracefully acknowledges the debt he owes to his chief councillor; cf. note ll. 14–16 above. The change from 'you' to 'thou' is significant of his desire to appear friendly. 'The K. positively coos over Laer., caressing him with his name four times in nine lines' (Harold Child; privately).

58–60. *wrung…consent* F1 omits these 2½ lines. MSH. pp. 22–3, 33.

60. *Upon his will…consent* A quibble upon 'will,' the legal document; 'hard consent' (v. G. 'hard') standing for the signet-ring. Cf. 3. 2. 402 for similar quibble.

65. *A little…kind.* 'Kin' echoes 'cousin' (= kinsman beyond the immediate family circle) and 'kind' 'son.' To paraphrase: 'a little more than kinsman, since you have married my mother, yet hardly your son, since the marriage is incestuous' (cf. 'kindless' 2. 2. 584). The audience take 'less than kind' as referring to the succession. They are not intended to see the whole point until after the First Soliloquy. Ham.'s first utterance is a riddle, like his character. Cf. *Introd.* p. xl, and Tilley *Proverbs* (1950) K.38.

67. *in the 'son'* Q 2 'in the sonne,' F 1 'i'th' Sun.' Another quibble, as the sp. of Q 2 makes clear: 'too much in the son' refers to the insult of being called 'son' by Claudius (l. 64); 'too much in the sun' (v. G. 'sun') refers to the proverbial 'in the sun' which means 'out of house and home, outlawed, disinherited,' as Ham. was by the usurpation of Claudius. Cf. *A.Y.L.* 2. 5. 37; *Lear* 2. 2. 168–69 'Thou out of heaven's benediction comest/To the warm sun,' Tilley, 287 and P. L. Carver in M.L.R. xxv. 478–81 and xxix. 173–76.

77–84. *'Tis not alone…might play* A bitter description of the mock funeral of his father, and of his mother's behaviour thereat.

82. *modes* (Capell) Q 2 'moodes,' F 1 'Moods'— a common sp. Cf. *Lov. Com.* 201 'the encrimson'd mood.'

102. *nature* v. G. and *Introd.* p. xxxiii.

105. *the first corse* Abel, killed by a brother! [J.C.M.]

108–109. *for let the world…our throne* An important political pronouncement, referred to again at 3. 2. 90–2 and 342–44: Ham., in full council, receives 'the voice of the king himself for his succession.' It is a bid for acquiescence in the *fait accompli*.

112. *impart* The vb. lacks an object. Johnson writes 'I believe "impart" is "impart myself," "communicate" whatever I can bestow.'

113. *school in Wittenberg*, i.e. the university of Wittenberg, Luther's university, indicating that Ham. was of Protestant upbringing. v. *Introd*. p. li.

120. *I shall...madam* Spoken, I suppose, in a tone of utter weariness. The K. makes the best of it.

125.* *No jocund health* etc. Referring to the marriage and coronation feast to follow.

129–59. *O, that this...hold my tongue*. For the Q 2 punctuation of this speech, v. MSH. pp. 197–200. There are only two stops in Q 2 heavier than a comma, viz. semi-colons, which make pauses of great dramatic force before the two climaxes: 'frailty thy name is woman!' and 'to post/With such dexterity to incestuous sheets.' The second climax reveals the monster present in Ham.'s mind from the beginning of the soliloquy; 'a birth, indeed, Which throes him much to yield' and, when uttered at last, suggesting a brood of serpents in the hissing of its sibilants.

129.* *too too sullied* (George Macdonald; Dowden) Q 2 'too too sallied,' Q 1 'too much grieu'd and sallied,' F 1 'too too solid.' For a full discussion of the graphical, linguistic, literary and dramatic issues involved in this crux, v. MSH. pp. 307–15. Cf. misp. 'sallies' for 'sullies' below, 2. 1. 39, and 'vnsallied' for 'unsullied' in *L.L.L.* 5. 2. 352. 'Sullied flesh' is the key to the soliloquy and tells us that Ham. is thinking of the 'kindless' (v. note l. 65) incestuous marriage as a personal defilement. Further, 'sullied' fits the immediate context as 'solid' does not. There is something absurd in associating 'solid flesh' with 'melt' and 'thaw'; whereas Sh. always uses 'sully' or 'sullied' elsewhere (cf. 1 *Hen. IV* 2. 4. 84; *Wint*. 1. 2. 326; 1 *Hen. VI* 4. 4. 6;

M.W.W. 2. 1. 102; *L.L.L.* 5. 2. 352; *Son.* 15. 12, 69. 14) with the image, implicit or explicit, of dirt upon a surface of pure white; and the surface Ham. obviously has in mind here is snow, symbolical of the nature he shares with his mother, once pure but now befouled.

132. *His canon 'gainst self-slaughter* Apparently the sixth commandment is meant. Cf. notes 5. 1. 9, 10–20 below and *Cymb.* 3. 4. 78–80:

> Against self-slaughter
> There is a prohibition so divine
> That cravens my weak hand.

150. *discourse of reason* v. G. A common expression in Florio's *Montaigne*.

157.* *incestuous* The marriage of a woman with her deceased husband's brother was so regarded by the Church, whether Catholic or Protestant. Cf. 1. 5. 42, 83; 3. 3. 90; 5. 2. 323. The horror of this 'incest' haunts Ham. throughout the play.

160. *I am glad to see you well;* Overcome with the emotion of the soliloquy, Ham. does not at first see who has entered. When he does, he throws himself almost hungrily upon Hor. The Q2 semicolon is noteworthy. MSH. pp. 200, 202. Edd. ask where Hor. can have been, and why Ham. had not met him before, if he arrived for the funeral. The theatre does not give time for the posing of such questions. Cf. *Introd.* pp. xlviii–xlix.

161. *self* Very emphatic.

163. *I'll change...with you* i.e. 'No talk of "servant"! the only name between us is "friend."' The emphatic word is 'that.' Cf. note l. 254 below.

167. —*good even, sir.* Q2 '(good euen sir).' The brackets denote a change of voice, and indicate a more distant form of salutation, to one who is perhaps a junior officer and personally unknown to the Prince. MSH. pp. 202–3.

180. *Thrift, thrift* To catch the full scorn of this, cf. 3. 2. 60 'Where thrift may follow fawning,' and 182 'base respects of thrift, but none of love.'

186. *I saw him once*, etc. Cf. *Introd*. p. xlviii. Percy Simpson (M.L.R. xiii. 321) suggests that Hor. is about to refer to some particular occasion when he had seen him, but that Ham. interrupts. He would read, therefore, 'I saw him once—a' was a goodly king—'

198. *the dead waste* (Q2, F1) Q1 'the dead vast,' which most edd. follow, quoting *Temp*. 1. 2. 327 'that vast of night.' The two words are variant forms, and the sense is the same, i.e. the desolate hours about midnight when all nature sleeps. MSH. p. 290. Marston, *Malcontent*, 2. 3. ''Tis now about the immodest waist of night,' seems to be a parody of this and 3. 2. 391.

204. *his truncheon* Cf. *M. for M*. 2. 2. 61 'the marshal's truncheon.' As commander-in-chief of the Danish forces the King was of marshal's rank.

211. *knew* = recognised. Cf. 5. 2. 7 and G.

212. *are not more like* i.e. than the apparition was to the late king. Hor. is careful not to identify the two, and generally calls the Ghost 'it.'

213. *watch* (Q2: some copies) F1 'watcht.' MSH. pp. 93–4, 267. The platform was the regular station for the guard. Cf. head-note 1. 1.

216. *it head* The old genitive.

222. *writ down in our duty* i.e. part of our prescribed obligation as soldiers. Cf. *Cor*. 1. 7. 1 'keep your duties/As I have set them down.'

224. *Indeed, indeed* Bradley (pp. 148–49) notes the habit of iteration as a characteristic of Ham.'s brooding speech. Cf. l. 237 below, and 2. 2. 193, 219–20; 3. 1. 92. MSH. pp. 79–82.

226. *Armed, say you?* This 'troubles' Ham.; cf. note 1. 1. 39 S.D. In the rapid dialogue that ensues he tests the witnesses searchingly on the point.

229. *Then...his face.* Not a question in Q2, but

a deduction: 'uttered,' suggests Dowden, 'in a tone of disappointed expectation'; rather, I think, in one of keen examination.

243. *war'nt* (Q2) Cf. note 2. 1. 38.

244–45. *If it assume...gape* The words show that at this stage Ham. is entertaining the idea that perhaps the spirit 'may be a devil' (2. 2. 603). Cf. *Introd.* pp. li–lii.

248–50. *Let it be...no tongue* Note the emphasis Ham. lays upon secrecy. Cf. note 1. 5. 136–40.

249. *whatsomever* A favourite form with Sh. MSH. p. 243.

254. *Your loves...to you* i.e. not 'duty' but 'love' as between friends. Cf. note l. 163 above. This courtesy towards his inferiors in rank is characteristic of Ham.

255. (*in arms!*) Q2 '(in armes)' The brackets, denoting change of voice, throw great emphasis upon these words. Cf. MSH. p. 203, and notes 1. 1. 39 S.D. and 1. 2. 226.

1. 3.

S.D. Q2 'Enter Laertes, and Ophelia his Sister.' The description of Oph. indicates that this is her first appearance in the play. Cf. head-note 1. 2.

6. *toy in blood* v. G. 'toy,' 'blood.'

12–13.* *temple...inward service* Cf. 2 Cor. vi. 16. Having used the word 'temple' Sh. characteristically goes on to think of 'service,' with its secondary meaning of 'allegiance.' Cf. *Introd.* pp. xxxv–xxxix.

18. *For he...birth* (F1) Q2 omits. MSH. p. 244.

20. *Carve for himself* v. G. We should say 'pick and choose for himself,' using another metaphor of the table.

21. *sanity* (Theobald, Hanmer) Q2 'safty,' F1 'sanctity.' Cf. misp. 'sanctity' for 'sanity' 2. 2. 212. Johnson endorsed Theobald's emendation; the alternatives are to supply (with Warburton) a second 'the'

before 'health,' or to read 'safety' as a trisyllable (though it has only two syllables in l. 43 below). MSH. p. 316. 'Sanity' = welfare, soundness, v. G.

23. *voice and yielding* = approval and acquiescence.

36–42. *The chariest maid...imminent.* The inverted commas, which denote 'sentences,' i.e. proverbial or sententious remarks, come from Q2, which however prints them only at the beginning of ll. 36, 38, 39. They prob. indicated in a playhouse MS. ponderous or solemn delivery by the actor. Cf. P. Simpson, *Shak. Punct.* pp. 101–103, and (for B. Jonson's concern with such inverted commas) *Ben Jonson*, iv. 335–36 (Oxford). Cf. notes below ll. 59–80; 4. 5. 17–20, and MSH pp. 204–5. For 'chariest' v. G.

44. *rebels* v. G.

50. *primrose path* Cf. *Macb.* 2. 3. 21; *All's Well,* 4. 5. 52–4 (*Matt.* vii. 13–14).

54. *Occasion smiles...leave* = It is an excellent opportunity for a second leave-taking.

S.D. Capell reads 'Kneeling to Polonius.'

57. S.D. Theobald reads 'Laying his hand on Laertes's head.'

58. *these few precepts* The similarity of these to precepts left by fathers like Burleigh or Sir Henry Sidney to their sons, and on the other hand to the advice given by Euphues to Philautus in *Euphues,* has been noted by many (v. Furness, and Bond, i. 165). Sh. evidently intended the speech as an epitome of paternal worldly wisdom; every precept is hedged with caution and pointed with self-interest.

59–80. *Give thy thoughts...any man* Q1 prints its version of the speech in inverted commas, which appear in another speech by Pol. at the end of the scene. No commas are found here in Q2 or F1; but if the Q1 pirate was an actor who had seen the players' parts, they may have stood therein. Cf. note ll. 36–42 above and MSH. pp. 204–5.

63. *unto thy soul* (Q2) F1 'to thy Soule'—and most edd. follow.

65. *courage* (Q2, Q1) F1 'Comrade' The Q2 reading is correct, and means spark, brave, blood; cf. N.E.D. 'courage,' 1c, quoting Hoby's *Castiglione's Courtier* (1577) 'the prowes of those diuine courages.' MSH. pp. 295–96.

74.* *Or* (Q2) F1, Q1 'Are'—which all edd. follow. MSH. pp. 317–19.

of a most...chief in that (Q2, F1, Q1) Despite the agreement of all three texts, corruption is indisputable. Most edd. omit 'of a,' which (if the F1 'Are' be correct) I conjecture may be a misp. for 'often' (sp. 'ofen' or 'ofn'), v. MSH. pp. 317–19, and Greg (Aspects), pp. 152–53, 200–201. Dowden suggests 'Or of a most select, *are* generous, chief in that'—which retains Q2's 'Or' and has attractions. A third alternative (Collier) is to follow F1 but alter 'chief' to 'choice.'

109. *Running* (Collier) Q2 'Wrong,' F1 'Roaming.' Cf. *K. John* 2.1.335, where F1 prints 'rome' for 'run' (sp. 'ronne'). MSH. p. 315. The emendation carries on the image of the overtaxed hound in the previous line.

tender me a fool i.e. make a fool of yourself in my eyes, or (as Dowden suggests) present me with a baby. The latter interpretation would make Oph.'s next speech an indignant rejoinder. For 'fool' (= darling) v. G. and as applied to a baby v. *Rom.* 1. 3. 31, 48.

117. *blazes* v. G.

122–23. *entreatments...parle* Terms of diplomacy. v. G.

128. *investments* = vestments. With a quibble on monetary investments, after 'brokers' (itself used quibblingly). v. G. for both words.

130. *bonds* (Q2, F1) Most edd. follow Theobald and read 'bawds.' The emendation makes Pol. say the very opposite of what he intends, which is that these

'unholy suits' pretend to be, not 'bawds' (what is a 'pious bawd'?), but sacred pledges. Malone declared for the original text, and quoted *Son.* 142 'sealed false bonds of love.' Cf. also 3. 2. 158 below 'most sacred bands' (= bonds). MSH. p. 290.

133. *moment leisure* Cf. 'region kites' 2. 2. 582, 'his music vows' 3. 1. 159.

1. 4.

S.D. For the localisation, and the absence of Barnardo v. head-note 1. 1.

6. S.D. Q2 'A florish of trumpets and 2. peeces goes of.'

8–9.* *The king...reels* i.e. the king is making an all-night feast of it, after the blustering fashion of the new-fangled revels. Cf. G. 'wake,' 'upspring,' 'reels.' In 'swagg'ring' Ham. refers to the braying of the trumpets and kettle-drums, and the firing of ordnance (cf. 1. 2. 125–28). Dowden (4th ed.) quotes Marlowe, *Dr Faustus* 4. 1. 19 'He took his rouse with stoups of Rhenish wine.'

12. *Is it a custom?* Cf. *Introd.* p. xlviii.

13. *Ay marry is't* i.e. it is no innovation by Claudius; the late King had also indulged in 'heavy-headed revels.' Cf. note 1. 5. 11.

17–38. *This heavy-headed...scandal.* Omitted in F1, possibly because it was considered politically dangerous after 1603 with a Danish Queen (Anne, the consort of James I) on the throne. MSH. pp. 25–6.

19–20. *with swinish...addition* A poetical way of saying 'they call us drunken swine.' v. G. 'addition.' Some have supposed a reference to 'Sweyn' a common name of Danish kings; Q2 gives the word an initial capital, which lends possible support to the idea.

24. *mole of nature* = natural blemish.　26. *his* = its.

27–8.* *some complexion...forts of reason* The 'complexion' (v. G.) Ham. has in mind is that of melancholy, which often led to madness. Cf. note l. 33.

29–30. *by some habit...manners* To 'o'er-leaven' (v. G.) is to have too much of a good thing. The habit spoken of, therefore, is one that makes pleasing manners appear excessive, or that allows men to place a sinister interpretation on what is nothing but personal charm. The whole passage, ll. 27–30, is applicable to Ham. himself; but the 'judicious' in an audience of 1601 would, I think, have detected a reference to the popularity of the late Earl of Essex, had the lines been spoken.

32. *nature's livery, or fortune's star* 'a blemish they were born with or one wrought by mischance' (Herford). 'Livery' = badge, and 'star' may also refer quibblingly to the mark or star on a horse's forehead.

33. *His virtues* (Q2) Theobald and later edd. read 'Their virtues.' As Ham. is thinking of himself, the transition from plur. to sing. is natural. MSH. p. 291.

36. *evil* (Keightley) Q2 'eale.' Dowden prints 'evil.' There can be little doubt, I think, that Sh. wrote 'eule' (= evil), of which 'eale' would be a simple *a* : *u* misreading. Cf. MSH. pp. 320–23, and notes 2. 2. 603; 3. 2. 127, which give us 'deule' and 'deale' for 'devil.'

37.* *of a doubt* With Dowden, I believe the emendation 'often dout' (=often put out, obliterate), to be the best solution of this crux. It was first advanced by Collier, though 'dout' has been proposed by many. For 'of a' as misp. of 'often' v. note 1. 3. 74, and Greg (Aspects), pp. 152–53, 200–201, while for 'doubt' as a sp. of 'dout' v. note 4. 7. 190. Cf. also MSH. pp. 320–23 for detailed discussion of the crux, a crux which has strangely attracted immense critical attention, though the general sense of the passage is quite clear.

38. S.D. Ham.'s long disquisition has lulled the audience to rest, so that the apparition takes them all the more by surprise.

39–42. *Angels...charitable* Ham.'s first words to his father's spirit express the accepted theory of Pro-

testant theologians that ghosts must be either angels, or
devils; he gives no hint of Purgatory. Cf. *Introd.* p. lii.

43.* *in such a questionable shape* =in at any rate a
form I can talk to.

53. *Revisits* (Q2, F1, Q1) Most edd. read
'revisit'st,' but Sh. commonly omitted 't' of 2nd pers.
sing. when it would be ugly or difficult to pronounce.
Cf. 1. 5. 84, and MSH. p. 291.

54. *fools of nature* = nature's dupes, i.e. the realm of
natural phenomena is an illusion, as we realise when
faced by the supernatural.

68. *waves me forth* Sh. is thinking in terms of the
theatre. The 'platform' is out of doors in Elsinore, but
at the Globe the Ghost stands by one of the stage exits
and 'waves forth.' Cf. 1. 1. head-note and notes 3. 2.
378; 3. 4. 49–51 below.

73.* *deprive...reason* =dethrone your reason from
its sovereignty over the mind. Cf. 'your cause of
distemper' 3. 2. 338.

75–8. *The very place...beneath.* F1 omits these
lines; Delius fantastically suggests that Sh. wished to
use the substance of them for his description of the cliff
at Dover in *King Lear*.

82. *artere** Q2 'arture,' F1 'Artire,' Q1 'Artiue.'
For Sh. the word was a dissyllable; 'artere' is a normal
sp. of the period. MSH. p. 288. [1954. v. G.]

91. *direct it* = direct 'the issue.' Hor. answers his
own question.

Nay i.e. 'let us not leave it to heaven, but do something ourselves' (Clar.).

1. 5.

S.D. The scene takes place on the front stage; the
Ghost disappears down the trap, and then 'cries under
the stage.' Chambers, who does not think that the upper-
stage 'was used for the platform at Elsinore Castle,' gives
as his reasons: 'There would be hardly room "above"

for the Ghost to waft Ham. to "a more removed ground"
(1. 4. 61), and the effect of 1. 5. 148, where "Ghost
cries under the Stage," would be less' (*Eliz. Stage*, iii.
116). The first point is disputable; the second I do not
understand. *the hilt...before him* The sword, drawn
to threaten his friends in the previous scene, is now used,
I suggest, as a protection against the powers of evil. Cf.
note 1. 5. 147 and Lavater, p. 247.

11.* *fast in fires* This has puzzled many; but Dante
(*Purg.* xxiii, esp. ll. 64–9) describes how the intem-
perate in food and drink are condemned to suffer
agonies of hunger and thirst in the cleansing fires of
Purgatory. It seems to follow that the 'foul crimes' of
which the Ghost speaks were those of intemperance;
cf. 3. 3. 80 'A' took my father grossly, full of bread' and
note 1. 4. 13 above.

19. *an end* (Q2, F1) v. G. Many edd. read 'on end.'

20. *Like quills...porpentine* A striking model of a
porcupine with quills erect, the crest of the Sidney
family, faces one as one enters the court of the Leicester
Hospital founded at Warwick in 1571 by the Earl of
Leicester. Sh. must have seen it when a boy; and if so
could hardly have forgotten it, while the memory would
naturally suggest 'blazon' (v. G.) in l. 21. The 'porpentine' was also used as a sign in London (v. MSH.
p. 260).

21. *eternal blazon* = revelation of the secrets of
eternity. v. G. 'blazon.' Schmidt notes that Sh. often
uses 'eternal' to express extreme abhorrence. Cf.
Jul. Caes. 1. 2. 160; *Oth.* 4. 2. 130.

33. *rots* (F1) Q2, Q1 'rootes.' Cf. *A. & C.* 1. 4.
45–7:

> Like to a vagabond flag upon the stream
> Goes to and back, lackeying the varying tide
> To rot itself with motion.

MSH. p. 282.

42–57.* *Ay, that...prey on garbage* The burden of

the passage is that Gertrude had been 'false to her husband while he lived' (Bradley, p. 166). With this view I concur despite the arguments of W. Keller (*Shak. Jahrb.* 1919, p. 152) and van Dam (*Text of Sh.'s Hamlet*, pp. 55–6). Cf. my article M.L.R. xiii. 140–42, and v. below 5.2.64 'whored my mother' and 5.2.379–83 (note). Had the Ghost been speaking only of the incestuous marriage, the reference to 'traitorous gifts' and the comparison of the physical powers of the two brothers would lose much point. Moreover, *The Hystorie of Hamblet* twice refers in unequivocal terms to the adultery of Fengon (= Claudius), who 'before he had any violent or bloody handes, or once committed parricide upon his brother, had incestuously abused his wife,' and who had used Geruth 'as his concubine during good Horvendile's life' (Gollancz, *Sources of Hamlet*, pp. 187, 189).

62.* *hebona* (Q2, Q1) F1 'Hebenon' v. MSH. p. 273. Sh. prob. found the word in Marlowe's *Jew of Malta*, iii. 271 'The juice of hebon and Cocytus' breath,' and Marlowe prob. took it from Gower, *Conf.* iv. 3017 'Of hebenus, that slepy tre.' But Gower did not mean (as Marlowe assumed) that 'hebenus' was soporific or poisonous; he in his turn borrowed from Ovid (*Met.* xi. 610 ff.), who speaks of ebony as the wood used by the God of Sleep for the walls of his chamber. Moreover, Sh. unconscious of these misapprehensions added yet another by associating 'hebona' with henbane and attributing to it all the properties which were commonly ascribed to the herb (v. Sh. Eng. i. 509 and note in M.L.R. xv. 85–7 by Henry Bradley, who unravels the whole history, but is challenged on the last point in M.L.R. xv. 305–7).

64–73. *The leperous...smooth body* The effects of poison are described in very similar fashion in a ballad of Deloney's, 'Of King Edward the second, being poysoned' (v. F. O. Mann, *Deloney's Works*, p. 405).

81. *nature in thee* i.e. any natural affection at all. v. G. 'nature' and *Introd.* p. xxxiii.

84. *howsomever* v. note I. 2. 249, *pursues* v. note I. 4. 53.

85. *Taint not thy mind* An ominous injunction; cf. *Tw. Nt.* 3. 4. 13 'tainted in's wits.'

85–8. *nor let thy soul...sting her* This means that Ham. must strike at his uncle without in any way harming his mother, a condition which complicates the task greatly.

91. S.D. *falls upon his knees* Ll. 94–5 make it clear that Ham. rises from his knees.

92–3. *O all you host...O fie!* Cf. *Introd.* p. lii.

93–7. *heart...sinews...distracted globe* By a natural transition Ham.'s mind turns in upon himself and his own distraught and half-paralysed condition; as he strives to rise, he presses his hand first to his heart, then to his head.

96. *whiles* (Q1) F1 'while'

100. *forms...pressures* i.e. sketches...impressions.

107–109. *My tables* The whole speech is built up round the 'tables,' the note-book which young men of the age carried to record sights or sayings of interest, especially when on travel. The image is first applied metaphorically to the memory; ll. 99–101 then describe the usual contents of such table-books; lastly at the thought of his uncle's face Ham. takes out the actual tables he has about him and in bitter jest sets down Smiling Villainy as one of the wonders of Denmark, shutting the book with a snap at 'So, uncle, there *you* are!' He may re-open it for what follows; but it seems more appropriate that the 'Word' (v. next note) should be only inscribed 'within the book and volume of his brain'; more seemly to the occasion of a solemn oath and more ironical. Cf. *Introd.* pp. xli–xliii.

110.* *Word* Q2, F1 'word.' Hitherto not satisfactorily explained. Steevens suggests 'watchword' and

Dowden 'command' (cf. *Jul. Caes.* 5. 3. 5); but neither accounts for the inclusion of 'adieu, adieu' or for the oath that follows. I interpret it heraldically as the motto or 'word' on a knight's coat of arms or shield, which expressed, often in riddling or cryptic fashion, the cause or ideal to which the life of its bearer was sworn. Cf. the joust in *Pericles*, 2. 2. at which six knights appear, each with a device on his shield, together with a 'motto' or 'word,' these terms being used interchangeably (v. N.E.D. 'motto,' 1*b*). Ham. solemnly dedicates himself to the service of the quest which the Ghost has laid upon him, adopting as his motto his father's parting words. By a touch at once of supreme irony and of profound psychological insight, the 'Word' his creator gives him is 'Adieu, adieu, *remember me!*'

114. *So be it!* A fervent Amen to Hor.'s prayer.

115. *Illo, ho, ho* Mar. in despair halloos at the top of his voice; Ham. mockingly echoes him, turning the cry into a falconer's call.

121. *once* = ever. Cf. *A. & C.* 5. 2. 50.

126–32. *Why right,...I will go pray* The speech, which begins in a manner as 'wild and whirling' as those which have gone before, suddenly changes tone as the words 'business and desire' remind Ham. of the task that lies before him. But the hysterical hilarity returns with the Ghost's cries. Cf. *Introd.* p. lxii.

135. *offence* v. G.

136–40. *Yes...as you may* These words, spoken to Hor. alone, should I think be an aside, 'And now, good friends' (v. note ll. 139–40), marking the point where Mar. is brought into the conversation. Mar. is Ham.'s problem in this scene, as Dowden (taking his cue from Irving) alone among critics seems to have realised (cf. his notes on 'Denmark' l. 123 and 'truepenny' l. 150). Ham. will tell Hor. everything later; but Mar. must know nothing except what he knows already, and on that he must be sworn to secrecy.

136. *by Saint Patrick* Various explanations offered. It is, I have no doubt, a reference to the legendary Purgatory of St Patrick; v. N.E.D. 'purgatory,' 1*b*; T. Wright, *St Patrick's Purgatory*, and a rev. of Lavater in T.L.S. (Jan. 9, 1930), to which last I owe this explanation, though Tschischwitz noted it in 1869 (Furness). Furness also quotes Dekker's *Honest Whore*, 1. i., 'St. Patrick, you know, keeps Purgatory.' In the late middle ages St Patrick was regarded as the chief witness to the existence of Purgatory, since according to legend he found an entrance thereto in a cave near Lough Derg and was thus able to convince the doubting Irish. Ham. is hinting to the Protestant 'philosopher' Hor., who does not believe in Purgatory, that the Ghost is 'honest' and comes from Purgatory not Hell.

139–40. *For your desire...may* At the end of l. 138, I suppose, Ham. is just about to take Hor. into his confidence; but as Mar., curious to hear the facts, comes up, he speaks these words instead. An actor playing Ham. should, I think, make it clear to the audience that Hor. is to be told as soon as Mar. is out of the way.

147.* *Upon my sword* i.e. Upon the cross of the hilt. Cf. *Wint*. 2. 3. 167–68.

We have...already The asseveration 'in faith' was equivalent to an oath.

149. *Swear* Here Q2 and F1 read S.D. 'Ghost cries vnder the Stage.' Ham. now proceeds to address his father's spirit as if it were a devil, his attitude being that of a conjurer with his 'familiar.' The epithets 'old mole,' 'pioner,' and perhaps 'truepenny,' refer to the common superstition that devils might work like miners beneath the ground and that their rumblings could be heard. Cf. Lavater, p. 73 'Pioners or diggers for mettal, do affirme, that in many mines, there appeare straunge shapes and spirites, who are apparelled like vnto other laborers in the pit.' Cf. also (same book) pp. 191, xxv–

xxvi. Scot, *Discourse vpon Diuels* (ch. iii), tells us that a particularly dangerous sort of devil known as the Subterranei 'assault them that are miners or pioners, which use to worke in deepe and darke holes under the earth.' Mar. who has taken a threefold oath in the presence of a powerful devil, as he supposes, will keep Ham.'s secret. Cf. note l. 182 S.D. below.

150. *truepenny* 'It is (as I learn from some Sheffield authorities) a mining term, and signifies a particular indication in the soil of the direction in which ore is to be found' (Collier). There is nothing of this in N.E.D.

156. *Hic et ubique?* 'The repetition of the oath, the shifting of the ground, and the Latin phrase are taken from the ceremonies of conjurers' (Tschischwitz). Cf. note 1. 1. 42.

159–61. *Swear...sword* (Q2) For F1 arrangement, which most edd. follow, v. MSH. p. 69.

163. *pioner* v. note l. 149 above.

165. *as...welcome* A glance at Hor.'s scepticism. Dowden quotes Middleton, *Women Beware Women*, 2. 2. 'She's a stranger, madam. The more should be her welcome.'

167. *your philosophy* 'Your' is prob. used in the impersonal colloquial sense (cf. 'your worm' 4. 3. 21); but the rebuke to 'philosophy' (= science, v. G.) is intended for the 'philosopher,' Hor.

177. *There be...might* i.e. Some could tell a tale if they were permitted.

179–80. *this do swear...you!* (Q2) F1, Q1 'this not to doe...you: Sweare' MSH. p. 70.

182. S.D. *they swear a third time* Scot, *Discoverie* (bk. 15, ch. xvii), speaks of 'Promises & oaths interchangeablie made betweene the conjuror & the spirit,' oaths which were sworn three times, and for the violation of which eternal penalties were exacted. Cf. note l. 149 S.D. above. The first oath seals their mouths

upon what they have *seen*, the second upon what they have *heard*, and the third upon the 'antic disposition'; cf. Bradley, pp. 412–13, who notes that the 'removing' during oath-taking occurs also in Fletcher's *Woman's Prize*, v. iii.

184. *so poor a man* Ham. does not harp upon his loss of the crown but he drops many hints of his lack of means and of power; cf. 2. 2. 272 'I am most dreadfully attended'; 275 'Beggar that I am'; 3. 2. 276 and note 1. 2. 67.

188–90. *The time…together* The first two lines are spoken broodingly; at 'Nay' Ham. recollects the others.

190. *Some weeks pass* Cf. note 2. 1. 1.

2. I.

1. *Give him this money* etc. The dialogue between Pol. and Rey. serves to mark the passage of time, a period of several weeks during which Laer. has been able to reach Paris from Denmark (in those days a long journey), spend the money he took with him, and send for more. This impression is strengthened by the return of the ambassadors from Norway, which follows immediately after. Cf. Aspects, pp. 215–16.

7. *Danskers* v. G.

25. *fencing* Cf. Pol.'s condemnation with the K.'s 4. 7. 74–6 (note).

30. *That…incontinency* Pol. does not object to a little private 'drabbing,' inevitable with most young men ('of general assault'); but for his son to be notoriously incontinent ('open to incontinency') is a very different thing.

38. *warrant* (F 1) Q 2 'wit' MSH. pp. 107–8. Q 2 gives sense; but F 1 is certainly the true reading. Cf. note 3. 4. 6.

39. *sullies* (F 1) Q 2 'sallies' Cf. note 1. 2. 129 and MSH. pp. 108, 308.

44. *closes...consequence* = comes to grips with you as follows.

48–50. *And then...I leave* Malone and mod. edd. print as prose; but the lines, as Q2 gives them, will pass as Polonian verse.

60. *takes* (F1) Q2 'take' MSH. p. 236.

carp With a quibble on 'carp' = talk, discourse, v. G. Dowden (4th ed.) quotes Chapman's *For stay in Competence*: 'caught with *carps of sophistry*.' The carp is a difficult fish to land. v. Sh. Eng. ii. 374.

62. *windlasses* v. G.

63. *directions*, i.e. how to proceed.

66. *God bye ye* Q2 'God buy ye' F1 'God buy you'—the regular Shakespearian forms, for which F4 reads 'God b'w' you' and most mod. edd. 'God be wi' you.' I print 'God bye' throughout.

68. *in yourself* i.e. by personal observation, as well as by hearsay.

75. *with his doublet all unbraced* etc. Edd. quote Rosalind's list of the marks of a man in love:

A lean cheek...a blue eye and sunken...an unquestionable spirit...a beard neglected....Then your hose should be ungartered, your bonnet unbanded, your sleeve unbuttoned, your shoe untied, and everything about you demonstrating a careless desolation (*A.Y.L.* 3. 2. 365–72).

But cf. note 2. 2. 159 S.D. ('*disorderly attired*'). For 'no hat upon his head' v. note 5. 2. 96–7.

80. *As if...out of hell* v. Introd. p. lxii.

103. *sorry*— The dash is Capell's. Pol. continues with his sentence at l. 108.

115–16. *being kept close...utter love* i.e. if we conceal it we may cause more grief (by Ham.'s 'fordoing' himself; cf. l. 101) than the displeasure we may incur by suggesting an alliance between a prince of the blood royal and a councillor's daughter.

2. 2.

S.D. *a lobby* v. l. 161 and note l. 159 S.D.

11. *of so young days* Cf. *Acts* viii. 11 'of long time he had bewitched them.'

52. *fruit* 'the dessert after the meat' (Johnson).

59. *Valtemand* (Q2) Cf. *Names of the Characters*, p. 141.

61. *Upon our first* i.e. 'at our first representation' (Verity).

71. *majesty:* The colon marks the pause of self-satisfaction at the success of the mission: perhaps the court murmurs applause.

73. *threescore* (Q2) F 1, Q 1 'three' The 'score' disturbs the metre, but is required by the sense. 'Three thousand crowns' would be a very poor allowance for a prince embarking upon a campaign that was esti-mated to cost 'twenty thousand ducats' (4. 4. 25). Cf. 'a poor thousand crowns' *A.Y.L.* 1. 1. 3. MSH. p. 274. Perhaps Sh. forgot to delete 'him.'

79. *regards...allowance* i.e. 'terms securing the safety of the country and regulating the passage of the troops through it' (Clar.).

103. *For this effect...cause* 'for this madness *has* some cause, i.e. is not due to mere accident' (Verity).

110. *beautified* = endowed with beauty. Cf. *Two Gent.* 4. 1. 55; *Rom.* 1. 3. 88; *Luc.* 404 and Nashe, ded. of *Christ's Tears* 'To the most beautified lady, the lady Elizabeth Carey.' The jest is that Pol. who himself uses such far-fetched vocabulary should boggle at an innocent word. Some connect it with 3. 1. 145–47 'I have heard of your paintings' etc., and suppose the whole letter ironical. I see no grounds for this; it is just the love-letter of a young man, beginning *à la mode*, containing a rather forced jingle for which he apologises, and ending on a note of genuine passion. The student comes out in the word 'machine,' v. note l. 124.

113. *in her...bosom* 'Women anciently had a pocket in the fore part of their stays, in which they not only carried love-letters and love-tokens, but even their money and materials for needlework' (Steevens). Cf. *Two Gent.* 3. 1. 250.

117. *Doubt...move* According to the accepted astronomy the sun, fixed in its sphere, moved round the 'centre,' which was the earth; 'doubt' in l. 118 means 'suspect.'

124. *machine* i.e. body, v. G. Dowden refers to Bright (*Melancholie*, pp. 61–2) who describes the body as a machine connected with the 'soul' by the intermediate 'spirit'; cf. note 2. 2. 300–301.

136. *played...table-book* i.e. noted the matter privately and kept it secret. Cf. 'tables' 1. 5. 107–109 (note).

137. *working* (Q2) F1 'winking'—which all edd. follow. Cf. *L.L.L.* 4. 1. 33 'the working of the heart'; *Son.* xciii 'thy heart's workings'; 1 *Hen. VI*, 5. 5. 86 'working of my thoughts'; above 1. 1. 67 'In what particular thought to work I know not'; and below l. 557, where Ham. speaks of the 'working' of the 'soul.' Thus 'working' = mental operation of any kind. MSH. pp. 74–5.

141. *out of thy star* The modern 'out of thy sphere' preserves the same astrological notion. Cf. *Tw. Nt.* 2. 5. 156; *All's Well*, 1. 1. 87–91.

145. *fruits* 'She took the fruits of advice when she obeyed advice, the advice was then made fruitful' (Johnson).

146. *repelléd* Q2 'repell'd.' Cf. 2. 1. 106.

156. S.D. Theobald added 'Pointing to his head and shoulder.' Dowden suggests that Pol. refers to his official staff of office and the hand that bore it.

159. *Centre* i.e. the centre of the earth, which was the centre of the Ptolemaic universe. Cf. note l. 117 and *M.N.D.* 3. 2. 53–4. Both Q2 and F1 print the capital.

S.D.* *Hamlet...reading a book*, etc. Q2, F1 and Q1
all give Ham.'s entry at l. 167 below, where it is needed
for an entry on to the outer-stage. That Sh. himself
intended Ham. here to enter on the inner-stage is I think
shown by Ham.'s first words to Pol., which gain point
only if we suppose ll. 159–67 to have been overheard
by him. v. *Introd*. pp. lvi–lix. If Sh.'s manuscript
contained a double-entry, it is easy to see how the earlier
one came to be omitted. MSH. pp. 186–87.

disorderly attired Cf. Oph.'s description at 2. 1.
75–8, obviously designed to prepare us for this entry,
and Anthony Scoloker, *Daiphantus* (1604), cited by
J. Q. Adams (*Life of Shakespeare*, p. 310):

> Puts off his clothes, his shirt he only wears,
> Much like mad Hamlet—

which gives us the contemporary stage-effect.

160. *four hours* The 'four' is indefinite; cf. *Wint*.
5. 2. 132 'any time these four hours.'

161. *Here in the lobby* He indicates, I suggest, the
inner-stage. v. *Introd*. pp. lvi–lix.

162. *I'll loose my daughter to him* v. *Introd*. pp.
lvii–lviii and G. 'loose.'

166. *assistant for a state* Cf. *Names of the Characters*,
'Polonius,' p. 141.

167. S.D. Q2 'Enter Hamlet.' F1 'Enter Hamlet
reading on a Booke.' Cf. note l. 159 S.D.

170. *O give me leave* The regular formula for
politely saying good-bye esp. to social superiors, or
requesting them to go away; cf. ll. 217–20 below and
K. John, 1. 1. 230. Led astray by F1, in which the lines
have become disarranged, all mod. edd. make Pol.
speak them to Ham. Cf. MSH. pp. 218–19.

174. *fishmonger* i.e. fleshmonger, bawd. Malone
quotes Barnaby Rich's *Irish Hubbub*, 'Senex fornicator,
an old fishmonger'; and Dowden, his *Herodotus*, 1584
(ed. Lang, p. 131) 'Such arrant honest women as are

fishe for every man [i.e. harlots].' Cf. also B. Jonson's
Masque of Christmas, in which Venus plays a 'tire-
woman' and 'a fishmonger's daughter,' and Middleton's
Anything for a Quiet Life, in which Margarita, the
French bawd, is likewise the daughter of a fishmonger.
A 'fishmonger's daughter' therefore = a prostitute, and
a 'fishmonger' = 'a seller of woman's chastity' (Herford). Cf. note l. 159 S.D. The epithet has an added
point as applied to one fishing for secrets.

181–82. *For if the sun...daughter* Such is Ham.'s
first direct reference to Oph. in the text. (Cf. *Cymb.*
1. 4. 147–48 'If you buy ladies' flesh at a million a dram,
you cannot preserve it from tainting.') Ham. is playing
upon 'loose' and 'fishmonger'; the usual word of the
time for 'flesh' in the carnal sense being 'carrion'; cf.
N.E.D. 'carrion,' 3; *Troil.* 4. 1. 71; and *M.V.* 3. 1. 32–4
'*Shy.* My own flesh and blood to rebel! *Sol.* Out upon
it, old carrion, rebels it at these years?' For the general
idea of the sun breeding from corruption, very prevalent
at this time and going back to Diogenes Laertius and
Tertullian, v. Tilley, 604 and an article by the same
writer in M.L.R. xi. Cf. also note 2. 2. 252–53;
M.W.W. 1. 3. 62 'Then did the sun on dunghill shine';
A. & C. 1. 3. 68–9 'By the fire That quickens Nilus'
slime'; *Meas.* 2. 2. 165–68:

> ...it is I
> That, lying by the violet in the sun,
> Do as the carrion does, not as the flower,
> Corrupt with virtuous season;

and *Edward III* (1596, *Sh. Apocrypha*, ed. Tucker
Brooke), 2. 1. 438–39:

> The freshest summers day doth soonest taint
> The lothed carrion that it seemes to kisse.

182. *a good kissing carrion* (Q2, F1) i.e. flesh good
enough for kissing purposes. Warburton read 'a god,
kissing carrion,' and many edd. follow, quoting *Cymb.*

3. 4. 166 'common-kissing Titan' and 1 *Hen. IV*,
2. 4. 133–34 'Didst thou never see Titan kiss a dish of
butter?' Tilley (v. previous note) supports the emendation as being in keeping with the incorruptible or divine
nature of the sun, insisted upon in all proverbial or
literary expressions of the idea, especially in that of
Tertullian, which occurring in an attack upon the
theatre may have been familiar to Shakespeare. The fact
that 'god' and 'good' are sometimes confused in this
(cf. notes 4. 5. 40, 71; 5. 2. 342) and other Qq. seems
at first sight to lend support also. But 'good' is far more
often spelt 'god' than vice versa; and 'good kissing' is
textually very difficult to set aside. The two versions give
different meanings, both convenient to the context; but
the cynicism of the unemended text is more appropriate
to Ham.'s mood than Warburton's 'noble emendation,'
as Johnson called it. Cf. also next note.

184.* *Let her not walk i'th'sun* 'Oph. is likewise
"a good kissing carrion"; therefore let her not walk
i'th'sun' (Herford). That Ham. has in mind the
proverbial 'Out of God's blessing into the warm sun,'
which is applicable to fallen women as to outcasts in
general (cf. note 1. 2. 67 and G. 'sun'), is shown by
'conception is a *blessing.*'

185. *but as your daughter* (Q2) F1 'but not as your
daughter' The Q2 reading is subtler and more in Ham.'s
manner; cf. MSH. pp. 256–57.

195. *Between who?* Again harping on the daughter;
cf. 'country matters' (3. 2. 114).

197. *Slanders, sir* etc. The old man, as appears from
'if like a crab you could go backward,' retreats in fright
as the 'mad' Ham. bears down on him enforcing point
after point of the 'satirical rogue' with an accusing
finger. (Cf. Capell, *Notes*, i. 131.) For the 'rogue'
Warburton suggests Juvenal (e.g. *Sat.* x. 188).

199–200. *eyes...plum-tree gum* Cf. Greene's *Tu
Quoque*, 1611 (Hazlitt, *Dodsley*, xi. 282) 'Surely I was

begotten in a plum-tree, I ha' such a deal of gum about mine eyes' (Dowden).

208. *Will you walk out of the air, my lord?* Fresh air was thought bad for an invalid, and Pol. is thus politely suggesting that Ham. is not quite himself. v. Tilley, 751. Cf. Jonson, *E.M.I.* 2. 3. 40–8 '*Dame*. What aile you sweet heart, are you not well... for loues sake, sweet heart, come in, out of the aire. *Kitely*. How simple, and how subtill are her answers!' There is clearly borrowing here, prob. unconscious, by either Jonson or Sh.; *E.M.I.* was first acted, with Sh. in the cast, in the autumn of 1598.

209. *grave*. (Q 2) F 1 'graue?'

210. *that's* (Q 2) F 1 'that is.'

212. *sanity* (F 1) Q 2 'sanctity' Cf. note 1. 3. 21 and MSH. p. 107.

227–28. *My excellent...you both?* Ham.'s greeting is at first most friendly and natural; his manner cools and his 'disposition' grows more 'antic' as his suspicions grow.

236. *privates* i.e. intimate friends (with a quibble).

239–40.* *the world's grown honest* Hardly a tactful remark to the dispossessed heir of Denmark; it arrests his attention and leads him to 'question more in particular.'

242–72. *Let me question...dreadfully attended* (F 1) Q 2 omits, possibly because the talk of Denmark as a 'prison' was thought dangerous with a Danish queen on the throne. MSH. pp. 96–8.

252–53. *there is...makes it so* A commonplace of the age; cf. Spenser, *F.Q.* VI. ix. 30 'It is the mind that maketh good or ill'; *Euphues* (Bond, i. 193) 'it is ye disposition of the thought yt altereth ye nature of ye thing. The Sun shineth vppon the dungehill and is not corrupted' (the juxtaposition of the two sentiments is interesting, cf. note 2.2.181–82 above); *Oth.* 1. 3. 322–23 ''tis in ourselves that we are thus or thus,' etc.

255.* *your ambition* No one seems hitherto to have observed the significance of this talk about Ham.'s ambition, continued for 14 lines, and then abruptly broken off by Ham. The two 'friends' acting on the K.'s suggestion are probing Ham. to 'gather so much as from occasion' they may glean (2. 2. 16) of what is in his mind. Ham. refuses to be drawn; but he has seen the point, and makes use of it later. Cf. notes 3. 1. 125; 3. 2. 243, 341, 345. To the Eliz. 'ambition' (v. G.) meant the ostentation of glory as well as the desire for it.

259. *bad dreams* Cf. Bright, p. 124, 'giuen to fearefull and terrible dreames.'

266–67. *Then are...shadows* Ham. reduces the argument to an absurdity: if ambition is but a shadow's shadow, then kings and bombastic heroes, the very type of ambition, are shadows, and their antitype, the beggars, the only real men (after Herford).

268.* *Shall we to th' court?* i.e. this sort of hair-splitting would do well enough at court, but is no pastime for sensible persons.

269. *wait upon you* = accompany you. But 'wait upon' also means 'watch' and 'lie in wait for,' as they prob. show by a significant glance at each other. Ham. pretends to take it in the sense of 'act as your servants.'

272. *most dreadfully attended* i.e. my retinue is a sorry one. Cf. 'Beggar that I am' (l. 275) and note 1. 5. 184. Generally taken as referring to the 'bad dreams' (l. 259); but Ham. is speaking of his 'servants.'

272–73. *in the beaten way of friendship* i.e. as old friends (ironical).

275. *Beggar that I am* Ham. identifies himself with the real men ('bodies') of l. 266.

275–77. *I am even poor...too dear a halfpenny* He can only afford a ha'p'orth of thanks, and yet even that is over-payment, since what they give in exchange is worth nothing. Cf. *A.Y.L.* 2. 3. 74 'too late a week.'

278. *come, come* (Q2) F1 'Come'

283. *your modesties* = your sense of shame.

288–90. *by the rights...love* Cf. 2. 2. 11–12.

290. *love, and by what* Q2 'loue; and by what'

290–91. *by what more...withal* = by any more moving appeal a better speaker than I could think of. *can charge* (Q2) F1 'could charge.'

300–301.* *custom of exercises* v. G. 'exercises.' Dowden finds the phrase in Bright, p. 126. Cf. note 2. 2. 124.

302–12. *this goodly frame...of dust* This famous passage prob. owes something to Florio's *Montaigne*, ii. ch. 12 (pp. 296–97). G. B. Harrison (*Sh. at Work*, pp. 277–78) quotes from W. Parry's *Travels of Sir Anthony Shirley* (pub. Nov. 1601): 'those resplendent and crystalline heavens over-canopying the earth.' But Montaigne seems the more likely source.

303. *a sterile promontory* In a 'sea of troubles.'

305. *roof fretted with golden fire* Cf. note 3. 2. 378. In *M.V.* 5. 1. 59–60 ('the floor of heaven...thick inlaid with patens of bright gold') the firmament is considered from the other side, as it were; the stars being balls of fire fixed in transparent spheres which revolved within the firmament. 'Fretted' (v. G.) = embossed —an architectural term.

305–306. *it appeareth...but* (Q2) F1 'it appeares no other thing to mee, then.'

307–11. *What a piece of work...animals* Such is the pointing of Q2. Cf. that of the F1 text, accepted by all edd., substituting notes of exclamation for the orig. queries, the two being alternatives in old printing:

What a piece of worke is a man! how noble in Reason! how infinite in faculty! in forme and mouing how expresse and admirable! in Action, how like an Angel! in apprehension, how like a God! the beauty of the world, the Parragon of Animals;

This is rhetorical, the declamation of a player; Q2, without an exclamation of any kind, gives us the brooding

Ham. The sense too is different, to the bewilderment of some critics. But the absolute 'how like a god' makes a fine climax, esp. as followed at once by 'this quint-essence of dust'; 'how like an angel in apprehension' recalls 'with wings as swift/As meditation or the thoughts of love' (1. 5. 29–30); while 'how infinite in faculties, in form and moving' may be paraphrased 'how infinitely varied in his bodily powers: in sight, hearing and other qualities of sense (cf. "the very faculties of eyes and ears" 2. 2. 569); in facial expression and gesture (cf. "his whole function suiting/With forms to his conceit" 2.2.559–60); and in the motion and activity of his body.' The traditional (F1) rendering, on the other hand, involves two grave difficulties: (i) To a thinking Eliz. angels were discarnate spirits whose only form of action was 'apprehension' (cf. Aquinas, *Summa*, i. 50–8). To make Ham. compare human action to that of an angel is, therefore, to make him talk nonsense. (ii) The epithet 'express' goes so awkwardly with 'form and moving' that N.E.D. has had to devise a nonce-use, i.e. 'well framed' or 'modelled' to explain it; whereas its ordinary meaning, i.e. 'direct and purposive' is exactly suited to 'action.' MSH. pp. 210–14.

307. *piece of work* = masterpiece, work of art. v. G. 'piece.'

308. *faculties* (Q2) F1 'faculty.'

323–29. *He that plays the King* etc. Ham.'s retort to Ros.'s talk of 'lenten entertainment.' The stock dramatic types of the age are glanced at, each in ironical fashion. As Sh. is reputed to have 'played some kingly parts' himself there may be 'a sly undercurrent of allusion' in the opening words (v. Sh. Eng. ii. 248).

325. *foil and target* i.e. for stage-fights, which were frequent in Eliz. drama, v. G. 'foil'; cf. L. B. Wright, *Stage Duelling* etc. (M.L.R. xxii. 265 ff.).

325–27. *the Lover...peace* i.e. I will applaud the sighs of the Lover and not interrupt the sallies of the

'Humorous Man.' The latter = the fantastic, like
Jaques, whose supposed topical or personal references
were often in danger of interruption by victims or
their partisans (cf. *A.Y.L.* 2. 7. 48–87). The F 1 list of
players at the end of 2 *Hen. IV* describes Falstaff and his
companions as 'irregular humorists.' W. J. Lawrence
(*Sh.'s Workshop*, p. 101) suggests a reference to trouble
caused by the ending of Jonson's *E.M.O.* in 1599
(v. Chambers, *Will. Shak.* i. 423, *Eliz. Stage*, iii. 361).

328–29.* *the Lady...halt for't* 'The lady, of course,
will have indecent words to utter; if she omits them, the
halting blank verse will betray her delicacy' (Dowden).

332. *the tragedians of the city* Generally taken as a
topical reference; if so, more appropriate to the Lord Admiral's men, with its famous tragic player, Edward Alleyn
and its Marlowe repertory, than to Sh.'s company, who
at this date had made their reputation in comedy rather
than in tragedy. Cf. notes 2. 2. 335–36, 339, 395–96,
451, and G. B. Harrison, *Sh. at Work*, pp. 273–76.

333. *residence* i.e. in the city.

335–36. *their inhibition...innovation* Much discussed, but without agreement. A few points may be
made: (i) The 'innovation' has nothing to do with the
'little eyases,' as many have assumed, since it is expressly
stated to be the cause of an 'inhibition,' i.e. a prohibition
of playing by authority. (ii) As Boas (*Sh. and the Universities*, p. 23 n.) shows, 'innovation' always means a
political upheaval of some kind in Sh. He quotes
1 *Hen. IV*, 5. 1. 78 'hurlyburly innovation' and *Oth.*
2. 3. 42, to which I may add *Cor.* 3. 1. 175 'a traitorous
innovator' and *More* (Sh.'s Addition), ll. 92–3 'You
shall perceive how horrible a shape/Your innovation
bears.' And if the passage (as I think) was written in
1601, the 'innovation' can hardly be other than that of
the Earl of Essex in Feb. of that year. (iii) Sh.'s company
were certainly not inhibited on account of the Essex
rising, since they were acting at court on the eve of the

Earl's execution. Nor have we any direct evidence that the Admiral's men were inhibited; but they seem to have ceased playing for a time in Feb. and March, 1601, and were involved in legal troubles of some kind in the same year (v. Chambers, *Eliz. Stage*, ii. 174–75). Cf. also Chambers, *Will. Shak.* i. 65, 423.

339. *No, indeed, are they not.* It is surely absurd to suppose that Sh.'s company would thus bluntly proclaim themselves unpopular. That they were financially affected 'too' is hinted at in ll. 364–65 (v. note).

340–65. *How comes it...his load too* (F1). Q2 omits, perhaps because, as De Groot suggests, when Q2 was printed in 1604 Anne of Denmark was Queen of England and had taken the Children of the Chapel under her protection (v. Chambers, *Will. Shak.* i. 414 and MSH. pp. 96, 98). The 'little eyases' were, of course, these Children, and the passage refers to the Poetomachia or 'War of the Theatres' begun by Jonson's *Cynthia's Revels*, acted by the Children late 1600, and his *Poetaster*, belonging to the spring of 1601, to which Dekker and Marston replied in *Satiromastix* acted by Sh.'s company in the summer of the same year. Sh. therefore can hardly have written the words before the summer of 1601. Cf. *Introd.* pp. xxi–xxii. (For the 'War of the Theatres' v. Chambers, *Eliz. Stage*, i. 381; iii. 363–64, 293, and R. A. Small, *Stage-Quarrel*, Breslau, 1899.)

343. *that cry out...question* i.e. whose shrill voices are heard above all others in the controversy. v. G. 'top,' 'question' and l. 443 below.

345. *the common stages* i.e. the public playhouses. The Children of the Chapel played at the Blackfriars, a 'private' playhouse.

345–47. *that many...come thither* 'Fashionable gallants are afraid to visit the common theatres, so unfashionable have the writers for the children made them' (Dowden).

351–52. *as it is like most will* (anon. apud *Camb. Sh.*) F1 'as it is like most.' Pope and most edd. 'as it is most like.' MSH. p. 303.

352. *not better* (F2) F1 'no better'—with a trace of the 't' type. MSH. pp. 291–92.

357–59. *no money bid...question* Generally explained: 'the theatre managers would offer nothing for the plot of a play, unless it concerned the controversy' (v. G. 'argument'). Verity suggests: 'the public... would not give a rap for any other subject of debate,' a rendering which seems less caviary to the general.

364–65. *Hercules and his load too* This could not have been penned before late 1599 when the Globe Theatre, with its sign of Hercules carrying the globe, was first opened. The 'too' is noteworthy, implying that 'the tragedians of the city' were not identical with Sh.'s company, v. note 2. 2. 332.

366. *It is not very strange* etc. The fickleness of popular favour brings Ham. back from Sh.'s London to Elsinore.

371. S.D. Q2 'A Florish,' F1 'Flourish for the Players.' Trumpets were used as a means of advertisement by Eliz. players both in the streets of London and when travelling in the country.

374. *Your hands? come then* Q2 'your hands come then,' F1 'your hands, come:'—which many edd. follow. The Q2 'then' makes all the difference. It is not Ham. but the others who offer to shake hands. He 'complies' for fashion's sake, hinting that he prefers the company of the players. MSH. pp. 260–62.

379–80. *but my uncle...deceived* Q2 'but my Vncle-father, and Aunt-mother, are deceaued' The emphasis-capitals and comma-pauses indicate the pointed irony of the sally. MSH. p. 202.

382–83.* *I am but mad...I know a hawk from a handsaw.* One of Ham.'s pregnant quibbles. 'Handsaw' is generally taken as a corruption of 'hernshaw' (= heron), but the word, occurring in both Q2 and F1, is textually very strong, and must be accepted as it stands. Moreover, 'hawk' like 'handsaw' is the name of a workman's tool, while the expression was doubtless proverbial and is actually included (in slightly different form) in Ray's *Proverbs* (1768, p. 196), without any reference to Sh. Mr J. A. Barlow, then of the Ministry of Labour, first suggested this to me privately in March, 1924, and interpreted 'hawk' as a plasterer's mortar-board, still in everyday use under that name. Dowden, I find, anticipates this suggestion, and offers as alternative 'hawk' or 'hack,' an Eliz. word meaning a heavy cutting tool of the mattock or pick-axe type (v. N.E.D. 'hawk,' 'hack,' sb. 1), which both in weight and manner of operation would form a more appropriate contrast to the light neat-cutting 'handsaw.' Anyhow, we need not hesitate to take Ham.'s words as meaning on the surface, 'I am only mad on one point; in other respects I have wit enough to tell chalk from cheese.' But as usual he has a second purport, which Ros. and Guild. are not intended to catch. 'Handsaw' is not a corruption of 'hernshaw,' but it is certainly a quibble upon it, since the whole passage (as all have noted) can be readily understood in terms of falconry. Hawking at herons was a favourite sport; and a north wind driving the two birds towards the south, i.e. into the sun, would make it difficult to distinguish between them at a distance despite their difference in size (v. Clar. note, and Madden, pp. 206–7). Thus Ham. also implies that he has 'an eye of' his seeming friends and knows them to be birds of prey. Finally, cf. Bright, p. 257 'the ayre meet for melancholicke folke, ought to be thinne, pure and subtile, open, and patent to all winds: in respect of their temper, especially to the South and South-east.'

386–87. *baby...swaddling-clouts* Perhaps a jest at something comical in the costume or figure of Pol.

392–93. *You say...indeed* Spoken to Ros. as Pol. comes within earshot.

395–96. *When Roscius...Rome* i.e. 'Queen Anne is dead' (as we should now say); cf. G. 'buz.' A reference to the famous actor of Rome, whom Eliz. and later writers took for a tragic actor though he was really a comic one, and with whom E. Alleyn the leading player of the Admiral's men was often compared (v. Chambers, *Eliz. Stage*, ii. 297, citing Nashe, Weever, B. Jonson, Fuller), would inevitably remind Sh.'s audience of the latter; and I have strong suspicions that, when the troupe appeared, 1 Player was 'made up' as Alleyn. Cf. note 2. 2. 332.

400. *Then came...ass* Prob. a line from some lost ballad; also, as Elze pointed out, a rude quibble on Pol.'s words 'upon my honour.'

401–407. *The best actors...the only men* The speech is characteristic of Pol.'s filing-cabinet type of mind, still found in some public officials. It was also intended, I suspect, as a satirical epitome of the repertory and perhaps even of the play-bills of the Admiral's men. It may be taken as axiomatic that praise from Pol. implies criticism on Sh.'s part.

404. *scene individable* i.e. a play which observes the unity of place, as distinct from 'poem unlimited' which ignores the unities altogether.

405–407. *Seneca...men* I preserve in effect the punct. of Q 2 with which F 1 substantially agrees. Most edd. follow Theobald (v. next note), and thus render the passage unintelligible. I take 'the law of writ' and 'the liberty' as terms defining the jurisdiction of the Sheriffs in and about the city of London (a jurisdiction very important for players), quibblingly applied to types of drama. 'The law of writ' refers to those districts where the sheriff's writ ran and where no play-houses would be erected. Sh. associates these with Seneca, who was for the Elizabethans a paragon of dramatic propriety, so that the phrase may be paraphrased 'plays written under strict regulation.' On the other hand, the lively and careless genius of Plautus is connected with 'the liberty' (i.e. districts within or without the city exempt from the sheriff's jurisdiction, and therefore convenient for the erection of playhouses), and may in turn be paraphrased as 'plays out of all bounds' (cf. Chambers, *Eliz. Stage*, ii. 477–80). The sentence 'These are the only men' stands apart from the rest. Pol. is repeating in other words 'The best actors in the world' after his pompous fashion.

406. *light for the law of writ and the liberty...* *These* Q2 'light for the lawe of writ, and the liberty: these' F1 'light, for the law of Writ, and the Liberty. These' Theobald 'light. For the law of writ and the liberty, these'

408.* *Jephthah, judge of Israel* If the repertory satirised in the previous speech be that of the Admiral's men, Ham.'s change of subject is not so abrupt as it seems, since a play called *Jephthah* by Dekker and Munday was being acted by them in July 1601 (v. Chambers, *Eliz. Stage*, ii. 179). The play is lost, but the 'pious chanson' survives, and the first 'row,' or stanza, runs (according to Halliwell):

> I read that many yeare agoe,
> When Jepha Judge of Israel
> Had one fair Daughter and no more,
>   whom he loved so passing well.
> And as by lot God wot,
> It came to passe most like it was,
> Great warrs there should be,
>   and who should be the chiefe, but he.

Dramatically 'Jephthah,' who sacrificed his daughter, harks back to 2. 2. 162. The reference to 'warrs' is omitted as beside the point, but 'as by lot...like it was' was intended, I think, to recall 2. 2. 184–86. Cf. 3 *Hen. VI*, 5. 1. 90–1, and *Book of Homilies*, 1574 ("A sermon against swearing and perjury"), ed. 1850, p. 75.

414. *Still on my daughter* 'Still' here, as ever, means 'always.'

426–33. *You are welcome* etc. Ham. greets the players as a whole first, and then addresses himself to 1 Player and the principal boy separately. All women's parts were, of course, played by boys in Sh.'s day.

432–33. *like a piece...the ring* v. G. 'cracked within the ring.'

434. *French falconers* The French were the master-falconers of the age. Turbervile's *Booke of Faulconrie* (1575), the best Eliz. book on the subject, was ad-mittedly drawn from French sources, while Sir T. Browne, writing *Of Hawks and Falconry* in 1684, declares that 'the French Artists...seem to have been the first and noblest Falconers in the Western part of Europe,' and relates how one of his favourite authors, Julius Scaliger, 'an expert Falconer,' saw a gerfalcon of Henry of Navarre in one day 'strike down a Buzzard, two wild Geese, divers Kites, a Crane and a Swan' (Sayle, *Works of Sir T. Browne*, iii. 297, 299). It is prob. that Southampton, Shakespeare's patron, and the friend of the Earl of Essex who had served with Navarre, knew all about the exploits of this gerfalcon. Madden (p. 140) wrongly interprets Ham.'s words as a sneer at the French.

441. *caviary* (Q2) The original form of the word.

443. *cried in the top of mine* = exceeded mine (v. G. 'top' and 2. 2. 343).

445. *with as...cunning* = with as much restraint as skill. The 'modesty' is enlarged upon in what follows.

448. *honest* = free from wantonness, clean.

449–50. *more handsome than fine* = a dignified ('handsome'), straightforward style without subtlety or artistry.

451. *Æneas' tale to Dido* Critics are agreed neither

upon the purpose of the episode that follows nor whether
Sh. himself approved of the Pyrrhus speech. Two titles
of a dramatic rendering of the Dido story have come
down to us from that period: the extant *Dido, Queen of
Carthage*, printed 1594, ascribed on the title-page to
Marlowe and Nashe, and *Dido and Aeneas*, of which
we know nothing except that it was acted on Jan. 8, 1598
by the Admiral's men, and prob. acquired by them from
the Pembroke men, for whom Nashe wrote (v. Chambers, *Eliz. Stage*, ii. 132). The former contains a
Pyrrhus speech; but Sh.'s speech is better poetry, tells
a different story, and draws from Vergil in other ways
than Marlowe's, to which, apart from one striking
parallel (v. note 2. 2. 476–78), it seems to owe nothing
at all. Fleay (v. Furness) and H. D. Gray (M.L.R. xv.
217 ff.) contend that Sh. is quoting from an old play of
his own, written in rivalry to Marlowe's. The materials
are too scanty to admit of dogmatism; but I tentatively
suggest as an alternative that the two Dido plays were
really two stages of the same play-book, the play performed in 1598 being a revision, perhaps by Chapman
or Drayton, of the 1594 text (v. notes ll. 487–91,
506, 521, 580–83), and that Sh., who had admired this
performance with reservations, set out to show that he
could better its style and criticise it at the same time.
I have no doubt at all that the speech is Sh.'s (cf. notes
ll. 487–91, 499–501). It should be noted that Alleyn
appears to have been absent from the Admiral's men in
Jan. 1598; if so he did not play Aeneas (v. Chambers,
Eliz. Stage, ii. 157; Greg, *Alcazar and Orlando*,
p. 92).

454. *like th'Hyrcanian beast* Cf. *Aen*. iv. 367
'Hyrcanaeque admorunt ubera tigres'—a phrase used
by Dido to 'perfidious' Aeneas. v. G. 'Hyrcanian.'

456–67. *The rugged Pyrrhus...hellish Pyrrhus*
There seems no basis either in Vergil or Marlowe for
this description. The nearest to ll. 459–63 we have is

Aen. ii. 551 'in multo lapsantem sanguine nati,' which refers to Priam not Pyrrhus. It is noteworthy that Dryden clearly had Sh.'s lines in mind in translating Vergil's account of Pyrrhus.

460. *heraldy* v. G.

461. *gules...tricked* Heraldic terms; v. G.

473–75. *Striking...command* Cf. *Aen.* ii. 509–11, and 544–46:

> arma diu senior desueta trementibus aevo
> circumdat nequiquam umeris et inutile ferrum
> cingitur.

> sic fatus senior telumque imbelle sine ictu
> coniecit, rauco quod protinus aere repulsum,
> et summo clipei nequiquam umbone pependit.

473. *antique* Either (*a*) ancient, or (*b*) 'antic' = ludicrous.

476–78. *in rage...father falls* The lines owe nothing to Vergil and must be borrowed from *Dido, Queen of Carthage* (v. note l. 451), 2. 1. 253–54:

> Which he disdaining, whisk'd his sword about,
> And with the wind thereof the king fell down.

478–80. *then senseless Ilium...his base* Cf. *Aen.* ii. 554–56:

> haec finis Priami fatorum, hic exitus illum
> sorte tulit Troiam incensam et prolapsa videntem
> Pergama.

487–91. *But as we often see...region* This studied simile, so like Chapman in manner (cf. *Bussy*, 2. 1. 94 ff. 'Then, as in Arden I have seen an oak' etc.), is in diction pure Sh., e.g. the words 'rack,' 'region,' 'hush' (for wind or weather) are favourites of his; cf. *Ado*, 2. 3. 37–8 'How still the evening is,/As hushed on purpose to grace harmony'; *Temp.* 4. 1. 207; *Oth.* 4. 2. 79; *John*, 5. 1. 20; *Son.* 102. 10. For 'region' cf. 2. 2. 582.

493–94. *the Cyclops' hammers* etc. Cf. 'Vulcan's stithy' 3. 2. 82.

499–501. *Break...fiends.* For this image of a
great wheel rolling down a hill cf. 3. 3. 17–22. The
style is different, but the two passages come from the
same corner of Sh.'s brain.

504–505. *he's for a jig...sleeps* i.e. the only thing
in a play he can appreciate is the Clown's jig (which
commonly took place at the end) or some bawdy jest—
he sleeps out the rest. Kempe, who left Sh.'s company
in 1599, was famous for his jigs, which were prob.
discontinued after his departure. v. G. 'jig.'

506.* *But who, ah woe!* Q 2 'But who, a woe,' F 1
'But who, O who,' MSH. p. 73.

mobled v. G. This far-fetched and, with its homely
association, rather ridiculous word, together with Ham.'s
shying at it and Pol.'s praise, was prob. introduced to
excite critical attention to what follows, e.g. to equally
far-fetched expressions like 'threat'ning the flames With
bisson rheum' and 'made milch the burning eyes of
heaven,' which I suggest were intended to parody the
style of *Dido and Aeneas.* Cf. note l. 451.

512. *o'er-teeméd loins* Perhaps suggested through
misunderstanding of *Aen.* ii. 503 'quinquaginta illi
thalami, spes ampla nepotum.'

521. *made milch* v. note l. 506 and cf. Drayton,
Polyolbion, xiii. 171 'exhaling the milch dew' (Steevens).

523. *whe'r* (Capell) Q 2, F 1 'where' Malone and
mod. edd. read the expanded form 'whether.' MSH.
p. 232.

528–30. *the abstracts...you live* Developed in
3. 2. 20–24 on 'the purpose of playing.' Here, as there,
it is the play rather than the players Sh. has chiefly in
mind. This repeated emphasis on the 'topicality' of
drama is significant in view of the prevailing belief in
Sh.'s 'impersonality.' For 'abstracts' (F 1) v. MSH.
p. 239.

533. *bodkin* (Q 2) F 1 'bodykins.' A recognised
variant, v. N.E.D.

534. *who shall 'scape whipping?* Referring to the Act of 1572 for the punishment of rogues and vagabonds, among which were named (as Puritan enemies of the stage rejoiced to point out) stage-players, though only those 'not belonging to any Baron of this Realme.' Under this act vagabonds were to 'bee grevouslye whipped and burnte through the gristle of the right Eare with a hot Yron of the compasse of an Ynche about' (v. Chambers, *Eliz. Stage*, iv. 269–70). Burleigh shared the puritan dislike of players, and believed in rewarding poets also 'according to their desert.' Fuller (*Worthies*, 1662, p. 220) writes:

There passeth a story commonly told and believed, that Spenser presenting his poems to queen Elizabeth, she, highly affected therewith, commanded the lord Cecil, her treasurer, to give him an hundred pounds; and when the treasurer (a good steward of the queen's money) alledged that sum was too much; 'Then give him,' quoth the queen, 'what is reason'; to which the lord consented, but was so busied belike about matters of higher concernment, that Spenser received no reward.

541. *The Murder of Gonzago* Cf. *Introd.* pp. xxii–iv.

544. *dozen or sixteen lines* Furness prints over four pages of speculation on the position of these lines in the interlude that follows. It is doubtful whether Sh. himself gave the matter much thought; but cf. note 3. 2. 1.

551. S.D. Q2, F1 'Exeunt' Most edd. print the S.D. after 'Ay, so, God bye to you!' Q2 and F1 show Ham. uttering the good-bye in a tone of sarcastic relief after the two have gone.

553. *rogue and peasant slave* Ham. has just been referring to the statute against 'rogues and vagabonds' (v. note l. 534).

559. *function* v. G. and cf. Daniel, *Civil Wars* (1599), vi. 93 'His hand, his eye, his wits all present, wrought/The function of the glorious Part he beares.'

560. *forms* v. G. and note 2. 2. 307–11.

566. *cleave the general ear* Cf. 3. 2. 10 'split the ears of the groundlings.'

567. *Make mad...free* An exact description of what Ham. effects in the play-scene. It leads on to ll. 592–98. *free* = innocent.

569. *yet I* 579. *Ha* Johnson and most mod. edd. print these as separate lines; I follow Q2 and F1. MSH. p. 222.

573. *property* Cf. 1. 5. 75 'of crown, of queen.'

580. *pigeon-livered* v. G. Cf. Bartholomew Anglicus, quoted in Robert Steele, *Mediaeval Lore*, p. 79, 'by the gall we are wroth.'

580–83. *lack gall...offal* Cf. Chapman, *Bussy*, 2. 1. 3–5:

> Less than either
> Will make the gall of Envy overflow;
> She feeds on outcast entrails like a kite.

The conjunction of 'gall,' 'kite' and 'offal' or 'outcast entrails' seems to make borrowing certain on one side or the other. *Bussy* was being acted c. 1600–1604. v. Chambers, *Eliz. Stage*, iii. 253.

582. *ha' fatted* Q2 'a fatted'

584. *kindless* = incestuous, v. G.

587. *a dear father* (Q4) Q2 'a deere,' F1 'the Deere' MSH. pp. 301–2. The coincidence of Q2 and F1 suggests that Sh. himself may have omitted the word 'father.'

588. *Prompted...by heaven and hell* Cf. ll. 602–607 below, and *Introd.* pp. l–liii.

591. *A stallion...foh!* Q2 prints this with l. 590. *stallion* Q2 'stallyon,' F1 'Scullion'—which edd. follow. Q1 'scalion' MSH. p. 71. With 'whore' and 'drab' in the context, 'stallion' (= courtesan or male whore) is undoubtedly the word Sh. intended. v. G.

592. *About* = Bestir! set about it! *brains* (Q2) F1 'Braine.'

593–96. *guilty creatures sitting at a play* etc.

A commonplace of the age. Heywood in his *Apology for Actors* (a reply to puritan critics of the theatre) cites a number of examples.

601. *blench* Not 'turn pale' but 'flinch,' i.e. from the 'tenting' (= probing). Often used of the eye.

602–607. *The spirit...damn me* Le Loyer, *IIII Livres des Spectres*, 1586, bk. ii, declares that the Devil is apt to appear in the guise of the dead to the weak and the melancholy, and that while his intent is always to delude he often seems to speak the truth (v. Lavater, pp. 234–35). Cf. *Introd.* pp. l–liii.

603. *a devil...the devil* Q2 'a deale...the deale,' MSH. pp. 108, 116.

605. *my weakness and my melancholy* An important testimony to Ham.'s true state of mind. Cf. *Introd.* pp. lxii–lxv. In l. 606 'such spirits' refers, of course, to the weakness and melancholy. v. G. 'weakness.'

609. S.D. For 'A day passes' v. above l. 543 'to-morrow night' and 3. 1. 21 'this night.'

3. 1.

S.D. For 'the lobby' and the 'arras' v. 2. 2. 161–63. The 'faldstool' is needed for Oph.'s devotions and for the K.'s in 3. 3.

1. *drift of conference* (Q2) i.e. leading him on in conversation. Cf. 'drift of question,' 2. 1. 10 and G. 'drift.' The K. implies that they have been ordered to catch Ham. in his talk (cf. 2. 2. 15–18). Most edd. read the comparatively pointless 'drift of circumstance' (F1). MSH. pp. 62–3.

4. *turbulent...lunacy* Cf. *Introd.* p. lxiv. The words prepare us for the ravings at the end of the scene.

5–14. *He does confess...his reply* Dowden comments:

The courtiers between them try to piece out an account, which will not discredit them, of an unsuccessful interview;

Ros. would suggest that they have not wholly failed; Guild. that this was in spite of much difficulty. They wish to turn off any enquiry as to Ham.'s sharp examination of them and his discovery that they were sent for.

8–10. *with a crafty madness...state* Referring to their failure to probe him on the score of his ambition (v. note 2. 2. 255).

12. *much forcing* A clue to the actor how to play 2. 2. 373–83.

13–14. *Niggard of question...reply* = slow to talk, but quite prepared to answer our questions. v. G. 'question.' Ros. is prevaricating, v. note 5–14.

19. *they are here about* (Q2) F1 'they are about,' MSH. p. 261.

26–7. *give him...delights* It is the K.'s policy to cure Ham. of his 'melancholy' (which he does not believe to be madness) so that he will cease to brood over his ambitions.

27. *into* (Q2) F1 'on to.'

49–54. *O, 'tis too true...burden!* The first indication that the K.'s conscience is uneasy. It links 2. 2. 592–602 with the Play-scene and the Prayer-scene later.

51–3. *The harlot's cheek...painted word* An anticipation of the theme elaborated by Ham. later in the scene. 'To' = in comparison with (cf. 'Hyperion to a satyr' 1. 2. 140).

55. S.D. Pol. had said (l. 43) 'walk you here' to Oph., but Ham.'s 'Nymph, in thy orisons' etc. (l. 89) proves, I think, that she kneels and does not merely walk to and fro with a book, else how could he know she was praying?

56. *To be, or not to be* Johnson, Dowden and others contend that Ham. is meditating upon his task, the fulfilment of which will prob. involve his own death; but I think ll. 75–6 rule this out, and show that he is thinking of suicide, as in the First Soliloquy (1. 2. 129–32), and as Malone, Bradley and most critics assume.

57. *in the mind* The words go with 'suffer.'

58. *slings* v. G.

59. *take arms...troubles* Herford notes:

To take up arms and rush upon the waves of the sea was a custom attributed by several classical writers to the Celts. Sh. prob. read of it in Fleming's trans. of Ælian's *Histories* (1576), bk. xii, where it is said that 'they throw themselves into the fomey floudes with their swordes drawn in their handes, and shaking their javelines as though they were of force and violence to withstand the rough waves.'

But prob. Sh. means no more than 'troubles as many as the waves of the sea.' Dowden cites 'sea of glory' (*Hen. VIII*, 3. 2. 360), 'sea of joys' (*Per.* 5. 1. 194) and 'sea of care' (*Luc.* 1100), and notes that 'take arms' continues the metaphor from battle in 'slings and arrows.'

60–4. *To die, to sleep...sleep* Brandes (*Shak.* p. 354) quotes a close parallel from Montaigne's summary of the Apology of Socrates (Florio, bk. iii, ch. 12): 'If it [i.e. death] be a consummation of ones being, it is also an amendement and entrance into a long and quiet life. Wee finde nothing so sweete in life, as a quiet rest and gentle sleepe, and without dreames.' For other possible sources of the Soliloquy v. Dowden's note on 'action' l. 88.

63. *heir to; 'tis* This semi-colon, which gives a different sense and rhythm to the speech from those traditionally accepted by edd., marks the only pause longer than a comma in Q 2 down to 'life:' (l. 69). For the ease of the modern reader I have printed in place of commas a period after 'them' (l. 60) and an exclamation after 'sleep' (l. 64), a dash after 'pause' (l. 68), and a query for a period at the end of l. 82, while I have removed a comma from the end of l. 86. Apart from these changes, the Q 2 pointing has been left intact. MSH. p. 210.

67. *coil* = fuss, v. G., with a quibble upon 'coil' (= a winding of rope). v. *Introd.* p. xxxiv.

69. *of so long life* = so long-lived.

70. *the whips and scorns of time* Life is thought of as a beadle whipping us through the streets, like the vagabond or the whore, with jeering mobs around. Cf. *Lear*, 4. 6. 164–65, and note 2. 2. 534 above.

72. *disprized* (F1) Q2 'despised' MSH. pp. 118, 279, 281.

79–80.* *The undiscovered country...returns* Why, it is asked, does Sh. give these words to one who has actually conversed with such a traveller? And modern critics reply that he forgot, or was careless. The true explanation (which Dowden alone has caught sight of) is that in this mood of deep dejection Ham. has given up all belief in the 'honesty' of the Ghost, and that Sh. wrote the lines to make this clear to the audience. Cf. *Introd.* p. lii.

83. *conscience*=reflection, consciousness. Bridges has restored this meaning in *The Testament of Beauty*. Cf. Bradley, p. 98 n.

85. *thought* = melancholy, v. G.

86. *pitch* (Q2) Many edd. read 'pith' with F1; but 'pitch' (= the highest point in a falcon's flight, just before it swoops upon its prey) gives a much finer image. MSH. p. 274. Cf. *Rich. II*, 1. 1. 109 'How high a pitch his resolution soars.'

88.* *The fair Ophelia* Ham. uses the same words at 5. 1. 236; there is no warmth in them.

89–90.* *Nymph...remembered* The touch of affectation in 'nymph' and 'orisons' (both pretentious words) and of sarcasm in 'all my sins' shows that Ham. speaks ironically, and not as Johnson maintained in 'grave and solemn' mood. Dowden sees 'estrangement in the word "Nymph."'

92. *I humbly thank you* 'He answers as to a stranger' (Dowden), with the same form of address he uses to the Captain in 4. 4. 29 and to Osric in 5. 2. 83.

well, well, well Does the repetition imply 'impatience' (Dowden) or indifference?

103. *Ha, ha! are you honest?* The change of manner is due to Ham.'s recollection of the plot laid at 2. 2. 160–67. Oph. has overplayed her part: it was not he who had jilted her but she him, at her father's command; her little speech, 'sententious' and 'couched in rhyme, has an air of having been prepared' (Dowden); finally, though he meets her 'by accident' (l. 30), she is ready with her trinkets. Ham. is now on his guard; he knows that both the K. and Pol. are listening; and what he says for the rest of the scene is designed for their ears; though, 'lapsed in passion,' he oversteps the mark towards the end. He begins in the 'fishmonger' vein, cf. 2. 2. 174–86.

107–108. *your honesty...beauty* i.e. your modesty ought to have guarded your beauty better than to allow it to be used as a decoy in this fashion (harking back to 'loose my daughter' 2. 2. 162). Oph. naturally misunderstands and supposes him to mean that her beauty and his honesty ought not to discourse together.

111–15. *Ay truly...gives it proof* Accepting her words, he twists them back to his own meaning by declaring that Beauty can transform Virtue itself into an opportunity for the gratification of lust. He is thinking not only of Oph.'s behaviour but his mother's, as is clear from the talk of 'our old stock' that follows.

115. *once* i.e. before my mother married again.

117–19. *You should not...I loved you not* i.e. a son of Gertrude is 'rank and gross in nature' and so incapable of anything but lust. Cf. 'this too too sullied flesh' 1. 2. 129, and G. 'inoculate,' 'relish.'

121.* *Get thee to a nunnery.* 'Nunnery' was a cant word for a house of ill fame and that Ham. has this meaning in mind is, I think, clear from his final speech. Cf. Fletcher, *Mad Lover*, 4. 2. 'There's an old Nunnerie at hand. What's that? A bawdy-house' and v. N.E.D. for other instances.

122. *a breeder of sinners* Carrying on the thought

of ll. 117–19 and of 'Conception is a blessing' etc.
2. 2. 184 ff.

125. *proud, revengeful, ambitious* No three adjectives less appropriate to Ham. could be found; but they will please Uncle Claudius and lead on to 3. 2. 243 (note).

125–27. *more offences...act them in* This sounds very terrible, but considered carefully it amounts to nothing.

130–31. *Where's your father?* The question gives her one last chance; she answers with a lie, as it would seem to him, though she is of course only humouring one whom she takes to be mad.

137–52. *If thou dost marry...nunnery, go* In these last two speeches Oph. has become that Frailty whose name is 'woman.' Ham. returns to emphasise his madness, and perhaps in hope of catching the eavesdroppers emerging. The madness is not all put on; he is indulging in one of his fits of passion. v. *Introd.* pp. lxii–lxv.

142. *monsters* i.e. horned cuckolds. Cf. *Wint.* 1. 2. 123–28, and *Oth.* 4. 1. 63 'a horned man's a monster.'

145–48. *I have heard...lisp* v. Tilley (R.E.S. v. pp. 312 ff.) for contemporary denunciations of face-painting, etc. Stubbes, *Anatomy of Abuses*, treats the matter at great length (v. ed. Sh. Soc. pp. 63–89); he insists that such paintings 'adulterate the Lord his woorkmanship' (p. 64), and writes 'it is a world to consider their coynesse in gestures, their minsednes in woords and speaches, their gingerlynes in trippinge on toes like yong goats, their demure nicitie and babishnes' (p. 78)—phrases very like Ham.'s.

148. *you nickname* (Q2) Most edd. follow F1 'and nickname,' MSH. p. 264. Ham. seems to allude to indecent names given to fruit and vegetables; Dowden cites *Rom.* 2. 1. 35–6 'that kind of fruit As maids call medlars when they laugh alone.'

150–51. *no mo marriage* (Q2) F1 'no more Marriages.' The abstract subs. is more in keeping with the context. v. G. 'mo.'

157. *observed of all observers* i.e. 'the object of all men's worthy deference' (Herford). v. G. 'observer.' Cf. *Wint.* 4. 4. 8 'the gracious mark o'th' land,' and 2 *Hen. IV*, 2. 3. 31–2 'He was the mark and glass, copy and book, That fashioned others.'

164. S.D. The K. and Pol. have waited a little in case Ham. should return once more. Some copies of Q2 give Oph. an 'exit' here. It is I think an unwarranted addition by the press-corrector. She does not hear the K.'s speech that follows, but she is certainly aware that the two have been behind the arras (v. 3. 1. 28–44): she sees no harm in it; for her Ham. is a madman.

165. *affections* v. G.

169. *disclose* v. G.

172–78. *he shall...of himself* The journey is for curative purposes only; it is not until after the Play-scene that the K. decides on Ham.'s death.

3. 2.

S.D. Q2 'Enter Hamlet, and three of the Players.' There are three speaking parts in the play: the 'King,' the 'Queen,' and Lucianus. It is evident from what follows that 1 Player is to take Lucianus. For the performance of plays on the dais of halls v. Chambers, *Eliz. Stage*, i. 229.

1. *the speech* Clearly intended to refer to the lines Ham. himself has written (v. note 2. 2. 544). It is a passionate speech (v. ll. 5–11), and Ham. is anxious that it shall produce its full effect. Cf. notes ll. 252, 253–54.

3–14. *but if you mouth...avoid it* This I take to be a criticism of the acting of the Admiral's men, and suspect Alleyn to be the 'robustious periwig-pated fellow'; 1 Player as Lucianus commits all the faults here condemned. Cf. 2. 2. 332 (note).

10–14. *tear...Herod* Cf. *M.N.D.* 1. 2. 25–6 'I

could play Ercles rarely, or a part to tear a cat in, to make all split.' Referring to the violent action of the old miracle plays. v. G. 'Termagant,' 'Herod.'

12. *inexplicable dumb-shows* This express condemnation of Dumb-shows proves that Ham. must not be held responsible for the Dumb-show that follows.

20. *from the purpose* = contrary to the purpose.

20–24. *whose end...pressure* This famous declaration has relevance to the Gonzago play, to *Hamlet* itself, and to the whole question of 'topicality' in Sh. Cf. note 2. 2. 528–30. 'Playing' includes the art of the playwright; 'scorn' = that which should be scorned, v. G., for 'body of the time' cf. *A.Y.L.* 2. 1. 58–9.

21–2. *hold...nature* = not 'reflect nature' but 'show human nature the ideal.'

26–7. *the judicious...of the which one* The singular suggests reference to a special patron. Southampton, who is known to have frequented plays assiduously in 1599, was in the Tower after Feb. 1601.

28–34. *O there be players* etc. Another hit at the 'robustious periwig-pated fellow' (cf. note 3. 2. 3–14). Lucianus later makes 'damnable faces' and Ham. sarcastically bids him 'bellow' (v. ll. 252–54).

34. *abominably* Q2 'abhominably.' The mod. sp. conceals the quibble; the word being supposed to derive from 'ab homine.'

35–6. *I hope...indifferently with us* This dubious assurance of reformation is a confession that Ham.'s strictures refer to him and his company.

37–43.* *and let those that play your clowns* etc. No clown appears in the Gonzago play, so that these words seem directed against a real clown recognisable by Sh.'s audience. This is supported by an extension of the passage in *Hamlet*, 1603 (Q1), which runs (in mod. spelling):

And then you have some again that keep one suit of jests, as a man is known by one suit of apparel; and gentlemen quote his jests down in their tables before they come to the play, as thus: 'Cannot you stay till I eat my porridge?' and 'You owe me a quarter's wages,' and 'My coat wants a cullison,' and 'Your beer is sour,' and 'Blabbering with his lips'; and thus keeping in his cinquepace of jests, when God knows the warm clown cannot make a jest unless by chance, as the blind man catcheth a hare: masters, tell him of it.

Whatever be its source, this addition must be a personal attack upon a particular clown, who is accused of using very stale material, since two of the 'cinquepace of jests' occur in *Tarlton's Jests* (pub. c. 1600), v. ed. Shak. Soc. 1844, pp. 5, 12. Collier suggested that the Clown was William Kempe, who left Sh.'s company in 1599.

45. *piece of work* i.e. masterpiece. Ham. speaks jocularly. Cf. 2. 2. 307.

52.* *just* =equable, well-balanced (as is clear from ll. 64–70). Cf. *M. of V.* 4. 1. 323 'a just pound.'

58–60. *candied tongue...fawning* The image is that of a spaniel at table, its tongue 'candied' with sweetmeats, yet 'fawning' for more (Spurgeon, *Sh.'s Iterative Imagery* in Aspects, pp. 266 ff.). For 'thrift' v. G.

59. *pregnant* 'because untold thrift is born from a cunning use of the knee' (Furness). v. G.

62–3. *distinguish her election, Sh'hath* (Q2) F. 'distinguish, her election Hath'—which all mod. edd. follow. MSH. pp. 274–75.

66–70. *blest...passion's slave* Ham. admires Hor. for being what he himself is not; the passage is an important piece of self-criticism, and also a hint from Sh. to the audience for the appraisement of Ham.'s conduct in what follows. With 'passion's slave' cf. 'lapsed in time and passion' 3. 4. 107. Ham. compares himself to a 'pipe' again at 3. 2. 354 ff. Cf. also *Introd.* pp. l–liii.

67. *co-medled*, Q2 'comedled,' F1 'co-mingled'—which all edd. follow. MSH. pp. 271, 278.

75. *I have told thee* v. note 1. 5. 139–40.

79. *in one speech* Cf. notes 3. 2. 1; 2. 2. 544.

80. *It is a damnèd ghost* v. *Introd.* p. li.

85–7. *Well, my lord…theft* Hor.'s tone is light. Does Sh. wish to suggest that he is still sceptical about the Ghost's 'honesty'?

88. *I must be idle* i.e. I must assume my antic disposition. v. G. 'idle,' 3. 4. 11, and *Lear*, 1. 3. 16. Clar., Dowden and Onions agree in this interpretation.

89. S.D. Q2 'Enter Trumpets and Kettle Drummes, King, Queene, Polonius, Ophelia.' F1 adds 'Rosincrance, Guildensterne, and other Lords attendant, with his Guard carrying Torches. Danish March. Sound a Flourish.' The 'Danish March' was prob. added after the accession of Queen Anne of Denmark in 1603. MSH. p. 40. The 'Torches' mark the scene as evening (cf. note 3. 2. 269). The 'Guard' are the 'Switzers' (4. 5. 97). If Sh. intended their entry here, it suggests that the K. prefers (after the Nunnery-scene) to be guarded in Ham.'s presence.

91–2.* *Excellent…capons so* Ham.'s first 'idle' speech is an elaborate quibble. He catches up 'fare' by the wrong end, to harp on the note of thwarted ambition (already sounded in the K.'s ears with 'I am very proud, revengeful, ambitious,' 3. 1. 125), by referring to the promise of the succession (v. note 1. 2. 108–9). For 'chameleon' v. G., and cf. *Two Gent.* 2. 1. 164–5 'Though the chameleon, love, can feed on the air,' and 2 *Hen. IV*, 1. 3. 28 'Eating the air on promise of supply.' 'Air' is a pun on 'heir' and 'promise-crammed' leads on to 'capon'; 'capon-crammed' (i.e. stuffed like a capon) being a common expression for 'over-fed' (cf. mod. slang 'fed up'). In 'capons' Ham. hints that the K. is plying him with empty promises in preparation for having him quietly removed from his path, since the word means young cocks stuffed for killing. It also stands for a type of stupidity. 'Even capons,' he says in effect, 'are not so stupid as to grow fat on air.'

93. *have nothing with*=can make nothing of. Cf.
2. 1. 65 'you have me, have you not?'

94. *are not mine*=have nothing to do with me.

96. *i'th'university* For playing at the universities v.
F. S. Boas, *Univ. Drama in the Tudor Age*.

99. *What did you enact?* Ham. is repeating some
garrulity of Pol. (cf. 'you say' l. 96), and knows very well
the answer to his question; but it suits his book to refer
to the death of Caesar at this point: the K. may think him
a 'capon,' but there are precedents for the assassination
of tyrants.

101. *Capitol* The error (repeated in *Jul. Caes.*) as
to the place of Caesar's death is as old as Chaucer;
v. *Monkes Tale*, l. 713.

104–105. *stay upon your patience*=await your permission (to begin).

107–108. *here's...attractive* Ham. sits by Oph.
because she sits opposite the K. whom he must watch,
and being there under the eye of Pol. he passes the time
by playing the distraught lover. His first words seem to
lend strong support to Pol.'s theory and precipitate (as
I think) a whispered colloquy with the K.

110. *shall I lie in your lap?* Ham.'s obscenity
would, he knew, be interpreted as the natural outbreak
of a madman crazed for love (cf. Oph.'s song 4. 5. 57 ff.);
at the same time he enjoys insulting Woman in her
person. Cf. note l. 251 and *Introd.* pp. lvi–lix.

114. *country matters* Cf. 2. 2. 195 (note) and
Dowden 'I suspect...some indelicate suggestion in
"country." In *Westward Hoe*, 5. 1. I find: "Though we
lie all night out of the city, they [our husbands] shall not
find country wenches of us."'

116. *a fair thought* A quibble = (*a*) a pretty trifle
(v. G. 'thought'), and (*b*) a modest idea.

119. *Nothing* Cf. *Rom.* 3. 3. 90; *Cymb.* 2. 5. 17.

124–25. *look...two hours* This 'idle' reference to
'his father's death' and the 'o'er-hasty marriage'

(cf. 2. 2. 57) causes the Queen to hide her confusion by turning away and joining in the conversation with the K. and Pol.

127–28. *let the devil...sables* A quibble on the two meanings of 'sable,' v. G.: (*a*) a suit trimmed with expensive furs, brown in colour, worn by elderly gentlemen to keep them warm; cf. 4. 7. 79 'settled age his sables,' (*b*) black mourning garment; cf. 1. 2. 242; 2. 2. 456. Dowden alone has noticed the connexion between 'sables' and 'So long?' and paraphrases 'What an age it is since my father died! I am quite an old gentleman!' Black was, of course, the native colour of the Devil.

127. *the devil* Q2 'the deule.' Cf. note 1. 4. 36.

132. *suffer not thinking on* = be forgotten.

the hobby-horse v. G. Symbolical of the old May-games, which the godly at this period were trying to suppress all over England. To be remembered nowadays, says Ham., one must be a pious benefactor, for the pious are becoming the only power in the land and are sweeping away the harmless old pleasures. 'For O... forgot' was a line from a popular ballad, as frequently quoted and jested upon as the refrain of a music-hall song to-day, partly no doubt because of the equivocal meaning of 'hobby-horse' (cf. *Oth.* 4. 1. 160 and *L.L.L.* G.).

133.* S.D. For the S.D. of the Dumb-show which differs in Q2 and F1 v. MSH. pp. 184, 359–60. I follow Q2, supplying words from F1, where they seem to have been omitted by the Q2 compositor, and altering the punctuation slightly.

Hamlet seems troubled etc. The apparent indifference of the K. to the Dumb-show, which reproduces all the particulars of his crime, although he rushes from the room when the poisoning is repeated in the spoken play, has long been a crux. My solution follows a hint from Halliwell, who wrote: 'If the King had seen the dumb-show, he must have known that there was offence in it. Is it allowable to direct that the King and Queen should be whispering confidentially to each other during the dumb-show, and so escape a sight of it?' The whispering is naturally accounted for by Ham.'s conduct; cf. notes ll. 107–108 and 124–25 above. The Dumb-show is, in Oph.'s words, the 'argument of the play,' and as such is unique in Eliz. drama (v. G. and Creizenach, *Eng. Drama*, p. 390). That the K. did not see it is, I think, proved by his question at l. 231 'Have you heard the argument? is there no offence in't?' It is equally certain that Ham. did not expect it; he had told 1 Player what he thought about dumb-shows at 3.2.12, and his anxiety after the show is over is evident (v. notes ll. 135, 139–40).

135.* *miching mallecho* v. G. Ham. refers to the mischievous behaviour of the players in surreptitiously interposing a dumb-show which almost ruins his plot by prematurely disclosing the Mouse-trap.

137–38. *the argument of the play* v. note l. 133 S.D. (*Hamlet seems troubled* etc.). Sh. thus informs us of *his* purpose in introducing the Dumb-show, i.e. to tell his audience what they are to expect, and so sharpen their anticipation. v. G. 'dumb-show.'

138. S.D. Q2 'Enter Prologue.' After a dumb-show the stage-practice was to bring on a Presenter or Chorus to explain its meaning (cf. 'inexplicable dumb-shows,' l. 12). Thus when 'this fellow' enters both Ham. and Sh.'s audience take him for a Presenter, and Ham.'s fears lest he should divulge his secret in words are clear from ll. 139–40.

139–40. *The players...tell all* If the K. had seen the dumb-show, the players would already have told him all. Ham.'s fears for what 'this fellow' may say show that so far the secret is safe.

142. *Ay, or any show* etc. Cf. Jonson's *Conversations with Drummond* (Jonson, i. 140, l. 293) and note ll. 245–46 below.

147–49. *For us...patiently* The jingling posy-prologue may be taken as another of the Players' dramatic gimcracks.

150. *the posy of a ring* Cf. *M. of V.* 5. 1. 149–50 'whose posy was For all the world like cutler's poetry.'

152. *As woman's love* Ham. himself prologues the play.

153–58. *Full thirty times* etc. The repeated insistence upon 'thirty' years of married life agrees with Ham.'s age given 5. 1. 143–57 (note).

165. *For women...love* F1 and many edd. omit. MSH. p. 27. There is no rhyme to 'love.'

167. *In neither aught* (F1) Q2 'Eyther none, in neither ought.' The first two words in Q2 prob. represent a false start by Sh. MSH. p. 27. Capell explains: 'They either feel none of these passions, or feel them both in extremity.'

170–71. *Where love...grows there* F1 omits these lines, which merely repeat the sense of l. 167. It is clear that Sh. wrote this Gonzago play hastily, leaving several tangles for the prompter to unravel.

180. *That's wormwood, wormwood.* Q2 'That's wormwood,' F1 'Wormwood, Wormwood,' Q1 'O wormewood, wormewood!' MSH. p. 302. Q2 prints this and the interruption at l. 223 in the margin, which suggests that they may have been added after the Gonzago play had been composed.

191–92. *Most necessary...is debt.* 'Our resolves are debts to ourselves; why embarrass ourselves with inconvenient payments?' (Dowden).

203. *The great man...flies* 'Had Sh. in mind the fall of the great Essex and his treatment by Bacon?' (Verity).

217–18. *To desperation...scope* Two more superfluous lines omitted by F1; cf. note ll. 170–71. For 'cheere' v. G.

231–32. *Have you...offence in't?* Cf. note l. 133

S.D. The K. grows restive at the repeated reference to second marriages. In his reply Ham. quibbles on 'offence' as at 1. 5. 136. v. G.

236. *The Mouse-trap* N.E.D. quotes many instances of this in the 'tropical' sense of 'a device for enticing a person to his destruction or defeat.'

Marry, how?—tropically (F 1) Q 2 'mary how tropically,' Q 1 'mary how trapically.' Q 1 suggests a quibble on 'trap,' perhaps in reference to 'marry trap' (= 'an exclamation of insult when a man was caught in his own stratagem,' Dr Johnson), cf. *M.W.W.* 1. 1. 155–56 'I will say "marry trap" with you,' i.e. I will give you tit for tat. v. G. 'tropically.'

238. *Gonzago* v. *Introd.* p. xxiii.

241–42.* *let the galled...unwrung* Tilley (525) quotes *Euphues* 'well I knowe none will winch excepte shee bee gawled, neither any bee offended vnlesse shee be guiltie' (Bond, i. 257), and 'rubbe there no more, least I winch, for deny I wil not that I am wroung on the withers' (*ibid*. ii. 151). The coincidence of 'winch' (v. next note), 'galled,' 'guilty,' 'offended' (offence), 'wrung' and 'withers' suggests borrowing.

241.* *wince* (Q 1) Q 2, F 1 'winch' MSH. p. 288. 'winch' = obs. form of 'wince.' In Sh.'s day 'wince' = kick.

243.* *nephew to the king* i.e. the Hamlet not the Claudius of the Gonzago story. Bradley (137 n.) points out that though the court, as is clear from 3. 2. 300 ff., 3. 3. 1–26, and 4. 7. 1–5, 30 ff., see 'in the play-scene a gross and menacing insult to the King...no one shows any sign of perceiving in it also an accusation of murder.' And he adds 'surely that is strange.' The clue is in this passage. Ham. arranges *two* meanings to the Play, one for the K. (and Hor.), the other for the rest of the spectators, who see a king being murdered by his nephew. In other words Ham. prepares the Court for the assassination of Claudius which was intended to follow, just as *Rich. II*, with its deposition scene, was performed by Sh.'s company on Feb. 7, 1601 to prepare London for the rising of the Essex party next day. I make little doubt that Lucianus should be dressed like Ham. Cf. notes ll. 91–2; 2. 2. 255; 3. 1. 125.

244. *chorus* Or 'presenter,' to explain the action of the play; cf. the Chorus in *Hen. V* and note l. 138 S.D. above.

245–46. *I could...dallying* Referring to the showman of the puppets, who 'recited a suitable dialogue as an accompaniment to their gestures' (Chambers, *Med. Stage*, ii. 159). Cf. *Two Gent.* 2. 1. 90–91 'O excellent motion, O exceeding puppet, now will he interpret to her.' Both Speed and Ham. prob. imply something indecent; cf. ll. 142–44 above. *your love* = your lover.

247. *You are keen* i.e. You mock in cruel fashion.

250. *Still better and worse* 'more keen and less decorous' (Caldecott). There is prob. a quibble on 'bitter.'

251. *mis-take* Q2 and F1 'mistake,' Q1 'must take' —which many edd. follow. Ham. refers to the marriage service in which man and wife 'take' each other 'for better for worse.' The pl. 'husbands' shows that here as elsewhere Oph. stands for Woman in general in his mind.

252. *damnable faces* Cf. Ham.'s warning against mouthing, sawing the air with the hand, strutting and bellowing, ll. 3–33 above.

253–54. *'the croaking...revenge'* As R. Simpson showed, these words are 'a satirical condensation' of the following passage from *The True Tragedy of Richard III* (an old Queen's company play, printed in a garbled version 1594):

> The screeking Rauen sits croking for reuenge.
> Whole heards of beasts comes bellowing for reuenge.

The lines, which occur in a speech by Richard describing the terrors of his conscience, were prob. familiar to Sh.'s audience as a stock absurdity of the revenge drama. Ham. ironically exhorts the strutting Player to bellow in Termagant fashion. On June 22, 1602 Henslowe, the financial director of the Admiral's company, advanced money to Jonson in earnest of a play-book called 'Richard Crookbacke' (Jonson, i. 33).

260. *usurps* (Q2, Q1) F1 'vsurpe,' MSH. pp. 267–68.

S.D. F1 'Powres the poyson in his eares,' Q2 omits.

262–63. *written ... Italian* Cf. *Introd.* p. xxiii.

266. *What.. .fire!* (F1) Q2 omits. MSH. p. 245. v. G. 'false fire.'

267. *How fares my lord?* The K. had asked Ham. the same question at the opening of the scene: the tables are turned.

269. *Give me some light* This call for light, i.e. to the torch-bearers to bring him to his chamber (cf. note l. 89 S.D. above), has a symbolical point.

271–74. *Why...world away* Prob. a stanza from some ballad, now lost.

272. *ungallèd* Cf. 'the galled jade,' l. 241 above.

275. *a forest of feathers* Plumes were worn by tragic actors and contemporary references to the fact are frequent. Cf. note 5. 2. 96–7 for a passage from *The Malcontent* in which Sh.'s fellow-actors appear decked out with feathers, prob. in mockery of some other company. v. G. 'Provincial roses,' 'razed.'

276. *turn Turk* v. G. Another reference to Ham.'s lack of means, cf. note 1. 5. 184.

277–78. *a fellowship...players*=a partnership in a theatrical company, v. G. 'cry,' 'share.'

281–84. *For thou...peacock* Prob. another stanza from the ballad quoted above, which should end, of course, with the word 'ass.'

284. *peacock* Q2 'paiock,' F1 'Paiocke.' Most edd. now read 'pajock' (F2), which Dyce explained as a Sc. dialect word. But 'paiock' is almost certainly a

misprint due to an old-fashioned sp. 'pacock,' MSH. pp. 306–7. 'Peacock,' typifying lechery as well as vanity, is an apt term of abuse for the K. Alternatively, Dowden suggests that the word may be intended for "patchcocke" or "patchcoke," Spenser's name for the degenerate English in Ireland. (Cf. N.E.D. 'paiocke' and 'patchcocke,' quoting 3. 4. 102 'A king of shreds and patches.')

290. S.D. Q2 gives the entry at l. 295, F1 here. The F1 position explains Ham.'s laugh, while his sending for music exhibits him deliberately ignoring them, as Guild.'s 'vouchsafe' suggests he is doing. MSH. p. 184.

293–94.* *For if...perdy* Another ballad-snatch.

303. *With drink, sir?* A deadly thrust (cf. 1. 4. 8–22, etc.), quibbling upon 'distempered,' v. G.

304. *rather with choler* i.e. at Ham.'s outrageous behaviour in the Play-scene, v. note l. 243 above.

306–308.* *for me...more choler* Ham. interprets 'choler' (v. G.) as a bilious attack following drunkenness, needing a purge, and then quibbles on 'purgation' (v. G. and 3. 3. 85) in the legal sense (cf. *Rich. II,* 1. 1. 153 and *Wint.* 3. 2. 7). Ros. and Guild., of course, understand nothing of this; but it is clear from what follows that they no longer believe him mad except 'in craft.'

307–308. *more choler* (Q2) F1 'farre more Choller,' MSH. p. 258.

310. *start* Like an untamed horse.

311. *pronounce* i.e. what are your orders?

318. *your pardon* = your permission to leave; cf. 1. 2. 56.

321. *What, my lord?* F1 assigns this to Guild. and all edd. follow but Capell, who explains that Guild. retires in dudgeon at l. 319, leaving Ros. to deliver the message (*Notes,* i. 138).

328. *amazement and admiration* v. G. Cf. 'most

great affliction of spirit,' ll. 312–13 and note l. 243
above. The Queen knows nothing of the murder
(v. note 3. 4. 30).

329. *stonish* (Q2) F1 'astonish.'

337. *And do still* (Q2) F1 'So I do still.'

by these pickers and stealers i.e. by these hands,
referring to 'keep my hands from picking and stealing'
(Church Catechism), and intended to recall what
follows, viz. 'and my tongue from evil speaking, lying
and slandering'—which he imputes to them; cf. l. 360.

338–39. *your cause of distemper* Cf. l. 4. 73 note.

339–40. *you do surely...friend* A threat, meaning
'your reticence may lead to your being shut up like a
madman.'

341. *I lack advancement* He gives them the answer
they desire, and strengthens the interpretation he wishes
the world to place upon his actions; cf. note l. 243.

343. *the voice...Denmark* A reference to 1. 2.
108–109.

345. '*While the grass grows*' Malone quotes
Whetstone's *Promus and Cassandra*, 1578: 'Whylst
grass doth growe, oft sterves the seely steede' and adds,
'Ham. means to intimate that whilst he is waiting for the
succession to the throne of Denmark, he may himself be
taken off by death.' But there is dramatic irony also:
the grass is also growing under Ham.'s own feet while
the K. acts.

351–52. *if my duty...unmannerly* i.e. if my behaviour seem a little bold, you must set it down to the
impetuosity of my affection. Ham. refuses to understand
this, not because it is 'an unmeaning compliment'
(Clar.), but because of its obvious insincerity. Guild.,
separated from Ros. and taken aback by Ham.'s sudden
question, answers stammeringly.

360. *lying* Referring to ll. 351–52.

361.* *fingers and thumbs* Q2 'fingers, & the vmber,'
F1 'finger and thumbe,' MSH. pp. 323–24. Most edd.

read 'fingers and thumb,' but it takes two thumbs to play a recorder.

372–73. *easier...played on than a pipe* Dramatic irony; cf. note 3. 2. 66–70.

374. *though you can fret me, you* (F 1) Q 2 'though you fret me not, you,' MSH. p. 283. v. G. 'fret.'

378. *yonder cloud* Ham. speaks in the royal palace, but also in the unlocalised Eliz. theatre open to the sky; thus he can point upwards to a cloud or to 'this brave o'erhanging firmament' (2. 2. 304), and the audience is conscious of no incongruity.

380. *and 'tis, like a* (Q 2) The position of the comma gives an effective turn to the obsequious assent.

382. *backed like a weasel* Particularly absurd after 'like a camel.'

385. *by and by* = before long (cf. 5. 2. 291), i.e. at my own time, not (as most interpret) 'immediately.'

386. *They fool...bent* 'They compel me to play the fool, till I can endure to do it no longer' (Dr Johnson). Ham.'s nerves are giving out.

390. *Leave me, friends* Addressed to Hor. and the Players. Q 2 and F 1 give no 'exeunt' for Ros. and Guild.

396. *nature* v. G.

397.* *The soul of Nero* i.e. the matricidal spirit; cf. *K. John*, 5. 2. 152. The violence of Ham.'s indignation against the Queen at this point is an important clue to the mood in which he goes to her bedroom in 3. 4. He fears 'the soul of Nero,' and forgets the spirit of Brutus.

401. *somever* Cf. note 1. 2. 249 and MSH. p. 243.

402. *give them seals* i.e. 'make them "deeds"' (Knight). A legal quibble; cf. note 1. 2. 60.

<h3 style="text-align:center">3. 3.</h3>

S.D. I place the scene in 'the lobby' because (i) it is on the way from the hall to the Queen's bedroom

(cf. 4. 3. 35), and (ii) the faldstool used by Oph. in 3. 1.
is now needed by the K.

1–26. *I like him not* etc. That the K. should thus
openly speak with Ros. and Guild. of his danger from
Ham. is proof that the Gonzago play was recognised by
all as a threat to his life; cf. note 3. 2. 243.

2–4. *prepare you...along with you* This implies a
change of plan, v. note 3. 4. 200.

5. *The terms...endure* i.e. it is impossible to conduct
the government of the country (while he is at large).

7.* *brawls* Q2 'browes,' F1 'Lunacies.' I emend
Q2 rather than adopt the makeshift reading of F1.
MSH. pp. 9–11, 169, 324. Cf. 'turbulent and dan-
gerous lunacy' 3. 1. 4. See p. 304.

14. *depends and rests* Confusion of proximity; cf.
Abbott, § 412, and above 1. 2. 38 'allow.'

15. *cess* Q2 'cesse,' F1 'cease.'. v. G. Cf. De Foe,
The Original Power of the People, 1703, 'If Power at
any time meets with a Cess, if Government and Thrones
become Vacant...' (v. N.E.D. 3), and MSH. p. 275.

17. *O, 'tis* Q2 'or it is,' F1 'It is.' MSH. p. 325.
Cf. note 5. 1. 117. For 'a massy wheel' v. note 2. 2.
499–501.

26. *We will haste us* Q2 heads this '*Ros.*,' F1 '*Both.*'
S.D. Q2 'Exeunt Gent.'/'Enter Polonius.'

30. *And as you said* etc. Pol. made the suggestion
(3. 1. 184–88), but he astutely attributes it to the King
(Herford).

33. *of vantage* prob. = 'in addition' not 'from a
convenient place'; v. G.

39. *Though inclination...will* i.e. he is not forcing
himself to pray; he wishes fervently to do so.

43–4. *this cursèd hand...blood* Cf. *Macb.* 2. 2.
60–3; 5. 1. 56–8.

46–7. *whereto...offence?* i.e. 'where is there scope
for mercy save in the very presence of sin?' (Verity).

56. *retain th'offence* 'He that does not amend what

can be amended retains his offence. The King kept the crown from the right heir' (Dr Johnson). Cf. *Introd.* p. liii.

58. *gilded* = furnished with bribes.

shove by = thrust aside.

61–2. *the action...true nature* = the deed is seen in its true colours. A quibble on the legal terms 'action,' 'lie,' v. G. 'lie.'

68–9. *O limèd soul...engaged* Bond (i. 173) quotes *Euphues*, 'Like the bird in the limebush which the more she striueth to get out, ye faster she sticketh in.'

73. *a' is a-praying* (Q2) F1 'he is praying.' MSH. p. 231. The familiar 'a'' adds a significant touch of contempt to Ham.'s words.

75. *would be scanned* = 'calls for scrutiny' (Herford).

scanned: Q2 'scand.'

79. *Why, this* (Q2) F1 'Oh this.'

bait and salary Q2 'base and silly,' F1 'hyre and Sallery.' Again I emend Q2 (assuming the sp. 'bate') rather than adopt a word of quite different graphical formation from F1; v. MSH. pp. 325–6 for discussion. 'Bait' = refreshment on a journey (in the K.'s case, to the next world); cf. Nashe (McKerrow's ed. ii. 222) 'gone to heauen without a bait,' i.e. without the last sacrament. It anticipates 'grossly, full of bread' in the next line, as 'salary' anticipates 'audit' in l. 82.

80.* *grossly, full of bread* (F1) Q2 omits comma. Cf. note 1. 5. 11.

81. *broad blown* v. G. 'blown' and cf. 1. 5. 76 'in the blossoms of my sin.'

83. *in our circumstance...thought* i.e. as all evidence and speculation shows; cf. G. 'circumstance' and 2. 2. 157.

88–95.* *Up, sword...it goes* Johnson and others have found these lines 'too horrible to be read or to be uttered.' They would not have shocked an ordinary Elizabethan; the quiet Kentish gentleman, Iden, expresses very similar sentiments in 2 *Hen. VI*, 4. 10. 84–6, while they are scarcely more barbarous than Ham.'s own words at 2. 2. 582–83, or than what the K. and Laer. say at 4. 7. 123–27. Ham., too, takes good care that Ros. and Guild. shall be allowed no 'shriving-time' (5. 2. 47).

88. *hent* A quibble; v. G.

89. *drunk asleep*, (F1) Q2 'drunke, a sleepe,' MSH. p. 206. i.e. dead drunk. Johnson read 'drunk-asleep.'

96. *This physic* i.e. prayer; cf. 'purging' l. 85.

97–8. *My words* etc. The K.'s prayer is closely paralleled by Angelo's, *Meas.* 2. 4. 1–7.

98. *never to heaven go* Cf. ll. 74–8. After all, there is no 'relish of salvation' in the K.'s prayer.

3. 4.

2–4. *Tell him...heat and him* A significant glimpse of the council of war after the Play-scene and of the Queen's part therein.

4. *I'll silence me* (Q2, F1) Q1 'I'le shrowde my selfe.' Hanmer and most mod. edd. read 'I'll sconce me.' 'The "foolish prating knave" Pol. can be "most still" only in death'; and the word 'silence' here 'may have an ironical relation to the occasion of his death, his loud "What, ho!"'' (Dowden). MSH. p. 292.

6. *war'nt* F1 'warrant,' Q2 'waite.' Cf. note 2. 1. 38 and MSH. pp. 107–108.

7. S.D. *Polonius...arras* and later S.D.'s at ll. 23–26 are derived from Rowe and Capell.

17. *Nay then...speak* This prob. leads Ham. to suspect that the K. is eavesdropping again, a suspicion easily conveyed on the stage by a significant glance around.

30. *As kill a king!* 'The astonishment...is evidently genuine' (Bradley, p. 166).

it was my word (Q 2) F 1 "'twas my word.'

37. *damnèd custom* Cf. ll. 161–70 below.

38. *sense* = feeling, sensibility. Cf. ll. 71–81 below.

40. *Such an act* etc. The 'act' is not named, but what follows suggests that Ham. has both adultery and incest in mind; cf. note 1. 5. 42–57.

43. *forehead* Cf. 4. 5. 118–20. It was a common idea that the character was written on the brow (cf. *Ado*, 3. 5. 12 'honest as the skin between his brows,' *Meas.* 4. 2. 152–53), which is perhaps why malefactors and harlots were branded on the forehead; hence 'blister' (l. 44). For 'rose' v. G.

46–7. *from the body…soul* i.e. by desecrating the most solemn type of agreement, that of marriage, it reduces all human contractual relations to empty form. The same thought is expressed in 'and sweet religion… words.'

49–51.* *And this…the act* Q 2 'Ore this…the act,' F 1 'Yea this…masse With tristful visage…the act.' Most edd. follow F 1 which may give us Sh.'s own emendation; I attempt to restore his original text. Cf. note 1. 3. 74 and MSH. p. 327. The 'compound mass' I take to be the moon to which Ham. points (cf. note 1. 4. 68 and 3. 2. 378). He is referring to some contemporary lunar eclipse; v. note 1. 1. 122–25, and cf. 'as against the doom is thought-sick' with 'sick almost to doomsday with eclipse' (1. 1. 125).

53.* *upon this…and on this* Ll. 58–9 indicate full-length portraits, and in *Der bestrafte Brudermord* they are referred to as in a 'gallery.' Cf. Sh.Eng. ii. 11.

56. *Hyperion's curls* Cf. 1. 2. 140.

Jove himself Cf. 3. 2. 283.

59. *New-lighted…hill* Malone suggests derivation from *Aen.* iv. 246 ff., the description of Mercury alighting upon Atlas, whence *Par. Lost*, v. 285–87 is certainly drawn.

64–5. *a mildewed ear…brother* Blasting and mildew

are often associated in Biblical references to corn; cf.
1 Kings viii. 37; Amos iv. 9; Haggai ii. 17.

67.* *moor* Q2 'Moor.' Prob. a quibble upon
'blackamoor' which to Elizabethans typified the physically repulsive.

71–6. *Sense sure…difference* F1 omits. MSH.
pp. 28, 167. For 'sense,' 'motion,' 'ecstasy,' v. G. 'In
ll. 71–2 the emotional aspect of the word (sense) is
prominent, in ll. 72–3 the intellectual' (Herford).

74–6. *Nor sense…difference* i.e. Feeling (or sen-
sation) has never been so dominated by the delusions of
madness that it did not retain some small portion of discrimination, enough at any rate to see the gulf that divides
these two men.

78–81. *Eyes…mope* F1 omits. MSH. pp. 28, 167.

88. *reason pandars will* Cf. *V.A.* 792 'When reason
is the bawd to lust's abuse.'

92. *enseaméd* v. G. and *Introd.* p. xxxviii.

95. *like daggers* Cf. 3. 2. 399 'I will speak daggers
to her.'

99–101. *A cutpurse…pocket* A clear indication
that Ham. thinks of the K. as a usurper; cf. 5. 2. 65 and
Introd. pp. liii–liv. 'He stole the crown "from a shelf"
like a petty thief, and h'ad not even the courage to take
it by violence' (Clar. after Warburton).

102. *of shreds and patches* Referring to the motley of
the 'vice' (v. G.) or clown.

S.D.* I adopt the S.D. from Q1, which almost
certainly informs us of what took place on Sh.'s stage.
'Night-gown' = dressing-gown (cf. *Macb.* 2. 2. 70),
appropriate to the Queen's bedroom as the armour was
to the battlements. Cf. l. 135 'in his habit as he lived.'

103–104. *Save me…guards!* Cf. 1. 4. 39 'Angels
and ministers of grace defend us!'

107. *lapsed in time and passion* Hitherto unex-
plained, because it has been forgotten that 'time' in
Sh. often means 'circumstance, the conditions of the

moment' (cf. 4. 7. 110–13 'love is begun by time' and 148 'convenience both of time and means'). Further, 'lapsed' (v. G.) in the only other place Sh. uses it (*Tw. Nt.* 3. 3. 36) means 'arrested' or 'taken prisoner.' Thus Ham. describes himself as 'the prisoner of circumstance and of passion,' repeating 'passion's slave' of 3. 2. 70, and referring to those fits of morbid excitement which so often take possession of him. Cf. *Introd.* p. lxiv and notes 3. 1. 137–52; 3. 4. 180; 5. 1. 278; 5. 2. 230. Schmidt, also citing *Tw. Nt.* 3. 3. 36, interprets the whole passage: 'who, surprised by you in a time and passion fit for the execution of your command, lets them go by.'

108. *important* = urgent. A significant admission; cf. note 3. 2. 372–73.

110–11. *this visitation Is but to whet* etc. i.e. the only purpose of my appearing is to whet etc. (v. *Introd.* p. lxi). His appeal on behalf of the Queen is an after-thought, due to the pitiable state in which he finds her.

120–22. *as the sleeping...stand an end* The hairs are compared with soldiers who leap from their beds at the alarm and stand stiff and erect for action.

121. *hairs* (Rowe) Q2, F1 'haire.' MSH. p. 300.

125–28. *how pale he glares...this piteous action* Ham.'s words suggest that he sees some strange agitation in the Ghost's face and actions; v. note l. 132.

126–27. *preaching to stones...capable.* v. Luke xix. 40; 'capable' (v. G.) implies softening.

129. *effects* = outward symptoms (of my stern purpose), v. G.

132. *Nothing at all* Bradley (p. 140) believes that the Ghost remains invisible and inaudible to the Queen in order to spare her. A more plausible reason is furnished by *Der bestrafte Brudermord*, viz. that she is 'no longer worthy to look on his form' (v. Furness, ii. 133); and since in Heywood's *Iron Age* (Pt. ii) Act 5, Scene 1, Orestes takes Clytemnestra's blindness to

Agamemnon's ghost as evidence of her guilt, the notion seems to have been a common one at the period. I suggest that the 'piteous action' Ham. speaks of is one of hands outstretched in supplication to Gertrude and that the Ghost's agitation conveys, first his amazement that she cannot see or hear him, and then his horror as he realises the cause. It is only after she has declared herself completely insensible of his presence that he 'steals away' in shame.

145. *unction* v. G.

152–53. *Forgive me this my virtue...times* i.e. Forgive the sermon; this degenerate age is so morally flabby that etc. Both 'fatness' and 'pursy' = out of condition physically, v. G.

155. *curb and woo* 'bend and truckle' (Johnson).

161–65. *That monster...put on* F1 omits. MSH. pp. 28–9, 167.

162. *Of habits evil* (Theobald aft. Thirlby) Q2 'Of habits deuill.' The misprint would be easy (v. MSH. pp. 320–1), especially as the compositor, like all edd. since Johnson, may have been misled by a supposed antithesis between 'devil' and 'angel,' whereas Sh. intends, I think, to contrast 'monster' with 'angel' and 'habits evil' with 'actions fair and good.'

164. *frock or livery* Two sorts of uniform: 'frock' of a monk, suggesting religion, and 'livery' of a servant, suggesting duty. The image springs from 'assume' (v. G.) and 'habits' (in a quibbling sense) just before.

167–70. *the next...potency* F1 omits. MSH. pp. 28–9, 167.

169. *And either...the devil* Q2 'And either the deuill.' The compositor has prob. as so often elsewhere omitted a word. It is conceivable, on the other hand, that 'either' (sp. 'eyther') may be a misprint or miscorrection of 'exorcise,' a word which suits the context and must come near Sh.'s meaning. For want of a better, it may serve to fill the gap in the text. MSH. pp. 302–3.

171. *desirous to be blessed* i.e. truly repentant, and so, ready for Heaven's blessing.

174. *To punish me with this* Cf. l. 211 'This man shall set me packing.' The death of Pol. has placed Ham. within the power of the K.

175. *their scourge and minister* i.e. at once the officer of Heaven's justice and the lash he wields. A reference to the public flogging of criminals; cf. note 3. 1. 70 and Matth. v. 25 (Bishops' Bible, 1572) 'Least...the iudge deliuer thee to the minister.' Ham. is a 'fell sergeant' (5. 2. 334) for the arrest of Pol., but with a 'scourge' for his own back. Heaven is plur., as often in Sh.

178–79. *I must be...behind* The couplet sums up the scene: the first line referring to his treatment of the Queen, the second to the death of Pol.

179. *This bad* (Q2) F1 'Thus bad'—which all edd. read. But 'This,' i.e. the corpse (cf. l. 174), makes sense of the couplet, which has hitherto eluded explanation. In 'worse remains behind' Ham. expresses his fears of what may come of his rash act (cf. note l. 174 above), and these fears lead on naturally to the lines that follow. MSH. p. 275.

180. *One word more, good lady* Cf. *Introd.* p. lxiii.

190. *paddock...bat...gib* The toad, the bat and the tom-cat—all forms assumed by spirits attendant on witches (Clar.).

191. *dear concernings* i.e. 'matters that concern him so closely' (Verity). v. G. 'dear.'

194. *the famous ape* The story is lost, but Ham. makes the outline clear; the ape carries a cage of birds to the top of a house, releases them by accident, and, surprised at their flight, imagines he can also fly by first creeping into the cage and then leaping out. The point for the Queen is the publicity of the proceeding ('on the house's top' = in full view of everyone), and that letting the cat out of the bag will involve her own destruction. For 'try conclusions' v. G. and *M. of V.* 2. 2. 34.

200. *I must to England* Ham.'s knowledge of this has puzzled critics; but the K. had decided on the mission (for the sake of Ham.'s health) before the Play-scene (v. note 3. 1. 172–78), and Ham. would naturally be informed of the royal pleasure in order that due preparations might be made. Moreover, Ham.'s words in ll. 204–205 imply that Ros. and Guild. have been instructed to precede him, taking the sealed commission with them, in accordance with the usual practice of such political missions. What Ham. does not know is that orders have already been issued for his leaving at once, and that Ros. and Guild. are now to accompany him as his guards (3. 3. 2–4).

202–10. *There's letters...meet* F1 omits. MSH. p. 28.

204. *the mandate* Cf. 5. 2. 18 ff.

211. *packing* A quibble, v. G. Ham. recognises that the death of Pol. will hasten his departure.

213. *good night indeed* (Q2) F1 'good night. Indeed' The F1 period brushes away a delicate point; the 'indeed' echoes l. 159.

216. *to draw...with you* i.e. let me finish my conversation with you ('foolish prating knave').

217. S.D. F1 'Exit Hamlet tugging in Polonius.'

4. 1.

Rowe, following Q. 1676, introduced this act-division, which is 'not very happy, for the pause is made at a time when there is more continuity of action than in almost any other of the Scenes' (Johnson).

S.D. Q2 'Eenter [*sic*] King, and Queene, with Rosencraus and Guyldensterne.' F1 'Enter King.' The S.D. in Q2 is doubly remarkable, seeing that Gertrude is already 'on' at the end of 3. 4., and that Ros. and Guild. are brought in to be dismissed at once. Perhaps some intervening scene or episode has been omitted. MSH. pp. 38, 91–2.

4. *Bestow...while* F1 omits. v. head-note. Q2 gives no exit.

.7. *Mad as the sea* Obedient to Ham.'s implied command at 3. 4. 186–88, the Queen insists upon his madness for the rest of the play; cf. 5. 1. 278–82.

12–23. *O heavy deed* etc. The K. gently points out her unwisdom in 'screening' Ham. after the Play-scene; cf. note 3. 4. 2–4.

25–6. *some ore...metals base* = a vein of gold in a mine of base metal. v. G 'ore.'

27. *a' weeps* The falsehood testifies to her fidelity. Cf. Bradley, p. 104 *n.*

40. [*so haply slander*] (Capell, Theobald) Q2, F1 omit the half-line, so that we have no clue to what Sh. wrote. MSH. p. 30.

41–4. *Whose whisper...air* F1 omits. MSH. p. 30.

44. *the woundless air* Cf. 1. 1. 145 'the air invulnerable' and *Temp.* 3. 3. 63–4.

4. 2.

7. *Tell us where 'tis* etc. The tone is insolent, to 'the son of a king.'

11–12. *keep your counsel...own* i.e. follow your advice and not keep my own secret. A quibbling retort to Ros.'s rudeness. v. G. 'counsel.'

12. *replication* A legal term = an answer to a charge (v. N.E.D. 2).

15–20. *that soaks up...dry again* The notion of sycophants and extortioners as a monarch's sponges, which derives from Suetonius (*Vespasian*, c. 16), is a commonplace of the time; v. Marston, *Scourge of Villainy* (1599), vii. 58–60; Webster, *Duch. of Malfi*, 3. 2. 249–51, etc. (v. Furness). Vespasian deliberately bestowed high office upon rapacious persons 'so that the common talk was he used them as sponges, letting them soak when they were dry and squeezing them out again when they were wet.'

16. *his authorities* A hint that they were taking too much upon them.

17. *like an apple* (Q 2) F 1 'like an Ape,' Q 1 'as an Ape doth nuttes.' Q 2 gives perfectly good sense. Sh. is thinking, not of apes, but of the groundlings gnawing or sucking little pippins in the theatre; cf. *Hen. VIII*, 5. 4. 63–4. MSH. p. 72.

22–3. *a knavish speech...foolish ear* Cf. a similar hit at 3. 2. 337. Ham. means, of course, that his speech is foolish and Ros. knavish.

26–7. *The body is with the king*, etc. One of Ham.'s riddling quibbles, like 'A little more than kin, etc.,' intended prob. to set the audience guessing. I interpret: the body, i.e. Polonius, is in the next world with the king, my father, but the other king, my uncle, has not yet joined him there. The reference to Ps. cxliv. 4 (v. next note) and the drift of Ham.'s remarks in 4. 3. bear this out.

27–9. *a thing...Of nothing* Cf. Ps. cxliv. 4 (Prayer Book) 'Man is like a thing of nought, his time passeth away like a shadow.' Ham. at once insults the K. and hints that his days are numbered. v. *Introd*. pp. xl–xli.

29–30. *Hide fox...after* The cry in some game like 'hide and seek'; cf. 'the hid-fox' (*Ado*, 2. 3. 41), and 'All hid, all hid, an old infant play' (*L.L.L.* 4. 3. 76). The 'fox' is Pol., and Ham. runs off the stage as he speaks.

4. 3.

S.D. Q 2 'Enter King, and two or three.' The 'two or three' are, I take it, the K.'s 'wisest friends' (4. 1. 38).

4. *distracted multitude* = mobile vulgus, v. G. 'distracted.'

6. *scourge* i.e. punishment.

9. *Deliberate pause* The delay in calling Ham. to account for Pol.'s murder must seem the result of policy, not panic.

11. S.D. Q2 'Enter Rosencraus and all the rest.'

15. *Ho...the lord* (Q2) F1 'Hoa, Guildensterne?
Bring in my Lord.'

S.D. Q2 'They enter.'

19–34. *Not where he eats...yourself* An elaboration
of 'The body is with the king, but the king is not (yet)
with the body' at 4. 2. 26–7.

20. *convocation of politic worms* Prob. a glance at
the Diet of Worms (Singer); cf. 'emperor for diet.'
'Politic worms' is a pregnant phrase, 'politic' suggesting
craftiness and 'worm' an insidious prying into another's
secrets. Brandes (*Will. Shak.* p. 354) quotes Florio's
Montaigne, ii. 12 'The heart and life of a mighty and
triumphant Emperor, is but the break-fast of a Seely little
Worm.'

23–4. *variable service* = different courses, v. G.

25–7. *Alas...that worm* F1 omits. MSH. p. 23.

30. *progress* = state journey, v. G.

35–6. *nose him...lobby* Perhaps derived from the
Belleforest story in which the body of the spy, killed in
the Queen's closet, is cut up into pieces by Hamblet and
'then cast...into an open vaulte or privie, that so it mighte
serve for foode to the hogges' (Gollancz, *Sources of
Hamlet*, pp. 207, 229). The 'politic worms' play the
part of the 'hogges.'

45. Hamlet. *For England.* (Q2) F1 adds a query,
and mod. edd. print an exclamation mark. But Ham.
is not surprised at 'this sudden sending him away'; he
accepts it as a matter of course (cf. 'Good'), which is
far more effective, and takes the K. aback.

47. *I see a cherub* etc. Cf. 3. 4. 202–209. The
Cherubim were the watchmen or sentinels of Heaven,
and therefore endowed with the keenest vision; cf. *M.V.*
5. 1. 63 'the young-eyed cherubins'; *Macb.* 1. 7. 22–4;
Troil. 3. 2. 74–5; *Par. Lost*, iv. 778–80, xi. 128;
Il Penseroso, 54 'The Cherub Contemplation'
(Verity).

61. *coldly set* = undervalue, lightly regard. v. G. 'set.'

63. *congruing* (Q2) F1 'coniuring.' MSH. p. 60.

4. 4.

9–66. *Good sir…nothing worth* F1 omits. MSH. pp. 30–1.

18.* *a little patch of ground* From July 2, 1601 till the spring of 1602 the sand-dunes of Ostend were valiantly defended against the Spaniards in many battles and with great loss of life by an English force under Sir Francis Vere, which returned home on March 18. The siege actually continued until Sept. 1604, but the London public would only be interested in the earlier stages. There can be little doubt that Sh. is here alluding to these events, which points to the late summer or autumn of 1601 as the date for *Hamlet*, as we have it in Q2. v. G. B. Harrison, *Last Elizabethan Journal*, pp. 190–270 and *Sh. at Work*, pp. 279–81. The earliest news-pamphlet on Ostend was entered in the Stat. Reg. on Aug. 5, 1601, v. A. W. Pollard, *Short Title Catalogue*, Ostend.

26. *straw!* Q2 'straw,'

27–9. *This is th'imposthume…dies* Nashe expresses a similar idea in *Pierce Penilesse* (McKerrow's *Nashe*, i. 211), 'There is a certaine waste of the people for whome there is no vse, but warre…if the affayres of the State be such, as cannot exhale all these corrupt excrements.' Cf. also 'Sedition is an aposteam, which, when it breaketh inwardly, putteth the state in great danger of recovery' (Sir John Cheke, quoted in Ben Jonson's *English Grammar*, ch. iii).

40–1. *some craven scruple…th'event* Cf. 3. 3. 75 ff. *event* = consequence.

53–6. *Rightly to be great…at the stake* i.e. Fighting for trifles is mere pugnacity, not greatness; but it *is* greatness to fight instantly and for a trifle when honour is at stake (after Furness).

63. *Whereon...try the cause* i.e. The plot did not even afford room for the contending forces to give battle.

64–5. *not tomb enough* etc. Perhaps suggested by the fact that Vere for some time occupied an old churchyard outside Ostend, v. note l. 18, and Harrison, *Journal*, pp. 191–92.

4. 5.

The interval of time between 4. 4. and 4. 5. has been variously estimated at 'a week' and 'two months.' It is most improbable that Sh. made any estimate himself.

6. *Spurns enviously at straws* i.e. 'Conceives hatred of the most trivial and innocent things' (Clar.). v. G. 'enviously.'

16. *Let her come in* Q2 assigns this to 'Hora.'; MSH. p. 189.

17–20. *'To my sick soul...spilt.'* Q2 marks the lines with inverted commas to signify 'sentences'; cf. note 1. 3. 36–42. The aside accounts for the Queen's reluctance to see Oph. and gives us the only glimpse of her real state of mind after Ham.'s departure to England. v. G. 'toy,' 'jealousy,' 'spill'; 'artless jealousy' may be rendered 'uncontrollable suspicion.'

20. S.D. Q2 'Enter Ophelia,' F1 'Enter Ophelia distracted,' Q1 'Enter Ofelia playing on a Lute, and her haire downe singing.' Cf. note 3. 4. 102 S.D.

23–6. *How should I* etc. This first stanza was not likely to ease the Queen's 'sick soul.' None of Oph.'s ballad-snatches, except that at l. 186, are known elsewhere.

25–6. *cockle hat...shoon* The garb of a pilgrim assumed by the conventional lover sworn to worship at the shrine of his 'saint'; cf. *Rom.* 1. 5. 95–112.

36. *Larded all with* (Q2) F1 'Larded with'— which all edd. follow. But Sh. gives Oph. stumbling verse in this stanza to exhibit the wandering of her mind; cf. next note.

37 *did not go* (Q2, F1, Q1) Pope omitted 'not' and most edd. follow, which 'seems rash...lest Sh. may have meant a distracted allusion to the "obscure burial" (l. 211) of Pol.' (Dowden). The unmetrical 'not' would direct the attention of the audience to her wandering.

40–1. *Well...a baker's daughter* i.e. Well, thank you; I am transformed, but not into an owl like the baker's daughter. The allusion is to a folk-tale, acc. to Douce current in Gloucestershire, in which Jesus asks for bread at a shop, and is given short weight by the baker's daughter, for which she is changed into an owl. For a recent treatment of the story in verse, v. *The Fleeting* by Walter de la Mare.

God dild you (F1) Q2 'good dild you.'

42. *God be at your table!* Prob. a form of salutation by a guest before partaking of hospitality; but connected, as Verity notes, in Oph.'s distraught mind with the inhospitality of the baker's daughter to God.

43. *Conceit upon her father* The K. refers to the general drift of Oph.'s remarks. Cf. ll. 74–5 below.

46–65. *To-morrow is Saint Valentine's day* etc. 'This song alludes to the custom of the first girl seen by a man on the morning of this day being considered his Valentine, or true-love' (Halliwell). Its immodesty is attributed by most commentators to the influence of madness.

50. *clo'es* Q2 'close,' F1 'clothes.'

63. (*He answers*) F1 omits. Cf. note l. 167 below.

68. *they would lay* (Q2) F1 'they should lay.'

71–2. *Good night* (F1) Q2 'God night.' Cf. notes ll. 40–1 above and 2. 2. 182.

74–6. *O, this...Gertrude* Q2 prints this as prose; F1 regularises but omits 'and now behold.' MSH. p. 218.

74–5. *it springs...death* i.e. from Ham.'s violence. The K. never loses an opportunity with the Queen of stressing the danger of her son being at large.

77–8. *spies...battalions* As an army advances, the spies come first and the battalions follow.

82–3. *death—and...him—poor* Q2 'death: and ...him: poore'

91–2. *Wherein necessity...arraign* i.e. In which the speakers, gravelled for other matter, are compelled to attack me.

93. *In ear and ear* Suggesting a chain of whisperers.

96. *Attend!* F1 and mod. edd. omit. MSH. p. 261.

100. *impiteous* Q2 'impitious,' F1 'impittious.' v. G. Most edd. follow F2 'impetuous.' N.E.D. gives the two forms as doublets, but notes that the older one 'suggests association with "piteous."' It seems best to retain Sh.'s sp. MSH. pp. 287–88.

105. *The ratifiers...word* This has puzzled all, because they have not seen that 'word' (v. G.), as often elsewhere in Sh., means 'promise, pledge, undertaking.'

118–19. *brands...brows* Cf. note 3. 4. 43. *brows* (Grant White) Q2, F1 'browe.' MSH. pp. 299–300.

124.* *can but peep...would* i.e. dare not openly show its true aims.

125. *his will* = its will.

137. *world's* (Pope) Q2 'worlds,' F1 'world.' Clar. suggests that 'worlds' refers back to 'both the worlds' (l. 134), but while 'both the worlds' conforms well enough with Eliz. cosmology, 'all the worlds' would strike too modern a note.

141. *father* (Q2) F1 'Fathers death'—which most edd. follow, unnecessarily. MSH. p. 254.

142. *sweepstake* (Johnson) Q2, F1 'soopstake,' Q1 'Swoop-stake-like.' Most edd. read 'swoopstake.' MSH. pp. 287–88.

151. *'pear* (Johnson) Q2 'peare,' F1 'pierce.' Day does not pierce the eye; it reveals everything to its gaze, as the K. offers to do with Laer. v. G. 'level,' MSH. pp. 275–76.

153. S.D. Q2, F1 'Enter Ophelia.' Q1 'Enter
Ofelia as before.' Rowe 'Enter Ophelia, fantastically
drest with Straws and Flowers.' Delius and Poel (*Sh. in
the Theatre*, p. 172) suggest that the flowers spoken of
in ll. 174–83 are imaginary.

154.* *O heat* etc. The 'bravery' of Laer.'s grief is as
evident in this scene as at the funeral later.

161–63. *Nature...it loves* (F1) Q2 omits. MSH.
pp. 96–7. A high-flown sentimental way of saying that
Oph.'s sanity has followed Pol. to the grave. No one
seems to have noticed that 'nature' here = natural or
filial affection (cf. *Introd*. p. xxxiii; 1. 5. 81; 3. 2. 396;
5. 2. 229, 242 and *2 Hen. IV*, 4. 5. 39 'nature, love and
filial tenderness'). To paraphrase: Filial love is exquisite
in its working, and will sacrifice its most precious
possession as a proof of its affection for the dear departed.
v. G. 'fine,' 'instance.'

167. *Fare...dove!* Q2, F1 do not distinguish this
from the song; Capell first printed it as if it were an
observation on the part of Oph., addressed to Laer. as
she recognises his presence. MSH. pp. 227–28.

170–71. *You must sing...adown-a* Again Q2, F1
make no distinction in type between speech and song,
and there have been many attempts to differentiate them.
I take it that Oph., addressing Laer., bids him sing
'adown, adown' as the refrain to her song, if he indeed
agrees that Pol. is 'adown,' i.e. fallen low. This interpretation leads on to 'the wheel' in l. 171. MSH.
pp. 228–29.

171. *O, how the wheel becomes it!* Variously explained as referring to the refrain (v. N.E.D. 'wheel'
16), or to the spinning-wheel, as an accompaniment to
ballad-song; cf. *Tw. Nt*. 2. 4. 45. The former fits the
context well, but I suggest that Oph. is also thinking of
Fortune's wheel which has brought the leading statesman
of Denmark low 'adown'; if so 'becomes it' means that
a wheel (= refrain) corresponds well enough with his

condition. Technically 'wheel' = a stanza of at least 4 lines, but it might apparently be used vaguely for any kind of refrain or chorus, v. J. Schipper, *Hist. of Eng. Vers.* pp. 280 ff.

172. *the false steward...daughter* The reference has not been traced in folk-tale or ballad. It seems to refer back to the song at ll. 46–65.

174–83. *There's rosemary...some violets* Each flower has its meaning and is presented to an appropriate person. *Rosemary* = remembrance, used both at weddings and funerals (cf. *Rom.* 4. 5. 79; *Wint.* 4. 4. 74–6), she gives to Laer. *Pansies* = thought, esp. love-thoughts, she keeps, I think, for herself. *Fennel* = flattery and *columbines* = cuckoldry (from their horned shape) were appropriate to the K. *Rue* = sorrow (for herself) and repentance (for the Queen); *herb of grace* is another name for 'rue,' though actually with no religious significance. *Daisy* = dissembling (cf. Greene, *Quip for an upstart courtier*, 'Next them grewe the dessembling daisie, to warne such light of loue wenches not to trust euery faire promise that such amorous batchelers make them'), which she would place next the 'pansies' in her own bosom as a warning. *Violets* = faithfulness; these she cannot give to anyone, as there are no more left in the world. Some suppose she addresses herself to Hor. here; but he is not on in this scene. (v. Furness for much of the material of this note.)

182. *with a difference* i.e. for a different reason (v. 'Rue' in previous note), with a quibble on 'difference,' the heraldic term. v. G.

186. *For bonny sweet Robin* etc. From a well-known ballad, mentioned again as sung by the mad girl in *Two Noble Kinsmen* (4. 1. 134).

187. *Thought...passion* = melancholy...suffering, v. G.

199.* *And of...souls* 'The common conclusion to many...monumental inscriptions' (Steevens).

213. *No trophy...bones* 'When a man of good family was buried in a church it was usual to hang his casque, sword and coat armour in its tinctures over his tomb, special funeral armour often being made for the purpose,' Sh. Eng. ii. 150.

4. 6.*

S.D. There seems no good reason why edd. should locate Scenes 6 and 7 in different 'rooms in the castle' as following Capell they have commonly done.

15. *him...Ere* Q2 'him: Ere'

26. *too light for the bore* The size of the bore determines the weight of the projectile.

31. *give you way* (F1) Q2 'will you way.' Most edd. read 'make you way' (Q4); v. MSH. p. 293, and G. 'give way.'

4. 7.

S.D. Readers ask: does the previous scene allow time enough to the K. to convince Laer.? Hardly if Laer. had first to 'make choice' among his 'wisest friends' (4. 5. 203). An audience might be relied upon to forget the point and would be untroubled by such problems.

5. *Pursued my life* v. note 3. 2. 243.

7. *crimeful* (F1) Q2 'criminall.' MSH. pp. 163–4, 280.

8. *greatness* (Q2) F1 omits and mod. edd. follow to avoid an alexandrine, though, as Clar. observes, 'the next line is an alexandrine also.'

14. *conjunctive* Dowden notes that this word (v. G. and also 'sphere') 'seems to have suggested the line that follows.'

20. *the spring...stone* Harrison's *Description of England* (ed. Furnivall, p. 349) states that the baths of King's Newnham, Warwickshire, turn wood into stone (Dowden).

21. *Convert...graces* i.e. regard his fetters (had we put him under arrest) as an honour to him. Cf. 4. 3. 3–7.

22. *loud a wind* Steevens quotes Ascham's *Toxo-philus*, 1598 (ed. Arber, p. 151) 'Weake bowes, and lyghte shaftes can not stande in a rough wynde.'

27. *if praises...again* = if I may praise her as she once was.

37. *These* (Q2) F1 'This.' Cf. 1. 41 'you shall hear them.' The term 'letters' was often used with a sing. meaning. Q2 misprints the second 'these' as 'this.' MSH. p. 242.

50. *Naked* v. G.

52. *devise* (Q2) F1 'aduise'—which all edd. read. v. G. and MSH. p. 278.

57. *As how...otherwise?* i.e. He was safely shipped off; how can he have returned? And yet here is his letter in my hand!

67–80. *My lord, I will...graveness* F1 omits. MSH. p. 31.

74–6. *in my regard...of youth* The K. is of the old-fashioned school which disliked the new-fangled French or Italian rapier play; cf. note 5. 2. 222 S.D. and Silver, pp. ix–x.

80. *health* = prosperity. v. G.

83. *can well* = are most expert.

88–9. *That I...he did* i.e. That I could never have imagined the 'tricks and shapes' (v. G.) he performed.

89. *A Norman* The reputation of Normandy for horse-breeding and horsemanship stood high (v. Sh. Eng. ii. 411).

91. *Lamord* (Q2) F1 'Lamound.' Most read 'Lamond'; Malone conjectures 'Lamode,' Grant White 'Lamont.' Possibly 'Le Monté' was intended. Dowden follows Q2, 'having noticed in Cotgrave "*Mords*, a bitt of a horse."' I agree with Verity that some personal allusion is prob., more esp. as the whole passage (80–93) 'does not arise naturally out of a context in which the accomplishment dwelt on is fencing, not horsemanship.'

Sh.'s patron, the Earl of Southampton, was created Master of his Horse by Essex in 1599, while in Ireland; and this may be the point of the allusion. 'The brooch indeed And gem of all the nation' would suit well with Southampton's reputation at this period.

94. *confession* i.e. 'the unwilling acknowledgment by a Frenchman of a Dane's superiority' (Dowden).

96. *art and exercise* = skilful exercise.

99–101. *the scrimers...opposed them* F1 omits. MSH. p. 31. For 'motion' v. G.

110–22. *But that I know...easing* The Player King's speech (3. 2. 185–214) expands this notion; *Son.* 116 contradicts it.

110. *begun by time* = created by circumstance. Cf. note 3. 4. 107.

113–22. *There lives...by easing* F1 omits. MSH. p. 31.

116–22. *plurisy...ulcer* Sh. here indulges in an elaborate quibble. v. *Introd.* p. xxxvii.

117–22. *That we would do...easing* As many have noted, these words point the whole moral of *Hamlet,* and are a comment (unconscious on Claud.'s part, but intentional on Sh.'s) upon Ham.'s character, as indeed much of the action in Act 4 is likewise. Cf. *Introd.* p. lxi.

121. *spendthrift sigh* Sighing was supposed to drain the blood; cf. *M.N.D.* 3. 2. 97.

125. *To cut his throat i'th'church* An unconscious reflexion upon Ham.'s conduct in the Prayer-scene; cf. note ll. 117–22 above.

128. *keep close within your chamber* 'And now the K. has but one anxiety—to prevent the young men meeting before the fencing match. For who can tell what Ham. might say in his defence, or how enchanting his tongue might prove?' (Bradley, p. 143).

135–37. *the foils...unbated* v. note 5. 2. 222 S.D.

137. *a pass of practice* A quibble: (*a*) a bout for

exercise, (*b*) a treacherous thrust; cf. l. 66 above, note 5. 2. 299 and G. 'practice.'

139–40. *anoint...unction* With a poss. quibble upon extreme unction: v. G.

143–4. *Collected...moon* Herbs were thought to be more efficacious if gathered by moonlight.

149.* *fit us to our shape* i.e. mould our plans to suit our ends.

158. *preferred* (Q2) F1 'prepar'd'—which most mod. edd. read. MSH. p. 278.

161. *But stay, what noise?* (Q2) F1 omits and reads instead 'How now, sweet queen'—which most edd. follow although some adopt both readings. Q1 supports F1 by reading 'How now Gertred.' MSH. pp. 246–7.

165–82. *There is a willow* etc. C. C. Stopes and E. I. Fripp conjecture that Sh. may have drawn upon memories of the drowning of 'Katherine Hamlett spinster,' in the Avon on Dec. 17, 1579/80 (cf. Fripp, *Minutes of the Corp. of Stratford*, iii. 50), but the time of year makes it impossible for 'the setting' to have been drawn upon also, as Chambers (*Will. Shak*. i. 425) seems to suggest. Cf. also Harrison, *Sh. at Work*, pp. 272–73.

165. *askant* Q2 'ascaunt,' F1 'aslant'—which most mod. edd. read. MSH. p. 278.

167. *Therewith...make* (Q2) F1 'There with... come'—which mod. edd. read, and so miss the fact that the garland was made of willow, the emblem of disconsolate love; cf. *Oth*. 4. 3. 51 'Sing all a green willow must be my garland.' MSH. p. 276.

171. *crownet* Q2 'cronet,' F1 'coronet.' Cf. *A. & C*. 5. 2. 91.

176. *lauds* (Q2) F1, Q1 'tunes'—which nearly all edd. read. MSH. pp. 71–2. In 'snatches of old lauds' Sh. seems to refer to the *laude* or vernacular hymns of praise sung by wandering bands or guilds of singers in Italy from 13th to 16th c., though it is not clear that they were ever the fashion in England (v. A. W. Pollard, *Old*

Picture Books, pp. 15–22). Perhaps Sh. also had in mind Pss. cxlviii–cl, the psalms of praise sung at the service of Lauds. Oph. dies crowned with flowers and singing hymns of praise to God.

188. *The woman will be out* i.e. When these tears are shed I shall have got rid of the woman in me. Cf. 'And all my mother came into mine eyes,' *Hen. V*, 4. 6. 31.

190. *douts* (Knight) F1 'doubts,' Q2 'drownes,' MSH. pp. 51, 137. Cf. *Hen. V*, 4. 2. 11 (F1) 'doubt' (= dout), and above note 1. 4. 37.

5. 1.

1–2. *when she* (Q2) F1 'that.'

4. *straight* = immediately (with a quibble on 'narrow').

6–7. *unless...her own defence* He is thinking of the law of homicide.

8. *found so* i.e. by the 'crowner.'

9. *se offendendo* The sexton means 'se defendendo,' i.e. the verdict in justifiable homicide (unless he is making a shot at 'felo de se').

10–20. *if I drown myself...his own life* An echo of the famous case of *Hales v. Petit*, heard 1554, of which reports were pub. in 1571, 1578, and which settled for the period the law as regards suicide, recognising it as homicide and so distinct from some kind of felony for which there was a forfeiture. Sir James Hales, the suicide, was a Common Law judge, and consequently the case would be noteworthy on that score; in any event it presents some striking parallels with the words of the sexton, e.g. (i) Hales committed suicide by walking into a river at Canterbury (cf. 'if the man go to this water' etc.). (ii) The counsel for the defence argued that

the act of self destruction consists of three parts. The first is the imagination, which is a reflection or meditation of the man's mind whether or no it be convenient to destroy himself and in what way it may be done; the second is the resolution, which is the determination of the mind to destroy himself and to do it in this or that particular way; the third is the perfection, which is the execution of what the mind has resolved to do. And this perfection consists of two parts, viz. the beginning and the end. The beginning is the doing of the act which causes the death, and the end is the death, which is only a sequel of the act.

(iii) There was much discussion as to whether Hales was the 'agent' or the 'patient,' in other words whether he went to the water or the water came to him; and the verdict was:

Sir James Hales was dead. And how came he by his death? It may be answered by drowning. And who drowned him? Sir James Hales. And when did he drown him? In his lifetime. So that Sir James Hales being alive caused Sir James Hales to die, the act of the living was the death of the dead man. And for this offence it is reasonable to punish the living man, who committed the offence, and not the dead man.

These parallels were first noted by Sir John Hawkins, the friend of Dr Johnson (v. Furness). The same arguments are likely to have been repeated at any inquest upon a drowned person and so might come to Sh.'s knowledge. Cf. Sir D. Plunket Barton, *Links between Sh. and the Law*, 1929, pp. 51–4, and *The Hist. of the Common Law*, 1934, pp. 307–8, by Dr Harold Potter, to whom I am indebted for the first half of this note.

12. *argal* A corruption of 'ergo'; cf. 'argo,' 2 *Hen. VI*, 4. 2. 31, and Sh.'s 'Addition' to *Sir Thomas More*, l. 5, and v. R. W. Chambers in M.L.R. xxvi. 256–57.

28–9. *even-Christen* (Q2) F1 'euen Christian.' v. G. and cf. Chaucer, *Persones Tale*, 24 'of his neighebore, that is to seyn, of his evene-cristene.' Here used collectively. MSH. pp. 276–77.

34–7. *Why, he had...without arms?* (F1) Q2 omits. MSH. p. 97.

38–9. *confess thyself*—'and be hanged' is the rest of the sentence.

43. *that frame* v. G. 'frame.' The Clown quibbles.

52. *unyoke* 'after this great effort you may unharness the team of your wit' (Dowden).

60. *get thee to Yaughan, and fetch* Q2 'get thee in, and fetch,' F1 'get thee to Yaughan, fetch.' Nicholson suggested that 'Yaughan' was the name of the keeper of a tavern near the Globe, which he identified with 'deaf John's' dark alehouse spoken of in Jonson's *Alchemist*, 1. 1. This, which is plausible prima facie, assumes that mine host was a German and that 'Yaughan' was an attempt to give a Welsh form to 'Johan' (or 'Yohan' as Jonson renders the name of a German Jew in *E.M.O.* 5. 6. 48). But it is not necessary to bring in a German at all, seeing that 'Johan' is also the Danish for John, and that if 'deaf John's' was the house intended, Sh. would naturally wish to translate it to Elsinore, just as he gives the Danish name Yorick to the K.'s jester, and Osric to the fop. Sh. prob. spelt it 'Yohan' as Jonson did, for the form 'Yaughan' belongs to the corrupt F1 text, while the notion quoted by Furness that it can be a Welsh name is apparently quite unfounded. That no name appears in Q2 may be set down to omission on the part of the compositor. MSH. pp. 259–60.

S.D. Q2 'Enter Hamlet and Horatio.' (at l. 64) F1 'Enter Hamlet and Horatio a farre off.' (at l. 55). It is clear from Ham.'s first words that they have over-heard the song. Cf. note 3. 2. 290 S.D. and MSH. p. 184. 'Clad as a sailor' is a suggestion by Mr William Poel (v. *Sh. in the Theatre*, pp. 173–74), quoting 'naked' (4. 7. 44) and pointing out that the Sexton does not recognise him and that he has to declare himself at l. 251.

61–4. *In youth when I* etc. The three stanzas of the sexton's song are a blundering and half-remembered

version of Vaux's 'The Aged Lover renounceth Love'
from *Tottel's Miscellany*, a volume which Slender in
M.W.W. possessed. The relevant verses, which are apt
for a grave-digger, run in Arber's reprint:

> I lothe that I did loue,
> In youth that I thought swete:
> As time requires for my behoue
> Methinkes they are not mete.
>
> My lustes they do me leaue,
> My fansies all are fledde:
> And tract of time begins to weaue
> Gray heares upon my hedde.
>
> For age with stelyng steppes,
> Hath clawed me with his crowch:
> And lusty life away she leapes,
> As there had bene none such.
>
> . . . .
>
> A pikeax and a spade
> And eke a shrowdyng shete
> A house of claye for to be made,
> For such a gest most mete.
>
> Me thinkes I heare the clarke,
> That knols the carefull knell:
> And bids me leue my wofull warke
> Er nature me compell.
>
> . . . .
>
> Loe here the bared scull,
> By whose bald signe I know:
> That stoupyng age away shall pull
> What youthfull yeres did sowe.
>
> For beauty with her bande
> These croked cares hath wrought:
> And shipped me into the lande
> From whence I first was brought.
>
> And ye that bide behinde
> Haue ye no other trust:
> As ye of claye were cast by kinde
> So shall ye waste to dust.

The original, which seems to us absurd enough in itself, must have been very familiar to Sh.'s audience for them to enjoy its perversion to the full.

63. *To contract o'the time* Q 2 'To contract ô the time.' MSH. pp. 304–5. An echo of 'And tract of time.' Some have taken the 'o' as a grunt of the digger at work; Clar. is prob. right in explaining the 'a' in this line and the next as 'the drawling notes in which he sings' (cf. *Wint.* 4. 3. 121, 123, 'stile-a,' 'mile-a').

67–8. *a property of easiness* Most interpret 'a peculiarity that comes easy.' But N.E.D. glosses 'easiness' as indifference, which would give 'a characteristic of indifference,' and Ham.'s reply shows that this is the sense intended. Bright, p. 78, speaking of the 'custom of life in saylers, butchers and ploughmen,' declares that

their instruments of action through continuall practise of such artes, maketh them in common sense, imagination, and affection, to deliuer thinges vnto the minde after an impure sort, alwayes sauouring of their ordinary trade of life.

77–8. *Cain's jaw-bone...this ass* Skeat (*N. & Q.* Aug. 21, 1880) showed that acc. to legend (mentioned in *Cursor Mundi*, 1071–74) Cain 'did the first murder' with the jaw-bone of an ass. Ham. implies that it is now the ass's turn to 'o'er-reach' Cain, v. next note.

79. *circumvent God* Cain was the first 'politician'; he denied that he was his brother's keeper, and when God asked him where Abel was he quibbled.

87. *chopless* (Q 2) F 1 'Chaplesse.'

90. *with them* (Q 2) F 1 'with 'em.'

96–7. *quiddities...quillities* Q 2 'quiddities... quillites,' F 1 'Quiddits...Quillets.' MSH. p. 268.

101–103. *his statutes...recoveries* v. G. for these terms, which suggest the sleights employed by the lawyer to get his neighbours' land into his own possession. Cf. Potter, *Hist. of the Common Law*, 1934, pp. 449–56.

103–105. *is this the fine...dirt?* A series of quibbles.

To paraphrase: is this the end of his fines, and the upshot of his recoveries, to have his egregious head full of unadulterated dirt? v. G. 'fine,' 'recovery.'

107–108. *a pair of indentures...this box* The box is the skull, the top of which Ham. turns towards the audience as he speaks, displaying its parchment-like surface and its serrated sutures, strikingly similar to the indented lines which divide 'a pair of indentures' (v. G.) into its parts. For 'inheritor' v. G.

109. *ha?* = eh? v. G.

114. *assurance* A further quibble. v. G.

117. *O, a pit* (F1) Q2 'or a pit.' MSH. p. 325.

134. *equivocation* A reference to the Jesuit doctrine of 'equivocation,' much discussed 1600–1601, owing to the famous 'Archpriest Controversy.' v. Harrison, *Last Eliz. Journ.* pp. 111, 218–19. For 'by the card' v. G. 'card.'

135. *this three years* (Q2) Dowden suggests an allusion here 'to the great Poor Law...of 1601,' which established 'the principle of taxation for the relief of the poor....The purses, if not the kibes, of needy courtiers were galled by the assessments of the overseers.' This seems likely. The act was actually passed late in 1597 (v. E. P. Cheyney, *Hist. of Eng.* 1588–1603, ii. 262, 270) and only re-enacted in 1601 with slight changes, which makes the 'Three years' precise if the passage was written in 1600 or 1601.

have took note (Q2) F1 'haue taken note.'

143–57. *that very day that young Hamlet...thirty years* This, together with the insistence upon 'thirty' years of married life for the Player King and Queen (v. note 3.2.153–58) and the precise reference to 'three and twenty years' since Yorick's death (l. 167), fixes the age of Ham. in so pointed a fashion that as most agree Sh. clearly attached importance to it; and yet this age does not at all tally with the impression of youth and inexperience which Ham. gives us at the opening of the play. The discrepancy, prob. due to revision, has occasioned much discussion, for which v. *Introd.* p. xlvii, and Furness, and cf. Østerberg, *Prince Hamlet's Age* (Copenhagen, 1924) for an opinion differing from that just given.

166–67. *Here's a skull...hath lien you* Q2 'heer's a scull now hath lyen you,' F1 'Heres a Scull now: this Scull, has laine.' The sexton turns it over in his hands, as he speaks. MSH. p. 257.

175. *skull, sir, was, sir* (Q2) F1 'Scull Sir, this same Scull sir, was.' MSH. p. 257.

Yorick's The Danish name 'Georg' sounds rather like 'Yory' or 'Yorig,' and it seems prob. (as Ainger pointed out) that this is the name intended. Many have taken it as referring to Tarlton: but he died in 1588, which makes 'three-and-twenty years' impossible; his name was Richard; and he was a stage-clown not a court jester.

205–206. *loam...beer-barrel* N.E.D. ('loam' 2) quotes from 1759 'A cake of plaisterers stiff loam, or such as the brewers use to stop their beer barrels.' The loam was commonly mixed with horse dung, which renders the 'use' still more 'base.'

207. *Imperious* v. G.

211. *awhile* (Q2) F1 'aside.' MSH. pp. 245, 267.

212. S.D. Q2 'Enter K. Q. Laertes and the corse,' F1 'Enter King, Queene, Laertes, and a Coffin, with Lords attendant.' The latter was expanded by Capell and Malone to 'Enter Priests, &c. in procession; the Corpse of Ophelia, Laertes and Mourners following: King, Queen, their trains, &c.'—which all mod. edd. read, though it suggests candles, incense and the full Catholic ceremony, and thus flies in the face of Ham.'s talk of 'maiméd rites' immediately after (v. Sh. Eng. ii. 271). Moreover, instead of 'Priests &c.' Q2 gives us a single Protestant minister (v. note l. 220). The 'Cour-

tiers' are mentioned by Ham. (l. 212), and the 'open coffin,' required by l. 244, was the common if not the usual practice of the time, the corpse being covered with a 'sable cloth' (cf. *Knight of the Burning Pestle*, 4. 4. 62 and above 4. 5. 164 'They bore him barefaced on the bier').

217. *That is Laertes* etc. v. *Introd.* p. xlviii. Sh. has been careful to keep Hor. and Laer. from meeting hitherto on the stage, and as Hor. had hurried to greet Ham. at the end of 4. 6. he would not have heard of the death of Oph.

220. *Her obsequies* etc. Q2 heads this and the priest's other speech '*Doct.*' which I interpret Doctor of Divinity, i.e. an Eliz. cleric. Canon Dearmer, who agrees, writes privately, 'he would wear a gown and a tippet over his cassock, and a square cap, as ordered in the canon of 1604, the tippet being what we call a black scarf' (cf. note 1. 2. 113).

221. *Her death was doubtful* Clearly the coroner's verdict (5. 1. 1–5) and the account of the drowning told to the Queen (4. 7. 165–82) have not satisfied the rigid ecclesiastical authorities. 'The rubric before the Burial Office forbids it to be used for persons who have laid violent hands upon themselves' (Clar.). The rubric was not inserted until 1662 but the practice was traditional. Cf. next note.

223–25. *She should...thrown on her* It was formerly the practice (abol. in 1823) to bury those convicted of felo de se beneath a pile of stones at the cross-roads with a stake driven through them. Cf. J. H. Blunt, *Book of Church Law* (ed. G. Edwardes Jones, 1899), pp. 182–4, which also makes clear that the verdict of a coroner was not binding upon the ecclesiastical authorities.

227–28. *bringing home...burial* i.e. laying to rest with the passing-bell and a grave in consecrated ground. 'Funerals during Eliz.'s reign' retained 'many of the traditional ceremonies and rites of pre-Reformation

times, the passing-bell being one of these' (Sh. Eng.
ii. 148); cf. *V.A.* 701–702.

231. *sage requiem* (F1) Q2 'a Requiem'—which
all mod. edd. follow. MSH. p. 11. Cf. *Il Penseroso*
'In sage and solemn tunes have sung.' For 'requiem,'
which means solemn music (v. Sh. Eng. ii. 150) and
not a mass, v. G., and cf. *The Phœnix and the Turtle*:

> Let the priest in surplice white,
> That defunctive music can
> Be the death-divining swan,
> Lest the requiem lack his right.

Here the words 'surplice white' show that the
'priest' is not a Roman one. I owe much of this note
to Canon Dearmer.

236. *liest howling* i.e. in Hell.

244. S.D. F1 'Leaps in the graue,' Q2 omits.
MSH. pp. 185–6. Graves at this time were much shal-
lower and wider than the neat deep-sunk pits of our
modern burial-grounds, which would allow no room for
a man to leap in beside the coffin (and that an open
one), still less for two to struggle therein. On the Eliz.
stage graves were represented by the open 'trap' (v.
Chambers, *Eliz. Stage*, iii. 107 and cf. head-note
1. 5.).

250. *the wand'ring stars* = the planets.

252.* *Hamlet the Dane* It is noteworthy that at this
first announcement to the Court of his return from
England Ham. assumes the royal title; cf. 'liegemen to
the Dane' (1. 1. 15).

S.D.* Q1 'Hamlet leapes in after Leartes,' Q2, F1
omit. MSH. p. 186. It is obvious from ll. 254–58
that Q1 preserves the stage-business. Rowe read
'Grappling with him' and (at l. 259) 'The Attendants
part them' to which latter Capell and Malone added
'and they come out of the grave.'

257. *wiseness* (F1) Q2 'wisdome'—which many

edd. follow. The more unusual F1 word gives an edge to Ham.'s irony. MSH. pp. 162–64.

268–78. *'Swounds...as well as thou* This speech clearly owes much to Florio's *Montaigne*, i. ch. 4: 'How the soule dischargeth her passions upon false objects, when the true faile it'; e.g.

The philosopher Byon was very pleasant with the king, that for griefe tore his haire, when he said, 'Doth this man thinke, that baldnesse will asswage his griefe? who hath not seene some to chew and swallow cardes, and wel-nigh choake themselves with bales of dice, only to be revenged for the losse of some money?' Xerxes whipped the Sea, and writ a cartell of defiance to the hill Athos.

269. *Woo't* I follow other edd. in retaining the sp. of Q2 and F1 here, and of Q2 in 'thou't' (Q2 'th'owt'), l. 268, though Sh. prob. intended nothing special by it; cf. 'wooll' for 'will' 2 *Hen. IV*, 3. 2. 308 (Q), and 'woot' for 'wilt' *A. & C.* 4. 2. 7; 4. 15. 59.

270. *eisel* (Theobald) Q2 'Esill,' F1 'Esile,' Q1 'vessels.' The reading 'eisel' is much discussed, but N.E.D. has no hesitation in accepting it, while, as F. L. Lucas (letter T.L.S. 29. 7. '26) shows, the sense (vinegar) suits the context well. What will you do for her (i.e. to show your grief)? asks Ham.; will you weep? fight (as you have just been doing)? fast (a ceremonial sign of grief)? tear yourself (i.e. rend your clothing)? drink vinegar to induce melancholy? or eat a crocodile to catch his trick of hypocritical tears?—a crescendo of sarcasm. Critics who imagine that 'Esill' is the name of some river have been led astray by the latter part of the speech: Ham. does not begin to outbid Pelion and Olympus until l. 274. Dowden comes near to the true interpretation, though missing the point about the croco-dile, and quotes W. Vaughan, *Directions for Health*, 1600, which states that vinegar while it allays choler and heat, 'hurteth them that be sorrowfull' (p. 47, ed. 1633), and L. Joubert, Physician to the French King, *Seconde*

Partie des Erreurs Populaires (Rouen, 1600), 'le vinaigre
est la mort de la colère et la vie de la mélancholie.' Cf.
also *Son.* 111. 10 'Potions (= doses) of Eysell gainst my
strong infection' and Bright, *Melancholy*, p. 30.

276. *the burning zone* v. G. 'burning zone.'

277. *Make Ossa like a wart* Ham. heaps 'Ossa' upon
Laer.'s 'Pelion.'

278. *This is mere madness* etc. Gertrude pointedly
stresses the madness, but the symptoms she describes are
genuine enough. Cf. *Introd.* pp. lxiii–lxiv.

285–86. *Let Hercules...day* Dowden paraphrases:
'Laertes must have his whine and his bark...if Hercules
cannot silence dogs, much less I, who am little like that
hero (1. 2. 153).' I prefer: 'Bluster away, my young
Hercules: but poor Hamlet's turn will come' (Verity),
since Laertes with his thrasonical brag of o'er-topping
Pelion and Olympus is surely the Hercules of the situation. Hercules is reputed to have disliked dogs and flies,
which were not allowed within his temple at Rome.
N.E.D. ('day' 15) quotes Queen Elizabeth, as reported
by Strype, saying in 1550 'Notwithstanding, as a dog
hath a day, so I may perchance have time to declare it
in deeds,' which seems to come close to Ham.'s meaning;
cf. also Jonson, *Tale of a Tub*, 2. 1. 4 'a man has his
hour and a dog his day.'

289. *the present push* i.e. the instant test (with a
quibble on 'push' = rapier-thrust), v. G. 'push.'

291. *a living monument* = an enduring memorial
(with a quibble on 'monument' = prodigious event,
cf. *Shrew*, 3. 2. 93). The K. hints at Ham.'s death.

5. 2.

S.D. For 'the hall' v. l. 174.

1. *So much...the other* They enter in the midst
of a conversation, the beginning of which we do not
hear. Cf. 2. 2. 392–93 'You say right...then indeed.'

7–11. *let us know...we will* A parenthesis enlarging 'praised be rashness.' The sentence 'Rashly... rashness for it' is continued in l. 12. For 'rashly' and 'know' v. G.

15. *Fingered* v. G. The mod. slang 'pinched' is almost an exact equivalent.

22. *such bugs...life* Usually explained by mod. edd. as 'threatening them with such terrors if they allowed me to live' (cf. 4. 3. 57–64); but the K. would rather persuade than threaten, and I prefer Johnson's suggestion that the 'bugs and goblins' were crimes attributed to Ham.

30. *Or* (Q2) F1 'Ere.' MSH. p. 243. The meaning is the same.

32. *wrote it fair* Referring to the elaborate Italian calligraphy employed in state letters addressed to sovereign princes at this period. Ham. is contemptuous of a style that marked the trained clerk rather than the gentleman (v. Maunde Thompson, Sh.Eng. i. 287). Cf. Florio's *Montaigne* (i. ch. 39):

I have in my time seene some, who by writing did earnestly get both their titles and living, to disavow their apprentissage, marre their pen, and affect the ignorance of so vulgar a qualitie.

Cf. also in the same ch. of Montaigne 'I commonly begin [letters] without project: the first words begets the second' etc. with ll. 30–31 above.

42. *a comma 'tween their amities* Much discussed, and many emendations of 'comma' proposed. But Ham. talks of writing and speaks as a scribe, a 'comma' being the shortest of all pauses in punctuation. N.E.D. quotes an exact parallel from Fuller's *Worthies*, 1662, 'Though a truce may give a comma or colon to the war, nothing under a peace can give a perfect period.' The word 'amities' is ironical, like 'faithful tributary' and 'love between them'; Ham. means that the two nations

are inveterate foes who will, after the briefest possible pause, be at each other's throats again.

43. *'as'es'* A pun on the preceding conjunctions which, with their weighty-looking (though empty) clauses are like a string of asses bearing heavy burdens ('great charge'). Cf. *Tw. Nt.* 2. 3. 174–76 for the same quibble.

57. *Why, man...employment* (F1) Q2 omits.

59. *insinuation* cf. 4. 2. 15–16.

63. *think thee* (Q2) F1 'thinkst thee.' MSH. p. 268.

65. *Popped in...hopes* Cf. note 3. 4. 99–101. For 'election' v. 5. 2. 353–54 and *Introd.* pp. liii–liv.

68–80. *To quit him...passion* (F1) Q2 omits. MSH. pp. 97–8.

69–70. *To let this canker...evil* i.e. To let this cancerous ulcer of humanity continue its foul existence. For 'in' = into, cf. 5. 1. 272.

74.* *a man's...say 'One'* This, which is passed over in silence by edd., refers I think to the single thrust of a rapier; cf. *Rom.* 2. 4. 23 'one, two, and the third in your bosom,' and below 5. 2 278 'One!'

80. S.D. For 'diminutive' v. note l. 84. The 'winged doublet' (i.e. with projections from the shoulders), then much in the fashion (v. N.E.D. 'wing' 8), is suggested by 'water-fly' (l. 84) and 'lapwing' (l. 186), while an absurd hat (cf. 'shell on his head' ll. 186–87) provides much of the business during the dialogue. Cf. Sh.Eng. ii. 105.

84. *water-fly* i.e. gnat, a tiny creature. 'A water-fly skips up and down upon the surface of the water, without any apparent purpose or reason, and is thence the proper emblem of a busy trifler' (Johnson). Cf. *Troil.* 5. 1. 38–9 'waterflies, diminutives of nature.'

87–9. *let a beast...mess* i.e. an ass has only to possess so many head of cattle and he gets the entry at Court.

94–5. *diligence of spirit* Implying that it may try his spirits.

96–7. *Put your bonnet* etc. It was customary for the Elizabethans to wear their hats indoors. v. Sh. Eng. ii. 109 and cf. 2. 1. 76. Sh. often makes play with this business of remaining uncovered in the presence of a superior; cf. *L.L.L.* 5. 1. 95, *M.N.D.* 4. 1. 20 (note), *A.Y.L.* 3. 3. 68 (note). Webster's Induction to Marston's *Malcontent* (1604), which is full of echoes from *Ham.*, contains the following dialogue between the members of Sh.'s company:

Condell. I beseech you, sir, be covered.

Sly. No, in good faith, for mine ease: look you, my hat's the handle to this fan: God's so, what a beast was I, I did not leave my feather at home! Well, but I'll take an order with you. *Puts his feather in his pocket.*

Burbadge. Why do you conceal your feather, sir?

Sly. Why? Do you think I'll have jests broken upon me in the play, to be laughed at? this play hath beaten all your gallants out of the feathers: Blackfriars hath almost spoiled Blackfriars for feathers.

Sinklo. God's so, I thought 'twas for somewhat our gentlewomen at home counselled me to wear my feather to the play....

Steevens, noting that the opening words are 'from the part of Osric in *Ham.*,' suggests that 'Sly might have been the original performer of that character.' If so, the passage perhaps gives us a clue to the nature of Osric's hat, while it has obvious reference to the 'forest of feathers' (3. 2. 275), since not only Sly but Sinklo, and prob. the other members of the company, are represented as wearing ridiculous feathers.

111–46. *Sir, here is newly...he's unfellowed.* F1 abridges this to one sentence: 'Sir, you are not ignorant of what excellence Laertes is at his weapon'—an obvious playhouse cut. MSH. p. 31.

113. *of very soft society* After Laer.'s conduct in the previous scene this is esp. ludicrous.

114. *sellingly* (Q2 some copies) Other copies
'fellingly'—which is a press-corrector's emendation, cf.
MSH. pp.123–31. Most edd. read with Q4 'feelingly'
(= with discernment, cf. *Twelfth Night*, 2. 3. 172).
But I agree with Steevens, Jennens and Collier that
'sellingly' is right; cf. *L.L.L.* 4. 3. 240 'To things of
sale a seller's praise belongs,' and *Son.* 21. 14 'I will not
praise that purpose not to sell.' Osric has been speaking
like a shopman advertising his wares (e.g. 'excellent
differences...and great showing'); and the jest is that
he no sooner announces his intention of doing so than
he deserts the language of the shop for that of the ship.
Cf. note ll. 117–24.

card or calendar of gentry = the very map or register
of elegance (with a quibble on the shipman's 'card').
v. G. 'card,' 'calendar.'

115. *parts* (Nicholson) Q2 'part,' MSH. pp. 300–1.
No one has followed Nicholson; yet he is surely right.
Osric is deep in maritime metaphor: Laer. is the
'continent' of gentry and contains in himself all those
'parts' that a gentleman would wish to see (upon his
travels), v. G.

117–24. *Sir, his definement...nothing more* Osric
has mixed the metaphors of the shop and the ship; and
Ham. follows suit. To paraphrase: the specification
(definement) of his perfections has lost nothing at your
hands, though I know they are so numerous that to make
a detailed inventory of them (as a shopkeeper might)
would puzzle (dizzy) the mental arithmetic of the
ordinary commercial man, who would, moreover, be
left staggering ('and yet but yaw neither') by his quick
sale (with a quibble on 'sail'); but in truth I take him
to be a soul of great scope ('article,' with a commercial
quibble: 'the particulars of an inventory are called
articles,' Johnson), and his essence ('infusion') of such
costliness ('dearth') and rarity, that indeed I can compare him with nothing save his own looking-glass; for

what can better describe him than a shadow? The whole speech is rattled off and intended, of course, to be a rubbish-heap of affectation; but there is more in it than has hitherto been perceived. For the individual words v. G.

119. *yaw* Q2 (some copies). Others 'raw'— a press-correction. MSH. pp. 123, 129–32.

124. *trace* A quibble: (*a*) describe, depict, (*b*) follow (as a shadow does).

126. *The concernancy, sir?* = But what is it all about?

127. *more rawer* i.e. as compared with the exquisite refinement of the 'gentleman' it 'wraps.'

129. *in another tongue* i.e. in more reasonable language.

130. *You will to't, sir, really* = You will be able to tackle it if you try; cf. 'e'en to't,' 2. 2. 434.

134–35. *His purse...spent* i.e. He can no longer speak 'sellingly.'

142–44. *I dare not...himself* An elaboration of Matth. vii. 1 'Judge not, that ye be not judged.' Verity quotes Browne, *Religio Medici*, ii. 4 'No man can judge another, because no man knows himself.' v. G. 'compare with.'

146. *laid...unfellowed* Mod. edd. punctuate (after Steevens): 'laid on him by them, he's unfellowed in his meed,' thus taking 'in his meed' with 'unfellowed' and explaining 'without a peer in his particular excellence.' But this leaves 'by them' in the air. With Q2 pointing, 'by them in his meed' = 'by those in his pay, in his retinue,' and all is clear.

148. *Rapier and dagger* Despite Ham.'s jest Osric's reply is in correct form, since 'What's his weapon?' means 'What style of fence does he follow?' (cf. note 5. 2. 222 S.D.). At l. 152 'poniards' = daggers.

151. *impawned* (Q4) Q2 'impaund,' F1 'impon'd.' MSH. p. 267.

153. *as girdle, hangers, and so*   We should now say 'as the girdle, the hangers, and so on.' Each rapier had its girdle, with hangers attached, i.e. straps from which the weapon was hung; and fantastic fops, especially those wearing long rapiers (cf. note l. 263 below) attached great importance to these hangers or 'carriages.' Cf. Jonson, *E.M.I.* (1616), 1. 5. 82–3.

157–58. *I knew you...done*   F1 omits.

157. *edified by the margent*   A reference to the marginal commentary in books of the period, esp. theological books (hence 'edified').

160–61. *The phrase...cannon*   Cf. *Hen. V*, 3. Pro. 26 'Behold the ordnance on their carriages.'

166–68. *The king, sir, hath laid...twelve for nine* Johnson writes: 'This wager I do not understand. In a dozen passes one must exceed the other more or less than three hits. Nor can I comprehend how, in a dozen, there can be twelve to nine. The passage is of no importance; it is sufficient that there was a wager'—and later edd. have remained puzzled. We can be certain that to the Elizabethans the passage *was* important, and that Sh. would have given much thought to the details of a sporting event which was one of the major attractions of his play (cf. note 5. 2. 222 S.D.). And there is no real difficulty, once it is grasped that in 'He hath laid on twelve for nine' the 'he' is the 'he' of the previous sentence, viz. Laer.; and that 'laid' and 'laid on' mean, not 'laid a wager' as in l. 106, but 'laid down conditions' as at 5. 2. 259 (v. note and G.). These conditions are: on the K.'s side, that Laer. must win by at least three up (as a modern sportsman would put it); and on Laer.'s, that the match must be one of twelve bouts instead of the usual nine in order to give him more elbow room, since to win 'three up' in a match of nine would mean winning six bouts to Ham.'s three, with no allowance for 'draws,' which would be fearful odds to give. Q1 reads, 'that yong Leartes in twelue venies At Rapier and

Dagger do not get three oddes of you'—which supports this interpretation. v. Silver (Introd. pp. xi–xiii) for further discussion.

170. *answer* v. G.

177. *purpose, I will win* Q2 'purpose; I will winne.'

183. *Yours, yours* i.e. At your service!—uttered perfunctorily.

184. *He does well to commend it* etc. A quibble on Osric's 'I commend my duty,' i.e. I present my respects (a polite leave-taking). Ham., taking 'duty' as 'bow, obeisance' and 'commend' as 'praise,' says in effect 'He does well to praise his ridiculous bowing and scraping himself; no one else would.'

186–87. *This lapwing...head* Osric is one of the 'new-hatched, unfledged' courtiers (1. 3. 65), and the new-hatched lapwing was proverbially supposed to run about with its shell on its head. Hor. is referring to the hat which Osric has at last put on; cf. note 5. 2. 80 S.D.

188. *A' did comply,* Ham. caps Hor.'s new-hatched lapwing with a new-born baby. For 'comply' v. G. and 2. 2. 375.

190. *bevy* (F1) Q2 'breede,' MSH. pp. 149, 328. Many edd. follow Q2 but 'bevy' (= a covey of lapwing) must be the true reading.

191. *out of an habit of encounter* (Q2) F1 'outward habite of encounter'—which all edd. follow. MSH. pp. 277, 329. In Q2 the 'yeasty collection' is got 'out of an habit of encounter,' i.e. is the fruit of encounters and exchange of compliments with other gallants as absurd as himself. v. G. 'encounter.'

192. *yeasty* A 'yeasty collection' = an assortment of phrases, 'flourishes,' etc. which float upon the mind of these courtiers like froth upon a vat. The whole passage is a sustained metaphor from the fermentation of barley for brewing. Cf. *Introd.* p. xxxvii. A 'collection'

lit. = miscellaneous extracts of a literary or historical character, v. G.

192–93. *which carries...opinions* Hitherto misunderstood, partly through doubts concerning the text (v. next note). I explain: 'which enables them to impose upon tried and experienced men of the world.' The image is that of frothy bubbles on the vat passing over the malted barley, which has been previously winnowed (by the keen winds of experience). For 'winnowed' cf. G. 'unsifted.'

193. *profound and winnowed* (Tschischwitz) Q2 'prophane and trennowed,' F1 'fond and winnowed,' MSH. pp. 328–31. Warburton and many edd. read 'fanned and winnowed,' which is to emend F1 and gives tautological sense. The right principle is to emend Q2. If Sh. wrote 'profund' or 'profond,' misreading as 'profane' would be easy.

194. *and do but blow them* After 'winnowed' the word 'them' (= Osric and his like) is emphatic. One puff of breath, and the froth is blown out of the vat.

195–206. F1 omits, thus saving a small part.

197. *He sends to know* Apparently Osric had not been able to 're-deliver' Ham. to the 'effect' he intended (v. ll. 179–81).

209. *at the odds* i.e. with the handicap allowed me; cf. note ll. 166–68.

217–18. *There is...sparrow.* Cf. Matth. x. 29. As usual when Sh. quotes, the context should be borne in mind; e.g. 'And fear not them which kill the body, but are not able to kill the soul,' and 'But the very hairs of your head are all numbered.'

220. *the readiness is all* The whole speech, as Brandes notes (*Will. Shak.* p. 354), is a distillation of *Montaigne*, i. 19 'That to Philosophie is to learne how to die.' To quote one or two passages from Florio's trans.:

At the stumbling of a horse, at the fall of a stone, at the least prick with a pinne, let us presently ruminate and say with our selves, what if it were death itself? and thereupon let us take heart of grace, and call our wits together to confront her.... It is uncertain where death looks for us; let us expect her everie where.... I am ever prepared about that which I may be.... A man should ever, as much as in him lieth, be ready booted to take his journey, and above all things, looke he have then nothing to doe but with himselfe.... For why should we feare to lose a thing, which being lost, cannot be moaned?... what matter is it when it cometh, since it is unavoidable?

220–22. *Since no man...let be* Q 2 'since no man of ought he leaues, knowes what ist to leaue betimes, let be'; F 1 'since no man ha's ought of what he leaues. What is't to leaue betimes?' MSH. pp. 214–15. Most edd. follow F 1 but add 'Let be' from Q 2 as a separate sentence. No one has ever yet tried to make sense of Q 2 as it stands. To paraphrase: since no one can tell from anything on earth ('of aught he leaues') what is the right moment to die (v. G. 'betimes'), why trouble about it?

222. S.D.* Q 2 'A table prepard, Trumpets, Drums and officers with Cushions, King, Queene, and all the state, Foiles, daggers, and Laertes.' F 1 'Enter King, Queene, Laertes and Lords, with other Attendants with Foyles, and Gauntlets, a Table and Flagons of Wine on it.' Eliz. actors were expert swordsmen and a stage-duel or fence was for many spectators the chief feature of the play in which it occurred. It is important, there-fore, to try and understand here Sh.'s intentions in particular, together with Eliz. practice in general. The difference between 'Foiles, daggers' (Q 2) and 'Foyles and Gauntlets' (F 1) points to a change of fashion in fence between 1601 and 1623, when F 1 was printed. It is clear from ll. 148, 152, above that Sh. intended the daggers, which at the end of the 16th and the beg. of the 17th c. were held in the left hand and used to ward off the opponent's thrust with his rapier, the while one

thrust with one's own. Testimony to the vogue is afforded by Norden's Map of London (1600) which shows two men duelling with rapiers and daggers in St George's Fields. (I owe this evidence to the courtesy of Dr Wieselgren of the Royal Library, Stockholm.) Cf. *Rom.* 3. 1. 163–68:

> he tilts
> With piercing steel at bold Mercutio's breast,
> Who, all as hot, turns deadly point to point,
> And, with a martial scorn, *with one hand* beats
> Cold death aside, *and with the other* sends
> It back to Tybalt.

The 'foil' for fence was not the buttoned fleuret of modern fence (buttons prob. did not come in before c. 1670), but the kind of sword used in duelling, though with its edge and point blunted or 'bated.' Thus Laer.'s 'shuffling' with the foils and choice of 'a sword unbated' (4. 7. 136–37) or 'sharp,' as it was often called, would be far easier than under modern conditions. On the other hand, the type of sword, whether bated or unbated, in favour both for duelling and sword-play at this date, was not the English broadsword (used with a target in the left hand), but the French or Italian rapier, a longer weapon and designed for thrusting rather than cutting or slashing. The comparative merits of these two types were much debated, and Sh. is full of echoes of the controversy (cf. note 4. 7. 74–6). The classic on rapier-and-dagger play is *Vincentio Saviolo his Practise* (1595), which informs us that gloves of mail were worn on either hand, while shirts of mail or breast-plates and a kind of skull-cap were generally used for protection of the body and head. Sometime before the middle of the 17th c. daggers were given up, and leather gauntlets seem to have taken the place of mailed gloves. For details v. G. di Grassi's *True Arte of Defence*, 1594; Saviolo (*op. cit.*); Silver's *Paradoxes of Defence*, 1599 (Shak. Assoc. 1933), a book written in support of the English short sword; my Introd. to the same; Egerton Castle's *Schools and Masters of Fence*, 1892; and corresp. in T.L.S. Jan. 11, 18, 25, Feb. 1, 1934.

223. S.D. Johnson reads 'King puts the hand of Laertes into the hand of Hamlet.'

229. *nature, honour and exception* i.e. filial duty (cf. note 4. 5. 161–63), good name, and personal dislike.

230. *I here proclaim was madness* Dr Johnson and others take this to be a falsehood. Bradley (pp. 420–21) excuses it on the ground that there is 'no moral difference ...between feigning insanity and asserting it.' E. E. Stoll (*Art and Artifice in Sh.* p. 120) declares that Ham.'s explanation contradicts that given to Hor. at ll. 75–80. I believe the two passages are not inconsistent and that Ham. means what he says, which is not that he is insane but merely that he is subject to fits of madness. Cf. *Introd.* p. lxiv and notes 3. 1. 137–52; 3. 4. 107, 180; 5. 1. 278. If there is a suspicion of falsehood or deception, our sympathy with Ham. (which at this moment of the play Sh. is most concerned to enlist) is weakened.

242–44. *in nature...honour* Cf. note 1. 229 above. 'Ham. has referred to "nature" and "honour"; Laer. replies to each point' (Dowden). He also deals (hypocritically) with 'exception' in ll. 248–50. But Ham.'s frank statement and affectionate appeal, and his own treacherous reply make him uncomfortable, as is clear from l. 294.

244–48. *in my terms of honour...name ungored* Laer. is not speaking idly; in an age when a gentleman's 'honour' was as important (even financially) as a business man's 'honesty' is in ours, some kind of formal acquittal was a necessary precaution. Further, his reference to the decision of 'some elder masters' was acc. to custom; cf. Saviolo (*op. cit.* note 1. 222 S.D., sig. Aa, 4r):

Touching all such matters whereon anye controuersie or dissencion maye growe, men ought specially to beware, not to be self-willed, but are rather to take counsail and aduise both of their freends and experienced men, and if there be cause to iudge this course necessarie in anye matter, it ought cheefelye to bee in such cases, wherein a mans life and honour is touched, for we see that euen the wisest sorte to study and endeuour by all meanes possible to furnish themselues with men experienced and seene in chiualrye and armes, that they maye bee counsailed and aduised by them, and may in such sort wish them to the field, as may best stand with reason, which office may onely be executed by learned men and gentlemen, wherof the first are tearmed counsailors and the second Padrini.

247. *voice and precedent* i.e. 'authoritative pronouncement, justified by precedent' (Dowden).

253. *your foil* A quibble, v. G. 'foil.' There is dramatic irony too; the two men are 'foils' to each other.

257.* *Give them…Osric* I assume from l. 304 that Osric is an accomplice in the plot, the arrangements of which were, I think, as follows: the poisoned and unbated sword was brought in with the bated foils, from which it was indistinguishable except on close scrutiny, and placed upon a side-table; at the K.'s command Osric then brings forward a few of the latter and the fencers take their choice; whereupon the K. engages Ham. in conversation, while Laer., complaining of the foil he has selected, goes to the table and picks up the fatal weapon. It was the duty of the judges to see that everything was in order, so that the unbated sword could not have been introduced without the knowledge of one of them— a point the Eliz. audience would appreciate, while significant glances on the part of the K., Laer. and Osric while the scheme went forward would make everything clear.

259. *laid…side* = stipulated that the weaker should have odds, i.e. you were well-advised to secure me a good handicap.

261. *bettered* (F 1) Q 2 'better.' v. G. 'Not naturally superior, trained by Parisian fencers,' Dowden (cf.

4. 7. 94–101). 'Better' is a favourite vb. with Sh.; v. Schmidt's *Lexicon*. At one time I favoured Q2's reading, explaining it as 'the proposer of the bet'; but I think now that had Sh. intended this he would have written 'the better'; v. MSH. pp. 284–5 for discussion.

263. *These foils...length?* Rapier-blades at this time might vary in length from 3 ft. 8 in. to 5 ft. 5 in., and the length was supposed to give an advantage in thrusting (v. Castle, *Schools and Masters of Fence*, pp. 319–30 and Plates I, 12, VI, 7, 8). But Ham.'s enquiry is perfunctory; he does 'not peruse the foils' (cf. 4. 7. 133–35).

264. S.D. Q2 (none), F1 'Prepare to play'— a direction, I take it, not only to Ham. and perhaps Laer. to don the mailed gloves, breastplate, etc. (v. end of note l. 222 S.D. above), but also to the attendants to prepare a suitable arena. The K.'s next speech shows that flagons of wine are brought in at this point (not at l. 222 as F1 directs) and placed on a side-table while cups are set on some table or stand at his side. Poel (*Sh. in the Theatre*, p. 174) suggests that one of the cups already contains the poison. This would make the attendants accomplices. The poisoning was done by means of the 'union' in a fashion all the more effective that it was left to the imagination of the audience (cf. Creizenach, *Engl. Drama*, p. 219 for poisonings in other plays). Moreover, though the K. says 'give me the cups,' it is clear from ll. 269–70 that he uses one only.

266–67. *If Hamlet give...exchange* i.e. If he wins the first or second bout, or even draws the third ('quit in answer' = give as good as he gets). In any of these three events Ham. will still stand a chance, since if he scores a single hit in the first three rounds Laer. will only be one up, and even if the latter wins the first two straight off a draw in the third may mean a turn of the tide. As a matter of fact, it is Ham. who wins the first two, while he draws the third.

270.* *union* v. G.

285.* *fat, and scant of breath* Much discussed. The argument that 'fat' refers to the corpulence (entirely hypothetical) of Richard Burbadge, the actor who first played Ham., really cuts the other way; for if Burbadge in 1601 was getting over-stout for the part of a young student, Sh. would hardly deliberately call attention to the fact (cf. note 1. 2. 129). I have little doubt that 'fat' simply means 'sweaty,' an interpretation which suits the double use of the handkerchief (ll. 286, 292), and Ham.'s reluctance to drink; cf. 1 *Hen. IV*, 2. 4. 1 'come out of that fat (= sweaty, or stuffy) room,' and 2 *Hen. IV*, 2. 4. 234–35 'how thou sweatest! come, let me wipe thy face.' The trickling of sweat from the brows into the eyes might seriously embarrass a swordsman. J. C. Maxwell supplies me with an apt parallel from a seventeenth-century romance, quoted in Sir Charles Firth's *Essays Historical and Literary*, p. 158: "The sweat of the Gyants browes ran into his eyes, and by the reason that he was so extreame fatte he grew so blinde that he could not see to endure combat with him any longer."

293. *My lord...not think't* I do not know of any comment upon these asides. I interpret: '*Laer.* I intend to finish it off now—*King.* I doubt whether you will be able to get past his ward at all.' Ham. was doing very well; he had won two bouts and was showing fine form; what if Laer., in spite of holding the poisoned 'sharp' in his hand, found himself unable to wound Ham. with it before he lost the match? Another three wins for Ham., or two wins and a couple of draws, and it would be over.

297. *make a wanton of me* = trifle with me, v. G. 'wanton.'

299. *Nothing neither way* The third bout is a draw, i.e. the opponents either score a simultaneous 'touch'— so slight as not to cause a scratch from Laer.'s 'sharp,' or they catch each other's sword-points in the *pas d'âne*,

that is the hooks on the hilts of their daggers (cf. note l. 300 S.D.), and so 'lock.' The doubt, expressed by the K. in l. 293, now troubles Laer.; he has 'passed with his best violence' without result. Something must be done.

300. *Have at you now!* At the end of the bout, one of the judges, as was the custom, extends a rapier or staff between the fencers, to show that they must break off. Ham. does so; but Laer.—so I understand Sh.'s intention—seizes the opportunity for a treacherous attack, shouting 'Have at you now!' as he lunges. Thus, I am told by fencers who remember Irving's performance at the Lyceum in 1878, the scene was played under the direction of Alfred Hutton, the well-known and learned fencer. The line, however, is omitted in his acting version.

S.D. Q2 omits (v. MSH. p. 185). F1 'In scuffling they change Rapiers'; Q1 'They catch one anothers Rapiers, and both are wounded, Leartes falles downe, the Queene falles downe and dies.' The Q1 S.D., as often, tells us more than the other texts, though here not enough. Di Grassi (*True Arte*, sig. Bb. 1 *verso*) describes how in rapier-and-dagger play one may jerk the sword out of an opponent's hand by using one's own sword as a lever and striking his sword sharply with the dagger in the left hand. This, I at first thought, was how Ham. forced the poisoned weapon from Laer.'s grasp to the ground; and Burbadge's execution of such a trick would prob. win applause. Laer., I supposed, then replied by seizing Ham.'s sword with his empty right hand and wresting it from him, while parrying his dagger-thrust with the dagger in his left. Whereupon Ham. in his turn pounced upon the sword on the floor; and so the exchange was effected. Cf. Silver (Introd. pp. xvi–xx).

Mr Evan John, however, in T.L.S. Jan. 25, 1934, offers a better, because more dramatic, alternative, viz. that Ham. enraged at the wound throws down his own sword and closing with Laer. seizes the 'sharp' with his empty right hand and wrests it from him, whereupon he allows him in ironical politeness to pick up the discarded 'blunt' from the ground. One merit of this explanation is that it tallies with the Q 1 S.D. 'They catch one anothers Rapiers.'

301. *Nay, come again* As Bradley (pp. 422–23) points out, the K.'s command to 'part them' is an attempt to save Laer. after the exchange of rapiers. Ham. frustrates this by running Laer. through before the judges can intervene.

304–305. *Why...mine own treachery* This aside could hardly have been spoken if Osric was himself innocent of the treachery. Cf. note l. 257.

306. *She swoons to see them bleed.* The K.'s nerve is magnificent.

320. S.D. Q 2 omits. F 1 'Hurts the King.'

322. *but hurt* = only wounded.

324. *Is thy union here?* Caldecott suggests a quibble; 'the-potion (v. G.) effects the union of the King and Queen.' Cf. Bradley, p. 151.

333. *mutes or audience* = silent spectators, v. G. 'mute.'

334. *this fell sergeant, Death* Malone quotes Silvester's *Du Bartas*: 'And Death, drad Serjant of th'eternall Iudge.' Cf. *Son.* lxxiv: 'when that fell arrest Without all bail shall carry me away,' and G. 'sergeant.'

342. *O God, Horatio,* (Q2) Q1 'O fie Horatio,' F 1 'Oh good Horatio'—which all edd. but Capell, Malone and Furness read. The Q 1 reading lends support to Q2. MSH. p. 266.

347. S.D. Q 2 'A march a farre off,' F 1 'March afarre off, and shout within.' The 'shout' is prob. a misprint for 'shoot.'

354. *my dying voice* Claudius being dead, Ham. is now de facto king. It was the constitutional theory of the age that the 'voice' of the reigning monarch, when

he had no heir of his body, went some way to secure the rights of his successor. Cf. 3. 2. 343 'the voice of the king himself' and the concern of the Privy Council to obtain the voice of the dying Elizabeth in favour of James (Cheyney, *Hist. of Eng.* ii. 575). Cf. *Introd.* p. lv.

355. *more and less* = great and small. v. G.

356. *Which have solicited*—i.e. 'Which have incited me to—' (Malone).

silence After this F1 ludicrously adds 'O, o, o, o.' MSH. pp. 13, 78–9.

358. *And flights of angels...rest!* Malone writes:

The concluding words of the unfortunate Lord Essex's prayer on the scaffold were these: '—and when my life and body shall part, send thy blessed angels, which may receive my soule, and convey it to the joys of heaven.' *Hamlet* had certainly been exhibited before the execution of that amiable nobleman; but the words here given to Horatio might have been one of the many additions made to this play.

Cf. *Introd.* pp. lxv–lxvi.

362. *This quarry cries on havoc* A metaphor from the chase; lit. 'This heap of dead proclaims an indiscriminate and immoderate slaughter (of game).' Fortinbras is describing the 'sight'; there is no suggestion of vengeance, as many have supposed; cf. G. 'quarry,' 'cry on,' 'havoc.'

363. *feast* Death, the huntsman, will feast on the 'quarry.' The 'eternal cell' is, of course, the grave; cf. *Tit. And.* 1. 1. 93.

370. *his mouth* Hor. points to the body of the K.

375–78. *give order...came about* Steevens quotes Brooke's *Romeus and Juliet* (1562), ll. 2817–18:

The prince did straight ordaine, the corses that wer founde, Should be set forth vpon a stage hye raysed from the grounde.

379–83. *Of carnal...heads* Here l. 379 summarises the crimes of Claud.: adultery, murder, incest;

l. 380 refers to the death of Oph. (accidental) and of
Pol. (casual); l. 381 to the deaths of Ros. and Guild.;
ll. 382–83 to those that have just taken place.

387. *of memory* i.e. unforgotten.

390. *whose voice* v. note l. 354.

393. *On* = On top of.

393–98. *Let four captains...for him* Cf. Cor. 5. 6.
149–52:

> Take him up.
> Help, three o'th' chiefest soldiers; I'll be one.
> Beat thou the drum, that it speak mournfully
> Trail your steel pikes.

The Eliz. stage being without a drop-curtain, it was
necessary to remove the 'dead' in some such way as this;
cf. 3. 4. 217 S.D.

401. S.D. Q2 'Exeunt,' F1 'Exeunt Marching:
after the which, a Peale of Ordenance are shot off.'

GLOSSARY

Note. Where a pun or quibble is intended, the meanings
are distinguished as (*a*) and (*b*)

ABOUT! bestir! get to work!
2. 2. 592

ABRIDGEMENT, (*a*) dramatic pastime (cf. *M.N.D.* 5. 1. 39),
(*b*) that which cuts one short;
2. 2. 425

ABSOLUTE, (i) positive, self-assured,
free from uncertainty (cf. *Cor.*
3. 1. 89 'Mark you his absolute
"shall"?'); 5. 1. 133; (ii) perfect,
consummate; 5. 2. 112

ABSTRACT, epitome (cf. *A. & C.*
1. 4. 9 'A man who is the abstract of all faults'); 2. 2. 528

ABUSE (sb.), deception, imposture;
4. 7. 49

ABUSE (vb.), impose upon, deceive;
1. 5. 38; 2. 2. 607

ACT, effect, operation; 1. 2. 205

ACTION OF BATTERY, legal process
for unlawful attack by beating
or wounding; 5. 1. 100

ADDITION, (i) title, style of address;
1. 4. 20; 2. 1. 46; (ii) flourish,
lit. heraldic addition; 4. 4. 17

ADMIRATION, wonder, astonishment; 1. 2. 192; 3. 2. 328

ADVANTAGE, superiority; 1. 2. 21

AERY, nestful of young hawks;
2. 2. 342

AFFECTION, affectation (cf. *L.L.L.*
5. 1. 4); 2. 2. 448

AFFECTION, (*a*) malady, (*b*) emotion, state of mind; 3. 1. 165

AFFRONT, meet, confront (cf. *Wint.*
5. 1. 75 'Unless another…
Affront his eye'); 3. 1. 31

AIM (vb.), guess (cf. *Rom.* 1. 1.
211); 4. 5. 9

AMAZE, bewilder, confound (cf
K. John, 4. 2. 137); 2. 2. 568

AMAZEMENT, bewilderment, fear,
frenzy; 3. 2. 328; 3. 4. 112

AMBITION, (*a*) inordinate desire
for distinction, (*b*) ostentatious
glory; 2. 2. 255; 3. 3. 55

ANCHOR, anchoret, 'anchor's cheere'
= anchoret's chair (N.E.D.
quotes Hall, *Satires*, 1599, IV. ii.
103 'Sit seauen yeares pining in
an anchores cheyre'); 3. 2. 218

AN END, on end; 1. 5. 19; 3. 4. 122

ANGLE (sb.), fishing hook or line;
5. 2. 66

ANOINT, smear. Perhaps with a
quibble on the religious ceremony of consecration (cf. *unction*); 4. 7. 139

ANSWER (sb.), (*a*) acceptance of a
challenge, (*b*) reply; 5. 2. 170;
the return hit in fencing;
5. 2. 267

ANSWER (vb.), excuse, justify,
atone for; 3. 4. 176; 'be answered,' be defended; 4. 1. 16

ANTIC, odd, fantastic; 1. 5. 172

ANTIQUE. Meaning uncertain;
either (i) ancient or (ii) ludicrous
('antic'); 2. 2. 473

APOPLEXED, paralysed; 3. 4. 73

APPLIANCE. Medical term = remedy, application (cf. *Per.*
3. 2. 86 'Who was by good
appliance recovered'); 4. 3. 10

APPOINTMENT, equipment; 4. 6. 16

APPREHENSION, (a) imagination, conception, (b) seizure, grasp; 2. 2. 310; conception; 4. 1. 11

APPROVE, (i) corroborate; 1. 1. 29; (ii) commend; 5. 2. 139

APPURTENANCE, adjuncts; 2. 2. 374

ARGAL, a perversion of 'ergo' (v. note); 5. 1. 12, 19, 48

ARGUMENT, (i) the plot of a play; 3. 2. 231; (ii) reason, cause of contention; 2. 2. 358 (with a quibble on sense i); 4. 4. 54

ARITHMETIC OF MEMORY, mental arithmetic; 5. 2. 119

ARM (vb.), prepare; 3. 3. 24

ARREST, staying order; 2. 2. 67

ARTERE, artery. The old physiology regarded the arteries as the ducts or channels of the 'vital spirits,' not of the blood; 1. 4. 82

ARTICLE, (i) part of a state document; 1. 1. 94; 1. 2. 38; (ii) 'of great article' = of great scope, of great importance (with a quibble on 'article' = item in an inventory; v. note); 5. 2. 121

ARTLESS, unskilful, without control; 4. 5. 19

ASKANT, sidewise (N.E.D. quotes this passage as the only instance of the word as a prep.); 4. 7. 165

ASSAY (sb.), (i) assault; 2. 2. 71; (ii) trial, attempt; 3. 3. 69; 'assay of bias' = indirect attempt. A metaphor from bowls, lit. an attempt to hit the jack by taking a winding course, which the bias allows; 2. 1. 62

ASSAY (vb.), challenge to a trial; 3. 1. 14

AS'ES. Plural of (a) as, the conditional particle, (b) ass; 5. 2. 43

ASSIGNS, appendages. Affected; Osric is perhaps thinking of 'heirs and assigns'; 5. 2. 153

ASSUME, put or take on a garb, aspect or character. A technical term of demonology for devils' disguising themselves in the form of some dead person; 1. 2. 244; 1. 4. 72; 2. 2. 604; 3. 4. 160

ASSURANCE, (a) security, (b) conveyance of land; 5. 1. 114

AT FOOT, closely (N.E.D. quotes *Cursor Mundi*, 24031 (Cott.) 'We folud þam to fote'); 4. 3. 53

ATTRIBUTE, reputation (cf. *Troil.* 2. 3. 125 'Much attribute he hath'); 1. 4. 22

AUDIT, official examination of accounts. Commonly used in theol. sense of a solemn rendering of account to God (cf. Matth. xxv. 19, Luke xvi. 2); 3. 3. 82

AUSPICIOUS, cheerful; 1. 2. 11

BACK. Military term = rearguard, body of supporters. N.E.D. quotes Speed (1611) 'Scotland was a special backe or second to King Henry'; 4. 7. 152

BAIT (sb.), food, refreshment (v. note); 3. 3. 79

BAKED MEATS, pies and other pastry; 1. 2. 180

BANDS, bonds, obligations; 1. 2. 24; 3. 2. 158

BARBARY HORSE, or Barb. A well-known breed in England at this time; 'a little horse but swift, and...esteemed in the manage for its ability to make a long career'; prob. a favourite with Sh. (v. *Sh. Eng.* ii. 408); 5. 2. 151, 162

BARKED ABOUT, encrusted; 1. 5. 71

BARE, (a) unsheathed, (b) mere; 3. 1. 76

BARREN, unresponsive, intellectually sterile (the opposite of 'capable' q.v.); 3. 2. 40

BATED, excepted (cf. *Temp.* 2. 1. 99 'Bate, I beseech you, widow Dido'); 5. 2. 23

BEAT (vb.), think persistently 3. 1. 177

BEAUTIFIED, endowed with beauty (cf. *Two Gent.* 4. 1. 55 'you are beautified with goodly shape'); 2. 2. 110

BEAVER, visor (cf. *2 Hen. IV*, 4. 1. 120 and *Sh. Eng.* i. 130); 1. 2. 230

BEDDED, flat (as in bed), laid or strewn in a flat layer, matted; 3. 4. 121

BEETLE (vb.), overhang. Prob. derived from Sidney, *Arcadia*, 'A pleasant valley of either side of which high hills lifted vp their beetle-browis, as if they would ouer looke the pleasantnesse of their vnder prospect,' and 'apparently used as a nonce-word by Shakespeare, from whom it has been taken by later writers' (N.E.D.); 1. 4. 71

BEGET, produce (cf. *L.L.L.* 2. 1. 69); 3. 2. 7

BEND (vb.), incline; 1. 2. 115

BENT, the extent to which a bow may be bent or a spring wound up, limit of capacity; 2. 2. 30; 3. 2. 386

BERATTLE, fill with din (cf. *K. John*, 5. 2. 172); 2. 2. 345

BETEEM, allow; 1. 2. 141

BETIMES, in good time, at the right moment, before it is too late (N.E.D. quotes from 1545 'Repent betymes, and...fall diligently to prayer' and Milton, *Par. Lost*, iii. 186 'To appease betimes Th'incensed Deity'); 5. 2. 222

BETTER (vb.), improve, perfect oneself; 5. 2. 261

BEVY. Technical name for a covey of quails or lapwings (v. N.E.D.); 5. 2. 190

BIAS, v. *assay*; 2. 1. 62

BILBOE, a kind of stocks used on board ship, 'a long iron bar, furnished with sliding shackles to confine the ankles of prisoners, and a lock by which to fix one end of the bar to the floor or ground' (N.E.D.); 5. 2. 6

BISSON, lit. blind; (here) blinding (N.E.D.); 2. 2. 510

BLANK (sb.), mark, lit. the white spot in the centre of a target; 4. 1. 42

BLANK (vb.), to blanch; 3. 2. 219

BLAST IN PROOF, burst when tested (a metaphor from cannon-practice); 4. 7. 153

BLASTMENT, shrivelling up, withering; 1. 3. 42

BLAZE (sb.), momentary flash, e.g. of lightning, anger, passion (cf. *Rich. II*, 2. 1. 33 'His rash fierce blaze of Ryot cannot last' and Greene, *Never Too Late*, p. 71 'Lightning, that beautifies the heauen for a blaze'); 1. 3. 117

BLAZON, proclaiming, making public (orig. a term of heraldry); 1. 5. 21

BLENCH, flinch, quail (often of the eyes); 2. 2. 601

BLOOD, passions; 3. 2. 67; 'in blood' = in the vigour of youth (used of stags in rut; cf. *L.L.L.* 4. 2. 3 'the deer was...in blood'); 1. 3. 6

BLOWN, blooming; 3. 1. 162; 'broad blown,' in full bloom; 3. 3. 81

BOARD (vb.), accost; 2. 2. 170

BODKIN, dagger; 3. 1. 76

BODKIN, v. *God's bodkin*; 2. 2. 533

BOND (sb.), pledge, promise (cf. *band*); 1. 3. 130

BORE (sb.), lit. calibre of a gun; hence, size, importance; 4. 6. 26

BORNE IN HAND, deceived; 2. 2. 67

BOTCH UP, put together clumsily; 4. 5. 10

BRAINISH, 'headstrong, passionate' (N.E.D.), 'illusory' (Herford); 4. 1. 11

BRAVERY, bravado, ostentatious display; 5. 2. 79

BREATHE, speak, express oneself; 1. 3. 130

BREATHING TIME, time for taking exercise; 5. 2. 175

BRINGING HOME, burial, laying to rest (cf. *Tit. And.* 1. 1. 83–4 'These that I bring unto their latest home.' N.E.D. quotes the expression from a will of 1528); 5. 1. 227

BROAD, gross, unrestrained; 3. 4. 2

BROKER, (a) middle-man, commission-agent, (b) go-between, pander; 1. 3. 127

BROOCH, conspicuous ornament (because worn in the hat). Cf. Jonson, *Staple of News*, 3. 2 'The very broch o' the bench gem o' the City'; 4. 7. 92

BRUIT, (a) report, (b) celebrate; 1. 2. 127

BUG, bogy, imaginary horror; 5. 2. 22

BULK, bodily frame (cf. *Luc.* 467 'her heart...beating her bulk'); 1. 3. 12; 2. 1. 92

BURIAL, a grave. The orig. sense (cf. *M.V.* 1. 1. 29); 5. 1. 1, 228

BURNING ZONE, the belt between the tropics of Cancer and Capricorn in the celestial sphere acc. to the old cosmology; 5. 1. 276

BUTTON, bud; 1. 3. 40

BUZ. 'Used to be an interjection at Oxford, when any one began a story that was generally known before' (Blackstone); 2. 2. 398

BUZZER, secret tale-bearer; 4. 5. 89

CALENDAR, register; 5. 2. 114

CALF, dolt; 3. 2. 103; 5. 1. 113

CANDIED, sugared; 3. 2. 58

CANKER, (i) canker worm; 1. 3. 39; (ii) cancer, ulcer; 5. 2. 69

CANON, edict, esp. of ecclesiastical law; 1. 2. 132

CANONIZED, consecrated, sainted (cf. *Troil.* 2. 2. 202 'And fame in time to come canonize us'); 1. 4. 47

CAN WELL, can do well, are skilled; 4. 7. 83

CAPABLE, impressible (like wax), capable of feeling, susceptible; 3. 2. 11; 3. 4. 127

CAP-A-PE, from head to foot; 1. 2. 200

CAPON, lit. a castrated cock fattened for killing, a dull fellow; 3. 2. 92

CARBUNCLE, a precious stone of a red or fiery colour; 2. 2. 467

CARD, (i) chart; 5. 2. 114; (ii) 'by the card,' exactly to the point, lit. according to the points on the mariner's compass (cf. *Macb.* 1. 3. 17 'the shipman's card'); 5. 1. 134

CAREFULLY, attentively, (here) promptly; 1. 1. 6

CARNAL, fleshly, adulterous; 5. 2. 379

CARP, (a) a fish, (b) talk, discourse (cf. *All's Well*, 5. 2. 22, and N.E.D. 'carp' vb.); 2. 1. 60

CARRIAGE, (i) import; 1. 1. 94; (ii) (a) an affected word for 'hanger' (q.v.), (b) gun-carriage 5. 2. 153–59

CARRION, (*a*) dead flesh, (*b*) 'the flesh' 'in the Pauline sense' N.E.D. (v. note); 2. 2. 182

CARRY IT AWAY, carry the day, be victorious (cf. *Rom.* 3. 1. 79 '*Alla stoccata* carries it away'); 2. 2. 363

CARRY THROUGH, carry through difficulties, enable to pass muster; 5. 2. 192

CART, chariot (cf. Spenser, *F.Q.* v, viii, 34); 3. 2. 153

CARVE FOR ONESELF, help oneself at will, indulge oneself; 1. 3. 20

CAST BEYOND ONESELF, to overrun the trail in hunting (v. letter by K. M. Buck in *T.L.S.* Jan. 7, 1932); 2. 1. 112

CATAPLASM, plaster, poultice; 4. 7. 142

CAUTEL, deceit, craft (cf. *Lov. Com.* 303 'Applied to cautels' and *Cor.* 4. 1. 33 'With cautelous baits and practice'); 1. 3. 15

CAVIARY, caviare. The figurative use derives from this passage; 2. 2. 441

CENSURE (sb.), opinion, judgment; 1. 3. 69; 1. 4. 35; with a quibble on 'disapproval'; 3. 2. 26, 85

CENTRE, middle of the earth (v. note); 2. 2. 159

CEREMENTS, lit. wax wrappings for the dead, (hence) grave-clothes generally; 1. 4. 48

CESS (sb.), cessation, extinction (v. note); 3. 3. 15

CHAMELEON. 'From their inanimate appearance, and power of existing for long periods without food, they were formerly supposed to live on air' (N.E.D.); 3. 2. 91

CHANGELING, 'a child which the fairies are supposed to leave in the room of that which they steal' (Dr Johnson); 5. 2. 53

CHANSON, song, ballad; 2. 2. 424

CHARACTER (vb.), imprint, inscribe; 1. 3. 59

CHARGE (sb.), (*a*) importance, (*b*) weight, load (cf. 1 *Hen. IV*, 2. 1. 50 'great charge'); 5. 2. 43

CHARIEST, 'most fastidious, shy' (N.E.D.), cf. *M.W.W.* 2. 1. 102 'the chariness of our honesty' (= modesty); 1. 3. 36

CHECK AT, abandon a course. A term of falconry, lit. to swerve aside (cf. *Tw. Nt.* 3. 1. 64 'And, like the haggard, check at every feather'); 4. 7. 61

CHEERE, chair. v. *anchor*; 3. 2. 218

CHOLER, bile, hence (*a*) bilious disorder, (*b*) anger (N.E.D. 1 c, 2); 3. 2. 304, 308

CHOP-FALLEN, (*a*) chopless, q.v., (*b*) cast down, dejected; 5. 1. 186

CHOPINE, a shoe worn in Italy and Spain at the end of the sixteenth century, with cork soles and heels sometimes of great height; 2. 2. 432

CHOPLESS, without the lower jaw (chop or chap); 5. 1. 87

CHORUS, an actor who summarises the action or explains the meaning of a theatrical spectacle (v. *dumb-show*); 3. 2. 244

CHOUGH, a bird of the crow family, a jackdaw, (hence) a chatterer; 5. 2. 89

CICATRICE, scar of a wound; 4. 3. 59

CIRCUMSTANCE, (i) circumlocution, beating about the bush; 1. 5. 127; (ii) relevant facts, evidence; 2. 2. 157; 3. 3. 83

CLEPE, call, name; 1. 4. 19

CLIMATURE. A variant of 'climate'
= region. N.E.D. ('climate'
1 b) quotes from 1605: 'When
the Sunne is Eclipsed, all the
earth is not darkened, but onely
one Climat'; 1. 1. 121

CLOSE (adj.), secret; 2. 1. 115

CLOSE WITH, engage in conversation, lit. come to close quarters
in fight (cf. 2 *Hen. IV*, 2. 1. 20);
2. 1. 44

CLOSELY, secretly; 3. 1. 29

CLOUDS (IN), in obscurity; 4. 5. 88

CLOUTS, cloths, clothes; 2. 2. 387

COCK (BY), by God; 4. 5. 60

COCKLE HAT, 'a hat with a cockle
or scallop-shell stuck in it, worn
by pilgrims, as a sign of their
having been at the shrine of
St James of Compostella in
Spain' (N.E.D.); 4. 5. 25

COIL (sb.), (*a*) bustle, turmoil,
(*b*) with a quibble upon 'coil' of
rope (v. *Introd.* p. xxxiv); 3. 1.
67

COLLEAGUED, allied; 1. 2. 21

COLLECTION, (i) deduction, in-
ference, guess-work (from Lat.
collectio, deduction, a term of
rhetoric); 4. 5. 9; (ii) assortment
'of extracts, historical or literary
materials' (N.E.D. 3 a); 5. 2.
192

COLOUR (vb.), gloss, disguise;
2. 2. 284; 3. 1. 45

COLUMBINE, an emblem of cuckoldry (N.E.D.); 4. 5. 180

CO-MART, joint bargain (cf.
'mart' 1. 1. 74 and *Shrew*,
2. 1. 320 'a desperate mart');
1. 1. 93

COME AWAY, COME YOUR WAYS,
come along; 1. 3. 135; 4. 1. 28
etc.

COME TARDY OFF, fall short, to be
done inadequately; 3. 2. 25

CO-MEDLED, mixed or mingled
together; N.E.D. quotes only
one other instance, i.e. Webster,
White Devil (1612), 3. 3. 36
'Religion; oh how it is com-
medled with policie'; 3. 2. 67

COMMA, brief pause or interval
(v. note); 5. 2. 42

COMMEND, (*a*) offer respectfully,
(*b*) praise; 5. 2. 182, 184

COMMENT (sb.), critical observation; 3. 2. 77

COMMERCE, intercourse, conversation; 3. 1. 109

COMPANIES, companionship; 2. 2.
14

COMPARE WITH, vie with, rival;
5. 2. 142

COMPETENT, adequate, (here) equal;
1. 1. 90

COMPLEXION, disposition, constitution. One of the four tempera-
ments (sanguine, melancholy,
choleric and phlegmatic); 1. 4.
27; 5. 2. 103

COMPLY, 'observe the formalities
of courtesy' (N.E.D.); 2. 2. 375;
5. 2. 188

COMPOST, prepared manure; 3. 4.
151

CONCEIT, (i) imagination; 2. 2.
556, 560; 3. 4. 114; (ii) 'conceit
upon' = fanciful notion suggested by; 4. 5. 43; (iii) design;
5. 2. 155

CONCEPTION, (*a*) understanding,
(*b*) pregnancy (cf. *Lear*, 1. 1.
12–13); 2. 2. 184

CONCERNANCY, import, relevance;
5. 2. 126

CONCERNING, concern; 3. 4. 191

CONCLUSION, experiment; 3. 4.
195

CONDOLEMENT, grief; 1. 2. 93

CONFEDERATE, conspiring to assist;
3. 2. 256

CONFERENCE, talk, conversation; 3. 1. 1, 188

CONFINE (sb.), prison cell, place of confinement; 1. 1. 155; 2. 2. 249

CONGRUE, to agree, accord (cf. *L.L.L.* 1. 2. 13; 5. 1. 89 'congruent'); 4. 3. 63

CONJUNCTIVE, (*a*) closely united, (*b*) a technical term of astrology used of two planets in close proximity; 4. 7. 14

CONSCIENCE, consciousness, 'speculative reflexion' (Herford); 3. 1. 83

CONSIDERED, suitable for thought; 2. 2. 81

CONSONANCY, agreement; 'consonancy of our youth,' being of the same age; 2. 2. 288

CONSTANTLY, steadily; 1. 2. 235

CONTINENT (sb.), (i) receptacle, cover, anything that contains or covers; 4. 4. 64; (ii) (*a*) summary, embodiment, (*b*) geographical continent (to suit 'card'); 5. 2. 115

CONTRACTION, good faith, contractual relations in general (v. note); 3. 4. 46

CONVEYANCE, (i) convoy, conduct; 4. 4. 3; (ii) legal document for the transference of land; 5. 1. 107

CONVOY (sb.), means of conveyance, transport (cf. *All's Well*, 4. 4. 10 'We have convenient convoy'); 1. 3. 3

COPE (vb.), encounter, meet; 3. 2. 53

COTE, to outstrip (a coursing term); 2. 2. 321

COUCH (vb.), lurk, hide; 5. 1. 216

COUNSEL, (*a*) advice, (*b*) secret; 4. 2. 11

COUNT (sb.), account, reckoning; 4. 7. 17

COUNTENANCE, favour, patronage; 4. 2. 15

COUNTER (adv.), a hunting term, lit. in the opposite direction to the course taken by the game; 4. 5. 110

COUNTERFEIT (past part.), represented in a picture or image; 3. 4. 54

COUPLETS, the two fledglings of the dove; 5. 1. 281

COURAGE, a brave, a spark (of a person), v. note; 1. 3. 65

COUSIN, kinsman (of any kind except parent, child, brother or sister); 1. 2. 64

COZEN (vb.), cheat; 3. 4. 77

COZENAGE, (*a*) cheating, deception, (*b*) with a poss. quibble on 'cousinage' = kinship; 5. 2. 67

CRACKED WITHIN THE RING, (*a*) of a coin cracked within the circle surrounding the head of the sovereign and therefore no longer legal tender, (*b*) of a boy singer's voice, liable to crack on a high note. Cf. Beaumont, *Remedy of Love* (ed. Dyce, xi. 477) 'If her voice be bad, crack'd in the ring'; 2. 2. 433

CRANTS, garland. The word (from German 'Kranz' or Danish 'Krans') was in fairly common use in England in the sixteenth and seventeenth centuries (N.E.D. quotes Hardman, *Our Prayer Book* (1890) 'the "crants" were garlands which it was usual to make of white paper and to hang up in the church on the occasion of a young girl's funeral.... Some of these were hanging up in Flamborough Church, Yorkshire, as late as 1850'); 5. 1. 226

CRESCENT, growing (cf. 'crescive,' *Hen. V*, 1. 1. 66); 1: 3. 11

CROSS (vb.), cross the path of, come in the way of, obstruct (v. N.E.D. 'cross' 12); 1. 1. 127

CROWFLOWER, buttercup (but also applied occasionally to the ragged robin and the wild hyacinth); 4. 7. 168

CROWNER, coroner; 5. 1. 4; 'crowner's quest,' coroner's inquest; 5. 1. 22

CROWNET, coronet; 4. 7. 171

CRY (sb.), a pack of hounds; 3. 2. 277

CRY ON (trans. vb.), cry aloud, exclaim (in joy or terror). App. not the same as 'cry on' = exclaim against, or 'cry on' = yelp like a hound on the scent (cf. 4. 5. 109). Cf. *Oth.* 5. 1. 48 'what noise is this that cries on murder'; *Rich. III*, 5. 3. 231 'cried on victory.' N.E.D. misses this meaning; 5. 2. 362

CUNNING (sb.), skill, wisdom, dexterity; 2. 2. 445; 4. 7. 154

CURB (vb.), bow, bend; 3. 4. 155

CURRENT, unchecked course (cf. *M.V.* 4. 1. 64 'To excuse the current of thy cruelty' and 1 *Hen. IV*, 2. 3. 58 'currents of a heady fight'); 3. 3. 57

DAMON, a faithful friend (a reference to the classical story of Damon and Pythias); 3. 2. 281

DANSKER, a Dane. The correct Danish term, not found elsewhere in English though Danske (= Danish) occurs rarely; 2. 1. 7

DAYS OF NATURE, days of one's life (N.E.D. does not note this phrase). Perhaps suggested by 'course of nature'; 1. 5. 12

DEAR, (i) important, vital; 3. 4. 191; (ii) rare, precious, unusual; 5. 2. 154

DEAREST, direst, cruellest (of different origin from 'dearest' = most precious); 1. 2. 182

DEARTH, dearness (N.E.D. quotes Bishop Barlow, *Three Sermons*, 1596, 'Dearth is that when all ...things...are rated at a high price'); 5. 2. 122

DEBATE (vb.), dispute, contend; 4. 4. 26

DECLENSION, decline, deterioration; 2. 2. 149

DEFEAT, destruction; 5. 2. 58; 'to make defeat upon' = to bring about the ruin or destruction of; 2. 2. 574

DEFEATED, disfigured, marred (cf. *Oth.* 1. 3. 346 'Defeat thy favour with a usurped beard'); 1. 2. 10

DEFENCE, science of fence; 4. 7. 96

DEFINEMENT, description, specification; 5. 2. 117

DELATED, accusing ('delate' = report details of a crime to a judge); 1. 2. 38

DEVISE, explain, give an account (of); 4. 7. 52

DICTION, description; 5. 2. 122

DIET, a day's pay (v. *All's Well* note on 5. 3. 220); 1. 1. 99

DIFFERENCE, (i) a quibble on the heraldic term = an alteration or addition to a coat of arms to distinguish a junior member or branch of a family; 4. 5. 182; (ii) distinguishing qualities; 5. 2. 112

DIGESTED, ordered, disposed in an orderly way (cf. *Troil.* Prol. 29 'What may be digested in a play'); 2. 2. 443

DIRECTIONS, i.e. how to proceed; 2. 1. 63

DISAPPOINTED, ill-equipped (of a person), unprepared (cf. *appointment*. Theobald quotes *Meas.* 3. 1. 56–60, where 'appointment' = preparation for a journey); 1. 5. 77

DISASTER. An astrological term = an unfavourable aspect of a star or planet. Prob. here = partial eclipse (v. note); 1. 1. 123

DISCLOSE (vb. and sb.), hatch out (of young birds). N.E.D. quotes *Book of St Albans* (1486), A. ij a, 'First thay been Egges, and afterwarde they bene disclosed hawkys'; 3. 1. 169; 5. 1. 281

DISCOURSE, the reasoning faculty; 'discourse of reason' also = the reasoning faculty (cf. *Troil.* 2. 2. 116 'So madly hot that no discourse of reason...Can qualify the same'); 1. 2. 150; 4. 4. 36

DISCOVERY, disclosure; 2. 2. 298

DISMAL, calamitous; 5. 2. 365

DISMANTLE, divest, deprive one of the protection of; 3. 2. 282

DISPATCH (vb.), (i) deprive (cf. N.E.D. 7 b); 1. 5. 75; (ii) execute swiftly; 3. 3. 3

DISPRIZED, disparaged, held in contempt; 3. 1. 72

DISTEMPER (sb.), 'deranged or disordered condition of the body or mind (formerly regarded as due to disordered state of the humours)' N.E.D.; 2. 2. 55; 3. 2. 339; 3. 4. 123

DISTEMPERED, (*a*) disturbed in 'humour,' ill in body or mind, (*b*) intoxicated (cf. *Hen. V*, 2. 2. 54); 3. 2. 301

DISTRACTED, confused, agitated, unstable; 1. 5. 97; 4. 3. 4

DISTRUST (vb.), fear for; 3. 2. 163

DIVIDE INVENTORIALLY, classify in detail; 5. 2. 118

DIVULGING, becoming publicly known; 4. 1. 22

DIZZY (vb.), bewilder, make giddy; 5. 2. 119

DOCUMENT, lesson. A legal term, lit. a detailed proof set out in writing (cf. N.E.D. 3 quoting Raleigh, *Hist. World* 'This may serue as a document of Fortunes instabilitie'); 4. 5. 177

DOUBLE VOUCHER. v. *voucher*; 5. 1. 102

DOUBT (vb.), suspect; 1. 2. 256; 2. 2. 118; 3. 1. 169

DOUBT (IN), ambiguous; 4. 5. 6

DOUT (vb.), extinguish (v. note 1. 4. 37); 4. 7. 190

DOWN-GYVED, fallen down to the ankle, like gyves or fetters; 2. 1. 77

DRAW ON MORE, bring others with it; 5. 2. 390

DRIFT (sb.), (i) purpose, plot (cf. *Two Gent.* 2. 6. 43 'Wit to plot this drift'); 2. 1. 37; 4. 7. 150; (ii) leading one on in conversation; 2. 1. 10 ('drift of question'); 3. 1. 1 ('drift of conference')

DROSSY, worthless, frivolous; 5. 2. 190

DRUNK ASLEEP, dead drunk; 3. 3. 89

DUMB-SHOW. A device frequent in Eliz. drama for (i) foreshadowing the contents of a play or an act by means of a historical or symbolical tableau, or (ii) summarising a part of the action, not otherwise represented, in a living picture, which was then explained by a Presenter or Chorus. The Dumb-show in *Hamlet* belongs to neither type; 3. 2. 12, 133 S.D. (v. note)

Dup (vb.), open; 4. 5. 51

Duty, (i) conduct to a superior, respect; 3. 2. 351; (ii) (a) as at 3. 2. 351, (b) bow, obeisance (cf. L.L.L. 4. 2. 149 'Stay not thy compliment, I forgive thy duty'); 5. 2. 182

Eager, sharp, sour; 1. 4. 2; 1. 5. 69

Easiness, (i) facility; 3. 4. 166; (ii) indifference; 5. 1. 68 (v. note)

Ecstasy, madness; 2. 1. 99; 3. 1. 163; 3. 4. 74, 139

Edge (give), stimulate, incite; 3. 1. 26

Effect, (i) operative influence; 1. 5. 64; (ii) something obtained by an action; 3. 3. 54; (iii) outward symptom of a state of mind (cf. Ado, 2. 3. 110 'what effects of passion shows she?'); 3. 4. 129

Eisel, vinegar (v. note); 5. 1. 270

Enacture, fulfilment (N.E.D. quoting this passage); 3. 2. 196

Encompassment, 'talking round' a subject; 2. 1. 10

Encounter (sb.), manner of address or accosting (cf. A.Y.L. 2. 5. 24 'that they call compliment is like the encounter of two dog-apes'); 5. 2. 191

Encumbered, folded (N.E.D. with a query, quoting this passage). Possibly = 'striking a superior attitude'; 1. 5. 174

Ends, results; 3. 2. 212

Engaged, entangled; 3. 3. 69

Enginer, military engineer (cf. modern sapper); 3. 4. 206

Enseamed,* loaded with grease. 'Seam' = (a) fat used in cloth manufacture, (b) hog's-lard for frying (cf. N.E.D. 'seam,' sb.³ 1, 2); 3. 4. 92

Entreatment, conversation, interview (a diplomatic term); 1. 3. 122

Envious, malicious, spiteful; 4. 7. 172

Enviously, maliciously; 4. 5. 6

Equivocation, ambiguity (v. note); 5. 1. 134

Erring, wandering; 1. 1. 154

Eruption, an outbreak of calamity or evil; 1. 1. 69

Escot, pay a reckoning for, maintain; 2. 2. 349

Espials, spies (cf. 1 Hen. VI, 1. 4. 8 'The prince's espials have informed me'); 3. 1. 32

Essentially, really, in fact; 3. 4. 187

Estate, authority, rank; 3. 3. 5; 5. 1. 215

Eternal, pertaining to eternity (v. note); 1. 5. 21

Even, straightforward; 2. 2. 291

Even-Christen, fellow-Christians (coll. sb. v. N.E.D. 'Christen'); 5. 1. 28

Event, issue, consequence; 4. 4. 41, 50

Exception, disapproval, objection (cf. All's Well, 1. 2. 40 'Exception bid him speak'); 5. 2. 229

Excrement, outgrowth (such as nails, hair); 3. 4. 121

Exercise (sb.), act of devotion (cf. Rich. III, 3. 7. 64 'in holy exercise'); 3. 1. 45

Exercises, manly sports (cf. A.Y.L. 1. 1. 67 'Allow me such exercises as may become a gentleman'); 2. 2. 301

Expostulate, debate, discourse upon (cf. Two Gent. 3. 1. 251 'The time now serves not to expostulate'); 2. 2. 86

Express (adj.), direct, purposive (v. note); 2. 2. 309

EXTENT, 'condescension, the behaviour of a superior to an inferior when he makes the first advances' (Clar.); (cf. 'extend' in *All's Well*, 3. 6. 65 'The duke shall...extend to you what further becomes his greatness' and *Tw. Nt.* 4. 1. 53 'In this uncivil and unjust extent'); 2. 2. 376

EXTRAVAGANT, wandering out of bounds, vagrant; 1. 1. 154

EYAS, young hawk; 2. 2. 342

EYE, (i) 'in his eye,' in his presence; 4. 4. 6; (ii) 'I have an eye of you,' I have an eye on you, I am watching you; 2. 2. 294

FACULTY, 'an inherent power or property of the body or one of its organs' (N.E.D.); 2. 2. 308, 569

FALSE FIRE, fire-works, or blank discharge of fire-arms (N.E.D. 'false' 14 b, 'fire' 8 a); 3. 2. 266

FAMILIAR, friendly; 1. 3. 61

FANCY, (i) fantasticalness (cf. *L.L.L.* 1. 1. 170); 1. 3. 71; (ii) 'to fancy,' in taste or design; 5. 2. 154

FANTASY, imagination; 1. 1. 23, 54

FARDEL, package, bundle (cf. *Wint.* 4. 4. 713); 3. 1. 76

FARM, rent; 4. 4. 20

FASHION OF HIMSELF, his usual behaviour; 3. 1. 178

FAT, sweaty (v. note); 5. 2. 285

FATNESS, grossness, slackness; 3. 4. 153

FAVOUR (sb.), (a) beauty, (b) face, aspect; 5. 1. 188

FEAR (sb.), solicitude, anxiety; 3. 3. 8

FEAR (vb.), fear for; 4. 5. 122

FEAT, evil deed (cf. *Macb.* 1. 7. 80 'this terrible feat'; the variant

form 'fact' was in more common Elizabethan use); 4. 7. 6

FEATURE, comeliness of proportion (cf. *Rich. III*, 1. 1. 19 'Cheated of Feature by dissembling Nature'); 3. 1. 162

FEE, 'in fee' = in fee simple, with absolute possession, freehold; 4. 4. 22

FELL-INCENSED, fiercely angered; 5. 2. 61

FELLY or felloe, one of the curved pieces forming the rim of a wheel; 2. 2. 499

FETCH (sb.), device; 2. 1. 38

FIERCE, violent (cf. *K. John*, 5. 7. 13 'Fierce extremes In their continuance will not feel themselves'); 1. 1. 117

FIND, (i) discover the secret of; 3. 1. 188; (ii) return as a verdict; 5. 1. 8

FINE (adj.), (i) exquisite, subtle, highly wrought; 2. 2. 450; 4. 5. 161; (ii) (a) pure, unalloyed, (b) egregious, consummate (in a contemptuous sense; cf. *M.W.W.* 5. 1. 17 'the finest mad devil of jealousy' and *Oth.* 4. 1. 155 'I was a fine fool to take it'); 5. 1. 104

FINE (sb.), (a) a fictitious suit for the conversion of estate tail into fee simple (v. *fee*), (b) end; 5. 1. 102, 103

FINE (IN), finally; 2. 2. 69; 5. 2. 15

FINGER (vb.), filch; 5. 2. 15

FISHMONGER, bawd (v. note); 2. 2. 174

FLAW, a sudden squall of wind; 5. 1. 210

FLUSH (adj.), lusty; 3. 3. 81

FLUSHING, redness; 1. 2. 155

FOIL (sb.), bated or blunted rapier for fencing (v. note 5. 2. 222 S.D.); 2. 2. 325; (a) fencing foil, (*b*) anything that serves by contrast to set off another thing to advantage; 5. 2. 253

FOND, foolish; 1. 5. 99

FOOL, (i) ? baby (v. note); the word is commonly used by Sh. as a term of endearment; 1. 3. 109; (ii) dupe; 1. 4. 54

FOOT, v. *at foot*; 4. 3. 53

FOR A NEED, at need; 2. 2. 543

FORCED CAUSE (BY), by reason of compulsion; 5. 2. 381

FORDO, destroy; 2. 1. 100; 5. 1. 215

FOREST OF FEATHERS, the plumes worn by tragedians (v. note 5. 2. 96–7); 3. 2. 275

FORESTALLED, prevented; 3. 3. 49

FORGERY, invention (not in a bad sense; cf. *M.N.D.* 2. 1. 81 'These are the forgeries of jealousy'); 2. 1. 20; 4. 7. 88

FORM (sb.), (i) manners, gesture, facial expression; 1. 4. 30; 2. 2. 308, 560; (ii) sketch (cf. *K. John*, 5. 7. 32 'I am a scribbled form, drawn with a pen'); 1. 5. 100

FRAME (sb.), (i) form, order; 3. 2. 310; (ii) (*a*) the framework of the gallows, (*b*) the wooden frame made by a carpenter in building a house; 5. 1. 43

FRANKLY, freely, without constraint; 3. 1. 34

FREE, (i) guiltless; 2. 2. 567; 3. 2. 240; (ii) voluntary, unconstrained; 2. 2. 278; 4. 3. 60

FRET (vb.), (*a*) anger, irritate, (*b*) furnish with frets, i.e. rings of gut or bars of wood to regulate the fingering, as in a guitar (v. *Sh. Eng.* ii. 38); 3. 2. 374

FRETTED, embossed (cf. *Cymb.* 2. 4. 88 'The roof o' the chamber With golden cherubins is fretted'); 2. 2. 305

FRIENDING, friendship; 1. 5. 185

FRONT (sb.), brow; 3. 4. 56

FRONTIER, frontier town or fortress (v. N.E.D. 'frontier' 5); 4. 4. 16

FRUIT, dessert; 2. 2. 52

FUNCTION, bearing or action during performance (of any kind); 2. 2. 559

FUST, grow mouldy; 4. 4. 39

GAGED, engaged, staked; 1. 1. 91

GAINGIVING (sb.), misgiving; 5. 2. 213

GAIT, progress, going forward (a variant of 'gate'); 1. 2. 31

GALL (vb.), (i) make sore from rubbing or chafing; 5. 1. 137; (ii) vex; 1. 3. 39; (iii) graze; 4. 7. 146

GALLED, sore from rubbing or chafing (cf. *ungalled*); 1. 2. 155; 3. 2. 241

GAMBOL (vb.), leap or start. Used of a horse shying (v. N.E.D. 1); 3. 4. 144

GARB (sb.), manner, form of behaviour (cf. *Hen. V*, 5. 1. 80 'He could not speak English in the native garb'); 2. 2. 376

GATHER, infer, make deductions; 2. 2. 108

GENDER, sort, class, 'the general gender' = the common people; 4. 7. 18

GENERAL (adj.), of the public; 1. 4. 35; 2. 2. 566; 4. 7. 18

GENERAL (sb.), the public, the common people; 2. 2. 442

GENTRY, courtesy, elegance; 2. 2. 22; 5. 2. 114

GERMANE (adj.), relevant, appropriate; 5. 2. 160

GIB, tom-cat (a term of reproach) 3. 4. 190

GILD, supply with money (cf. *M.V.* 2. 6. 49 'gild myself with... ducats'); 3. 3. 58

GIS (BY), by Jesus; 4. 5. 57

GIVE, God give; 1. 1. 16

GIVE WAY, allow free scope (cf. 2 *Hen. IV*, 5. 2. 82 'I gave bold way to my authority' and *Temp.* 1. 2. 186); 4. 6. 31

GLIMPSE, momentary flash or gleam; thus 'the glimpses of the moon' = the earth by night (N.E.D.); 1. 4. 53

GO ABOUT, (*a*) make it one's business, (*b*) with quibble on naut. sense—change the course of a ship; 3. 2. 349

GOD BYE TO YOU, GOD BYE YE, God be with you, goodbye; 2. 1. 66 (v. note), etc.

GOD DILD, lit. God yield, God reward you; 4. 5. 40

GOD'S BODKIN. More commonly 'God's bodykins' = God's dear body (diminutive of endearment). An oath, referring to the sacramental bread; 2. 2. 533

GOOD NOW, please. A form of entreaty (cf. *Wint.* 5. 1. 19); 1. 1. 70

GRACE, 'do grace to,' reflect credit upon, do honour to; 1. 1. 131; 2. 2. 53

GRAINED, indelibly dyed; 3. 4. 90

GRIZZLED, grey; 1. 2. 240

GROSS AND SCOPE, general drift; 1. 1. 68

GROUND, 'upon what ground?' = from what cause?; 5. 1. 155

GROUNDLING, a spectator who paid a penny to stand on the floor of the playhouse, hence an uncritical or unrefined auditor; 3. 2. 11

GULES, the heraldic name for red; 2. 2. 461

GULF, whirlpool; 3. 3. 16

HA? eh? ('eh?' unknown before late 18th c.); 5. 1. 109

HANDSAW (v. note); 2. 2. 383

HANDSOME, stately, 'beautiful with dignity' (Dr Johnson); 2. 2. 450

HANGERS, the straps by which the rapier hung from the belt (often richly ornamented); 5. 2. 153

HAPPILY, haply; 1. 1. 134

HAPPINESS, appropriateness, felicity; 2. 2. 211

HARBINGER, lit. 'one that goes before and announces the approach of some one' (N.E.D.), a forerunner; 1. 1. 118

HARD, reluctant, unwilling (with a quibble); 1. 2. 60

HATCHMENT, an escutcheon, especially a tablet showing the armorial bearings of a deceased person; 4. 5. 213

HAUNT (OUT OF), out of the society of others (cf. *A.Y.L.* 2. 1. 15); 4. 1. 18

HAVE, understand; 2. 1. 65; 3. 2. 93

HAVIOUR, demeanour, behaviour; 1. 2. 81; 2. 2. 12

HAVOC, indiscriminate slaughter (it is noteworthy that Shakespeare often associates 'havoc' with the chase even when he is speaking of war; cf. *Hen. V*, 1. 2. 173 'To tear and havoc more than she can eat'; *Cor.* 3. 1. 275 'Do not cry havoc when you should but hunt With modest warrant'; *Jul. Caes.* 3. 1. 273 'Cry "Havoc" and let slip the dogs of war'); 5. 2. 362

HAWK, (*a*) mattock or pick-axe, (*b*) falcon (v. note); 2. 2. 383

HEAD (sb.), (i) source (lit. head of a stream; cf. *All's Well*, 1. 3. 169 'Your salt tears' head'); 1. 1. 106; (ii) an armed force (cf. 1 *Hen. IV*, 1. 3. 284 'To save our heads, by raising of a head'); 4. 5. 101

HEALTH, welfare, well-being (physical, mental or moral); 1. 3. 21; 4. 7. 80; 'spirit of health' = angel; 1. 4. 40

HEARSED, entombed; 1. 4. 47

HEAVY,* grievous, distressing; 3. 3. 84; 4. 1. 12

HEBONA, an imaginary poison, associated with henbane (v. note); 1. 5. 62

HECATE, Persephone, Queen of Hell, presiding over witchcraft and magic rites; 3. 2. 258

HECTIC (sb.), hectic or consumptive fever; 4. 3. 65

HEIGHT (AT), at the highest point of excellence; 1. 4. 21

HENT (sb.), (*a*) clutch, grasp (a rare sb. not found elsewhere in Sh.; more common as a vb.; cf. *Wint.* 4. 3. 121 and *Meas.* 4. 6. 14); (*b*) quibble on 'hint' = opportunity (sp. 'hent' in *Oth.* 1. 3. 142); 3. 3. 88

HERALDY. Old form of 'heraldry,' the law of arms; 1. 1. 87; 2. 2. 460

HERCULES AND HIS LOAD. Reference to the sign outside the Globe theatre; 2. 2. 364

HEROD, king of Judaea, represented in miracle plays as blustering and grandiose; 3. 2. 14

HEY-DAY, excitement of the spirits or passions; 3. 4. 69

HIC ET UBIQUE, here and everywhere (v. note); 1. 5. 156

HIDE FOX AND ALL AFTER, a cry formerly used in hide-and-seek; 4. 2. 29

HOBBY-HORSE, (*a*) a traditional figure or character in the old village festivals, esp. in the morris-dance, consisting of a man riding a pasteboard or wicker horse with his legs concealed beneath a footcloth (v. Douce, ed. 1807, ii. p. 470, for a cut and cf. Chambers, *Med. Stage*, i. 142, 258)); (*b*) a prostitute (cf. *L.L.L.* 3. 1. 28–30; *Oth.* 4. 1. 160); 3. 2. 132

HOIST, raise aloft, (here) blow up; 3. 4. 207

HOLD OFF, maintain a reserve; 2. 2. 295

HOLD UP, maintain, continue; 5. 1. 31

HOME (adv.), thoroughly; 3. 3. 29; 3. 4. 1

HONEST, (i) real, genuine; 1. 5. 138; (ii) chaste; 3. 1. 103; (iii) respectable, with a quibble upon sense ii; 2. 2. 176–78; 3. 1. 123

HOODMAN-BLIND, blindman's buff; 3. 4. 77

HORRID, horrible, dreadful; 2. 2. 566; 3. 3. 88

HORRIDLY, horribly, dreadfully; 1. 4. 55

HUGGER-MUGGER, secrecy; 4. 5. 83

HUMOROUS MAN, a fantastic dramatic character (like Jaques in *A.Y.L.*); 2. 2. 326

HUSBANDRY, thrift; 1. 3. 77

HYPERION, the sun god, Apollo; 1. 2. 140; 3. 4. 56

HYRCANIAN BEAST, the tiger. Cf. *Macb.* 3. 4. 101. Hyrcania was the classical name for the wild territory south of the Caucasus, which abounded in savage beasts; 2. 2. 454

IDLE, out of one's mind, crazy (N.E.D. quotes Hall, *Chron. Rich. III*, 55 b 'He...beganne a lytle to waxe ydle and weake in his wit'); 3. 2. 88; 3. 4. 11

IMAGE, likeness, representation; 1. 1. 81; 3. 2. 237

IMPART, bestow (v. note); 1. 2. 112

IMPARTMENT, communication; 1. 4. 59

IMPASTED, formed into a paste or crust; 2. 2. 463

IMPAWNED, staked, pledged as security; 5. 2. 151, 165

IMPERIOUS, imperial; 5. 1. 207

IMPITEOUS, pitiless, impetuous (v. note); 4. 5. 100

IMPLORATORS,* solicitors; 1. 3. 129

IMPORT (vb.), signify, make known; 3. 2. 137; 4. 3. 62

IMPORTANT, urgent (cf. *Ado*, 2. 1. 63 'If the prince be too important, tell him there is measure in everything'); 3. 4. 108

IMPORTING, concerning; 1. 2. 23; 5. 2. 21

IMPOSTHUME, lit. abscess, (hence) swelling of pride, insolence, etc.; 4. 4. 27

IMPRESS (sb.), enforced service (cf. *Troil.* 2. 1. 107); 1. 1. 75

IMPUTATION, repute; 5. 2. 145

INCAPABLE OF, insensitive to (cf. *capable*); 4. 7. 177

INCORPORAL, incorporeal, immaterial; 3. 4. 118

INCORPSED, made into one body (with); 4. 7. 86

INCORRECT, unchastened; 1. 2. 95

INDENTURES (A PAIR OF), a deed or legal document binding two parties, in duplicate, both copies being written on one piece of parchment or paper and then cut apart in a serrated or sinuous line, so that when brought together again at any time the two edges tally exactly and show that they are parts of the same original; 5. 1. 107

INDEX, table of contents at the beginning of a book, (hence) prelude; 3. 4. 52

INDIFFERENT (adj.), ordinary, neither good nor bad; 2. 2. 229

INDIFFERENT, INDIFFERENTLY, (adv.), moderately, fairly; 3. 1. 123; 3. 2. 35; 5. 2. 101

INDIRECTION,* roundabout method; 2. 1. 63

INDUED, endowed with appropriate qualities (cf. *Oth.* 3. 4. 146); 4. 7. 178

INFUSION, essence. A term of alchemy or medicine (cf. *Per.* 3. 2. 35–6 'The blest infusions That dwell in vegetives, in metals, stones'); 5. 2. 121

INGENIOUS, noble, high-minded, 'delicately sensitive' (T. Wright); 5. 1. 242

INHERITOR, possessor (cf. *L.L.L.* 2. 1. 5–6 'the sole inheritor Of all perfections'); 5. 1. 109

INHIBITION, prohibition (of plays) by authority; 2. 2. 335

INNOVATION, revolution, rebellion (v. note); 2. 2. 336

INOCULATE, to engraft (a term of horticulture); 3. 1. 118

INSINUATION, stealing into favour, ingratiation; 5. 2. 59

INSTANCE, (i) motive, cause; 3. 2. 181; (ii) token (v. N.E.D. 7); 4. 5. 162

INTIL, into; 5. 1. 73

INURN, inter. A use pec. to Sh. (cf. 'urn' = grave, *Hen. V,* 1. 2. 228); 1. 4. 49

INVENTORIALLY, as with a list of goods; 5. 2. 118

INVESTMENTS, (*a*) vestments (cf. 2 *Hen. IV,* 4. 1. 45 'Whose white investments figure innocence'); (*b*) money investments; 1. 3. 128

JEALOUSY, suspicion; 2. 1. 110; 4. 5. 19

JEPHTHAH, a Judge of Israel who sacrificed his daughter in fulfilment of a foolish vow; 2. 2. 408

JIG, a farce or entertainment of singing and dancing performed after a play (v. *Sh. Eng.* ii. 261 and Chambers, *Eliz. Stage*, ii. 551); 2. 2. 504

JIG-MAKER, a professional clown or stage fool who composed or performed jigs; 3. 2. 123

JOHN-A-DREAMS. Usually associated by edd. with John a Droynes, a country bumpkin, for whom v. McKerrow, *Nashe*, iii. 95 (note). There is nothing dreamy about this stock figure. I think Ham. is prob. alluding to some forgotten nursery character like Little Johnny Head-in-air; 2. 2. 571

JOINTRESS, a widow who holds a jointure or life-interest (N.E.D.); 1. 2. 9

JOURNEYMAN, lit. an artisan who is not a master of his trade but works for another, (hence) indifferent workman; 3. 2. 33

JOWL (vb.), strike, dash; 5. 1. 76

JUMP (adv.), just, exactly; 1. 1. 65; 5. 2. 373

JUST, sound, equable, well-balanced (v. note); 3. 2. 52

KEEN, (*a*) harsh, bitter, (*b*) with a strong appetite; 3. 2. 247

KEEP (vb.), lodge (a word still used at the older universities); 2. 1. 8

KEEP SHORT, keep rigidly confined or under strict discipline (N.E.D.); 4. 1. 18

KETTLE, kettledrum; 5. 2. 273

KIBE, a chilblain on the heel; 5. 1. 137

KIND, (*a*) sb. family, stock, (*b*) adj. natural, lawful, (*c*) adj. affectionate; 1. 2. 65; 4. 5. 146 (sense (*c*) only)

KINDLESS, unnatural, incestuous; 2. 2. 584

KNOW, recognise, acknowledge; 1. 2. 211; 2. 2. 173; 5. 2. 7

KNOWING (adj.), intelligent; 4. 7. 3; (sb.) knowledge; 5. 2. 44

LA, 'an exclamation...used to call attention to an emphatic statement' (N.E.D.); 4. 5. 55

LAPSED. Generally explained 'having let (time) slip'; better, I think, 'apprehended, arrested.' Cf. *Tw. Nt.* 3. 3. 36. N.E.D. (v. 'lap,' sb.[1] 6) commenting on the latter passage suggests association with 'laps' and quotes Strype (1558) 'fallen in the Lapse of the Law' and Daus (1560) 'fel into the lappes of their ennemies' (v. note); 3. 4. 107

LAPWING. Said to run about when newly hatched with its shell on its head; 5. 2. 186

LARDED, (i) stuck over with; 4. 5. 36; (ii) (*a*) garnished, (*b*) greased (to make it go down easily); 5. 2. 20

LAW OF WRIT AND THE LIBERTY (v. note); 2. 2. 406

LAY, (i) wager; 5. 2. 106; (ii) stipulate, lay down conditions; 5. 2. 166, 259; also 'lay on' (v. N.E.D. 'lay' v.[1] 28, 55); 5. 2. 168

LAYING IN, burial; 5. 1. 161

LAZAR-LIKE, like a leper; 1. 5. 72

LEAN ON, depend on (cf. 2. *Hen. IV*, 1. 1. 163–64 'The lives... Lean on your health'); 4. 3. 56

LEAVE, give up (cf. *M.V.* 5. 1. 173); 3. 4. 91

LECTURE, instruction; 2. 1. 64

LENTEN, meagre; 2. 2. 320

LET, hinder; 1. 4. 85

LETHE, the river of forgetfulness; 1. 5. 33

LEVEL (adj.), (i) with direct aim, straight; 4. 1. 42; (ii) plain, straightforward, readily accessible to (cf. 2 *Hen. IV*, 4. 4. 7 'everything lies level to our wish'); 4. 5. 151

LIBERAL, (i) frank, licentious; 4. 7. 169; (ii) 'liberal conceit,' elaborate design; 5. 2. 155

LIE (vb.), in the legal sense, to be admissible or sustainable; 3. 3. 61

LIGHTNESS, lightheadedness; 2. 2. 149

LIMED, caught (as with bird-lime); 3. 3. 68

LIST (sb.), (i) lit. catalogue of soldiers, hence company, troop; 1. 1. 98; 1. 2. 32; (ii) boundary, barrier; 4. 5. 99

LIVERY, (i) badge or cognizance worn by retainer; 1. 4. 32; (ii) clothes or uniform denoting some rank or calling; 3. 4. 164; 4. 7. 78

LIVING, enduring, eternal; 5. 1. 291

LOBBY, a passage or corridor outside a large room, often used as a waiting place or ante-room (v. N.E.D. 'lobby' 2 and cf. 2 *Hen. VI*, 4. 1. 61 'How in our voiding lobby hast thou stood'); 2. 2. 161

LOGGATS, a game, rather like nine-pins, in which missiles were thrown at wooden pins or bones fixed in the ground (v. *Sh. Eng.* ii. 465–66); 5. 1. 90

LONG PURPLE, early purple orchis, *Orchis mascula*; 4. 7. 168

LOOSE (vb.), (*a*) release (as a dog from a leash), (*b*) turn loose (in cattle or horse breeding); cf. *Temp.* 2. 1. 124 'loose her to an African'; *M.W.W.* 2. 1. 164 'turn her loose to him' (v. note); 2. 2. 162

LUXURY, lasciviousness, lust; 1. 5. 83

MACHINE, 'applied to the human and animal frame as a combination of several parts' (N.E.D., quoting from 1687 'What Nobler Souls the Nobler Machins Wear'); 2. 2 124

MAIN (sb.), (i) the main cause (cf. 2 *Hen. VI*, 1. 1. 208 'look unto the main'); 2. 2. 56; (ii) the chief or principal part, the main body; 4. 4. 15

MAINLY, forcibly, very greatly (cf. 1 *Hen. IV*, 2. 4. 222–3 'mainly thrust at me'); 4. 7. 9

MALLECHO = Spanish 'malhecho,' misdeed, iniquity. N.E.D. asserts that 'there is no evidence that the Sp. word was familiar in English,' but Dowden quotes Shirley, *Gentleman of Venice*: 'Be thou humble, Thou man of mallecho, or thou diest'; 3. 2. 135

MARGENT, margin, marginal note; 5. 2. 157

MARKET (sb.), profit, what one makes or gets in exchange for something else, or (perhaps) traffic; 4. 4. 34

MART, traffic, bargaining; 1. 1. 74

MATIN, daybreak, lit. the religious office recited at daybreak; 1. 5. 89

MATTER (sb.), (*a*) subject matter, (*b*) business, affair (v. note); 2. 2. 194; business; 2. 2. 485; ? love-affair, love-making (v. note); 3. 2. 114

MAZZARD, skull, head (lit. a drinking cup or bowl); 5. 1. 87

MEANS, manner; 4. 5. 212

MEED, wages, hire; 'in his meed' = in his pay (v. note); 5. 2. 146

MERE, pure, sheer; 5. 1. 278

MERELY, completely; 1. 2. 137

MESS, table; 5. 2. 89

METAL, a magnet (with a quibble on 'mettle'); 3. 2. 107

MICHING, sneaking (for mischievous or improper purposes); 3. 2. 135

MILCH, lit. giving milk, (hence) moist; 2. 2. 521

MINERAL (sb.), mine; 4. 1. 26

Mo, more in quantity. Rare (but cf. *Temp.* 5. 1. 235 'mo diversity'). Generally = more in number; 3. 1. 150

MOBLED, muffled ('survives in Warwickshire,' Onions); 2. 2. 506

MODEL, counterpart in miniature (cf. *Rich. II*, 3. 2. 153); 5. 2. 50

MODESTY, (i) sense of shame (cf. Lyly, *Mother Bombie*, 3. 1 'I can neither without danger smother the fire, nor without modestie disclose my furie'); 2. 2. 283; (ii) moderation, restraint; 2. 2. 445; 3. 2. 19; 5. 1. 202

MOIETY, portion; 1. 1. 90

MOLE, blemish; 1. 4. 24

MONUMENT, prodigy (v. note); 5. 1. 291

MOPE, be bewildered, 'move and act without the impulse and guidance of thought' (Schmidt); 3. 4. 81

MORE ABOVE, moreover; 2. 2. 126

MORE AND LESS, great and small (cf. *2 Hen. IV*, 1. 1. 209 'And more and less do flock to follow him' and *Macb.* 5. 4. 12 'Both more and less have given him the revolt'); 5. 2. 355

MOREOVER THAT, besides that; 2. 2. 2

MORTISED, closely and firmly fixed (as with mortise and tenon); 3. 3. 20

MOTION (sb.), (i) impulse, desire; 3. 4. 72; (ii) a fencing term signifying a practised and regulated movement of the body; 4. 7. 100, 156

MOULD (sb.), model; 3. 1. 156

MOUNT (ON), conspicuously, in view of all; 4. 7. 28

MOUNTEBANK, itinerant quack; 4. 7. 140

MOUSE, pet name for a woman or girl (cf. *L.L.L.* 5. 2. 19, *Tw. Nt.* 1. 5. 61); 3. 4. 183

MOUTH (vb.), utter in a pompously oratorical style, declaim; 3. 2. 3; 5. 1. 277

MOUTHS, 'make mouths at' = grimace in derision, scorn; 4. 4. 50

Mow (sb.), grimace; 2. 2. 367

MUDDIED, confused, agitated; 4. 5. 80

MUDDY-METTLED, thick-witted, dull; 2. 2. 570

MURDERING PIECE, a small cannon loaded with shrapnel, so as to inflict a number of wounds; 4. 5. 94

MUSTY, stale; 3. 2. 346

MUTE (sb.), an actor who has no speaking part; 5. 2. 333

MUTINE (sb.), mutineer; 5. 2. 6

MUTINE (vb.), mutiny, revolt; 3. 4. 83

NAKED, destitute, devoid of resources; 4. 7. 44

NAPKIN, handkerchief (cf. *Oth.* 3. 3. 290 'I am glad I have found this napkin'); 5. 2. 286

NATIVE (adj.), (i) closely related;
1. 2. 47; (ii) natural; 3. 1. 84

NATURE, natural affection (cf.
2 *Hen. IV*, 4. 5. 39; *Macb.*
1. 5. 46); 1. 2. 102; 1. 5. 81;
3. 2. 396; 3. 3. 32; 4. 5. 161;
5. 2. 229, 242

NAUGHT, improper, lewd; 3. 2. 145

NAVE, the hub of a wheel; 2. 2. 500

NEIGHBOURED TO, intimately associated with; 2. 2. 12

NEMEAN LION, a fierce lion killed
by Hercules (cf. *L.L.L.* 4. 1. 87);
1. 4. 83

NERO. The reference is to the fact
that Nero killed his mother,
Agrippina; 3. 2. 397

NERVE, muscle, ligament (as always
in Shakespeare; cf. *Cor.* 2. 1. 177
'Death...in's nervy arm doth
lie'); 1. 4. 83

NICKNAME (vb.), misname; 3.1.148

NIOBE, a daughter of Tantalus, who
wept unceasingly for her children slain by the gods, and was
finally turned into stone, from
which the tears still trickled;
1. 2. 149

NOBILITY, high degree, generosity;
1. 2. 110

NOYANCE, harm; 3. 3. 13

OBSEQUIOUS, 'dutiful in performing
funeral obsequies or manifesting
regard for the dead; proper to
obsequies' (N.E.D.); 1. 2. 92

OBSERVER, courtier, one who pays
respect (cf. *Jul. Caes.* 4. 3. 45);
3. 1. 157

OCCASION, opportunity; 1. 3. 54;
2. 2. 16

OCCULTED, hidden; 3. 2. 78

OCCURRENT, occurrence; 5. 2. 355

O'ER-CROW, triumph over, (hence)
overpower. A term from cock-
fighting; 5. 2. 352

O'ER-LEAVEN, lit. put too much
leaven in the bread, (hence)
'imbue to excess with some
modifying element' (N.E.D.);
1. 4. 29

O'ER-RAUGHT, overtook, came up
with; 3. 1. 17

O'ER-REACH, get the better of;
5. 1. 78

O'ER-SIZED, covered, painted; 2. 2.
466

O'ER-TEEMED, worn out by excessive breeding; 2. 2. 512

O'ERTOOK, overcome by drink;
2. 1. 56

OFFENCE, (*a*) anything offensive,
(*b*) crime, injury; 1. 5. 135;
3. 2. 232; (sense *b* only 3. 3.
36, 56, 58)

OMEN, ominous event (cf. Heywood, *Life of Merlin* 'His
country's omen did long since
foretell'); 1. 1. 119

ONCE, ever (cf. *A. & C.* 5. 2. 50
'If idle talk will once be necessary'); 1. 5. 121

OPEN TO, notorious for; 2. 1. 30

OPPOSITE (sb.), (i) a contrary or
hostile thing; 3. 2. 219; (ii) opponent; 5. 2. 62

OR (conj.), before; 1. 2. 183;
5. 2. 30

ORDINANT, guiding, directive; 5. 2.
48

ORE, gold. By confusion with 'Or'
the heraldic name for gold
(Dr Johnson; Cotgrave glosses
'ore' as 'gold'); 4. 1. 25

OSTENTATION, display (in a good
sense); 4. 5. 214

OUTSTRETCHED, 'strained, puffed
up, hyperbolical' (Schmidt; cf.
Meas. 2. 4. 153); 2. 2. 267

OVERPEER, tower above (cf. *M.V.*
1. 1. 12; *K. John* 3. 1. 23);
4. 5. 99

PACKING, (a) packing up, for a journey, (b) plotting; 3. 4. 211

PADDLE (vb.), finger idly or fondly (cf. *Wint.* 1. 2. 115 'paddling palms'); 3. 4. 185

PADDOCK, toad; 3. 4. 190

PALL (vb.), grow vapid, fail (cf. *A. & C.* 2. 7. 88 'I'll never follow thy palled fortunes more'); 5. 2. 9

PARAGON, 'the perfection, or flower of; the most complete, most absolute, most excellent peece, in any kind whatsoever' (Cotgrave; cf. *Two Gent.* 2. 4. 144 'She is an earthly paragon'); 2. 2. 311

PARDON (sb.), permission to depart; 1. 2. 56; 3. 2. 318

PARLE, (i) conference under a truce; 1. 1. 62; (ii) conversation, with a quibble on sense i; 1. 3. 123

PART (sb.), (i) (a) quality, characteristic, (b) actor's part; 3. 2. 102; (ii) capacity, talent; 4. 7. 72; (iii) (a) as at 4. 7. 72; (b) foreign parts; 5. 2. 115

PARTISAN, 'A spear with a broad head, the weapon of the guards, and at this day seen in the hands of the Yeomen of the Guard.' It was 'about nine feet with a staff of stiff ash' and was carried by officers (*Sh. Eng.* i. 137–38). Not the same as a halberd; 1. 1. 140

PASS (sb.), (i) bout (of fencing); 5. 2. 167; (ii) lunge, thrust; 5. 2. 61; 'pass of practice,' (a) a bout for exercise, (b) treacherous thrust; 4. 7. 137

PASS (vb.), thrust; 5. 2. 296

PASSAGE, passing to the next world, death; 3. 3. 86; 5. 2. 396

PASSAGES OF PROOF, well-attested cases; 4. 7. 111

PASSION, suffering; 4. 5. 187

PATIENCE, permission; 3. 2. 105

PEAK (vb.), mope about, 'make a mean figure, sneak' (Dr Johnson); 2. 2. 570

PEASANT (adj.), base; 2. 2. 553

PECULIAR, private. 'The single and peculiar life' = the life of the private individual; 3. 3. 11

PEEVISH, obstinate, perverse (cf. *Cymb.* 1. 6. 54 'He is strange and peevish'); 1. 2. 100

PELICAN. The female was said to feed or revive her young with her own blood; 4. 5. 146

PELION, a lofty range of mountains in Thessaly, famous in Greek mythology; 5. 1. 247

PERDITION, loss, diminution (cf. *Temp.* 1. 2. 30 'No, not so much perdition as an hair'); 5. 2. 117

PERDY, pardie, by God, verily; 3. 2. 294

PERIWIG-PATED, all wig and no brains. The wig was a mark of the actor at this period, when gentlemen still wore their own hair; 3. 2. 9

PERPEND, ponder; 2. 2. 105

PERUSAL, study; 2. 1. 87

PERUSE, examine, study; 4. 7. 135

PETAR, petard, mortar, a small engine of war used to blow up gates, walls, etc.; 3. 4. 207

PHILOSOPHY, natural philosophy, science as then understood (including demonology); 1. 5. 167; 2. 2. 371

PHRASE, phraseology, language; 2. 2. 447

PICKED, (a) fastidious, finical, exquisite (cf. *L.L.L.* 5. 1. 13 'He is too picked, too spruce, too affected'), (b) peaked, pointed (possibly in reference to 'picked shoes,' shoes with long projecting points; N.E.D. quotes instance of this use from 1615); 5. 1. 136

PICTURE IN LITTLE, miniature; 2. 2. 369

PIECE OF WORK, masterpiece, work of art. N.E.D. does not give this meaning, but it is clear that Sh. often uses 'piece' in the sense of 'supreme example,' good or bad (cf. *Wint*. 4. 4. 419–20; 5. 3. 38, 'O royal piece!'); 2. 2. 307; 3. 2. 45

PIGEON-LIVERED, meek, gentle. Pigeons were supposed to secrete no gall (v. note); 2. 2. 580

PIONER, miner; 1. 5. 163

PITCH (sb.), endeavour, lit. the highest point of a falcon's flight (v. note); 3. 1. 86

PLATFORM, a level place constructed for mounting guns, a terrace; 1. 2. 213, 252

PLAUSIVE, pleasing, gracious, popular—in a good sense (cf. *All's Well*, 1. 2. 53 'his plausive words,' and *Troil*. 3. 3. 43 'Why such unplausive eyes are bent on him'); 1. 4. 30

PLURISY, (*a*) pleurisy, (*b*) excess (v. *Introd*. p. xxxvii); 4. 7. 116

POCKY, infected with pox (syphilis); 5. 1. 160

POINT (AT), suitably, appropriately; 'at point exactly' = in every particular; 1. 2. 200

POLITIC, (*a*) political, (*b*) shrewd, cunning; 4. 3. 20

PORPENTINE, porcupine; 1. 5. 20

POSSET (vb.), curdle; 1. 5. 68

POSY, a short motto; 3. 2. 150

POTION, (*a*) dose of medicine or poison, (*b*) draught, drink; 5. 2. 324

POWERS, troops; 4. 4. 9

PRACTICE (sb.), (i) doings; 2. 2. 38; (ii) treachery, plot; 4. 7. 66; 5. 2. 315; 'of practice,' (*a*) skilful, (*b*) treacherous; 4. 7. 137

PRECURSE, heralding, foretokening; 1. 1. 117

PREGNANT, (i) full of meaning, apt; 2. 2. 210; (ii) (*a*) ready, prompt, (*b*) fertile in results; 3. 2. 59

PRESCRIPT, precept; 2. 2. 142

PRESENT, immediate (cf. *Wint*. 1. 2. 281 'My present vengeance'); 5. 1. 289

PRESENTLY, at once; 2. 2. 170, 595; 3. 2. 46

PRESSURE, image, impress; 1. 5. 100; 3. 2. 24

PREVENT, anticipate; 2. 2. 298

PRICKED ON, spurred on; 1. 1. 83

PRIMAL, original, pristine, (here) the curse of Cain; 3. 3. 37

PRIMY, in its prime or springtime; 1. 3. 7

PRIVATE (sb.), an intimate (v. N.E.D. 10, quoting from 1574 'men that be private and in favour'), with an indelicate quibble; 2. 2. 236

PROBATION, proof; 1. 1. 156

PROCESS, (i) relation, story (cf. *M.V*. 4. 1. 271); 1. 5. 37; (ii) procedure, indictment (leg.); 3. 3. 29; (iii) mandate, command; 4. 3. 62

PROGRESS, a royal or state journey, such as Queen Elizabeth made annually to different parts of England; 4. 3. 30

PRONOUNCE, (i) deliver a sentence or statement; 3. 2. 311; (ii) declare, proclaim; 2. 2. 515

PROOF, (i) tested strength (of armour or arms), invulnerability (cf. *A. & C*. 4. 8. 15 'Through proof of harness to my heart,' and *Shrew*, 2. 1. 140 'But be thou armed...Ay, to the proof'); 2. 2. 494; (ii) proof-armour; 3. 4. 38

PROPER, (i) own, very; 5. 2. 66; (ii) peculiar (to); 2. 1. 111

PROPERTY, (i) nature, characteristic quality; 2. 1. 100; 5. 1. 67; (ii) possessions; 2. 2. 573

PROPORTIONS, forces or supplies for war, contingents (cf. *Hen. V*, 1. 2. 137–8 'But lay down our proportions to defend Against the Scot'); 1. 2. 32

PROPOSER, one who states a proposition, or propounds a form of words; 2. 2. 290

PROVINCIAL ROSES, rosettes shaped or coloured like damask roses from Provins in N.E. France (v. N.E.D. 'Provence'); 3. 2. 276

PUFFED, (i) bloated (cf. *M.W.W.* 5. 5. 148 'A puffed man?'); 1. 3. 49; (ii) elated; 4. 4. 49

PURGATION, (*a*) judicial examination (cf. *A.Y.L.* 5. 4. 42–3 'put me to my purgation'), (*b*) medicinal purging; 3. 2. 307

PURGING, (i) exuding, discharging; 2. 2. 199; (ii) spiritual cleansing; 3. 3. 85

PURSY, lit. shortwinded, hence out of condition (physical or moral); 3. 4. 153

PUSH (sb.), (*a*) juncture, pinch (cf. *Wint.* 5. 3. 129), (*b*) rapier-thrust. The 'present push' = the immediate test; 5. 1. 289

PUT ON, (i) put to, impress upon; 1. 3. 94; (ii) ascribe to; 2. 1. 19; (iii) instigate; 4. 7. 130; 5. 2. 381; (iv) set to work; 5. 2. 395

PUT ONE FROM, remove, separate (cf. *Rom.* 3. 5. 109 'Put thee from thy heaviness'); 2. 2. 8

PYRRHUS, the son of Achilles, instrumental in the capture of Troy; 2. 2. 454

QUAINTLY, delicately, or (perhaps) artfully (cf. *M.V.* 2. 4. 6); 2. 1. 31

QUALITY, profession (esp. the acting profession); 2. 2. 349; with a quibble on 'quality' = ability; 2. 2. 437

QUANTITY, (i) proportion; 3. 2. 166; (ii) fragment (cf. *2 Hen. IV*, 5. 1. 69–71 'If I were sawed into quantities I should make four dozen of such bearded hermits' staves'); 3. 4. 75; (iii) amount, sum; 5. 1. 264

QUARRY, a heap of slain hart or deer after a hunt (cf. *Cor.* 1. 1. 202–4 'I'd make a quarry/With thousands of these quarter'd slaves, as high/As I could pick my lance'; *Macb.* 4. 3. 206; and Nashe, *First Part of Pasquils Apologie*, ed. McKerrow, i. 135 'like a quarrie of Deare at a generall hunting, hurled vppon a heape'); 5. 2. 362

QUEST, inquest; 5. 1. 22

QUESTION (sb.), (i) subject, matter; 1. 1. 111; 5. 2. 373; (ii) controversy; 2. 2. 343; (iii) conversation; 3. 1. 13

QUESTIONABLE, that may be interrogated or spoken to; 1. 4. 43

QUIDDITY, subtlety (from 'quid-ditas' = the distinctive nature of the thing, according to the scholastics); 5. 1. 96

QUIETUS, discharge, settlement of an account (a legal term; with a poss. quibble on 'quiet'); 3. 1. 75

QUILLITY, frivolous distinction, verbal nicety; 5. 1. 97

QUINTESSENCE, highly refined or concentrated essence. Lit. the 'fifth essence' of medieval science, supposed to be the ultimate substance of the universe, to extract which was the supreme object of alchemy; 2. 2. 312

QUIT, lit. repay, give as good as one gets; 'quit in answer' = exchange simultaneous hits with an opponent in fencing; 5. 2. 267

QUOTE, note, observe (cf. *Rom.* 1. 4. 30—1 'What care I What curious eye doth quote deformities?'); 2. 1. 109

RACK (sb.), 'a mass of cloud driven before the wind in the upper air' (N.E.D.); 2. 2. 488

RANK, gross, excessive; 2. 1. 20; 'ranker' = higher; 4. 4. 22

RASH, impetuous, reckless; 5.1.255

RASHLY, impulsively; 5. 2.6

RAVEL OUT, disentangle, make clear (cf. *Rich. II*, 4. 1. 228—9 'must I ravel out My weaved-up folly?'); 3. 4. 186

RAW, crude, unskilled; 5. 2. 127

RAZED, slit, slashed; 3. 2. 277

REACH (sb.), compass, capacity; 1. 4. 56; 'of reach' or 'of great reach' = of power or range of comprehension (v. N.E.D. 7 c); 2. 1. 61

REBEL (vb.), lust. This sense, not recorded in N.E.D., is common in Shakespeare (cf. *M.V.* 3. 1. 33, and *All's Well*, G.); 1. 3. 44

RECK (vb.), heed; 1. 3. 51

RECKON, count, enumerate; 2. 2. 121

RECOGNIZANCE, a kind of 'statute' (q.v.). 'Statutes' and 'recognizances' are commonly mentioned together in the covenants of purchase deeds; 5. 1. 102

RECORDER, the chief Elizabethan wind instrument, 'ancestor of the modern flageolet, constructed with eight holes, and generally made in sets, the lower-toned instruments being fitted with keys; their length varied from two to four feet, and their tone was peculiarly sweet and solemn' (*Sh. Eng.* ii. 31); 3. 2. 292

RECOVER THE WIND OF, get to windward of (so as to head off in the opposite direction). Madden, p. 32, quotes du Fouilloux, *La Venerie* (1561) 'prendre le vent; c'est soy ranger du costé qui vient le vent'; 3. 2. 349

RECOVERY, (*a*) 'the process, based on a legal fiction, by which entailed estate was commonly transferred' (N.E.D.), (*b*) attainment (v. N.E.D. 7); 5. 1. 103, 104

REDE, counsel, advice; 1. 3. 51

REECHY, filthy, foul; 3. 4. 184

REELS (sb.), revels (cf. *A. & C.* 2. 7. 100 'Drink thou; increase the reels'); 1. 4. 9

REGARD (sb.), (i) consideration; 2. 2. 79; 3. 1. 87; (ii) estimation; 4. 7. 74

REGION (sb. and adj.), the space of the air; 2. 2. 491, 582

RELATIVE, relevant; 2. 2. 608

RELISH (sb.), trace, suggestion; 3. 3. 92

RELISH OF (vb.), have a touch, taste or trace of (cf. *Per.* 2. 5. 60 'That never relished of a base descent'); 3. 1. 118

REMISS, careless; 4. 7. 133

REMOVED, remote, retired (cf. *A.Y.L.* 3. 2. 337 'so removed a dwelling'); 1. 4. 61

REPAST (vb.), feed; 4. 5. 147

REPEL, reject, repulse, jilt (cf. *V.A.* 573 'Foul words and frowns must not repel a lover'); 2. 1. 106; 2. 2. 146

REPLICATION, reply (v. note); 4. 2. 12

REPUGNANT, refractory; 2. 2. 475

REQUIEM, 'any dirge or solemn chant for the repose of the dead (chiefly *poet.*),' N.E.D. Cf. Beau. & Fletch. *Philaster*, 5. 1. 'sing sad requiems to your departing souls,' and v. note; 5. 1. 231

RESOLUTE (sb.), a bravado, a determined person; 1. 1. 98

RESOLVE (vb.), dissolve, disintegrate; 1. 2. 130

RESPECT (sb.), consideration; 3. 1. 68; 3. 2. 182

RESPONSIVE TO, well matched with; 5. 2. 154

RETROGRADE. An astrological term, lit. the movement of planets in a direction contrary to the order of the signs, or in the wrong direction, cf. *All's Well*, 1. 1. 196–8 'born under Mars ... When he was retrograde'; (hence) contrary to, opposed to; 1. 2. 114

REVOLUTION, alteration, change produced by time; 5. 1. 88

RHAPSODY, a medley, conglomeration, 'string'; 3. 4. 48

RHENISH, Rhenish or Rhine wine; 1. 4. 10; 5. 1. 174

RING, v. *cracked within the ring*; 2. 2. 433

RIVAL (sb.), partner, 'one who is in pursuit of the same object as another' (N.E.D.); 1. 1. 13

ROBUSTIOUS, boisterous; 3. 2. 9

ROMAGE, rummage, bustle, turmoil; 1. 1. 107

ROOD (BY THE), by the Cross; 3. 4. 14

ROSCIUS, a famous Roman actor (v. note); 2. 2. 396

ROSE, (i) perfection, paragon (formerly an epithet often applied to the Virgin Mary; cf. *Son.* 1. 2. 'Beauty's rose,' v. N.E.D. 5); 3. 1. 155; (ii) emblem of perfection and innocence; 3. 4. 42

ROUND (adj. and adv.), straightforward, open, without mincing matters; 2. 2. 139; 3. 1. 186; 3. 4. 5

ROUSE (sb.), (i) a draught of liquor, a bumper; 1. 2. 127; (ii) carousal, drinking bout; 1. 4. 8; 2. 1. 56

ROW (sb.), stanza; 2. 2. 424

RUB (sb.), impediment, obstacle (a term of bowls); 3. 1. 65

RUSSET, a coarse homespun cloth, or the colour of the same; hence, reddish-brown, grey; 1. 1. 166

SABLES, (*a*) expensive furs; 4. 7. 79; (*b*) black mourning garments with a quibble on sense *a*; 3. 2. 128

SAGE, 'grave, dignified, solemn' (N.E.D.); 5. 1. 231

SALLETS, lit. salads, (hence) anything sharp or tasty, spicy improprieties; 2. 2. 446

SANCTUARIZE, to protect as by sanctuary; 4. 7. 126

SANITY, soundness of condition generally; 1. 3. 21

SANS, without; 3. 4. 79

SAT ON, sat in inquest on; 5. 1. 4

SAVOURY, appetising; 2. 2. 447

SAW (sb.), maxim, saying; 1. 5. 100

SCONCE, head; 5. 1. 99

SCORN, folly. Lit. an object of derision (cf. *L.L.L.* 1. 1. 299 'These oaths and laws will prove an idle scorn'); 3. 2. 23

SCRIMER, fencer; 4. 7. 99

SCRUPLE, (*a*) doubt, (*b*) very small quantity; 4. 4. 40

SEA-GOWN, 'a coarse, high-collared and short-sleeved gown, reaching down to the mid-leg, and used most by seamen and sailors' (Cotgrave: 'esclavine'); apparently chiefly for night-wear (cf. N.E.D. 18 j. quot. 1699); 5. 2. 13

SEASON (vb.), (i) temper, moderate (a culinary metaphor); 1. 2. 192; 2. 1. 28; (ii) ripen, bring to maturity; 1. 3. 81; 3. 2. 208; (iii) prepare; 3. 3. 86

SECURE (adj.), unguarded, unsuspecting; 1. 5. 61

SEEMING, appearance, aspect; 3. 2. 85

SEIZED OF, possessed of; 1. 1. 89

SELLINGLY, in commercial language (v. note); 5. 2. 114

SEMBLABLE (sb.), likeness; 5. 2. 123

SENSE, feeling, perceptive sensibility; 3. 4. 38, 71, 161; (with a quibble on 'sense' = one of the five senses); 3. 4. 80

SENSIBLE, pertaining to the senses; 1. 1. 57

SENSIBLY, acutely, intensely; 4. 5. 150

SE OFFENDENDO, v. note; 5. 1. 9

SERGEANT, an officer whose duty is to summon persons to appear before a court; 5. 2. 334

SERVICE, (i) (*a*) allegiance, (*b*) religious service; 1. 3. 13; (ii) a course at a meal; 4. 3. 24

SET (vb.), value, estimate (v. N.E.D. 89 c); 1. 4. 65; 4. 3. 61

SHAPE* (sb.), (i) attitude; 4. 7. 88; (ii) plan of proceeding; 4. 7. 149

SHARD, fragment of earthenware; 5. 1. 225

SHARE (sb.), one of the parts into which the capital and profits of

a theatrical company were divided (v. Chambers, *Eliz. Stage*, i. 352–58); 3. 2. 279

SHARK UP, to sweep together greedily and indiscriminately (v. *Introd.* p. xxxvi); 1. 1. 98

SHENT, rated, put to shame or confusion; 3. 2. 401

SHOWING, 'great showing' = distinguished appearance (Schmidt) 5. 2. 113

SHUFFLE OFF, 'get rid of or evade,' 'shirk (a duty)' N.E.D. (v. *Introd.* p. xxxiv n. and cf. *Tw. Nt.* 3. 3. 16); 3. 1. 67

SHUFFLING, (i) mixing, jumbling together; 4. 7. 136; (ii) shifty or evasive dealing or conduct (with a quibble on sense i); 3. 3. 61

SIEGE, class, category; 4. 7. 75

SKIRTS (sb.), outlying parts (where authority is weakest); 1. 1. 97

SLANDER (vb.), bring disgrace upon (cf. *Ado*, 2. 3. 44); 1. 3. 133

SLEDDED, mounted on sleds or sledges; 1. 1. 63

SLING (sb.), field-gun, culverin (cf. *Sh. Eng.* i. 139–40, and Drayton, *Agincourt*, xcvi 'Their brazen slings send in the wildefire balls'); 3. 1. 58

SLIVER, a branch split from a tree (cf. *Lear*, 4. 2. 34; *Macb.* 4. 1. 28); 4. 7. 172

SOFTLY, slowly (cf. *Jul. Caes.* 5. 1. 16 'Lead your battle softly on'); 4. 4. 8

SOLICIT, incite, prompt; 5. 2. 356

SORT (vb.), come about, turn out; 1. 1. 109

SPHERE, 'one or other of the concentric, transparent hollow globes imagined by the older astronomers as revolving round the earth and respectively carrying with them the several heavenly bodies' (N.E.D.); 4. 7. 15

SPILL, destroy, kill; 4. 5. 20

SPLENITIVE, splenetic, liable to fits of anger; 5. 1. 255

SPRINGE, snare, trap; 1. 3. 115; 5. 2. 304

STAINED, dishonoured; 4. 4. 57

STALLION, courtesan or male whore (v. N.E.D. 2 b, 3); 2. 2. 591

STAND ONE UPON, be incumbent upon one (cf. *Rich. II*, 2. 3. 138 'It stands your Grace upon to do him right'); 5. 2. 63

STAR, 'a person's fortune, rank or destiny...viewed as determined by the stars' (N.E.D., cf. *Tw. Nt.* 2. 5. 147); 1. 4. 32; 2. 2. 141

STATE (sb.), (i) government; 1. 1. 101; 1. 2. 20; (ii) power, majesty; 2. 2. 515

STATION, attitude in standing; 3. 4. 58

STATIST, statesman, public official; 5. 2. 33

STATUTE, a legal document or bond in acknowledgment of debt, by virtue of which 'the creditor may immediately have execution upon the debtor's body, land and goods,' and which therefore gave him control over his land; 5. 1. 102

STAY UPON, await; 3. 2. 104

STICK OFF, show to advantage; 5. 2. 255

STILL (adv.), invariably, always; 1. 1. 118, etc.

STITHY, forge; 3. 2. 82

STOMACH (sb.), spice of adventure (lit. courage), with a quibble upon the physiological sense to suit 'food and diet'; 1. 1. 100

STOP (sb.), a finger-hole in the tube of a wind instrument, a metal key used for closing this hole; 3. 2. 363

STOUP, a drinking vessel (of varying dimensions); 5. 1. 60; 5. 2. 265

STRAIGHT (adv.), straightway; 2. 2. 436; with a quibble on 'straight' = narrow, 5. 1. 4

STREWMENTS, flowers strewn upon a grave (cf. *Cymb.* 4. 2. 285 'Are strewings fitt'st for graves'); 5. 1. 227

STRIKE (vb.). Astrol. term; planets 'in opposition' were supposed to blast or 'strike' objects beneath them; cf. mod. 'moon-struck' and *Cor.* 2. 2. 117–18 'struck Corioli like a planet'; 1. 1. 162

STUCK (sb.), thrust, lunge; 4. 7. 160

SUBJECT (THE), the people, the subjects of the realm (coll. sing. only found in Shakespeare; cf. *Meas.* 3. 2. 133 'the greater file of the subject'); 1. 1. 72; 1. 2. 33

SUN (IN THE). Ref. to proverb 'Out of God's blessing into a warm sun' = 'from an exalted, or honourable, state or occupation to a low or ignoble one' (P. L. Carver, v. note); 1. 2. 67; 2. 2. 184

SUPERVISE (sb.), the first reading; 5. 2. 23

SUPPLIANCE, diversion, lit. that which supplies or fills up (a minute); 1. 3. 9

SWAGG'RING, blustering, boastful; 1. 4. 9

SWEEP MY WAY, clear my path; 3. 4. 204

SWEEPSTAKE (adv.), in a clean sweep, lit. taking all the stakes in a game at once. A common name for a ship in that piratical age (N.E.D.); 4. 5. 142

SWITZERS, Swiss mercenaries (employed as bodyguard at several European courts at this period and still found at the Vatican); 4. 5. 97

TABLE(s), writing tablet, memorandum book; 1. 5. 98, 107

TABLE BOOK, v. table(s); 2. 2. 136

TAKE, strike with paralysis, bewitch (cf. Wint. 4. 4. 118–20 'daffodils, That come...and take The winds of March with beauty'); 1. 1. 163

TARGET, light shield; 2. 2. 325

TARRE, provoke to fight, set dogs by the ears (cf. Troil. 1. 3. 392); 2. 2. 356

TAX (vb.), (i) censure; 1. 4. 18; (ii) take to task; 3. 3. 29

TELLUS, the goddess of the earth; 3. 2. 154

TEMPER (vb.), concoct, compound; 5. 2. 326

TENABLE, kept back, retained; 1. 2. 248

TEND, attend, wait in readiness; 1. 3. 83; 4. 3. 44

TENDER (adj.), youthful; 4. 4. 48

TENDER (vb.), (a) have regard for; 4. 3. 40; (b) show, offer; 1. 3. 107, 109

TENT (vb.), probe (with the surgeon's knife); 2. 2. 601

TERMAGANT, 'an imaginary deity held in mediaeval Christendom to be worshipped by Mohammedans; in the mystery plays represented as a violent overbearing personage' (N.E.D.); 3. 2. 14

TERMS, condition; 3. 3. 5; 4. 7. 26

TETTER, an eruption of the skin; 1. 5. 71

THING, a term of contempt (cf. Wint. 2. 1. 82 'O thou thing!'); 4. 2. 27

THOUGHT,* (i) melancholy consideration (cf. Jul. Caes. 2. 1. 187; A. & C. 3. 13. 1 'Think and die'); 3. 1. 85; 4. 5. 187; (ii) (a) a trifle, a very little (cf. Ado, 3. 4. 13 'a thought browner'; N.E.D. quotes from 1617 'A thought of time'); (b) idea; 3. 2. 116

THRIFT, profit; 1. 2. 180; 3. 2. 60

THROUGH AND THROUGH, right through (cf. A.Y.L. 2. 7. 59–60 'through and through Cleanse'); 5. 2. 192

TICKLE O'TH'SERE. 'Sere' = part of the mechanism of a trigger, which if 'tickle' = ticklish, loose or unsteady, would 'go off' at a touch. Thus: 'tickle o'th'sere' = ready to laugh on the slightest provocation; 2. 2. 328

TIMBERED, 'too slightly timbered,' made of wood too light; 4. 7. 22

TIME, the present circumstance, the conditions of the moment; 3. 1. 114, 3. 4. 107 (v. note); 4. 7. 110, 148

TINCT, colour; 3. 4. 91

To, in comparison with; 1. 2. 140; 3. 1. 52

TOIL (sb.), net, snare; 3. 2. 350

TOO TOO. Emphatic reduplication of 'too'; like 'too much' capable of qualifying the vb. (N.E.D. quotes Sir T. More 'make us too too shrink'); 1. 2. 129

TOP. 'In the top of,' 'on top of,' lit. above, here louder than; 2. 2. 343, 443

TOP (vb.), excel, outdo; 4. 7. 87

TOUCHED, tainted, guilty (cf. A.Y.L. 3. 2. 343 'touched with ...offences'); 4. 5. 206

TOWARD, imminent, impending;
1. 1. 77; 5. 2. 363

TOY (sb.), idle fancy, impulse,
freak, trifle; 1. 3. 6 (for 'toy in
blood' v. *blood*); 1. 4. 75; 4. 5. 18

TRACE (vb.), (a) draw, (b) follow;
5. 2. 124

TRADE (sb.), business; 3. 2. 335

TRICK (sb.), (i) whim, toy, play-
thing; 4. 4. 61; (ii) wont, way
(cf. 2 *Hen. IV*, 1. 2. 240–41 'it
was...the trick of our English
nation'); 4. 7. 186; (iii) trickery;
4. 5. 5; 5. 1. 97; (iv) knack;
5. 1. 88

TRICK (vb.), a term in heraldry
= 'to indicate colours by means
of certain arrangements of dots
or lines'; hence, to smear, spot;
2. 2. 461

TROPHY, monument, memorial;
4. 5. 213

TROPICALLY, figuratively; 3. 2. 236

TRUEPENNY, trusty fellow; 1. 5.
150

TRUMPET, trumpeter; 1. 1. 150

TRUNCHEON, staff of office; 1. 2.
204

TRUSTER, one that believes or
credits, lit. creditor (cf. *Tim.*
4. 1. 10); 1. 2. 172

TRY CONCLUSIONS, make experiment, see what will happen;
3. 4. 195

TUNE, temper; 5. 2. 191

TURN THE BEAM, turn the scale,
preponderate (v. N.E.D. 'turn'
49); 4. 5. 157

TURN TURK, prove renegade, go to
the bad; 3. 2. 276

TYRANNICALLY, vehemently, out-
rageously (in the fashion of the
Herod (q.v.) of the mystery
plays); 2. 2. 343

TYRANNOUS, cruel, pitiless; 2. 2.
464

UMBRAGE, shadow; 5. 2. 124

UNANELED, unanointed, without
extreme unction; 1. 5. 77

UNBATED, not blunted at the edge
and point; 4. 7. 137; 5. 2. 315

UNBRACED, unfastened; 2. 1. 75

UNCHARGE, acquit; 'uncharge the
practice' = fail to suspect the
plot; 4. 7. 66

UNCTION, ointment, salve, with
a poss. reference to religious
unction (cf. *anoint*); 3. 4. 145;
4. 7. 140

UNCURRENT, unacceptable, invalid;
2. 2. 432

UNDERGO, bear the weight of,
support (cf. *Meas.* 1. 1. 22–3 'be
of worth To undergo such ample
grace and honour'); 1. 4. 34

UNEFFECTUAL, losing its effect;
1. 5. 90

UNFELLOWED, unmatched, un-
equalled; 5. 2. 146

UNFOLD, disclose, declare; 1. 1. 2

UNGALLED, ungrazed, unharmed;
3. 2. 272

UNGORED, unpierced, unharmed;
5. 2. 248

UNGRACIOUS, graceless (cf. 1 *Hen.
IV*, 2. 4. 490 'Swearest thou,
ungracious boy?'); 1. 3. 47

UNHOUSELED, without the Euchar-
ist; 1. 5. 77

UNIMPROVED, (a) unreproved, (b)
crude, untempered (lit. unculti-
vated, ref. to waste land), v.
N.E.D. 'improve' v. 2; 1. 1. 96

UNION, 'a pearl of large size, good
quality and great value'; 5. 2.
270, 324

UNKENNEL, force a fox from its
hole, bring to light (cf. *M.W.W*
3. 3. 156); 3. 2. 79

UNPREGNANT, lit. unimpregnated,
hence unquickened, not stirred
to action (cf. *Meas.* 4. 4. 18–19

'This deed unshapes me quite, makes me unpregnant and dull to all proceedings'); 2. 2. 571

UNPREVAILING, unavailing (prevail ='avail' in 16th c.); 1. 2. 107

UPROPORTIONED, inordinate; 1. 3. 60

UNRECLAIMED, untamed (a term in falconry); 2. 1. 34

UNSHAPED, unformed, uncontrolled; 4. 5. 8

UNSIFTED, untested, inexperienced; 1. 3. 102

UNSINEWED, nerveless, weak, feeble; 4. 7. 10

UNVALUED, worthless; 1. 3. 19

UNWRUNG, not pinched or galled; 3. 2. 241

UNYOKE, cease from labour, give over (a metaphor from the plough); 5. 1. 52

UPSHOT, issue, conclusion, lit. 'the final shot in a match at archery' (N.E.D.); 5. 2. 382

UPSPRING (adj.), upstart, newly come into fashion (N.E.D. quotes from 1591 'the new upspring nobilitie'); 1. 4. 9

USE (sb.), (1) usage, way; 1. 2. 134; (ii) practice; 3. 4. 163

USURP (vb.), (i) appropriate or use wrongfully; 1. 1. 46; (ii) exert an unlawful influence; 3. 2. 260

VAIL (vb.), lower, cast down; 1. 2. 70

VALANCED, fringed with hangings (like those round the sides and foot of a bed); 2. 2. 428

VALIDITY, strength; 3. 2. 188

VANTAGE (OF). Meaning doubtful; *Macb.* 1. 6. 7 'coign of vantage' suggests 'from a convenient corner' (i.e. behind the arras), but Onions cites *Oth.* 4. 3. 85–6 'a dozen: and as many

to th' vantage, as would store the world,' where 'to the vantage'= in addition, cf. N.E.D. 'vantage' sb. 2 b; 3. 3. 33

VARIABLE, diverse, various; 3. 1. 175; 'variable service' = different courses of food; 4. 3. 23

VENTAGE, finger-hole in a wind instrument; 3. 2. 360

VICE, riotous buffoon, orig. a clownish character in a morality play representing one of the vices. Here, a depraved example, a caricature; 3. 4. 98

VIDELICET, that is to say; 2. 1. 59

VIRTUE, (i) integrity; 1. 3. 16; (ii) strength, power (cf. *L.L.L.* 5. 2. 348 'The virtue of your eye'); 4. 5. 155

VOICE, (i) approval, nomination; 1. 3. 23; 3. 2. 343; 5. 2. 354; (ii) opinion; 5. 2. 247

VOUCH, guarantee the title to a property; 5. 1. 105

VOUCHER, and DOUBLE VOUCHER, legal devices for 'recovery' (q.v.) or converting estate entail into fee simple, involving fictitious actions and the summoning (vouching) of men of straw to warrant titles which all parties wish invalidated, and which become invalidated by the vouchees defaulting; 5. 1. 102, 105–6

VULCAN, the armourer of the gods; 3. 2. 82

VULGAR, (i) common, ordinary; 1. 2. 99; (ii) common, cheap; 1. 3. 61

WAG (vb.), move (without its mod. ludicrous associations); 5. 1. 261

WAIT UPON, attend, accompany (with a prob. quibble on 'wait upon' = watch or lie in wait

for, v. N.E.D. 'wait' 14 a, b);
2. 2. 269

WAKE (vb.), sit up late for pleasure,
turn night into day; 1. 4. 8

WAN (vb.), grow pale; 2. 2. 557

WANTON (sb.), a spoilt child, a
pampered pet; 5. 2. 297

WARRANT, 'of warrant' = warrant-
ed to succeed; 2. 1. 38

WASSAIL, carousal; 1. 4. 9

WASTE, the desolate hours about
midnight (v. note); 1. 2. 198

WATCH (sb.), insomnia, sleepless-
ness; 2. 2. 148

WATER-FLY, midge, 'busy trifler'
(Johnson); 5. 2. 84

WEAKNESS, weakmindedness; 2.
2. 148, 605

WEEDS, garments distinctive of a
person's state of life (N.E.D. 5);
4. 7. 79

WHARF, bank (of a river); 1. 5. 33

WHEEL, burden, refrain (with a
quibble on 'Fortune's wheel,'
v. note); 4. 5. 171

WHOLESOME, (i) sound, healthy;
1. 5. 70; 2. 2. 449; 3. 2. 260;
(ii) sensible, reasonable; 3. 2. 317

WHORESON, 'a coarsely abusive
epithet...also sometimes ex-
pressing familiarity or commendation' (N.E.D.); 5. 1. 166,
170

WILD, agitated, full of excitement;
5. 2. 392

WINDLASS, lit. a circuit to intercept
game in hunting, (hence) roundabout way, crafty device (not
related to 'windlass' = a me-
chanical device); 2. 1. 62

WINNOWED, tested, freed from
inferior or worthless elements;
5. 2. 193

WISENESS, wisdom ('ironical
N.E.D.); 5. 1. 257

WIT, understanding, acumen; 2. 2.
90; 3. 2. 322

WITCHING, appropriate to witchcraft or supernatural occurrences; 3. 2. 391

WITHDRAW WITH, take aside, be
private with; 3. 2. 348

WITHERS, the part of the back
between the shoulder blades;
3. 2. 241

WONDER (sb.), great distress or
grief (N.E.D. 5 c quotes from
1600 'As woe and wonder be
them amonge'); 4. 5. 88;
5. 2. 362

WOODCOCK, a bird very easily
caught in a snare; 1. 3. 115;
5. 2. 304

WOO'T, wilt. A frequent Shakespearian form (v. note); 5. 1. 269,
270

WORD, (i) motto (v. note); 1. 5.
110; (ii) promise, pledge; 4. 5.
105

WORK (vb.), think; 1. 1. 67

WORKING, action, operation, function (of the mind); 2. 2. 137
(v. note), 557

WOUNDLESS, invulnerable; 4. 1. 44

WRECK (vb.), ruin; 2. 1. 110

YAW, lit. (of a vessel) to deviate
from the course, to turn from
side to side, hence to proceed
unsteadily so as to fall behind
something else; 5. 2. 119

YEASTY, frothy, light and super-
ficial; 5. 2. 192

YIELDING (sb.), consent; 1. 3. 23

ZONE, v. burning zone; 5. 1. 276

CORRECTIONS AND
ADDITIONAL NOTES (1936)

In the compilation of these notes I have profited from the perusal of two important editions of the play and an interesting monograph, all unhappily unknown to me in 1934, viz. the text brilliantly edited for French schools by M. R. Travers (*Librairie Hachette*, Paris, 1st ed. 1929, 2nd ed. 1935), the no less remarkable *Hamlet* of Prof. J. Q. Adams (Houghton Mifflin Co., Boston and New York, 1929), and Prof. W. F. Trench's *Hamlet, a new Commentary* (Smith, Elder and Co., 1913). Each anticipates my findings at more than one important point, and to all three I tender my apologies with this belated recognition.

INTRODUCTION

p. xxi (l. 2 from top) Insert 'probably' after 'a play' and add the footnote 'v. E. K. Chambers' *Elizabethan Stage*, iii. 454.'

p. xxiii (footnote) Add 'Since this was written Prof. Bullough has suggested a plausible source in the murder, by means of poison administered through the ears, of Francesca Maria, Duke of Urbino, by Luigi Gonzaga, the kinsman of his wife, in 1538; v. 'The murder of Gonzago,' *Modern Language Review*, Oct. 1935.'

p. xxv (l. 12) '*Der bestrafte Brudermord* and *Hamlet*, Act v,' by A. H. J. Knight (*Modern Language Review*, July, 1936), furnishes the most recent account of this German version.

p. xxxiii (l. 2 from foot) L. L. Schücking (*Anglia Beiblatt*, vol. xlvi, no. 7, p. 205) points out that this meaning is given in Leon Kellner's *Shakespeare-Wörterbuch*, 1922.

p. xxxix Cf. 'Notes on a feature of Shakespeare's style' in *Suggestions*, by E. E. Kellett, 1923 (an important pioneer article); Caroline Spurgeon, *Shakespeare's Imagery*, 1935, and Wolfgang Clemen, *Shakespeares Bilder, ihre Entwicklung und ihre Funktionen im dramatischen Werk* (Bonn: Peter Hanstein, 1935).

p. xlii (l. 5 from foot) The following, from Dekker's *Gull's Hornbook* (1609), ch. vi, may be added to the passages quoted:

To conclude, hoard vp the finest play-scraps you can get, vpon which your leane wit may most sauourly feede, for want of other stuffe, when the *Arcadian* and *Euphuizd* gentlewomen haue their tongues sharpened to set vpon you.

p. xliv My *What happens in Hamlet* (Cambridge, 1935) deals more fully with the problems raised in §§ V and VI.

p. lvi (l. 13) For further discussion of this question v. corr. T.L.S. Jan. 4, 11, 18, 25, Sept. 26, Oct. 3, 10, 17, 1936.

p. lviii (l. 22) v. the add. note on 2. 2. 184 below. Adams (p. 255), commenting on the Nunnery Scene, writes:

Hamlet thinks that Claudius and Polonius, in their effort to discover whether he really is mad or not, are employing a familiar old medico-legal test of insanity. This test was to place some woman, whom the suspected person was known formerly to have loved, alone with him to offer him lewd temptations. If the supposed madman yielded to her temptations he was, it was believed, merely feigning insanity, for an insane person was thought to be incapable of the passion of love.

And he quotes from the *Historie of Hamblett* in support of this. The suggestion is very interesting and if the notion was commonly entertained by Sh.'s audience it would still further help to explain Ham.'s conduct to Oph.

(l. 5 from foot) It is important that the entry should be from some central point of the modern stage, corresponding with the inner stage of Shakespeare's theatre, so that it cannot escape notice by the audience, as an entry from the side, or from in front of the modern proscenium, is likely to do.

p. lx Cf. Émile Legouis, 'La réaction contre la critique romantique de Shakespeare,' *Essays and Studies*, English Association, vol. XIII.

p. lxi (last line) This is disputable, it being one of the moot points of scholastic theory whether 'angels and separate souls have a natural power to understand thoughts.' Donne was of opinion that they had not; cf. his *Dreame*:

> But when I saw thou sawest my heart
> And knew my thought, beyond an angel's art;

and H. J. C. Grierson's note in *Poems of John Donne*, ii. 34–5. But it can hardly be disputed that the audience was expected to 'take the Ghost's word' for it that his 'tardy son' was 'lapsed in time and passion' (cf. Travers, note on 3. 4. 111).

THE STAGE-HISTORY

p. lxxxii (l. 20) Garrick's version of *Hamlet*, 1772, has at last come to light in the Folger Shakespeare Library, and conjecture may now be set at rest. Full particulars are given by Mr George Winchester Stone, junior, in PMLA. xlix. 3, Sept. 1934.

p. xcvi (l. 25) The Elizabethan Stage Society was not founded by William Poel until 1895, and had no part, therefore, in the production of 1881.

NOTES

p. 140. *Names of the Characters* For 'perversions of Danish names' v. Brandes, pp. 357–58.

p. 142. *Rosencrantz* and *Guildenstern* v. letter in T.L.S. Jan. 28, 1926 for reference to 'one Frederik Rosenkrantz...a member of a Danish diplomatic mission sent

to Queen Bess....In 1593 he had married a Guildenstern and was accompanied to London by his wife's
brother, a Guildenstern. These two men were both
graduates of Wittenberg University and described as
dashing and accomplished men of the world.'

I. I.

36. *yon same star* etc. Schücking (*Der Sinn des
Hamlet*, p. 45) notes that Barnardo's words draw the
audience's attention to the spot at which the Ghost will
appear.

143–46. *We do it wrong...mockery* Cf. *Temp.*
3. 3. 61–6 and Lavater, p. 214:

Some others, when spirits appeare vnto them, will by and
by set on them, and driue them away with naked swords...
not considering with themselues, that spirites are nothing
hurte with weapons.

I. 2.

9. *imperial jointress* = royal widow who retains the
jointure or life interest in the crown. An expression
which points to the legal quibble by which Claudius
'popped in between th'election' and Hamlet's 'hopes.'

66. *you* not 'thee'; contrast l. 45 (Travers).

82. *shapes* A theat. term = 'make-up and costume
suited to a particular part' (N.E.D. 8, quoting Dekker
and Massinger). This adds a new touch of bitterness to
the speech; cf. 'actions that a man might play' (l. 84).

125. *No jocund health* etc. Cf. add. note 1. 4. 8–9
below.

129. *too too sullied* (end of note) Cf. 3. 3. 46 'white
as snow,' Isaiah v. 18 'though your sins be as scarlet,
they shall be white as snow,' and Psalm li. 7. Dr A. F.
Titley suggests (privately) that there was nothing
'absurd' in the idea of flesh melting into 'dew,' inasmuch
as acc. to the physiology of the time the human body was
mostly composed of the element water. Cf. *Dr Faustus*,
5. 2. 163–65, 187–90; *Macb.* 1. 3. 80.

153. *than I to Hercules* Travers notes that Ham. thinks of Hercules rather as the purifier of the world than as the strong man, and quotes *Antonio's Revenge*, 5.2:

> Thou art another Hercules to us
> In ridding huge pollution from our state.

This has the great merit of freeing us from the necessity of supposing that Ham. regards himself as a weakling—which he certainly was not.

157. *incestuous* Trench (pp. 55, 257–60) notes 'that the recent internal history and the existing international position of Sh.'s England turned largely upon that very point, the case of Gertrude being precisely parallel with that of Catherine of Aragon.'

1. 3.

12–13. *temple...service* E. E. Kellett, *Suggestions*, p. 74, anticipates me here.

74. *of a most...chief in that* (add at end) A fourth, suggested by Staunton and Ingleby (v. Furness) is to read 'cheefe' and 'sheaf' (=set, class). But this merely repeats 'of the best rank' (l. 73).

113. *almost all* =even all, v. G. (add.).

1. 4.

8–9. *The king...reels* (add.) Cf. 1. 2. 125–28, 5.2.273–76. For this Danish custom and contemporary English opinion upon it v. the account of 'The Earle of Rutland his Ambassage into Denmarke' (June and July, 1603), on the occasion of a royal christening and for the presentation of the order of the Garter to Christian IV (King James I's brother-in-law), given in Stow's *Annals* (pp. 1433–37) and based upon a note supplied by 'Maister William Segar, Garter King at Armes.' Two extracts may be quoted:

That afternoone the King [Christian IV] went aboord the English ship [lying off Elsinore] and had a banket prepared for him vpon the vpper decks, which were hung with an Awning of cloaths of Tissue; euery health reported sixe, eight, or ten shot of great Ordinance, so that during the King's abode, the ship discharged 160 shot.

Of a previous 'solemne feast to the embassadour' given by the King, Segar writes:

It were superfluous to tell you of all superfluities that were vsed; and it would make a man sicke to heare of their drunken healths: vse hath brought it into fashion, and fashion made it a habit, which ill bessemes our nation to imitate.

These last words come very close to Hamlet's in ll. 13–19. The passages were first noted by Furnivall in *New Shak. Soc. Trans.* 1874, p. 512.

27–28. *some complexion...forts of reason* Cf. Bright, p. 250, 'There keepe the straightest hand, where the lists of reason are most like to be broken through.'

37. *of a doubt* Commenting on my conj. emendation M. R. Ridley ('New Temple' *Hamlet*) writes:

A flame can be 'douted': but how can a 'noble substance' be 'douted,' and, if so, by a 'dram'? The sense required is infection rather than extinction.

But for Sh. and his contemporaries there was one 'substance,' and that most 'noble,' which *could* be 'douted,' douted by a dram, and douted after a fashion that was at once infection and extinction, viz. the gold which alchemists were always trying and always failing to make in their crucibles. Cf. N.E.D. 'noble' 7*b* ('Of precious stones, metals, and minerals'); and note that a dram was avoirdupois as well as apothecaries' weight with Sh. Ham. means that the character of his 'particular man' might have been pure gold but for the touch of evil or weakness which went to its composition and so brought him to ruin.

43. *shape* v. note I. 2. 82 (add.) above.

73. *deprive...reason* This warning prepares us for Ham.'s 'distemper' after the interview in the next scene.

I. 5.

11. *fast in fires* G. Bullough (M.L.R. xxx. 440) explains 'grossly full of bread' (3. 3. 80) as meaning that

Ham. 'would have wished to die fasting, with body, as well as mind, prepared for Judgment.' Perhaps this 'disappointed' condition of body is sufficient to account for the purgatorial fast in fires.

42–91. *Ay, that...remember me* Ham.'s silence during this long speech is noteworthy. 'Until the Ghost began to speak of Gertrude's sins, he was full of energy, constantly interrupting and quick to respond to his father's every utterance. Now, however, he is too over-come to speak a single word' (Adams, p. 215).

62. *hebona* Cf. *The Troublesome Reign of King John*, I, iii, 3:

> Morpheus, leaue here thy silent Ebon caue.

70. *The thin and wholesome blood* 'Melancholy blood is thicke and grosse,' Bright, p. 270.

110. *Word* Cf. Nashe (*Works*, ed. R. B. McKerrow, iii. p. 30, l. 20): 'resoluing to take vp for the Word or *Motto* of my patience, Perdere posse sat est,' and Mars-ton, *Antonio's Revenge*, 1. 3. (ed. H. H. Harvey, i. 77): 'Ile carrie for my deuice my grandfathers great stone hors, flinging vp his head, and ierking out his left legge. The word: *Wighy Purt*.'

147. *Upon my sword* Cf. *Span. Trag.* II. i. 87–93:

> *Lorenzo* Sweare on this crosse that what thou saiest is true
>   And that thou wilt conceale what thou hast tolde—

whereupon Pedringano takes an oath upon his sword.

151. *cellarage* This reference to the space under the stage is at once topical and metaphorical, since the cellarage was commonly called 'hell,' a name derived from the miracle plays. Cf. Travers, note 1. 5. 6 and Chambers, *Eliz. Stage*, ii. 528, n. 3, quoting Dekker, *News from Hell* (1606, *Works*, ii. 92, 139):

> Marry the question is, in which of the *Play-houses* he [the Devil] would haue performed his prize...Hell being vnder euerie one of their *Stages*, the Players (if they had owed him a spight) might with a false Trappe doore haue slipt

him downe, and there kept him, as a laughing stocke to al their yawning spectators.

179. *this do swear* The line lacks a syllable, and Pope read 'this do ye swear.' But 'this do swear,' spoken with a solemn emphasis upon each word, is more effective.

2. 2.

159. S.D. *disorderly attired* Travers notes (2.1.79) that the frontispiece to *Hamlet* in Rowe's ed. (1709), which illustrates the apparition in the Bedroom Scene (3.4.), shows Ham. with one stocking half-down.

172. *God-a-mercy* v. G. (add.).

173. *know me* =recognize me. Cf. 1.2.211.

184. *Let her not walk i'th'sun* v. pp. 105–106 in *What happens in Hamlet* for a further elucidation of this passage.

239–40. *the world's grown honest* Cf. ll. 178–79 above, which show what Ham. thought of the world's honesty. Cf. Adams, p. 240.

246–49. *Denmark's a prison...dungeons* Cf. Bright, p. 263: 'The house...seemeth vnto the melancholicke a prison or dungeon, rather than a place of assured repose and rest.'

255. *your ambition* Adams, pp. 240–41 and Trench, pp. 96–7 in part anticipate me here.

268. *Shall we to th' court?* Cf. *Span. Trag.* III. x. 104–105:

> Nay, and you argue things so cunningly,
> Weele goe continue this discourse at Court.

300–301. *custom of exercises* Add 'and 5.2.285. Cf. also Bright, p. 31, "exercises...wholy intermitted... causing the blood to be thicke through setling." '

301–307. *It goes so heavily...congregation of vapours* Cf. Bright, p. 106:

The body thus possessed with the vnchearefull, and discomfortable darknes of melancholie, obscureth the Sonne and Moone, and all the comfortable planetts of our natures, in such sort, that if they appeare, they appeare all darke, and more then half eclipsed of this mist of blackenes, rising from that hideous lake.

328–29. *the Lady...halt for't* Verity explains 'freely' as 'not very accurately,' and Travers paraphrases: 'not thinking herself tied down to the letter of the text, improvising (metrically) whenever her memory failed her.' This seems more satisfactory than Dowden's explanation. No doubt the boys who played women's parts often forgot their lines.

373. *Gentlemen* This 'sudden formality...tells them that they are no longer "good lads" and his "excellent good friends"' (Travers).

379. *You are welcome* i.e. to uncle-father and aunt-mother. The irony is repeated at l. 550.

382–83. *I know a hawk from a handsaw* Mr A. J. Eagleston (privately) notes that the inventory of Wolsey's goods taken after death included a tapestry depicting among other things 'a bow drawn and a heronsawe and a hawk in the compasse thereof' (Cal. Letters and Papers, Henry VIII, vol. iv. p. 3, No. 6748 (12) at p. 3045).

408. *Jephthah* Adams (p. 242) also links this with the Fishmonger passage.

484–96. H. W. Crundell (letter T.L.S. Nov. 23, 1935) notes that the ruthless Pyrrhus is, like Laertes and Fortinbras later, a foil to Ham., and Trench (pp. 106–107) writes: 'Especially is he [Ham.] concerned about the passage relating to Hecuba, about the horrible effect, that is to say, the deed would have upon his mother.'

506. '*mobled queen*' *is good* I suggest that Pol. should write the phrase in his tables, as he speaks.

549. *My good friends* 'Stressed with secret irony' (Travers); cf. add. notes 2. 2. 373, 379.

553 ff. *O, what a rogue* etc. A close examination of Hieronimo's speech at III. xiii. 95–123 of the *Span. Trag.* shows it to be in large measure the germ of this

soliloquy. For various interpretations of Ham.'s line of thought, v. Trench, pp. 111–25, Adams, pp. 244–45, W. W. Greg (M.L.R. xxxi. 151), and my *What happens in Hamlet*, p. 142. Adams and Greg independently suggest that Hamlet's first idea is to use *The Murder of Gonzago* 'as a sort of challenge to the king' and that it is only later (i.e. at the end of the soliloquy) that he thinks of making it 'a test of the king's conscience' and of introducing the poisoning through the ear to that end ('something like the murder of my father'). And Trench's theory is not dissimilar. To me the difference between these two intentions seems so slight as to be *dramatically* imperceptible.

562–63. *What's Hecuba...weep for her?* Prof. J. A. K. Thomson draws my attention, in a private letter, to an anecdote about Alexander of Pherae, a tyrant of the 'Cambyses' sort, in Plutarch's *Life of Pelopides* (North's Plutarch, ii. 323, Tudor Translations), which runs:

And an other time being in a Theater, where the tragedy of *Troades* of Euripides was played, he went out of the Theater, and sent word to the players notwithstandinge, that they shoulde go on with their playe, as if he had bene still amonge them: saying, that he came not away for any misliking he had of them or of the play, but bicause he was ashamed his people shoulde see him weepe, to see the miseries of Hecuba and Andromacha played, and that they never saw him pity the death of any one man, of so many of his citizens as he had caused to be slaine. The gilty conscience therefore of this cruell and heathen tyran, did make him tremble at the only name and reputacion of Epaminondas.

The story bridges Ham.'s soliloquy, as it were, since it deals with a remorseless tyrant, like Pyrrhus, who was also a 'guilty creature sitting at a play...by the very cunning of the scene...struck...to the soul,' and makes him weep for Hecuba. Sh., as Prof. Thomson says, 'must have read this story. Plutarch tells it for its psychological interest, and it would have a professional interest for Sh. There is a tyrant in it, and a tragic actor, and Plutarch's unspoken comment "What was Hecuba to him, that he should weep for her?"' The *Life* of Pelopides comes close to those of Coriolanus and Pericles (cf. add. note 3. 2. 360–74).

579–83. *for it cannot be...slave's offal* Ham. compares himself, I think, with a falcon refusing to kill.

585. *O, vengeance!* 'The word is out' (Travers)— but only when the mood is almost exhausted.

3. 1.

See Adams, pp. 250–61, for a different reading of this scene, which yet corresponds with mine at many points.

2. *puts on this confusion* Dr Greg suggests, privately, that this shows the true character of the K.'s suspicions.

60. *them.* Q2 'them,' F. 'them:' Rowe, Hanmer and Capell read 'them.'; but Pope read 'them?' and most mod. edd. follow.

79–80. *The undiscovered country* etc. Cf. Marlowe, *Edward II*, 5. 6. 65:

> Farewell, fair queen: weep not for Mortimer
> That scorns the world, and as a traveller
> Goes to discover countries yet unknown.

Trench (pp. 138–40) has, like Dowden, caught sight of the true explanation.

88. *The fair Ophelia* 'The phrase itself is too smooth for the utterance of a man in "the pangs of despised love"; and Ham. is speaking to himself, not acting indifference' (Travers).

89. *Nymph* Cf. Jonson's *Cynthia's Revels*, 3. 5. 75, 140 for 'nymph' in affected use. Travers plausibly argues that Ham. pretends not to recognize Oph. until l. 102.

121. *Get thee to a nunnery* Adams (p. 260) anticipates me here.

161. *Like sweet bells...harsh* Cf. Bright, p. 250: 'putting the parts of that most consonant and pleasant harmony [i.e. the body] out of tune, deliuer a note to the great discontentment of reason and much against the mindes will, which intendeth far other then the corporall instrument effecteth.'

3. 2.

37–43. *those that play your clowns* etc. Dr G. B. Harrison notes, in a private letter, that one of these jests is given to Sogliardo, 'the essential Clowne' in Jonson's *Every Man Out of his Humour*, 'first acted in the yeere 1599 by the then Lord Chamberlaine his seruants.' Cf. 1. 2. 145: 'Ile giue coats, that's my humour: but I lacke a cullisen,' which it seems possible was a glance at Kempe. N.B. his name does not appear in the list of 'principall comœdians' who acted the play in 1599.

52. *just* 'Finer than "honest" by all the united radiancy of classical and Biblical associations, such as the "vir justus" of Horace (*Odes*, III. iii. ll. 60–66) and "the path of the just is a shining light" (Prov. iv. 18)' (Travers).

68. *a pipe for Fortune's finger* Cf. note on ll. 360–74 below, quoting from North's Plutarch (*Life of Pericles*) words which seem to be the germ of both these passages.

71. *heart's core* N.E.D. 14 *b* suggests 'a play on *core* and Latin *cor*.' Cf. 'heart of heart.'

91–2. *Excellent...capons so* Verity has seen the connexion between this and 1. 2. 108–109.

133. S.D. *Hamlet seems troubled* etc. See B. R. Pearn, *Dumb-shows in Elizabethan Drama*, R.E.S. Oct. 1935, and a letter by J. Purves in T.L.S. Sept. 19, 1935. Trench (p. 159 n.) also adopts Halliwell's solution.

135. *miching mallecho* Cf. 1 *Rich. II* (l. 2648 Mal. Soc. Reprint): 'Com ye micheing Rascall.'

241. *let the galled jade wince* W. W. Greg paraphrases (M.L.R. xxxi. 150) 'Let your jade of a wife show her withers galled.' This would imply that the

Queen had been visibly disturbed by the references to second marriages in the interlude, which I think very likely.

wince Greg objects (M.L.R. xxx. 86) that the distinction between 'wince' and 'winch' (Q2, F1) is 'one of linguistic form and not merely of spelling, and that not even a modernising editor has the right to interfere.' Reference to N.E.D. 'wince' 1 *a* and 'winch' 2 *b* shows that both forms were used indifferently of the 'galled jade' in Sh.'s day.

243. *nephew to the king* Trench (p. 166, n. 2) anticipates my explanation here to the extent of suggesting that Ros. and Guil. may identify Lucianus with Ham. For second thoughts on Lucianus' costume v. *What happens in Hamlet*, p. 171 n.

293–94. *For if...perdy* This is not 'another ballad-snatch' but a parody (cf. note 253–54 above) of the *Span. Trag.* IV. i. 196–97:

> And if the world like not this Tragedie,
> Hard is the hap of olde Hieronimo.

'Just before, Hamlet has quoted two stanzas, probably from old ballads, and has clearly misquoted the last line of the second stanza...after which Horatio says "You might have rhymed." So Hamlet reverses the process of misquotation and rhymes where Kyd had not rhymed' (A. Clutton-Brock, *Shakespeare's Hamlet*, 1922, p. 17).

306–308. *for me...more choler* Purgation for bile or choler might be by bleeding (cf. *Ric. II*, 1.1.153)—the readiest way to cure Claudius.

316. *breed* v. G. (add.).

358. *I know no touch of it* = 'I cannot play a note on it' (Christopher Welch, v. note l. 361, below). Cf. 'touch' G. (add.).

360–74. *Govern...play upon me* Cf. North's Plutarch, *Life of Pericles* (Tudor Translations, ii. 22):

For as it falleth out commonly unto people that enjoye

so great an empire: many times misfortunes doe chaunce, that fill them full of sundrie passions, the which Pericles alone could finely steere and *governe* with two principall rudders, feare and hope....Wherein he manifestly proved, that rethorike and eloquence (as Plato sayeth) is an arte which quickeneth mens spirites at her pleasure, and her chiefest skill is, to knowe howe to move passions and affections throughly, *which are as stoppes and soundes of the soule, that would be played upon with a fine fingered hand of a conning master.*

The italics are mine. Cf. add. notes l. 68 above, and 2. 2. 562–63.

361. *fingers and thumb* It does *not* 'take two thumbs to play a recorder' as I asserted in my 'ignorance and conceit' (cf. MSH. ii. 296, 323–25). Several correspondents have written to point out the error, which I might have avoided had I known before of Ch. Welch's fascinating *Six Lectures on the Recorder* (Oxford, 1911), v. especially Lect. iii, 'Hamlet and the Recorder.' The intrusive 'r' in Q2's 'the vmber,' which led me astray, must now be attributed to misplaced ingenuity in the printing-house. I have corrected the text.

397. *The soul of Nero* Dowden notes that Agrippina, Nero's mother, was not only the wife of a Claudius, but was accused of poisoning a husband and of living in incest with a brother. If Sh. knew all this, perhaps it accounts for his choice of Claudius as the name for his king of Denmark.

3. 3.

7. *brows* In the 2nd ed. I suggested 'braves' as a likely emendation for the Q2 'browes.' The sense, 'impudent or defiant threats,' would suit the context well, and it would be easier than 'brawls' graphically. But it is safer to retain 'brows' in view of O.E.D. which cites late 17th century examples of 'brow' in the figurative sense of 'an unabashed brow, effrontery.'

80. Cf. note (add.) 1. 5. 11 above.

88–95. *Up, sword...it goes* Travers aptly quotes 1.2.152: 'Would I had met my dearest foe in heaven.'

3.4.

9–10. *thou hast...you have* The change is significant (Adams, p. 278).

42–4. *takes off...blister there* i.e. her act has destroyed his innocent love for Oph., v. *What happens in Hamlet*, p. 101.

49–51. *And this...the act* For a criticism of both the reading and the interpretation here v. rev. by W. W. Greg in M.L.R. xxx. 85.

53. *upon this...and on this* The picture of this scene in Rowe's ed. of 1709 shows half-length portraits on the wall; cf. add. note 2.2.159 S.D. And Stow (*Annals*, p. 1436) speaks of a great chamber in the palace at Elsinore 'hanged with Tapistary of fresh colourd silke without gold, wherein all the Danish kings are exprest in antique habits, according to their several times, with their armes and inscriptions, conteining all their conquests and victories.' But cf. Hazelton Spencer, 'How Sh. staged his plays', *Johns Hopkins Alumni Magazine*, xx, 205–21.

67. *moor* Cf. 'with a face like Vulcan,' which Q1 reads at the corresponding passage.

102. S.D. The picture in Rowe (v. add. note 1. 53) shows the Ghost in armour and with truncheon.

135. *in his habit as he lived* Cf. Lavater, p. 69, 'as he was wonte when he lived'.

4.4.

18. *a little patch of ground* The following sentences from Camden's *Elizabeth*, describing the siege of Ostend, 1601, come close to Sh.'s words here and in ll. 50–65 below:

There was not in our age any seige and defence maintained with greater slaughter of men, nor continued longer.... For the most warlike souldiers of the Low Countreys, Spaine, England, France, Scotland and Italy, whilest they most eagerly contended for a barren plot of sand, had as it were one common sepulcher, but an eternall monument of their valour.

The news-pamphlets, the number of which testifies to the public interest taken in the siege, all insist upon the terrific struggle, the magnitude of the sacrifice, the unexampled bravery of those taking part, and the insignificance and sterility of the little plot of sandy ground fought for. Perhaps the most interesting testimony is to be found in a volume of French poems on the siege, entitled *Ostende*, 1603 (B.M. press mark 1192. g. 6), of which the lines

> Tout le subiect de ce siege hazardeux
> N'est que ce champ infertile et poudreux

give the key-note of the whole. That Sh. had himself read the earliest news-pamphlet (ent. S.R. Aug. 5, 1601) looks probable from its reference to a man 'very miraculously saved...upon a piece of a mast' in the sea outside the town, which seems to have suggested Sebastian's escape in *Tw. Nt.* 1. 2. 12–14.

36–9. *Sure he...unused* Cf. Bright, p. 70:

Moreover, if a man were double fronted (as the Poets have fained Ianus)...the same facultie of sight would addresse it selfe to see both before and behind at one instant, which now it doth by turning.... So the mind, in action wonderful, and next vnto the supreme maiestie of God, and by a peculiar maner proceeding from him selfe...of present things determineth: and that which the eye doth by turning of the head, beholding before, behind, and on ech side, that doth the mind freely at once.

4. 5.

99–102. *The ocean...officers* Cf. Donne, *A Valediction: of the booke*, l. 25:

Vandals and Goths inundate us.

123–24. *There's such divinity...would* Travers quotes from Chettle's *England's Mourning Garment*, 1603, a description of Q. Eliz.'s bearing after an attempt upon her life: 'Such majesty had her presence, and such boldness her heart, that she despised all fear, and was, as all princes are or should be, so full of divine fullness that guilty mortality durst not behold her but with dazzled eyes.'

154. *O, heat* etc. 'Obviously all this is to be taken as uttered under the first shock of finding her mad....No "buzzer," it seems, had even told Laertes of Oph.'s condition' (Travers). A good instance of Sh.'s dramatic legerdemain: no questions arise in the theatre.

199. *And of...souls* A rev. in *Notes and Queries*, Dec. 22, 1934, suggests that Oph. here refers to 'the end of the Catholic formula,' viz. 'Of your charity pray for the repose...on whose soul and on all Christian souls may the Lord have mercy.'

4. 6.

Travers writes:

A scene to which justice has not always been done. Even its 'sea-faring man,' however briefly sketched and on merely typical lines, makes, for the moment, a breezy change. As to the news, why not accept them in the spirit that Sh. would expect from his audience: appreciation of their exciting nature, of the intricate opportuneness of the affair with the 'thieves of mercy,' of hero's valiancy and resourcefulness, of his epistolary style too, as sharp as any rapier?

4. 7.

43–7. *High and mighty* etc. Travers insists on the ironical solemnity of this letter; cf. also *What happens in Hamlet*, p. 267.

56 *diest* (F. A. Marshall conj.) Q2 'didst', F 'diddest', Q1 'thus he diest'. See W. W. Greg in *T.L.S.* June 28, 1957.

83–9. *but this gallant...he did* Cf. *Lover's Complaint*, ll. 106–12:

> Well could he ride, and often men would say
> "That horse his mettle from his rider takes:
> Proud of subjection, noble by the sway,
> What rounds, what bounds, what course, what stop
>   he makes!"
> And controversy hence a question takes,
> Whether the horse by him became his deed,
> Or he his manage by the well-doing steed.

It is possible that both passages refer to the same horseman, viz. Sh.'s patron.

149. *fit us to our shape* v. G. (add.) 'shape.' Johnson interprets: 'enable us to assume proper characters and to act our part.'

5. 1.

252. *Hamlet the Dane* Adams, p. 319, also notes this.
S.D. Cf. from *A Funerall Elegye on ye Death of the famous Actor Richard Burbedg*, 1618 (cited C. M. Ingleby, *Shakespeare, the Man and his Book*, ii. 169, and E. Nungezer, *A Dictionary of Actors*, 74):

> Oft haue I seene him leap into the Graue,
> Suiting the person which he seem'd to haue
> Of a sadd Louer, with soe true an Eye
> That theer I would haue sworne he meant to dye—

a vivid memory of how Burbage acted at this point.

5. 2.

10–11. *There's a divinity...we will* Mr J. P. Malleson writes (privately):

Years ago a country labourer astonished my father by saying as he sharpened stakes for fixing hurdles in the ground: 'My mate roughhews them and I shape their ends.'

Perhaps the image came to Sh. from the passage in Saxo or Belleforest which describes Amleth shaping the ends of little staves in the fire, v. Gollancz, *Sources of Hamlet*, pp. 103–105, 199.

74. *a man's...say 'One'* Adams (p. 321) concurs in this interpretation.

77–8. *For by the image...his* Cf. *Span. Trag.* III. xiii. 84–5:

> Whiles wretched I in thy mishaps may see
> The liuely portrait of my dying selfe.

108. S.D. Johnson gives 'Hamlet moves him to put on his hat.'

110. *for mine ease* Travers quotes from Florio's *Second Fruits*, 1591:

> Why do you stand bareheaded? you do yourself wrong.
> Pardon me, good sir, I do it for my ease.

222. S.D. (p. 251) Bated foils were still in use on the stage in 1668. Cf. Dryden, *Essay of Dramatic Poetry*, i. 62 (*Essays of John Dryden*, ed. by W. P. Ker).

> For what is more ridiculous than...to see a duel fought and one slain with two or three thrusts of the foils, which we know are so blunted that we might give a man an hour to kill another in good earnest with them?

(8 lines from foot) Between 'while' and 'shirts of mail' insert: 'Egerton Castle (p. 346, n. 1) states that there is internal evidence in many books of the period that.'

257. *Osric* A. H. J. Knight in '*Der bestrafte Brudermord* and *Hamlet*, Act v*' (M.L.R. July, 1936, pp. 385 ff.) shows that Phantasmo (Osric) was certainly an accomplice in the *Brudermord*.

270. *union* Adams (pp. 325–26) notes that Sir Thomas Gresham at the opening of the Royal Exchange in 1571 drank to the honour of Queen Elizabeth a cup of wine in which had been dissolved a pearl costing £1500.

285. *fat, and scant of breath* Cf. M. P. Tilley, *Journ. Eng. and Germ. Phil.* xxiv. 315–19, who calls attention to the popular belief of Sh.'s time that perspiration was oozing fat, and corr. T.L.S. May 26, 1927. Cf. above 3. 4. 92–3.

ADDENDA TO GLOSSARY

Almost, even; cf. *Temp.* 3. 3. 34 and *Cor.* 1. 2. 24 'ere almost Rome should know'; 1. 3. 113.

Breed, species, with a quibble on 'breeding' = manners (after 'courtesy'); 3. 2. 316.

Cast, tinge, shade of colour; 3. 1. 85.

[*Enseamed*] Cf. *Troil.* 2. 2. 186 'That bastes his arrogance with his own seam.'

Fruitful, copious (v. N.E.D. 3); 1. 2. 80.

God-a-mercy Lit. God reward you. 'Used in response to a respectful salutation or a wish, usually expressed by an inferior, for a person's welfare' (Onions); 2. 2. 172.

[*Heavy*] Before '4. 1. 12' insert 'wicked (cf. *K. John*, 4. 3. 58).'

Hence, in the next world (cf. *K. John*, 5. 4. 29); 3. 2. 221.

[*Implorators*] Add 'Not found elsewhere (cf. obs. Fr. 16. c. 'implorateur' in Cotgrave).'

[*Indirection*] After 'method' add 'crooked course (cf. *K. John*, 3. 1. 175).'

Remorse, compassion; 2. 2. 495.

[*Shape*] Delete 'plan of proceeding; 4. 7. 149' and read 'guise, make-up and costume, (hence) part to play (N.E.D. 8); 1. 2. 82 (v. note); 1. 4. 43; 1. 5. 54; 4. 7. 149.'

Suddenly, instantly; 2. 2. 214.

[*Thought*] Add 'Cf. Halle, *Chronicle*, ed. 1809, p. 5: "where he for thoughte and Melancholy deceased" (of Thos. Mowbray, Duke of Norfolk, temp. Ric. II).'

Touch, fingering (of a musical instrument), note. Cf. *Ric. II*, 1. 3. 163; *Merch.* 5. 1. 58, and Ch. Welch, *Six Lectures on the Recorder*, p. 174; 3. 2. 359.

[1954] *artere*, ligament (cf. O.E.D. 'artery' 5 and Lat. *artero*), 1. 4. 82.